IMPORTE

A READING SEMINAR

IMPORTED

A READING SEMINAR

A PROJECT EDITED BY

RAINER GANAHL

SEMIOTEXT(E)

Semiotext(e)

Editorial Offices:
522 Philosophy Hall, Columbia University, New York, NY 10027
55 South Eleventh Street, Brooklyn, NY 11211-0568 USA
Phone and Fax: (718) 963-2603

Imported: A Reading Seminar
is Semiotext(e) #18
(Volume VI, Issue 3)
ISSN 0-093-95779
ISBN 1-57027-076-7

Semiotext(e) is a not-for-profit publication.

Layout and design by Rainer Ganahl and Benjamin Meyers.

Distribution in North America:
Autonomedia Distribution, Brooklyn
Small Press Distribution, Berkeley
Left Bank Distribution, Seattle
AK Distribution, San Francisco
Last Gasp Distribution, San Francisco
Marginal Distribution, Canada

Distribution in Europe:
Central Books, London
AK Distribution, Edinburgh
Buchhandlung Walther König, Köln
Villa Arson, Nice

Printed in the United States of America

CONTENTS

RAINER GANAHL

Introduction 9

Vorwort 24

Introduction 42

序文 59

Japanese Version 75

KOJIN KARATANI – SABU KOHSO

Intercourse of Ideas 76

SABU KOHSO

Two Modes of Translation, or a Crossing over the Pacific 96

翻訳、満たされぬ愛、あるいは日本語を読むあなたへの手紙 106

US Version 115

BILL ARNING

Everyone is Gay (if Kurt Cobain said it, it's true) 116

DAN BACALZO

I'm Sorry, But I Don't Speak the Language 121

COCO FUSCO

Hustling for Dollars: Sex Work & Tourism in Cuba 139

EDWARD W. SAID

Traveling Theory 157

GAYATRI CHAKRAVORTY SPIVAK – RAINER GANAHL

Lost our language – Underneath the linguistic map 182

French Version 193

JULIA KRISTEVA
The Other Language or Translating Sensitivity 194
SYLVÈRE LOTRINGER — RAINER GANAHL
Agent de l'étranger (*Foreign Agent*) 211
SAMI NAÏR
Les identités aléatoires 221

Russian Version 231

ZEIGAM AZIZOV
Russification and the Terrain of "Self-Determination" 232
VICTOR TUPITSYN
ТЕЛО-БЕЗ-ИМЕНИ (ТЕРМИДОР ТЕЛЕСНОСТИ) 243

Californian Version 259

KAREN KELSKY
Flirting with the Foreign — Interracial Sex in Japan's "International" Age 260
EDWARD W. SOJA
Los Angeles 1965 - 1992: From Crisis-Generated Restructuring to Restructuring-Generated Crisis 281

German Version 317

BENJAMIN H. D. BUCHLOH - RAINER GANAHL
Böse Bemerkungen zwischen Moskau und Los Angeles 318
WULF SCHMIDT-WULFEN
"Teufelskreise" – geographische Vorstellungen deutscher Jugendlicher zum Thema afrikansiche "Entwicklungsländer" 340

Austrian Version 349

RAINER GANAHL

Sprechen, Lesen, Lernen, Lehren 350

DANA LEONARD, LISA ADKINS

Zur Rekonstrüktion des französischen Feminismus: Verdinglichung, Materialismus und Geschlecht. Die Verdinglichung des "französischen Feminismus" 364

BIBLIOGRAPHIES 397

CONTRIBUTORS 412

ACKNOWLEDGEMENTS

During the four years I have been working on this project many people and institutions gave me the benefit of their interest as well as their direct and indirect help. Next to all the institutions that hosted me – see below – and the participants from whom I learned, I am especially grateful to the following persons for helping me realize the reading seminar project: Timothy Blum, Thomas Nordanstadt, Roger Pailhas, Victor Missiano, Peter Weibel, Michael Cohen, Nancy Barton, Kenjiro Okazaki, Jade Dellinger, Christoph Gerozissis, Nicolaus Schafhausen, Michel Bourel, Patrick Aubouin, Axel Huber, Paul Devautour, Stella Rollig, Hema Schmutz, Marlene Ropac, and Nicola Hirner. For the realization of this book I am very thankful to Stella Rollig, Sylvère Lotringer, Jim Fleming, Ben Meyers, Michel Bourel, Catherine Queloz, Max Protetch and in particular to the contributors of this publication as well as to friends who gave me advice for it.

Also I would like to mention Judy Geib, Adrienne Day, and Ben Meyers for proof reading the English texts, Patrick Auboin and Maria Wutz for the French text, Christine Huber and Maria Mikl-Kaufmann for the German texts, and Sabu Kohso for the Japanese texts. Concerning the translations I am very thankful to Zeigam Azizov, Yuzo Sakuramoto and Mai-Thu A Perret.

Thanks to all the institutions where a reading seminar or a presentation was held: Contemporary Art Center, Moscow, January - March 1995; Otis School of Art, Los Angeles, April, May 1995; Blum & Poe, Los Angeles, May 1995 (presentation only); Haizuka Project, Hiroshima Prefecture, August, September 1995; Florida, Polk Museum of Art, November, December 1995; Künstlerhaus Stuttgart, Stuttgart, January 1996; Villa Arson, Nice, March, April 1996; Depot, Vienna, May, June 1996 (presentation only); Galerie Roger Pailhas, Paris, December 1996 (presentation only).

The photograph from the cover is entitled: *IMPORTED - A READING SEMINAR in Relationship with my "A Portable (Not so Ideal) Imported Library, Or How to Reinvent the Coffee Table: 25 Books for Instant Use (Californian Version),"* 1995. It was taken at Otis School of Art, Los Angeles, April, May 1995 during one of my reading seminars.

Sous-so, Ecole supériere d'arts visuels, Département de l'"Instruction Publique, Genève.

Diese Publikation ist gefördert im Auftrag des Österreichischen Bundesministeriums für Wissenschaft, Unterricht und Kunst, Kuratorin Stella Rollig.

Cette publication apparait suite à une exposition à la Villa Arson (directeur: Michel Bourel; secrétaire général: Jean-Louis Pastor), à Nice en 1996, avec le soutien du Centre National des Arts Plastiques, Ministère de la Culture.

Rainer Ganahl, Reading Seminars, 15 mars - 21 avril 1996

Cette exposition a été préparée et réalisée par Patrick Aubouin, Michel Bourel et Axel Huber.

INTRODUCTION

RAINER GANAHL

This publication concludes a public project entitled *IMPORTED—A READING SEMINAR in Relationship with my "A Portable (Not So Ideal) Imported Library, Or How to Reinvent the Coffee Table: 25 Books for Instant Use (7 Different National Versions)"* (1993-96). I conducted six reading seminars held in six different countries. I traveled around Asia, Europe, and the US, and, with the different libraries, established them for one- and two-month long seminars in universities, museums and art centers. This book is an extension of the project, gathering an independent collection of texts with the common theme of IMPORT. I have asked authors who have a direct relationship to the different places I held reading seminars for texts and interviews that deal with cultural exchange from a variety of perspectives. Each text is printed in its original language. This resulting volume includes texts in English, Japanese, Russian, German, and French. Significantly, some writers preferred to write in English since the chances of it being read are higher than if the text were in, for instance, Japanese or Russian. The "national" grouping of authors is partially incorrect and serves to organize texts only in an ironic way, alluding to the meandering necessary for my public reading projects. The bibliographies of the *IMPORTED* libraries I used when holding the reading seminars are included in the back, and a photograph from each of the reading groups marks the beginning of each section. In Austria, I was unable to organize a reading seminar, which explains why there is just a photograph of the books. The selection of sites was dependent upon invitation, based on previous connections, and funding was in most cases provided by the host organization.

Like the texts assembled in this volume, the reading seminar project touched upon the problems of exchange, globalization, nationalism, tourism, languages, theory, desires, identity, and politics. Although there is already a vast amount of literature in print on these issues, I nonetheless would like to make a few comments on their relation to educational and cultural politics. For centuries, dominant European nations developed their cultural apparatus as instruments for conceptualizing, implementing, and justifying internal and external hegemony and power. Cultural, ideological, and religious arrogance contributed to brutal subordination of entire populations and groups, abroad and at home.[1] We are left with tragic histories of exploitation and misrepresentations that, unfortunately, create an abusive infrastructure for a post-colonial *new world order* in which "business as usual" can continue without the need to directly apply force and violence.

Educational and linguistic programs were central to the formation of the national state in the 19th century; they homogenized the people and even anticipated territorial and political unity. Specifically in Germany, *Bildung* (bourgeois education with an ideological impact) was invented in order to celebrate national unity as an idea, before it became a political fact. A national language with national literature and theater, national history and national art, music, and opera were created, celebrated and instrumentalized. National education programs vigorously sought to create something Fichte could refer to as an "inner border" (*innere Grenze*), a metaphor that stood primarily for a national language and its culture. Today, this metaphor is again very significant if we think of the Schengen security treaties that are turning the entire European Union into a permanent border zone for policing people, or some propositions before the California legislature that want to police people automatically at any state office (post office, hospitals, schools, etc.). Independent of these obvious panoptic screenings that are largely biased by racial and class prejudices, "inner borders" are also visible, for example, in the possession of credit cards and in educational and professional qualifications. The tremendous impact of educational advantages in this contemporary, information-dense society reflects a history of discrimination based upon the exclusion of the majority population from higher education; regulated access to education has always reproduced social hierarchies. For example, until the end of the 19th century, education for African-Americans was forbidden by law in the USA, a fact that is not without relationship to today's racially disproportionate educational demographics.[2]

Education is not just a discourse of social reproduction and as such political, but is also an investment into a big market. Universities are generally very expensive, exclusive, and increasingly constituting an industry that reduces even critical thinking to commodity status. While Kant, Humboldt and others could conceive of a philosophical faculty that guaranteed critical autonomy, today any kind of critic has first to find sponsors. The discourse of critique tends to function as just another market, with all its attendent fluctuations and fashions. Political, ideological, gender, racial, and socio-economic discrepancies are also inscribed in this logic. What to teach, to whom, in which language, for what kind of interest group is no longer automatically guaranteed by a state *Bildungsauftrag*, a totalized educational aim presupposed as "natural" and national. Rather, these issues become the subjects of argument, necessary conflicts that inform us about open and hidden repressive histories and power struggles. Texts that fall into the category of "critical studies" are often concerned with the rewriting and analyzing of this kind of biased educational canon.

For a long time, traveling was a privilege reserved for wealthy and educated people. In fact, educational programs often included travel or even consisted solely of travel. Reaching out into the world, conquering, controlling, exploiting, studying, and representing the Other has also been the basis of wealth, power, and domination. Cultural arrogance mixed with a benevolent humanism and ignorance informed most missionary work, which was subsumed into the larger framework of rewriting the political, geographic, linguistic, and economic map around the globe. The trading of people—slavery—helped to finance and develop the mode of production and exchange now called industrialization and capitalism, where colonial resources and products alone originally had formed the basis for capitalism. Today the migration of people has new names, reasons, and practices: sex slaves turned into prostitutes, illegal immigrants, and tourists occupy different but overlapping realities. And it is not just people who are traveling freely or unfreely, pushed or lured around. So is nearly everything today: labor, production, raw materials, information, knowledge, technologies, trash, disease, gods, goods, images, desires, conflicts, and all kinds of consumption. Mobility, speed, and compatibility are becoming an aim in itself for the contemporary professional class, including artists and academics.

Today, the competition among states fighting for and over territories, colonies and their resources has decreased. Rather, we are dealing with an opaque net of transnational corporations (TNCs) whose power structure is not so easy to define. TNC power doesn't favor one place over another any more than it bows before any border or authority. TNCs even speak and adopt state rhetoric, since the state itself is being transformed more and more into a merely bureaucratic institution that delegates its power and monopolies. Prisons are as privatizable as national banks, health care, and educational systems. The dismantling and eroding of state power also dismantles the educational and cultural institutions that were at the heart of its creation. Although universities were, historically, complicit with state power and the disasters of nationalism, they also had a critical function. Now that too is fading. The model of TNC dynamics consists of nationless operations responsible and faithful only to the logic of transnational capital and its exclusive members and shareholders. This model has also been adopted by the culture industry as it has become more and more dependent on corporate collaborations and interests. In the case of the Guggenheim Museum in New York, for example, foreign investors sponsor activities in order to gain exclusive visibility and influence. In return, the museum is assured financial backing and can expand and open branches all over the world—a mini-TNC unto itself. The military too is trying to operate like the transnational companies, collaging materials and troops from several nations, as was shown in the Gulf War and is now the case with NATO and its expansionism. But this doesn't signal the end of colonialism and the disasters of nationalism. Quite the opposite: domination and exploitation are becoming an operative logic that is penetrating every larger social body.

My traveling reading seminar project is symptomatic of, if not complicit with, today's transnational situation. It would make sense to describe the international transfer of art and culture since the 1970s as a result of the *747-phenomenon,* which should also be analyzed in terms of its effects on cultural production. Today, the cultural world and its parameters span all the industrialized zones in the world: it seems that after achieving high industrialization, the model of western art is desired and needed everywhere for a touch of liberalism. Positioned within the connected world of relative privilege—culturally speaking—I was able to access institutions and funding in order to pursue my project: I conducted (mostly) public reading seminars and discussions with people who enjoy the relative privileges, freedom, and time to be interested in such discussions. I experienced a lot from discussing similar issues in changing contexts and languages (which I keep learning as my artwork—Basic Japanese, Korean, Russian, Modern Greek, etc.). Although all the reading seminars were taped and archived, the often surprising discussions and conflicts are not represented in this introduction. Rather I am interested in letting the voices that are somehow related to the places I went and the topics we discussed speak for themselves. It goes without saying that the texts assembled here are individual voices from which I have learned.

Because this volume doesn't include translations, hereforth follows a summary of each contribution, which provides some access to the texts written in a so-called "foreign language." The order of appearance parallels the itinerary of my *Portable (Not so Ideal) Imported Libraries...* The interview between Kojin Karatani and Sabu Kohso, entitled "Intercourse of Ideas," addresses a wide array of issues that concern contemporary society and thinking in a climate of interdependency. Japan, like any other Asian country, is constantly confronted with misrepresentations produced in the West and even in Asia itself. Associated with them are a biased rhetoric of "originality and copy," in which Karatani detects power relations. "Most of the books about Japan are written to fulfill the requirements of a representation which is formed around either aesthetic or religious realms, or economical and technological interests... Intellectual and ethical domains are omitted." Karatani's analysis of modernism and its various critiques is very productive since he approaches and studies it from the geographical margin. In relation to his critique of phonocentrism and politics, this interview addresses important economical and political aspects of language and its ideological instrumentality in the construction of nations and of race consciousness.

Some of Karatani's writings have been translated by Sabu Kohso, who contributes his text "Two Modes of Translation, or a Crossing over the Pacific" in English, and another slightly different essay, "*Honyaku, Mitasarenu-ai, aruiwa Nihongo-o-yomu Anata-eno-tegami*" ("Translation, an Unrequited Love, or a Letter to You Who Read Japanese") in Japanese. For the Japan-born Kohso, translating is an existential business, since he has been living in New York for many years. Translating between English and Japanese in both directions, for the translator, a "trafficking (that) involves totally different ways of thinking, performing, producing, and being.... The two ways produce two different personae in me." In an intriguing way, Kohso links not just the construction of his parallel identity with the act of translating, but also the construction of the Japanese identity in general with translation. "Translation has always been the main tool of shaping the nation...." He develops a theory of translation that serves as a critique of his native country which he describes as having a "national obsession with importing foreign cultures." His critique is not just directed at Japan's exchange economics but also at the biased Western attitude towards their own *translation* politics from Japanese: very little critical thinking "Made in Japan" gets translated and circulated outside Japan. "Aesthetic Japan as opposed to critical Japan [is favored].... Today, Japan's most powerful cultural exports are electronic game software and animation. They again reflect Japan's unbalanced profile: a military and high-tech superpower with an infantile mentality (and in a double sense: first, the media themselves are originally made for kids; second, they represent less ethical thinking than a libidinal flow in the techno-social network)." Here again, Kohso's critique goes in several directions, also targeting what became known to the critical community as "Orientalism." His in-between position explains why his text appears in parallel English and Japanese versions without their being necessarily identical translations.

In his text "Everyone is Gay (if Kurt Cobain said it, it is true)," Bill Arning describes himself as "one unemployed faggot-curator." With the shows he has curated, such as "The Anti-Masculine" or "Stonewall 25—Imagining the Gay Past," he has developed an open and remarkably outspoken image of a contemporary New York gay identity. Along with a very peculiar story reflecting the homophobic climate (in which it is not so much a question of a happy or unhappy ending, but of the circumstances that surround this anecdote), Arning tells us about some interesting encounters he had abroad while "exporting" his curating experience. It comes to this issue: "From my New York perspective, you can't be a good curator unless you're an honest curator, and you can't be honest if you're closeted." The more we read, the more the author shows us, in his seductive style, how he came to understand that "sexuality always has a cultural context"; that these contexts are constantly changing I saw quite clearly when reading texts on sexual and gay politics with different audiences in different places during my seminar-work.

Dan Bacalzo's "I'm Sorry, But I Don't Speak the Language," is a play I was fortunate enough to see performed by the author himself, a young Filipino-American standing alone on a bare stage at New York University. It addresses issues of sexuality and cultural context, in his case as a gay Asian-American. Bacalzo's play deals with his first violent same-sex experiences that reflect his culturally and racially biased new "foreign" homeland. He shows how sexual, linguistic and racial stereotypes blend and make up an aggressive reality which this writer addresses fluently: "And while he was fucking me, I wasn't thinking about representation. I wasn't thinking that Asians are always playing the role of the bottom in gay male sexual encounters. I wasn't thinking that this white male was playing out his colonial fantasies on my Asian body...." Or: "I'm a stupid fucker because I'm trying to speak several different languages at the same time. But unlike my grandmother, I lack fluency."

Geo-politics and sex are also at the core of Coco Fusco's text entitled "Hustling for Dollars: Sex Work & Tourism in Cuba": "My interest in the special role that women of color are playing in the burgeoning sex tourism industry there, coupled with my awareness that since 1993, there had been a marked increase in prostitution in Cuba, prompted me to write an article about the women involved. I was also particularly interested in the issues that prostitution raises for a third world socialist country that is in the process of making a difficult transition to capitalism." The global sex industry is an issue that is unfortunately not well studied or openly addressed, though it touches upon dimensions that are directly linked to other dark and abusive economies of forced exchange and "importation." Coco Fusco's historical and contemporary account of Cuba is not just factually rich and provocative, but also describes scenarios for many other countries and situations that suffer unequal exchange relationships.

"Like people and schools of criticism, ideas and theories travel—from person to person, from situation to situation, from one period to another. Cultural and intellectual life are usually nourished and often sustained by this circulation of ideas, and whether it takes the form of acknowledged or unconscious influence, creative borrowing, or wholesale appropriation, the movement of ideas and theories from one place to another is both a fact of life and a usefully enabling condition of intellectual activity." This is how Edward W. Said opens his article "Traveling Theory," from 1984, which discusses the particular case of Georg Lukács—author of *History and Class Consciousness* (1923), that elaborated his important theory of reification. Lukács' thinking "traveled" from revolutionary Hungary via post-World War II Paris (L. Goldmann) to Cambridge (R. Williams). In the tradition of Said's influential writings on cultural representation, this text also addresses questions of intellectual labor and the function of critique and critical consciousness: "The critical consciousness is awareness of the differences between situations, awareness, too, of the fact that no system or theory exhausts the situation out of which it emerges or to which it is transported. And above all, critical consciousness is awareness of the resistances to theory, reactions to it elicited by those concrete experiences or interpretations with which it is in conflict. Indeed I would go as far as saying that it is the critic's job to provide resistances to theory, to open it up toward historical reality, toward society, toward human needs and interests, to point up those concrete instances drawn from everyday reality, that lie outside or just beyond the interpretive area necessarily designated in advance."

Gayatri Chakravorty Spivak and I agreed to call our interview "Lost our Language—Underneath the Linguistic Map" to point out a reality that is often overlooked: that in the world there are not just a few dominant languages but innumerable regional languages and dialects, "languages of the soil," that are in many cases suppressed or regarded as inferior without any public acknowledgment in order to establish "a map." "Lost our language" is an expression Spivak learned from the peoples of Eastern Kimberley; its sentiment is a reality for many people today who no longer live in their own cultural idiom. "Language is here being used as a broader concept metaphor. They mean that they no longer make sense of their lives in terms of their cultural idiom. Foucault would say that their cultural idiom is no longer their *pouvoir savoir*, their ability to know." Spivak speaks about her relationship to languages growing up with a hegemonic Indian language and the colonial language English:

"That my own mother tongue was itself carrying within itself a history of imposition which we didn't know. And when we begin with the imposition of English, then we look at my mother tongue, for example, as a kind of victim language." Spivak criticizes even some social work that is informed by post-colonial theory: "For me, even to begin with the idea of the imposition of English is part of the problem."

Julia Kristeva presented her text "The Other Language or Translating Sensitivity" at a conference in New York in a language foreign to her: English. Though she is a French citizen, she didn't read her paper with a French accent but with a Slavic one, the accent of her mother tongue. The text, translated from French, opens almost immediately with the problem of "another language": "Immediately, but also fundamentally, the foreigner differs from someone who isn't, because he speaks another language. Looked at more closely, this fact is less trivial than it appears; it reveals an extravagant destiny: a tragedy as much as a choice. Tragedy, because the human being is a speaking being, and he naturally speaks the language of his people: the mother tongue, the language of his group, the national language. Changing languages is tantamount to losing something natural, betraying one's mother tongue or, at very least, translating it. A foreigner is, in essence, a translator." Kristeva unfolds a theory of translation from a psychoanalytical point of view that knows the conditions of exchange which produce the abject. She speaks about Proust and others but also about herself.

Sylvère Lotringer's interview is entitled "Agent de l'étranger (Foreign Agent)" and surprised me by the path it followed. I interviewed him in his role as founding editor of *Semiotext(e)*, the major organ for introducing so-called French Theory to the USA since the '70s, at a time when few editors were interested in publishing these authors. Lotringer gives a critical account of American academia and its publishing houses. Interested in a *"sémiotique 'matérialiste',"* he moved on to a *"sémiotique EN ACTE,"* an activism of signs that creates a delirium through the manipulation of texts and images, a "schizo-culture" that is closer to capitalism than to academia. Lotringer is not just reflecting the major intellectual and 'traveling' movements of post-structuralism, but also the tragic political disaster of fascism which he experienced as a hidden Jewish child, an experience which made him leave France: *"Un Vichy m'a suffi"*—"One

Vichy regime was enough for me." Lotringer has since looked very carefully at fascism, which he sees operating in many major literary, cultural, and religious productions which he names openly.

Crisis, deplacement of collective identities, and their representations are the subject of Sami Naïr's paper, "*Les identités aléatoire*" ("aleatory identities"). Sami Naïr is a Paris-based academic with an ethnic background that is very much in crisis, not just in northern Africa but also in France, through racist, ethnocentric, and repressive immigration politics that have a significant presence throughout Europe. The writer knows these well, and analyzes and criticizes them thoroughly. From his multifaceted cultural and intellectual perspective, Naïr develops a social critique that also indicts institutions: "The egalitarian norm masks an unequal reality," a structural inequality that is manifest between individuals and between different cultures. Naïr also focuses upon the negative effects of social crises on the perception of cultural and ethnic differences. Conflicts are not based on objective oppositions but on a "mobilization that is highly fantasmatic concerning the collective imaginary of the local people in relationship to the one that is perceived as foreign." Coming back to the title of his text, Naïr sees in "aleatory identities" not just a descriptive term for the individual in crisis, but also a concept of identifications that comes to terms with change, ambiguity, conflicts, singularity, and the Other without subscribing to fixed, universal, or national concepts of identity politics. It is not about universality or particularity, but about singularities that are subject to transformation and negotiation. He asks what it is to be "beur," to be Arab: "To be 'Arab' is thus to be in-between, and this is, through the force of things, because of the lack of choosing at the present between these cold monsters, these collective belongings. It is waiting, it is waiting for it 'to change.'"

Zeigam Azizov's text "Russification and the Terrain of 'Self Determination'" shows how the process of making an empire also meant the making of a language. Among other things, Azizov narrates a detailed history of the Russian language and its imperial career, the effects of this process during the Soviet era with its particular nomenclature, Lenin's theory of imperialism and his concept of "self-determination of nations" and its reality, Stalin's geo-linguistics and his book *Marxism and Linguistics*, and some interesting personal stories. Azizov—his name had to be

"Russified"—was born in Azerbaijan, studied later in Leningrad under racist pressure from institutions and individuals, and emigrated as an artist and writer to London where he lives now with a new language and a new passport. Today, post-perestroika, the independence of the former Soviet republics and satellite states also means an end to the Russian language that had served until recently as a *lingua franca* for more than a third of the geographical world. Now this function is being replaced by English. "For the 'free republics' *perestroika* turned history backwards: in trying to find their independence these republics had to look at their own histories and learn their own languages properly, that which had been cut off by the socialist revolution... the starting point of a complicated 'de-russification.'" The text ends with some critiques of the contemporary situation: "The 'iron curtain' which once hung between the Soviet empire and western capitalism is today multiplied and causes discrimination between cultures, languages, and relationships in the former republics of the Soviet Union."

The title of Victor Tupitsyn's text may be translated as "'Body Without Name': The Hero of his Time or of his Space?" It is written in Russian, though the author lives as a writer and academic in New York City. The Deleuzian "body without organs" is here turned into the "body without names." Here Tupitsyn is refering to the Russian art scene and to Russian intellectuals, some of whom have gained international recognition in spite of his argument, and this, unfortunately, of late, also by means of quasi-terroristic destructive actions (for example, the spraying of a Malevich painting in a museum). With a dense theoretical language—quotations from Hegel, Kant via Freud, Brecht, Bahktin, Deleuze, Derrida, etc.—intellectual relationships between the West and Russia after 1989 are investigated and criticized. This relationship is discussed as the center-periphery opposition. Tupitsyn qualifies this relationship as a particular kind of Orientalism. The author is very critical of the intellectuals left in his country; translated freely, he says: "If Moscow writers refer to Lacan, Foucault, Lyotard, Derrida, and Deleuze, it has only a decorative nature, or it is just a rudiment of their bureaucratic tradition of referring to authorities. In other words, in a text there are no theoretical models or methodologies, but arbitrarily taken sayings from these 'authoritarian comrades.' (Earlier such comrades were Stalin, Zhdanov, and Lisenko)."

Karen Kelsky's text "Flirting with the Foreign—Interracial Sex in Japan's 'International' Age" is a study of gender, racial, economic and libidinal dynamics in and outside contemporary Japan. Young, independent Japanese women—beyond the stereotypical so-called "office ladies"—discover and live their material mobility and desires in a touristic, international setting where they can play out their erotic, exotic, racial, and materialistic fantasies. This acting-out of female desires through the consumption of exotic male foreigners reflects upon fixed hierarchies in Japan. This paper doesn't bring heterosexual economies between interracial relationships to a happy end. Rather, it examines how old stereotypes on all sides are reinscribed, and how on "the global sex map, capital and the forces of commodification can dominate even as they liberate desire." Kelsky states: "What is 'recreated' within the *yellow cab* phenomenon (Japanese women, stereotyped by [Japanese] men) is not a brave new world of female empowerment and international intimacy, but rather old racism in a new guise."

Edward W. Soja's "Los Angeles 1965-1992: From Crisis-Generated Restructuring to Restructuring-Generated Crisis" gives a profile that encompasses the urban, social, industrial, technological, and demographic history between two major violent upheavals, the Watts rebellion and the L.A. riots in 1992. He thoroughly researches and relates economic decline and restructuring, industrialization and deindustrialization, large migrations, racial and ethnic oppression, poverty and richness, social upheavals, and traveling economies and productions. His studies of urban geography also touch upon "obsessive *Anglofication*," the role of the military, technology, segregation and racism. Soja describes the urban and suburban developments of L.A. in relationship to the global, transnational restructuring processes: "The local was becoming global... American manufacturing was not only leaving its metropolitan concentrations, it was leaving the country entirely," leaving a traumatized, urbanized suburbia behind without production but with conflicting demographics. Soja tries to "reconceptualize the very nature of urban studies, to see urban form more as a complex and polycentric regional mosaic of geographically uneven development affecting and affected by local, national, and global forces and influences. Studying Los Angeles (or Tokyo, or São Paulo, or Little Rock) thus becomes a window onto a wider panorama of subject matter than has traditionally been treated in the field of urban studies."

The interview I conducted with Benjamin Buchloh is in many ways revealing. Buchloh played a major role in introducing (mostly male—a fact on which he comments) European artists (Broodthaers, Buren, Richter) and theory (as editor of *October*) to the US over the last twenty years. He severely critiques European cultural institutions, cultural receptions, and state politics. "The European reception of American cultural praxis tends to isolate works from its context... Cultural praxis in Europe is still intensively built upon the reliability of cultural concepts (*Kulturbegriffe*) and cultural institutions." He also describes a significant example from Paris: the day the body of André Malraux, a leftist of his time, was transferred to the Pantheon, a Republican hall of cultural heroes, the French rap group NTM was sentenced to 6 months prison for their music texts. Touching upon a wide array of interesting issues—art historical and methodological problems, social art history, the museum, Critical Theory, Post-Colonial Theory etc.—identity politics becomes a focus. Buchloh discusses identity autobiographically as a German *émigré* to the USA and in terms of contemporary German politics: he fiercely criticizes Germany for retransforming Berlin into a capital centered around a traditional, nationalistic model of state identity at a time when big cities are internationally and globally interwoven. Consequently, we named this conversation "Mean remarks in between Moscow and Los Angeles," a title put together from two quotes.

Wulf Schmidt-Wulfen is a German geographer who for more than 20 years has been working on the representations of Africa in the context of German education. Unfamiliar with contemporary Anglo-American theory production, this academic has come to conclusions comparable to so-called post-colonial theory. "Vicious Circles—Geographical Imaginations/Representations of German Youth on the Subject of African 'Developing Countries'" is a text that synthesizes an empirical research project in which he asked more then 1,700 students, 10 to 17 years old, all over Germany to fill out a questionnaire on Africa. The results are devastating and reconfirm the most pessimistic accounts of the misrepresentation of the "cultural Other". Calling it a vicious circle is not just describing the average student's imaginings about Africa—"Because it is hot and dry, they are dark, black, poor, starving and underdeveloped and need help"—but also the way the media, school books and other representations function in order to perpetuate a catastrophic "geographic imagination" (E. Said) complicit with a colonial, post- and neo-colonial ideological status quo, which then informs daily politics and business. It must be added that in contrast to American academia and media, most mainstream European intellectuals and media are not familiar with critical debates about the power and the problems of representation. Schmidt-Wulfen's work is therefore a rather unique enterprise that has had only a tiny and skeptical reception within a purely academic realm.

The paper I contributed is entitled "Speaking, Reading, Learning, Teaching" (Sprechen, Lesen, Lernen, Lehren"). Once the institutional context is changed or removed altogether, all of these daily practices take on an "uncanny" dimension. Nobody would consider reading or learning as work if it were not done inside a context that justified it—school, university, profession, leisure time, etc. Behind this strangeness there is a critical dimension in which I am interested. I have been learning foreign languages continuously since the age of ten, mostly without or against the motivation of school. For a variety of reasons I have become very self-conscious about this practice in terms of its critical, social, psychoanalytical, and identity-specific implications. As an artist I have used speaking, reading, learning, and teaching strategically in order to open and stress discussion on the relationships of power, politics, institutions, knowledge, and technologies of the self. Furthermore, I have "imported" these basic cultural practices—speaking, reading, learning, teaching—into my artwork which as an institutional overlapping is worthy of reflection.

Dana Leonard and Lisa Adkins' text on French feminism was proposed by Isabelle Graw, who I also asked for a contribution as a founding member of *Texte zur Kunst*, a journal that has been translating and producing mostly so-called "cultural theory" for a German-speaking audience. *Texte zur Kunst* was about to translate and publish Leonard and Adkins' text on traveling feminist theory from France. Graw's contribution for my publication is not only ideally suited for this book, but also is significant regarding the German and Austrian situation of contemporary theory consumption: importation. Leonard and Adkins are British writers who name their text "Reconstructing French Feminism: Commodification,

Materialism, and Sex." The text shows in detail how such a category as "French feminism" was constituted in the American-English context through limited and reductive translation, editing, and publishing policy. Let me just quote one of the many reasons: "The 'curious synecdochic reduction' of French feminism to the work of deconstructionist and psychoanalytic writers is also crucially connected to the disciplinary background of most English-speaking specialists on France.... Such specialists usually have disciplinary backgrounds in linguistics and literature, and so find far greater connection with French feminists writing fiction or literary theory than with those from sociology, psychology, or anthropology." It is interesting to read how the materialistic and social-related works of French theorists were left out or reduced to limited reception. Besides the precise and carefully researched historical accounts of some of the powers that have defined "Feminism," the paper also presents and develops important arguments of the more social, materialistic, and gender-oriented debates that are far from finished.

Every critical discourse is dependent on the trafficking, evaluation, and reception of information, texts, and translations. The climate of cultural perceptions, critical debates, and the related art products ought to be constantly rearticulated and reinvestigated. One of the most striking experiences for me, when moving through different cultural contexts, different languages, and different reception milieu, is to observe how perceptions and the evaluating processes are changing and heterogeneous as well. This text volume is only an insufficient attempt to bring together some of the different voices in order to let them speak on a subject and for themselves.

New York, April 1997

1. See texts by Edward W. Said and others.
2. See Kenrick Ian Grandison, "Landscape of Terror: A Reading of Tuskee's Historic Campus" in Patricia Yaeger (ed), *The Geography of Identity*, Ann Arbor: The University of Michagan Press, 1996, p. 334 ff.

VORWORT

RAINER GANAHL

Das vorliegende Buch bildet den Abschluß eines Projektes mit dem Titel: *"IMPORTED - A READING SEMINAR in Relationship with my 'A Portable (Not So Ideal) Imported Library, Or How to Reinvent the Coffee Table: 25 Books for Instant Use (7 Different National Versions)'*, 1993-96". Ich bereiste mit den verschiedenen "tragbaren (nicht so idealen) importierten Bibliotheken" Asien, Amerika und Europa, um diese Seminare für einen oder zwei Monate lang an Universitäten, in Museen und Kunstzentren abzuhalten. Diese Publikation ist eine Fortsetzung des Projektes und enthält eine davon unabhängige Textsammlung zum Thema IMPORT. Ich habe Autoren, die jeweils einen direkten Bezug zu den von mir besuchten Orten haben, um Texte oder Interviews gebeten, die das Problem des kulturellen Austausches, des Kulturtransfers unter diversen Blickwinkeln behandeln. Jeder Text ist in seiner ursprünglichen Sprache abgedruckt. Deshalb umfaßt dieser Textband Beiträge in englischer, japanischer, russischer und deutscher Sprache. Es ist bezeichnend, daß es einige Autoren vorgezogen haben, in Englisch zu erscheinen, da die Wahrscheinlichkeit, in dieser Sprache gelesen zu werden, größer ist als z. B. in Japanisch oder Russisch. Das "nationale" Gruppieren der Autoren ist teilweise inkorrekt und hilft nur in ironischer Weise Texte zuzuordnen, was wiederum eine Anspielung auf das Mäandern meiner öffentlichen Leseprojekte ist. Die Bibliographien zu den verwendeten "importierten" Bibliotheken sind im Anhang. Ein Photo von jeder Lesegruppe markiert jede Sektion. In Österreich ist es mir nicht gelungen, ein Leseseminar zu veranstalten, was erklärt, wieso für den österreichischen Teil nur Bücher abgebildet sind. Die Auswahl der Orte war abhängig von bereits bestehenden Verbindungen und Einladungen. Die Projekte wurden finanziell vorwiegend von den einladenden Institutionen getragen.

Die Textsammmlung hier berührt, ebenso wie die mehrteiligen

Leseseminarprojekte, Probleme wie Transfer, Globalisierung, Nationalismus, Tourismus, Sprachen, Theorie, Wünsche, Identität und Politik. Obwohl schon eine umfassende Literatur zu diesen Themen vorhanden ist, möchte ich nichtsdestotrotz einige Überlegungen in Bezug auf Erziehungs- und Kulturpolitik beitragen. Über Jahrhunderte hinweg haben die dominierenden europäischen Nationen ihre kulturellen Apparate als wichtige Instrumente entwickelt und verwendet, um interne und externe Hegemonieansprüche zu konzeptualisieren, auszuüben und zu rechtfertigen. Kulturelle, ideologische und religiöse Arroganz hat sich als brutale Unterwerfung von ganzen Völkern und Gruppen im Ausland als auch im jeweils eigenen Land manifestiert. Verblieben ist eine Geschiche von tragischen Ausbeutungen und Mißrepräsentationen, die leider erneut eine Infrastruktur des Mißbrauchs für eine post-kolonialistische "neue Weltordnung" (new world order) abgibt, in der *business as usual* fortgesetzt werden kann, ohne Macht und Gewalt direkt anwenden zu müssen[1].

Für die Herausbildung der Nationalstaaten im 19. Jahrhundert waren Erziehungs- und Sprachprogramme zentrale Anliegen, weil durch sie das Volk homogenisiert und territoriale und politische Einheit antizipierbar wurde. Insbesonders im Fall Deutschland wurde das vorwiegend ideologische Konzept der Bildung erfunden, um die nationale Einheit als Idee der politischen Realität vorwegzunehmen. Eine Nationalsprache mit einem nationalen Theater, nationaler Literatur, Geschichte und Kunst als auch nationaler Musik und Oper wurden geschaffen, gefeiert und benutzt. Nationale Erziehungsprogramme garantierten etwas, das Fichte "innere Grenze" nennen konnte: eine Metapher, die zuerst für eine nationale Sprache und ihre Kultur stand. Heute ist diese Metapher wieder von besonderer Bedeutung: man braucht nur an das Schengener Sicherheitsabkommen zu denken, das die gesamte europäische Union in eine permanent Leute kontrollierende Grenzzone verwandelt, oder an die vieldiskutierte kalifornische Rechtslage, die die Bevölkerung beim Verkehr mit jedem staatlichen Amt (Postämter, Spitäler, Schulen usw.) automatisch einer Kontrolle unterziehen möchte. Unabhängig von diesen offensichtlichen Kontrolleinrichtungen, die meistens durch rassistische und klassenspezifische Vorurteile motiviert sind, werden "innere Grenzen" z. B. auch beim Besitz von Kreditkarten oder bei Ausbildungs- und beruflichen Qualifikationen geltend gemacht. Die enormen Auswir-kungen von Ausbildungsvorteilen in der aktuellen Informationsgesell-schaft reflektieren eine Geschichte der Diskriminierung als Folge eines Ausschlusses der Mehrheit der Bevölkerung von höherer Bildung, die immer schon einen beschränkten Zugang hatte und somit soziale Hierar-chien reproduzierte. So war z. B. bis zum Ende des 19. Jahrhunderts die Ausbildung von Afro-Amerikanern in den USA gesetzlich verboten, eine Tatsache, die nicht unabhängig gesehen werden kann von der heutigen Bildungssdemographie, die ethnische Unterschiede deutlich spiegelt[2].

Bildung ist nicht nur ein Diskurs gesellschaftlicher Reproduktion und als solche politisch, sondern auch eine Investition in einen großen Markt. Universitäten sind in der Regel sehr exklusiv und z. T. teuer. Sie konstituieren sich mehr und mehr als eine Industrie, die kritisches Denken in Ware verwandelt. Während Kant, Humboldt und andere eine philosophische Fakultät entwerfen konnten, deren kritische Autonomie garantiert war, so muß heute jede Form von Kritik zuerst ihre Sponsoren finden. Kritisches Denken tendiert dazu, nur als Markt mit all seinen Fluktuationen und Moden zu funktionieren. Politische, ideologische und die das soziale Geschlecht und die ethnischen und klassenspezifischen Zugehörigkeiten betreffenden Unterschiede sind dieser politischen Logik verschrieben. Was, wem, in welcher Sprache, für welche Interessensgruppe unterrichtet wird, ist nicht mehr eindeutig und schon gar nicht garantiert durch einen staatlichen Bildungsauftrag, ein Gesamtbildungsziel, das als "natürlich" und national vorausgesetzt wird, sondern ist selbst ein Streitobjekt, ein notwendiger Konflikt und reflektiert offene und verdeckte Repressionsgeschichten und Machtkämpfe. Texte der Kategorie *critical studies* sind deshalb oft beschäftigt mit dem Neu-schreiben und Analysieren eines voreingenommenen Erziehungskanons.

Reisen ist ein Privileg, das für lange Zeit wohlhabenden und gebildeten Leuten vorbehalten war. Frühere Bildungsprogramme beinhalteten Reisen oder bestanden überhaupt nur aus Reisen. In die Welt fahren, die anderen erobern, kontrollieren, ausnützen, studieren und repräsentieren stellte die Grundlage für Reichtum, Macht und Einfluß dar. Kulturelle Arroganz gemischt mit wohlwollendem Humanismus, Ignoranz und intellektueller Voreingenommenheit beeinflußte den Großteil der missionarischen Arbeit, die ihren eigentlichen Bezugsrahmen im Neuschreiben der machtpolitischen, geographischen, linguistischen und ökonomischen Karte der Welt hatte. Der Handel mit Menschen war als Sklaverei bekannt und half mit, jene Art von Produktion und Austausch zu finanzieren, die man Industrialisierung und Kapitalismus nennt und die ursprünglich nur mit kolonialen Resourcen und Produkten operierte. Heute finden sich für die Migration, die Massenwanderungen von Menschen, neue Namen, Gründe und Praktiken. Sexuelle Versklavung und Prostitution, illegale Einwanderer, die ökonomisch ausgebeutet werden, sowie Tourismus bezeichnen verschiedene, jedoch sich überlagern-de Realitäten. Aber nicht nur Menschen reisen frei oder unfrei, sind begrenzt oder werden herumgestoßen und herumgelockt. Das geschieht nun fast allem: Arbeit, Produktion, Rohmaterialien, Informationen, Wissen, Technologien, Abfall, Krankheiten, Göttern, Gütern, Bildern, Wünschen, Konflikten und jeder Form von Verbrauch. Mobilität, Geschwindigkeit und Austauschbarkeit werden zu einem Ziel an sich, und auch Künstler und Akademiker sind davon betroffen.

Heute kämpfen konkurrierende Staaten weniger direkt um Territorien, Kolonien und Resourcen. Vielmehr sind es nun schwer durchschaubare Netze transnationaler Konzerne (*TNC - transnational corporations*), deren Machtstrukturen nicht so einfach zu lokalisieren sind. *TNC*-Einfluß favorisiert keinen Ort und macht vor keiner Grenze oder Autorität halt. Transnationale Konzerne sprechen jede und passen sich jeder Staatsrhetorik an. Auch der Staat selbst verwandelt sich mehr und mehr in eine rein bürokratische Institution, die ihre Macht und deren Monopole delegiert. Gefängnisse sind ebenso privatisierbar wie Nationalbanken und das Gesundheits- und Erziehungswesen. Das Demontieren und Erodieren der Macht des Staates zerbricht auch seine Kultur- und Erziehungsinstitutionen. Obwohl Universitäten mit der Staatsmacht und dem Desaster Nationalismus geschichtlich komplizenhaft verbunden waren, nahmen sie auch eine kritische Funktion wahr, die jetzt ebenfalls am Schwinden ist, zur Ware mutiert und vermarktet wird. Das Modell der Dynamik von transnationalen Konzernen besteht aus national unspezifischen Operationen, die nur der Logik des transnationalen Kapitals und ihren exklusiven Mitgliedern und Aktionären gegenüber verantwortlich sind. Dieses Modell jedoch hat sich auch die Kultur-industrie zu eigen gemacht, die vermehrt von der Zusammenarbeit mit der Wirtschaft und ihren Interessen abhängig wird. Im Falle des Guggenheim Museums in New York sponsern ausländische Investoren, um sich exklusive Sichtbarkeit zu sichern und Einfluß zu gewinnen. Dafür wird dem Museum finanzielle Unterstützung gewährt. Es kann expandieren und Zweigstellen in der gesamten Welt eröffnen, die den Städten wiederum Prestigegewinn und Tourismus sichern. Das Militär versucht gleichfalls, wie eine transnationale Gesellschaft zu operieren. Truppen und Materialien werden von verschiedenen Nationen zu Gemeinschaftsaktionen zusammengeführt, wie das im letzten Golfkrieg der Fall war und bei der NATO und ihrer Expansion zutrifft. Aber all das bedeutet nicht, daß Kolonialismus und die durch Nationalismus produzierten Desaster der Vergangenheit angehören. Vielmehr das Gegenteil ist der Fall. Vorherrschaft und Ausbeutung werden zu einer operativen Logik, die jeden größeren sozialen Körper durchdringt.

Was mein reisendes Leseseminarprojekt betrifft, so ist auch dieses symptomatisch, wenn nicht sogar komplizenhaft mitbeteiligt an der heutigen transnationalen Situation. Überhaupt könnte man den internationalen Kunst- und Kulturtransfer seit den 70er Jahren als ein *Boeing 747-Phänomen* beschreiben und als solches auch auf seine Produktionsauswirkungen analysieren. Das Modell der westlichen Kunst scheint nach vollzogener Hochindustrialisierung überall in der Welt für einen begehrten Hauch von Liberalismus verwendbar zu sein. Ausgestattet mit Privilegien der vernetzten kulturellen Welt und ihrer Geographie, die nun die gesamte industrialisierte Zone der Erde einschließt, konnte ich Institutionen und finanzielle Mittel gewinnen, um mein Projekt frei durchzuführen: Leseseminare und Diskussionen mit Personen, die wiederum über das relative Privileg und die Freiheit verfügen, Zeit und Interesse an solchen, meistens öffentlichen Diskussionen zu haben. Ich erfuhr sehr viel aus den Gesprächen zu den mehr oder weniger gleichen Themen in verschiedenen Kontexten und Sprachen, die ich als meine Kunstpraxis lerne (*Basic Japanese, Korean, Russian, Modern Greek* ...). Obwohl alles auf Video aufgezeichnet und archiviert wurde, möchte ich hier keine Anekdoten der Diskussionen und Konflikte wiedergeben, hinter denen komplizierte Geschichten des jeweiligen Gastlandes stecken. Vielmehr bin ich interessiert, andere Stimmen sprechen zu lassen, die auf vielfältige Art zu den Orten, die ich besuchte, und zu Themen, die zur Diskussion kamen, in Beziehung stehen. Es versteht sich von selbst, daß ich aus den hier vereinten individuellen Texten gelernt habe.

Da dieser Band keine Übersetzungen anbietet, versuche ich, jeden Beitrag zu resümmieren, um auch einen gewissen Zugang zu jenen Texten zu gewährleisten, die in einer sogenannten Fremdsprache geschrieben sind. Die Reihenfolge der Texte ist abhängig vom Erscheinungszeitpunkt der jeweiligen "tragbaren (nicht so idealen) importierten Bibliotheken ...". Das Interview zwischen Kojin Karatani und Sabu Kohso hat den Titel "Ideenverkehr"(*Intercourse of Ideas*) und bezieht ein weites Spektrum von Belangen mit ein, die die heutige Gesellschaft und das Denken in einem Klima der gegenseitigen Abhängigkeit betreffen. Japan, wie jedes andere asiatische Land, ist ständig mit Mißrepräsentationen konfrontiert, die im Westen und auch in Asien selbst produziert werden. Damit in Zusammenhang steht eine Rhetorik der Originalität und Kopie, in der Karatani Machtverhältnisse festmacht: "Die meisten Bücher über Japan sind geschrieben, um Anforderungen einer Repräsentation zu erfüllen, die sich um ästhetische oder religöse, ökonomische und technologische Interessen formiert. ... Intellektuelle oder ethische Bereiche sind total außer acht gelassen." Karatanis Analyse des Modernismus und seine diversen Kritiken sind sehr produktiv, da er diese vom geographischen Rand her angeht und somit auch dieKehrseite des Modernismus studiert. In Bezug auf seine Kritik zum Bereich Phonozentrismus und Politik behandelt dieses Interview wichtige ökonomische und politische Aspekte von Sprachen, wie z. B. ihre ideologische Instrumentier-barkeit in der Konstruktion von National- und Rassenbewußtsein.

Einige von Karatanis Schriften wurden von Sabu Kohso übersetzt, der seinen Text "Zwei Arten der Übersetzung oder ein Überqueren des Pazifiks" in Englisch und leicht verändert auf Japanisch unter dem Titel "Übersetzung, eine unvergoltene Liebe oder ein Brief an Dich, der Japanisch liest" beisteuert. Übersetzen ist für den in Japan geborenen Kohso eine Lebensgrundlage, da er schon seit vielen Jahren in New York lebt. Das Übersetzen zwischen Englisch und Japanisch ist für den Übersetzer ein "'Verkehr', der völlig verschiedene Arten des Denkens, Agierens, Produzierens und Seins abverlangt. ... Die beiden Sprachen schaffen zwei verschiedene Personen in mir". In einer faszinierenden Art verbindet Kohso nicht nur die Konstruktion seiner Identität als einer Parallelidentität mit dem Akt des Übersetzens, sondern auch die Konstruktion der japanischen Identität an sich. "Übersetzen war immer das Hauptwerkzeug in der Ausformung der Nation ... ". Er entwickelt eine Theorie der Übersetzung, die nicht nur drei Wellen von kulturellem Import mit der Konstruktion der drei verschiedenen japanischen Schreibsysteme (chinesische Schriftzeichen, *Hiragana*, *Katakana*) erklärt. Seine Theorie liefert auch eine scharfe Kritik an seinem Geburtsland, das er als ein Land mit einer "nationalen Zwanghaftigkeit, fremde Kulturen zu importieren" beschreibt. Seine Kritik ist aber nicht nur auf Japans Austauschökonomie gerichtet, sondern auch auf die voreingenommene westliche Übersetzungspolitik aus dem Japanischen. Sehr wenig kriti-sches Denken *Made in Japan* wird übersetzt und außerhalb Japans in Umlauf gebracht. "Ein ästhetisches Japan wird gegenüber einem kriti-schen Japan [favorisiert] ... Heute besteht Japans bedeutendster kultureller Export aus der elektronischen *Software* für Spiele und Anima- tionen. Diese reflektieren wiederum Japans unausgeglichenes Profil: eine militärische und High-Tech Supermacht mit einer infantilen Mentalität (im doppelten Sinn: erstens sind die Medien für Kinder gemacht, zwei-tens repräsentieren sie weniger ethnisches Denken als vielmehr einen libidinösen Fluß in einem techno-sozialen Netzwerk)". Auch hier geht Kohsos konsistente Kritik in mehrere Richtungen, indem sie auch auf das abzielt, was einer kritischen Leserschaft als "Orientalismuskritik" be-kannt ist. Seine Mittelposition – auch eine Mittlerposition – erklärt, warum er seinen Text parallel auf Englisch und auf Japanisch geschrieben hat, ohne jedoch notwendigerweise zu übersetzen.

Bill Arning spricht in seinem Beitrag "Jeder ist schwul (wenn Kurt Cobain es gesagt hat, muß es wahr sein)" von sich selbst als "einem arbeitslosen, schwulen Ausstellungsmacher" (*faggot-curator*). Mit seinen organisierten Ausstellungen wie "The Anti-Masculine" oder "Stonewall 25 – Imagining the Gay Past" gibt er ein offenes und bemerkenswert prononciertes Bild der gegenwärtigen New Yorker Gay-Identität ab. Neben einer sehr seltsamen Geschichte, die ein anti-homosexuelles (homophobisches) Klima spiegelt - und es ist nicht so sehr eine Frage des *happy* oder *unhappy end*, sondern mehr der Umstände, die solche Geschichten entstehen lassen - erzählt Arning über einige interessante Treffen als Ausstellungsmacher im Ausland: "Von meiner New Yorker

Perspektive aus gesehen, kann man kein guter Ausstellungsmacher sein, solange man kein ehrlicher Kurator ist, und versteckt-schwul (*closeted*) kann man nicht ehrlich sein". Je mehr er fortschreitet, umso mehr zeigt uns der Text in seiner verführerischen Art, wie Arning verstanden hat, daß "Sexualität immer einen kulturellen Kontext hat". Während meiner Leseseminararbeit mit verschiedenen Beteiligten an verschiedenen Orten erlebte ich die Veränderbarkeit dieser Kontexte bei der gemeinsamen Lektüre von Texten zur Politik von Sexualität und Homosexualität.

Dan Bacalzos "Es tut mir leid, aber ich spreche nicht die Sprache" ist ein szenisches Sprechstück, welches ich vom Autor, einem jungen Philippino-Amerikaner, alleine auf einer leeren Bühne der New Yorker Universität vorgetragen, sehen konnte. Es thematisiert Belange der Sexualität und des kulturellen Kontexts, welche in Bacalzos Fall die Identität eines homosexuellen Asien-Amerikaners darstellen. Sein Text handelt von seinen ersten gewaltsamen, gleichgeschlechtlich-sexuellen Erlebnissen, welche sein kulturell und rassistisch voreingenommenes, "neues" "fremdes" Heimatland spiegeln. Er zeigt, wie sexuelle, sprachliche und ethnische Stereotypen einander überlagern und eine aggressive Realität abgeben, die der Schriftsteller "fließend" zu benennen weiß: "... Und während er mich fickte, dachte ich nicht an Repräsentationen. Ich dachte nicht, daß Asiaten immer die untere Rolle bei schwulen sexuellen Begegnungen spielen müssen. Ich dachte nicht, daß dieser weiße Typ seine kolonialen Phantasien auf meinem asiatischen Körper ausleben könnte ...." oder: "Ich bin ein dummer Idiot (*stupid fucker*), denn ich versuche, verschiedene Sprachen gleichzeitig zu sprechen. Aber anders als meine Großmutter spreche ich keine fließend".

Die Kombination von Geopolitik und Sex ist auch die Grundlage von Coco Fuscos Text mit dem Titel "Den Dollars nachjagen: Sexarbeit & Tourismus in Kuba": "Mein Interesse an der speziellen Rolle, die farbige Frauen in der wachsenden Sextourismusindustrie spielen, verbunden mit meinem Wissen, daß seit 1993 die Prostitution in Kuba markant angestiegen ist, hat mich dazu bewogen, einen Artikel über die betroffenen Frauen zu schreiben. Ich war auch besonders an den Problemen, die die Prostitution für ein sozialistisches Dritte-Welt-Land im Prozeß einer schwierigen Umstellung zum Kapitalismus darstellt, interessiert." Die Sexindustrie in der Welt ist ein Punkt, der leider kaum untersucht und erforscht ist, obwohl er Dimensionen annimmt, die direkt mit anderen dunklen und oppressiven Ökonomien des erzwungenen Austausches und Transfers in Verbindung stehen. Coco Fuscos historischer und gegenwärtiger Bericht zum besonderen Fall Kuba ist nicht nur reich an Fakten und provokativ, sondern beschreibt auch Szenarios, die andere Länder und Situationen, die an ungleichen Austauschverhältnissen leiden, gleichermaßen betreffen.

"Wie Personen und ganze Schulen von Interpretationen (*criticism*), so reisen auch Ideen und Theorien von Person zu Person, von Situation zu Situation, von einer Periode zur nächsten. Kulturelles und intellektuelles Leben ist gewöhnlich durch dieses Zirkulieren von Ideen unterstützt und unterhalten, egal ob es nun die Form eines zugegebenen oder eines unbewußten Einflusses, eines kreativen Zitierens oder einer großkalibrigen Aneignung annimmt. Die Bewegung von Ideen und Theorien von einem Ort zu einem anderen ist beides, sowohl eine Tatsache des Lebens als auch eine brauchbare fördernde Bedingung der intellektuellen Aktivität." So eröffnet Edward Said seinen Artikel "Rei-sende Theorie" ("Traveling Theory") von 1984, welcher den besonderen Fall von Georg Lukacs behandelt, Autor von "Geschichte und Klassenbewußtsein" (1923), worin dieser seine wichtige Theorie der Versachlichung entwickelt. Lukacs' Denken "reiste" vom revolutionären Ungarn über das Nachkriegs-Paris (L. Goldmann) nach Cambridge (R. Williams). In der Tradition von Saids einflußreichem Schreiben zum Thema kulturelle Repräsentation behandelt dieser Text auch Fragen zur intellektuellen Arbeit und der Funktion von Kritik und kritischem Bewußtsein: "Das kritische Wissen ist ein Bewußtsein über die Unterschiede von verschiedenen Situationen, ein Bewußtsein auch über die Tatsache, daß kein System oder keine Theorie die Situtation, aus der sie entsteht oder in die sie transportiert wird, komplett aufbraucht. Darüber hinaus ist kritisches Bewußtsein ein Bewußtsein des Widerstands gegenüber der Theorie und reagiert auf sie mit jenen ans Licht gebrachten konkreten Erfahrungen oder Interpretationen, mit denen es in Konflikt steht. Tatsächlich würde ich soweit gehen und sagen, daß es die Aufgabe des Intellektuellen (*critic's job*) ist, Widerstand gegenüber Theorie zu leisten, sie für geschichtliche Realität, für Gesellschaft, für menschliche Bedürfnisse und Interessen zu öffnen und auf jene konkreten Momente hinzuweisen, die der alltäglichen Wirklichkeit entstammen, die außerhalb oder jenseits des im vorhinein designierten interpretativen Bereichs liegen."

Gayatri Ch. Spivaks Interview mit mir nannten wir "Unsere Sprache verloren – Unterhalb der sprachlichen Karte. Es verweist auf eine Wirklichkeit, die oft übersehen wird: Es gibt nicht nur ein paar dominante Sprachen, sondern eine Unzahl von regionalen Sprachen und Dialekten, "Sprachen des Bodens" (*"languages of the soil"*), die, um eine "Karte" zu etablieren, in vielen Fällen unterdrückt und als minder angesehen werden. "Unsere Sprache verloren" (*"Lost our language"*) ist ein Ausdruck, den Spivak von den Menschen von Eastern Kimberley gelernt hat und der für etwas steht, was für so viele Menschen heute Realität ist: nicht mehr in ihrem eigenen kulturellen Idiom zu leben. "Sprache ist hier gebraucht als eine erweiterte konzeptuelle Metapher. Sie [die Menschen] meinen, daß sie nicht mehr länger den Sinn ihres Lebens aus ihrem kulturellen Idiom schöpfen. Foucault würde sagen, daß ihr kulturelles Idiom nicht mehr ihr *pouvoir savoir*, ihre Fähigkeit zu wissen, ist." Spivak spricht über ihr Verhältnis zu Sprachen. Sie wuchs in einer der vorherrschenden indischen Sprachen und in der Kolonialsprache Englisch auf: "Wir wußten nicht, daß meine eigene Muttersprache in sich selbst die Geschichte des Aufzwingens trug. Und wenn wir vom Aufzwingen des Englischen sprechen, dann betrachten wir meine Muttersprache als eine Art Sprache von Opfern." Spivak kritisiert auch einige jener sozialen Arbeiten, die von postkolonialer Theorie beeinflußt sind: "Es ist für mich sogar Teil des Problems, mit der Idee des Aufzwingens von Englisch zu beginnen". (*"For me, even to begin with the idea of the imposition of English is part of the problem."*)

Julia Kristeva präsentierte ihren Text "Die andere Sprache oder das Übersetzen von Sensibilität" auf einer Konferenz in New York in einer ihr fremden Sprache: auf Englisch. Als französische Staatsbürgerin las sie ihre Rede jedoch nicht mit einem französischen Akzent, sondern mit einem slawischen, dem Akzent ihrer Muttersprache. Der aus dem Französischen übersetzte Text beginnt fast konsequenterweise mit dem Problem einer "anderen Sprache": "Der Ausländer unterscheidet sich sofort, aber auch fundamental von jemandem, der keiner ist, denn er spricht eine andere Sprache. Näher betrachtet ist diese Tatsache weniger trivial als sie erscheinen mag; sie enthüllt ein extravagantes Schicksal: sowohl eine

Tragödie als auch eine Wahl. Eine Tragödie, weil ein Mensch ein sprechendes Wesen ist und somit natürlicherweise die Sprache seiner Landsleute spricht: die Muttersprache, die Sprache seiner Gruppe, die Nationalsprache. Der Wechsel von Sprachen ist gleichbedeutend mit dem Verlust von etwas Natürlichem, dem Verraten der eigenen Muttersprache oder zumindest mit der Notwendigkeit, zu übersetzen. Ein Ausländer ist essentiell ein Übersetzer." Kristeva entwickelt eine überraschende Theorie der Übersetzung aus einer psychoanalytischen Sicht, die jene Bedingungen des Austausches kennt, die totale Verachtung (*abject*) erzeugen. Sie spricht weiters über Proust, andere Schriftsteller und sich selbst.

Sylvère Lotringers Interview mit mir nennt sich "*Foreign Agent*" und überraschte mich mit der Richtung, die es einschlug. Ich interviewte ihn in seiner Funktion als Gründungsmitglied und Herausgeber der Zeitschrift *Semiotext(e)*, ein wichtiges Organ, das sogenannte französische Theorie seit den 70er Jahren in die USA einführt, also seit einer Zeit, in der noch kaum Interesse an der Publikation dieser Autoren in Amerika bestand. Lotringer gibt einen kritischen Bericht über die amerikanischen Universitäten und deren Publikationsorgane. Interessiert zuerst an einer "materialistischen Semiotik", verlagerte sich sein Interesse dann zu einer "Semiotik in Aktion" (*sémioitique EN ACTE*), ein Zeichenaktivismus, der durch die Manipulation von Texten und Bildern ein Delirium, eine "Schizokultur" kreierte, die dem Kapitalismus näher stand als den Universitäten. Lotringer reflektiert nicht nur die bedeutenden intellektuellen und "reisenden" Richtungen des Poststrukturalismus, sondern auch das tragische politische Desaster Faschismus, welches er als verstecktes jüdisches Kind erfahren mußte, eine Erfahrung, welche ihn Frankreich verlassen ließ: "*Un Vichy m'a suffi*" - ein Vichy-Regime hat mir gereicht. Lotringer hat seit damals den Faschismus sehr genau beobachtet, welchen er in einer großen Anzahl von bedeutenden litera-rischen, kulturellen und religiösen Produktionen, die er offen nennt, am Werk sieht.

Krise, Verschiebung von kollektiven Identitäten und ihre Repräsentationen sind die Themen von Sami Naïrs Schrift "Aleatorische Identitäten". Sami Naïr ist ein in Paris lebender Akademiker mit einem ethnischen Hintergrund, der nicht nur in Nordafrika sehr in die Krise geraten ist, sondern auch in Frankreich; als Folge einer rassistischen, ethnozentrischen und repressiven Immigrationspolitik, die bezeichnend ist für das gesamte Europa, was der Schriftsteller sehr gründlich zu analysieren und zu kritisieren weiß. Aus seiner multifacettierten, kulturellen und intellektuellen Perspektive entwickelt der Autor eine soziale Kritik, die es auch auf Institutionen absieht: "Die egalitäre Norm maskiert die inegalitäre Realität", eine strukturelle Ungleichheit, die sich nicht nur individuell auswirkt, sondern auch zwischen den verschiedenen Kulturen. Naïr beleuchtet u. a. die negativen Auswirkungen der sozialen Krise auf die Wahrnehmung von kulturellen und ethnischen Unterschieden. Konflikte basieren nicht auf objektiven Oppositionen, sondern auf einer "Mobilisierung, die höchst phantasmagorisch ist, in Bezug auf das kollektive Imaginäre der örtlichen Einwohner in Beziehung zu dem, was als fremd wahrgenommen wird." Auf den Titel seines Textes zurückverweisend, sieht Naïr in "Zufallsidentitäten" nicht nur einen deskriptiven Begriff für das in die Krise geratene Individuum, sondern auch ein Konzept für Identifikationen, das mit Veränderungen, Mehrdeutigkeit, Konflikten, Vereinzelung und dem Anderen fertig werden muß, ohne daß es sich fixierten, universalen oder nationalen Konzepten von Identitätspolitik verschreiben muß. Es geht nicht um Universalität oder Partikularität, sondern um Singularitäten, die Gegenstand von Veränderung und Diskussion sind. Naïr fragt in seinem Text, was es bedeutet, "*beur*", Araber zu sein: "Araber zu sein, bedeutet, durch die Macht der Dinge dazwischen zu sein. Es ist die Wahl mangels der Wahl, in der Gegenwart zwischen diesen zwei kalten Monstern zu wählen, die das kollektive Dazugehören ausmachen".

Zeigam Azizovs Text "Russifizierung und das Terrain der 'Selbstbestimmung'" zeigt, wie der Prozeß der Schaffung eines Impe-riums auch die Schaffung einer Sprache bedeutete. Azizov erzählt u.a. eine detailierte Geschichte der russischen Sprache und ihrer imperialen Karriere, von den Auswirkungen dieses Prozesses während der Sowjet-ära mit ihrer besonderen Nomenklatur, von Lenins Theorie des Imperia-lismus, seinem Konzept der "Selbstbestimmung der Nationen" und dessen Realität, von Stalins Geolinguistik und seinem Buch *Marxismus und Sprachlehre,* als auch von interessanten persönlichen Geschichten: Azizov - auch sein Name mußte russifiziert werden - geboren in Aser-baidschan, studierte in Leningrad, wo er unter persönlichen und institutionellen rassistischen Druck geriet. Er emigrierte als Künstler und Schrift- steller nach

London, wo er nun mit einer neuen Sprache und einem neuen Paß lebt. Heute, in einer Post-*Perestroika* Zeit bedeutet die Unabhängigkeit der ehemaligen sowjetischen Republiken und Satellitenstaaten auch ein Ende für die russische Sprache, die bis vor kurzem mehr als einem Drittel der geographischen Welt als *Lingua Franca* gedient hat. Nun ist diese Funktion ersetzt durch Englisch. "Für die 'freien Republiken' kehrte *Perestroika* die Geschichte um. Im Versuch, ihre Unabhängigkeit zu erlangen, mußten diese Republiken auf ihre Geschichte schauen und ihre eigenen Sprachen, von denen sie durch die sozialistische Revolution abge- schnitten waren, von Grund auf neu erlernen. Das leitete den Beginn einer komplizierten 'Entrussifizierung' ein." Der Text endet mit einer Kritik an der zeitgenössischen Situation: "Der 'Eiserne Vorhang', welcher einmal zwischen dem Sowjetreich und dem westlichen Kapitalismus hing, ist heute vervielfacht und bewirkt eine Diskriminierung von Kul-turen und Sprachen in den Beziehungen zwischen den früheren Repub-liken der Sowjetunion."

Die Überschrift von Victor Tupitsyns Text kann übersetzt werden mit "Körper ohne Name: Der Held seiner Zeit oder seines Raumes?". Der Text ist auf russisch verfaßt. Der Autor lebt jedoch schon seit langem als Schriftsteller und Universitätsprofessor in New York. Der deleuzianische "Körper ohne Organe" wird hier zum "Körper ohne Namen", wobei Tupitsyn sich auf die russische Kunstszene und die russischen Intellektuellen bezieht, von denen einige sehr wohl internationale Anerkennung gefunden haben, und das letzthin mitunter leider auch durch quasi-terroristische, destruktive Aktionen, wie z. B. das Besprühen eines Malevich-Gemäldes im Museum. In einer theoretisch dichten Sprache – Zitate von Hegel, Kant über Freud, Brecht, Bachtin zu Deleuze, Derrida usw. – werden die Beziehungen zwischen dem Westen und Rußland nach 1989 in Bezug auf das intellektuelle Leben hin untersucht und kritisiert. Diese Beziehungen sind als eine Zentrum-Peripherie-Opposition anzusehen. Tupitsyn möchte diese Beziehungen auch als eine besondere Art des Orientalismus qualifizieren. Der Autor ist gegenüber Intellektuellen, die in seinem Land zurückgeblieben sind, sehr kritisch. Frei übersetzt meint er: "Wenn sich Moskauer Schriftsteller in Artikeln auf Lacan, Foucault, Lyotard, Derrida und Deleuze beziehen, dann hat das nur dekorativen Charakter oder ist ein Überbleibsel der bürokratischen Tradition, auf Autoritäten zu verweisen. Mit anderen Worten gesagt: es gibt in einem

Text keine theoretischen Modelle oder Methodologien, sondern nur willkürlich angeeignete Zitate von diesen 'autoritären Kameraden' (früher waren diese Kameraden Stalin, Zhdanov und Lishenko)".

Karen Kelskys Text "Flirten mit dem Fremden, interethnischer[2] Sex in Japans 'internationalem' Zeitalter" ist eine Studie zur sozialgeschlechtlichen, ethnischen, ökonomischen und libidinösen Dynamik in und außerhalb des gegenwärtigen Japans. Junge und unabhängige japanische Frauen – nicht nur sogenannte *office ladies* – entdecken und leben ihre materielle und libidinöse Mobilität in einem internationalen touristischen Milieu, in welchem sie ihre erotischen, exotischen, ethnischen und materialistischen Phantasien ausleben können. Dieses weibliche Ausleben von Wünschen über das Konsumieren von exotischen ausländischen Männern reflektiert die starren Hierarchien Japans. Dieser Text bringt die heterosexuelle Ökonomie in Mischbeziehungen zu keinem *happy end*. Vielmehr zeigt er, wie alte Stereotypen auf allen Seiten sich neu einschreiben und wie auf "der globalen sexuellen Karte das Kapital und die Mächte der Verdinglichung dominieren, selbst dann, wenn sie Wünsche befreien." Kelsky: " ... das, was mit dem Gelben-Taxi-Phänomen [von (japanischen) Männern stereotypisierte japanische Frauen] 'neu kreiert' wird, ist keine tapfere neue Welt der weiblichen Ermächtigung und der internationalen Intimität, sondern eher ein alter Rassismus mit einem neuen Gesicht".

Edward W. Sojas "Los Angeles 1965 - 1992: Von der krisengenerierten Restrukturierung zur restrukturierungsgenerierten Krise" zeichnet das Profil der urbanen, sozialen, industriellen, technologischen und demographischen Geschichte zwischen zwei bedeutenden gewaltsamen Unruhen, nämlich der Wattsrebellion und der L.A. Revolte von 1992. Ökonomischer Niedergang und Restrukturierung, Industrialisierung und Industrieabbau, große Wanderbewegungen, rassistische und ethnische Unterdrückung, Armut und Reichtum, soziale Unruhen sowie reisende Ökonomien und Produktionen hängen zusammen und sind von Soja gut erforscht worden. Seine Studien zur urbanen Geographie berühren auch die *obsessive Anglofizierung* (*anglofication*), die Rolle des Militärs und der Technologie, als auch die von Ausgrenzung und Rassismus, um nur einige Punkte zu nennen. Soja beschreibt die städti- schen und vorstädtischen Entwicklungen von L. A. in Beziehung zu einem globalisierten transnationalen Restrukturierungsprozesses: "Das Lokale wurde global ... Amerikanische Produktionsstätten verließen nicht nur die großstädtischen Konzentrationen, sie verließen das Land überhaupt ganz" und hinterließen eine traumatisierte verstädterte Vor-stadtbevölkerung (*suburbia*) ohne Produktion, jedoch mit einer konfliktreichen Bevölkerungszusammensetzung. Soja versucht, "das Eigentliche des Urbanismus zu rekonzeptualisieren und die städtische Form mehr als ein komplexes und polyzentrisches regionales Mosaik von geographisch ungleicher Entwicklung zu sehen, das lokale, nationale und globale Mächte und Einflüsse mitbestimmt und von diesen beeinflußt wird. Das Studieren von Los Angeles (oder Tokio oder Sao Paulo oder Little Rock [Bill und Hillary Clintons Spekulationsland]) eröffnet so ein Fenster zu einem weiteren Panorama von Themen als die herkömmlicherweise im Feld der Urbanistik behandelten".

Das Interview, das ich mit Benjamin Buchloh geführt habe, überrascht in vielfacher Weise. Buchloh nahm und nimmt die letzten zwanzig Jahre hindurch eine bedeutende Rolle als Wegbereiter von (hauptsächlich männlichen – er nimmt dazu Stellung) europäischen Künstlern (Broodthaers, Buren, Richter) und Theorie (als Mitherausgeber von *October*) in den USA ein. Im Interview kritisiert er europäische kulturelle Institutionen, sowie deren Rezeption und Staatspolitik scharf. "Die europäische Rezeption amerikanischer Kulturpraxis hat immer die Tendenz, die Arbeiten aus ihrem eigenen Kontext herauszulösen ... kulturelle Praxis in Europa (ist) immer noch viel intensiver auf die Verläßlichkeit von Kulturbegriffen und Kulturinstitutionen aus". Er liefert auch ein bezeichnendes Beispiel aus Paris: Am Tag, an dem die Überreste von André Malraux, ein linker Aktivist seiner Zeit, in den Pantheon, eine republikanische Gedenksstätte für Helden der kulturellen Sphäre, überstellt wurden, an demselben Tag wurde auch die französische Rap-Gruppe NTM zu sechs Monaten Gefängnisstrafe für ihre Musiktexte verurteilt. Neben einem weiten Spektrum von interessanten Themen – kunstgeschichtliche und methodologische Probleme, soziale Kunstgeschichte, das Museum, Kritische Theorie, postkoloniale Theorie usw. – rückt Identitätspolitik in den Mittelpunkt. Der aus Deutschland emigrierte Kunstkritiker und Kunsthistoriker diskutiert Identität autobiographisch und in Beziehung zur gegenwärtigen deutschen Politik, die er heftig in Frage stellt. Vor allem kritisiert er die Umgestaltung Berlins zur Haupt-stadt, zentriert um ein traditionelles nationalistisches Modell von Staatsidentität, zu einer Zeit, in der Großstädte international und global vernetzt sind. Konsequenterweise nannten wir diese Konversation "Böse Bemerkungen zwischen Moskau und Los Angeles", ein Titel, der aus Fragmenten des Textes zusammengesetzt wurde.

Wulf Schmidt-Wulfen ist ein deutscher Geographiepädagoge, der seit mehr als zwanzig Jahren Arbeiten zur Repräsentation Afrikas im deutschen Ausbildungskontext verfaßt hat. Ohne besondere Kenntnis der aktuellen anglo-amerikanischen Theorieproduktion ist dieser Universitätsprofessor zu Resultaten gekommen, die vergleichbar sind mit den postkolonialen Theorien von Edward Said und anderen. "'Teufelskreise' – geographische Vorstellungen deutscher Jugendlicher zum Thema afrikanische 'Entwicklungsländer'" gibt die Synthese eines empirischen Forschungsprojektes wieder, für das er mehr als 1700 Mittelschüler – zehn bis siebzehn Jahre alt – aus ganz Deutschland bat, Fragebögen zu Afrika auszufüllen. Die Ergebnisse sind erschütternd und bestätigen die pessimistischsten Berichte über die Mißrepräsentierung des kulturell anderen. Teufelskreis ist jedoch nicht nur eine angemessene Metapher, die die Vorstellungen eines durchschnittlichen Schülers zu Afrika beschreibt: "Weil es dort heiß und trocken ist, sind sie dunkel, schwarz, arm, hungernd und unterentwickelt und brauchen deshalb Hilfe". Das Wort Teufelskreis ist auch bezeichnend für die Art und Weise, wie Medien, Schulbücher und andere Repräsentationen funktionieren, um eine katastrophale "geographische Imagination"[3] zu perpetuieren, die mit dem kolonialen, post- und neokolonialen, ideologischen Status-Quo komplizenhaft kompatibel ist und täglich in Politik und Wirtschaft Eingang findet. Es muß noch dazugesagt werden, daß, anders als im Umfeld der Universitäten und Medien Nordamerikas, in den meisten europäischen intellektuellen und medialen Kontexten kritische Debatten zu diesen Fragen über Macht und Repräsentation kaum stattfinden. Schmidt-Wulfens Arbeit ist deshalb ein ziemlich einzigartiges Unternehmen und hat bis dato nur eine limitierte, skeptische und rein akademische Rezeption erfahren.

Mein eigener Beitrag ist bezeichnenderweise mit "Sprechen, Lesen, Lernen, Lehren" überschrieben. Hinter all diesen alltäglichen

Praktiken verbirgt sich auch eine "unheimliche" Dimension, ist einmal der institutionelle Kontext verändert oder überhaupt entfernt. Niemand würde Lesen oder Lernen als Arbeit betrachten, wenn es nicht innerhalb eines dafür vorgesehenen Zusammenhanges stattfindet, der es rechtfertigt: Schule, Universität, Beruf, Freizeit, usw. In dieser Befremdung aber steckt eine kritische Dimension, die mich interessiert. Ich lerne schon seit meinem zehnten Lebensjahr Fremdsprachen und dies meistens ohne oder entgegen jede schulische Motivation. Aus einer Reihe von Gründen wurde ich mir dieser Praxis in Bezug auf ihre kritischen, sozialen, psychoanalytischen und identitätsspezifischen Implikationen sehr bewußt. Vor etlichen Jahren fing ich an, in der Funktion als Künstler Sprechen, Lesen, Lernen und Lehren strategisch einzusetzen, um Diskussionen über die Beziehungen von Macht, Politik, Institutionen, Wissen und Technologien des Ichs zu eröffnen und zu forcieren. Weiters versuche ich, diese elementaren kulturellen Praktiken in meine künstlerische Arbeit zu "importieren", was als Vermischung von institutionellen Kontexten interessant ist, reflektiert zu werden.

Dana Leonard und Lisa Adkins' Text über französischen Feminismus wurde mir von Isabelle Graw vorgeschlagen, nachdem ich sie in ihrer Funktion als Gründungsmitglied von *Texte zur Kunst* gebeten hatte, einen Text zu dieser Publikation beizusteuern. *Texte zur Kunst* selbst übersetzt und produziert vorwiegend sogenannte *cultural theory* für einen deutschsprachigen Kontext. Diese Zeitschrift war gerade dabei, den Text von Leonard und Adkins über die Rezeption französischer Theorieproduktion zu übersetzen. Graws Angebot paßt nicht nur zum Thema dieser hier vorliegenden Publikation, sondern ist auch signifikant für den deutschen und österreichischen Theoriekonsum: Import. Leonard und Adkins sind zwei in England arbeitende Theoretikerinnen, die ihren Text "Zur Rekonstruktion des französischen Feminismus: Verdinglichung, Materialismus und Geschlecht. Die Verdinglichung des 'französischen Feminismus'" nennen. Der Text zeigt im Detail auf, wie die Kategorie "französischer Feminismus" sich im englisch-amerikani- schen Kontext aufgrund einer beschränkten und verkürzten Übersetzungs-, Redaktions- und Veröffentlichungspolitik konstituierte. Ich zitiere hier nur einen der vielen Gründe: "Die 'merkwürdige synekdochische Reduktion' des französischen Feminismus auf die Arbeiten der dekonstruktiven und psychoanalytischen Autorinnen hängt auch wesentlich mit dem fachlichen Hintergrund der meisten englischsprachigen Frankreich-Expertinnen ... zusammen. Ihr fachlicher Hintergrund liegt meistens in der Sprach- oder Literaturwissenschaft, sodaß sie weitaus eher eine Verbindung zu denjenigen französischen Feministin-nen finden, die Literatur oder Literaturtheorie schreiben, als zu denen aus Soziologie, Psychologie und Anthropologie." Es ist interessant nach-zulesen, wie die materialistischen, sozialen und anthropologischen Arbeiten der französischen Theoretikerinnen übergangen oder auf eine beschränkte Rezeption reduziert wurden. Neben dem genauen und sorg-fältig recherchierten historischen Bericht über einige der Definitionen, die "Feminismus" konstituiert haben, nimmt dieser Text wichtige soziologische, materialistische und geschlechtsspezifische Argumente wieder auf, die noch lange nicht ausdiskutiert sind.

Jeder kritische Diskurs ist abhängig vom Zirkulieren, Bewerten und Rezipieren von Informationen, Texten und ihren Übersetzungen. Das Klima von kulturellen Rezeptionen, kritischen Debatten und seinen kunstbezogenen Produktionen muß ständig neuformuliert und neu untersucht werden. Eine der beeindruckendsten Erfahrungen beim Durchqueren verschiedener kultureller Kontexte, verschiedener Sprachen und verschiedener Rezeptionsmilieus ist für mich das Beobachten der Veränderbarkeit von Texten, Ideen und kulturellen Produktionen in Bezug auf deren vielfältige Bewertungen. Dieser Textband ist nur ein kleiner Versuch, verschiedene Texte zu diesen Themen zusammenzubringen.

New York, April 1997

1. vgl. die Texte von Edward W. Said und anderen.
2. vgl. Kenrick Ian Grandison, "Landscape of Terror: A Reading of Tuskee's Historic Campus" in Patricia Yaeger (ed), *The Geography of Identity,* Ann Arbor: The University of Michigan Press, 1996, p. 334 ff.
3. Das Wort "*interracial*" übersetze ich mit "interethnisch", weil ich es trotz der neutralen Konnotationen des Englischen oder Französischen vorziehe, die deutschen Wörter "rassisch", oder "Rasse" nicht zu verwenden.
3. siehe Edward W. Said.

INTRODUCTION

RAINER GANAHL

Cette publication conclut un projet de lectures consistant en six séminaires donnés dans six pays différents et intitulé : *Importé – un séminaire de lecture en relation avec ma "bibliothèque portable (pas vraiment idéale) importée ou comment réinventer la table café: 25 livres pour utilisation instantanée (7 versions nationales différentes)" 1993-96. [IMPORTED – A Reading Seminar in Relationship with my 'A Portable (Not So Ideal) Imported Library, Or How to Reinvent the Coffee Table: 25 Books for Instant Use (7 Different National Versions)' (1993-96)"].* J'ai voyagé en Asie, Europe et aux États-Unis avec différentes bibliothèques pour donner dans des universités, des musées et des centres d'art, des séminaires d'une durée de un à deux mois. Ce livre est une extension de mon projet. Il réunit des textes indépendants qui ont pour préoccupation commune le problème de l' IMPORT-EXPORT. J'ai demandé à des auteurs en relation directe avec les pays où se sont déroulés ces séminaires de fournir des textes et des interviews sur l'importation, le transfert culturels et leurs diverses implications sociales, géo-économiques, matérielles, linguistiques, idéologiques et psychologiques. Chaque texte est reproduit dans sa langue originale. Ainsi, ce volume comprend des textes en langue anglaise, russe, allemande, japonaise, et française. L'indexation des auteurs sous des bannières nationales est partiellement incorrecte, mais sert de manière ironique au regroupement des textes. Elle fait allusion au parcours nécessaire pour réaliser ce projet. En fin de volume, j'inclus les bibliographies des bibliothèques importées que j'ai utilisées dans chaque pays. Une photographie des groupes de lecture illustre chaque chapitre. Pour l'Autriche, où je n'ai pas pu tenir le séminaire prévu, il n'y qu'une photographie des livres. La localisation des séminaires tenait aux invitations faites par des institutions, et le financement était dans la plupart des cas assuré par les organisations d'accueil.

Tout comme les textes assemblés dans ce volume, le projet touche aux problèmes des frontières et des échanges; de la globalisation, du nationalisme, du tourisme, des langues, de la théorie, des désirs, de l'identité et de la politique. Même s'il existe déjà une vaste littérature sur ces thèmes, je voudrais juste ajouter quelques remarques sur ces questions et sur leur rapport avec la politique de la culture et de l'éducation. Depuis des siècles les nations européennes dominantes ont développé et utilisé leurs appareils culturels et éducatifs comme instrument pour concevoir, la justifier et approfondir une hégémonie intérieure et extérieure au bénéfice des pouvoirs en place. Cette arrogance culturelle, idéologique et religieuse, dans les cas les plus extrêmes, a contribué à une subordination brutale, tant à l'étranger que sur les sols nationaux. Aujourd'hui, nous nous retrouvons avec l'héritage tragique d'une histoire de représentations érronées *(misrepresentations)* et d'exploitations perpétuant une infrastructure d'abus qui permet à un "nouvel ordre mondial" post-colonial de se développer, *business as usual*, sans avoir besoin de recourir à l'usage direct de la force et de la violence.

Les programmes linguistiques et éducatifs ont partout joué un rôle déterminant dans la formation de l'Etat-nation au dix-neuvième siècle: ils ont permis d'homogénéiser les populations et d'anticiper, au niveau imaginaire, l'unification territoriale et politique. Par exemple, dans le cas allemand, la Bildung (éducation bourgeoise à fort impact idéologique) a été inventée pour célébrer l'unité nationale comme idée avant même qu'elle ne devienne un état de fait politique. Une langue nationale, avec sa littérature et son théâtre nationaux, son histoire nationale et son art national, son opéra et sa musique, fut ainsi créée, développée et instrumentalisée. Les programmes éducatifs garantissaient ainsi l'existence de ce que Fichte appelait la "frontière intérieure" (*innere Grenze*), métaphore désignant avant tout une langue nationale et sa culture. Aujourd'hui, cette métaphore est de nouveau importante comme l'indiquent les traités de Schengen qui transforment l'Europe entière en une zone frontière où la police contrôle les populations, ou bien les récentes propositions pour une législation californienne exigeant le contrôle automatique d'identité à toute administration d'état, postes, hôpitaux, écoles, etc. Indépendamment de ces contrôles panoptiques évidents, directement dictés par des préjugés sociaux et raciaux, la présence de ces "frontières intérieures" se manifeste aussi, par exemple, dans la ségrégation qui permettent les cartes de crédit et les compétences éducatives et professionnelles. L'impact énorme des avantages éducatifs dans la société d'information contemporaine est le reflet, le prolongement d'une logique de reproduction sociale basée sur une restriction de l'accès à l'éducation qui bénéficie aux couches dominantes de la société. C'est l'éducation qui garantit la reproduction des hiérarchies sociales, tout en jouant un rôle idéologique comme outil de légitimation, de "naturalisation" de l'ordre établi. Jusqu'à la fin du 19e siècle, par exemple, l'éducation des Afro-Américains était interdite par la loi, un fait qui n'est pas sans relation avec l'exclusivité raciale de la démographie éducative américaine aujourd'hui.

L'éducation n'est pas seulement un discours de reproduction sociale, et donc un fait politique, elle est aussi un marché gigantesque. En plus de leurs caractères exclusifs et coûteux, les universités actuelles constituent une industrie qui menace toujours plus de réduire la critique elle-même à l'état de marchandise. Si Kant, Humboldt et leurs contemporains pouvaient concevoir une faculté de philosophie dont l'autonomie critique était garantie, aujourd'hui tout critique doit d'abord trouver ses sponsors. L'université actuelle tend dès lors à fonctionner comme un marché, avec ses modes et ses fluctuations. Des écarts idéologiques, politiques, raciaux et sociaux-économiques s'inscrivent eux-aussi dans cette logique politique. Quoi enseigner, à qui, dans quelle langue, et dans l'intérêt de quel groupe.La réponse à ces questions n'est plus automatiquement garantie par un *Bildungsauftrag*, un objectif éducatif global et supposé naturel, elle devient au contraire une querelle, un conflit nécessaire qui révèle des histoires répressives et des conflits de pouvoir latents et occultés. Les textes compris dans la partie anglo-saxonne (*critical studies)* sont ainsi souvent engagés dans un projet d'analyse et de réécriture de ce genre de canons éducatifs dominants, eurocentristes, hétérosexistes et racialement biaisés.

Voyager a été pendant longtemps un privilège réservé aux gens riches et éduqués. Les programmes d'éducation d'autrefois comprenaient des voyages, quand ils ne consistaient pas uniquement en voyages. S'répandre dans le monde, conquérir, étudier, contrôler, exploiter et représenter l'Autre, toutes ces actions ont aussi été la source de richesses, du pouvoir, et de la domination. Une arrogance culturelle mêlée d'humanisme charitable, une ignorance et un sentiment de supériorité intellectuelle ont régi la majorité des expéditions missionnaires, alors que leur véritable rôle se jouait au niveau conceptuel et politique, dans la réécriture de la carte géographique, économique et linguistique. Le commerce d'êtres humains (esclavage) a aidé au financement du mode de production et d'échange capitaliste . La révolution industrielle, ne l'oublions pas, à été tout d'abord fondée uniquement sur l'exploitation des produits et des ressources coloniales. Aujourd'hui, les migrations humaines ont de nouveaux noms, des pratiques et des raisons nouvelles. L'esclave sexuelle devenue prostituée, l'immigrant illégal exploité économiquement et le touriste, désignent des réalités différentes du même ordre. En fait tout voya-ge aujourd'hui, et pas seulement les êtres humains: travail, production, matériaux bruts, information, savoir, technologies, déchets, maladies, divinités, possessions, images, désirs, conflits, et consommations de toutes ordres, poussent, attirent, bloquent et séduisent à l'échelle de la planète entière. La mobilité, la vitesse, la compatibilité sont en train de devenir des qualités propres aux classes professionnelles contemporaines, dont les universitaires et les artistes font aussi partie.

Dans la situation politique actuelle, les conflits entre nations en rivalité pour des territoires, des colonies et leurs ressources, ont diminué. Bien plus souvent, il s'agit de négociations à l'intérieur d'un réseau opaque de sociétés transnationales (*TNC*) dont la structure de pouvoir est bien plus difficile à localiser. Le pouvoir des *TNC* ne hiérarchise pas les lieux, il traverse le pouvoir des États et les déterminations géographiques. Les *TNC* peuvent même adopter la rhétorique de l'état, puisque l'état lui-même se transforme de plus en plus en une simple institution bureaucratique déléguant ses pouvoirs et ses monopoles à des entreprises privées. On privatise les prisons au même titre que les banques, les services sociaux et les systèmes d'éducation. Le démembrement et l'érosion du pouvoir de l'état implique aussi celui de ses institutions culturelles et éducatives, puisqu'elles étaient au coeur de sa création. Malgré leur complicité avec le pouvoir de l'état et les désastres du nationalisme, les universités avaient aussi une fonction critique qui s'efface actuellement, se transformant en marchandise. Le modèle de la dynamique des *TNC* consiste en opérations sans allégeances nationales, garantes uniquement de la logique d'un capital transnational fidèle aux intérêts exclusifs de ses membres et actionnaires. Ce modèle est aussi adopté par l'industrie culturelle qui dépend de plus en plus de collaborations avec des corporations qui y trouvent leur intérêt.C'est le cas du Musée Guggenheim à New York, financé par des investisseurs étrangers qui espèrent ainsi gagner en termes d'exclusivité, visibilité, et influence. En retour, le Musée s'assure un soutien financier; il peut s'étendre et ouvrir des filiales partout dans le monde. L'armée tente elle aussi de fonctionner comme une société transnationale quand elle intervient avec le matériel et les troupes de plusieurs nations, comme cela a été le cas dans la guerre du Golfe et dans l'expansionisme actuel de l'OTAN. Ceci ne signifie cependant pas que nous en ayions fini avec le colonialisme et les horreurs du nationalisme. En fait, le contraire semble se produire: domination et exploitation s'articulent en une logique opératoire capable de pénétrer n'importe quel corps social.

Mon projet de séminaires itinérants de lecture et les préoccupations qui s'y attachent sont aussi symptomatiques, sinon complices, de la situation transnationale actuelle. Aujourd'hui, l'industrie culturelle et ses ramifications s'étendent dans toutes les zones industrialisées de la planète. Il semble qu'après la réussite de la haute industrie le modèle de l'art occidental soit partout désiré et sollicité comme une touche de libéralisme. Positionné à l'intérieur d'un réseau connecté, relativement privilégié (le monde de la culture), j'ai eu accès à des institutions et à des fonds pour poursuivre mon projet librement. Les séminaires de lecture et les discussions ont impliqué des gens qui eux-aussi jouissent du privilège relatif et de la liberté nécessaire pour s'intéresser à de telles discussions. J'ai beaucoup appris en discutant de problèmes similaires dans des contextes et des langues différentes (je continue à apprendre de nouvelles langues pour mon travail artistique - *Basic Japanese, Korean, Russian, Modern Greek, Japanese,* etc.). Bien que tout ait été enregistré et archivé, cette introduction n'a pas pour but de présenter ou de résumer les discussions et les conflits que j'ai rencontrés. Ceux-ci sont le produit d'histoires complexes dans les contextes d'accueil différents. Je veux plutôt essayer de laisser parler par eux-mêmes les sujets abordés et les voix liées aux lieux visités.

Étant donné que ce volume ne comprend pas de traductions, ce qui suit est un simple sommaire de chaque contribution destiné à faciliter l'accès à ces textes écrits dans des langues dites étrangères. Leur ordre d'apparition suit l'itinéraire de mes *Bibliothèques portables et importées (pas vraiment idéales)*. L'interview entre Kojin Karatani et Sabu Kohso, intitulée "Rapport d'idées" (*Intercourse of ideas*) traite un ensemble de questions concernant la société contemporaine et la réflexion dans un contexte d'interdépendance. Comme tout pays asiatique, le Japon est constamment l'objet de représentations fautives produites à l'Ouest voire même en Asie. À ces représentations falsifiés s'associe une rhétorique biaisée, celle de l'opposition entre "original et copie", où Karatani détecte des rapports de force. "La plupart des livres sur le Japon sont écrits pour satisfaire les demandes d'une représentation groupée soit autour de sphères religieuses et culturelles, soit autour de questions et d'intérêts économiques et technologiques... Les domaines intellectuels et éthiques sont oblitérés". L'efficacité de l'analyse du modernisme fournie par Karatani provient du fait qu'il aborde le problème à partir d'une zone marginale. En relation avec sa critique du phonocentrisme et du politique, cette interview examine des aspects économiques et politiques de la langue et son instrumentalité idéologique dans la constitution de l'État-nation et de la conscience raciale.

Une partie des écrits de Karatani a été traduite par Kosho qui contribue deux textes à ce volume, "*Two Modes of Translation, or a Crossing Over the Pacific*" en anglais, et un article légèrement différent, "Honyaku, Mitasarenu-ai, aruiwa Nihongo-o-yomo-eno-tegami" ("Traduction, un amour non désiré, ou lettre à vous qui lisez le japonais"), en japonais. Pour Kosho, qui est né au Japon, la traduction est une réalité existentielle, car il habite à New York depuis plusieurs années. Traduire de l'anglais en Japonais et vice versa, est pour le traducteur "un trafic qui implique deux manières complètement différentes de penser, de jouer, de produire, d'être même... Les deux manières produisent deux personnages différents en moi". De façon curieuse, Kohso associe l'acte de traduire non seulement à la construction de son identité propre comme identités parallèles, mais aussi à l'identité japonaise en général. "La traduction a toujours été l'outil principal pour former la nation". La théorie de la traduction qu'il développe constitue une critique sévère de son pays d'origine, qu'il décrit comme ayant "une obsession nationale pour l'importation de cultures étrangères". Sa critique est autant dirigée contre l'économie japonaise d'échange que contre l'attitude biaisée de l'ouest quant à sa politique relative aux textes traduits du japonais: très peu de travail critique "*made in Japan*" est traduit et circule à l'extérieur du Japon. "Le Japon esthétique est favorisé aux dépens du Japon critique. Aujourd'hui, les exportations culturelles japonaises les plus puissantes sont les logiciels des jeux électroniques et des dessins animés. Elles reflètent à nouveau le déséquilibre du profil japonais: une superpuissance militaire et économique à la mentalité infantile (ceci dans un double sens: premièrement ces médias sont originairement conçues pour les enfants; deuxièmement, ils représentent non pas une pensée éthique mais plutôt un courant libidineux dans le réseau techno-social)". La critique de Kohso est également orientée dans plusieurs directions, visant ce qui est désormais désigné par la communauté critique sous le nom d'*Orientalisme*. Sa position d'entre-deux explique pourquoi Kohso a écrit ses textes en anglais et en japonais sans nécessairement traduire de l'un à l'autre.

Dans son texte "Tout le monde est gay (si Kurt Cobain l'a dit c'est vrai)", Bill Arning se décrit comme un "conservateur pédé au chômage". Avec les expositions qu'il a organisées, dont "L'Anti-Masculin" ou "Stonewall 25 – Imaginer le Passé Gay", entre autres, il a développé une image ouverte et remarquablement distincte d'une identité homosexuelle new yorkaise. En même temps qu'il nous raconte une histoire étrange reflétant le climat homophobe – et ce qui compte ici ce n'est pas vraiment que la fin soit triste ou heureuse, mais plutôt les circonstances qui l'entourent – Arning nous fait part de quelques rencontres significatives qu'il a faites à l'étranger alors qu'il "exportait" son expérience d'organisateur d'exposition. Ce qui est en jeu, c'est ce dilemme: "De ma perspective new yorkaise, on ne peut pas être un bon organisateur d'expositions si on n'est pas honnête, et on ne peut pas être honnête si on est 'pédé-caché' (*closeted*)." Plus nous lisons, plus l'auteur nous montre, dans un style séduisant, comment il en est arrivé à comprendre que "la sexualité a toujours un contexte culturel". Je suis devenu très conscient moi-même du changement constant de ces contextes en lisant des textes sur la politique du sexe et de l'homosexualité avec des audiences différentes dans des lieux différents pendant mon travail de séminaires.

J'ai eu la chance d'assister à la performance "Je suis désolé, je ne parle pas la langue" par l'auteur, Dan Bazalco, un jeune philipin-américain debout sur une scène vide à la New York University. La pièce explore des questions de contexte sexuel et culturel, dans son cas l'identité d'un homosexuel asiatique-américain. Ses premières expériences homosexuelles violentes reflètent le préjugé culturel et racial du nouveau pays "étranger" qu'il habite. Il montre comment les stéréotypes sexuels, linguistiques et raciaux se mélangent et forment une réalité agressive dont il a l'expérience: "... et pendant qu'il me baisait, je ne pensais pas à la représentation. Je ne pensais pas que les asiatiques jouent toujours un rôle passif dans les rencontres homosexuelles mâles. Je ne pensais pas que ce mâle blanc était en train de projeter ses fantasmes coloniaux sur mon corps asiatique ..." Ou encore: "Je suis un putain d'imbécile parce que j'essaie de parler plusieurs langues à la fois. Mais contrairement à ma grand-mère, je ne peux le faire couramment"

La géopolitique et le sexe sont aussi au centre du texte de Coco Fusco, intitulé "Racoler pour des dollars: Travail Sexuel et Tourisme à Cuba": "L'intérêt que je porte au rôle spécial que les femmes de couleur jouent dans l'explosion du tourisme sexuel là-bas, allié à ma conscience de l'accroissement marqué de la prostitution à Cuba depuis 1993, m'a poussé à écrire un article sur les femmes concernées. Je m'intéresse aussi particulièrement aux questions que la prostitution pose pour un pays socialiste du tiers-monde sur le point de faire une transition difficile en direction du capitalisme." L'industrie globale du sexe est un problème qui n'est malheureusement que peu étudié et abordé, bien qu'elle touche à des dimensions directement liées à d'autres économies d'échange forcé et d'importation sombres et abusives. L'analyse historique et contemporaine de Cuba proposée ici par Coco Fusco est non seulement riche et provocatrice au niveau des faits, mais elle décrit aussi un scénario applicable à beaucoup d'autres pays soumis à des relations d'échange inégales.

"Comme les gens et les écoles critiques, les idées et les théories voyagent– de personne à personne, de situation à situation, d'une période à une autre. La vie intellectuelle et culturelle est normalement nourrie et souvent soutenue par cette circulation d'idées, sous forme d'influence manifeste ou inconsciente, d'emprunt créateur, ou d'appropriation pure et simple, le mouvement des idées et des théories d'un lieu à un autre étant à la fois un fait vécu et la condition de possibilités utiles à toute activité intellectuelle". Ceci constitue l'ouverture d'un article d'Edward Said publié en 1984, intitulé "Travelling Theory", où il discute du cas particulier de Georg Lukacs – auteur, entre autres, d'"Histoire et conscience de classe" (1923) où est élaborée son importante théorie de la réification. La pensée de Lukacs a voyagé de la Hongrie révolutionnaire via le Paris d'après la seconde guerre mondiale (L. Goldman) jusqu'à Cambridge (R. Williams). Dans la tradition importante des écrits de Said sur la représentation culturelle, ce texte aborde aussi la question du travail intellectuel et de la fonction de la critique et de la conscience critique: "La conscience critique est une concrétisation des différences entre les situations, une concrétisation aussi du fait qu'aucun système théorique n'épuise la situation dont il est issu ou bien celle où il est transporté. Et par-dessus tout, la conscience critique est une concrétisation des résistances à la théorie, des réactions antagonistes provoquées par ces expériences concrètes ou ces interprétations avec lesquelles la théorie est en conflit. En fait, j'irais jusqu'à dire que le travail du critique est d'offrir des résistances à la théorie, de l'ouvrir à la réalité historique, à la société, aux besoins et aux intérêts humains, de montrer ces instances concrètes tirées de la réalité quotidienne, et qui se tiennent en dehors ou juste au-delà de l'aire d'interprétation nécessairement désignée à l'avance."

Nous nous sommes mis d'accord, Gayatri Spivak et moi, pour appeler notre interview "Notre langue perdue - Sous la carte linguistique" pour attirer l'attention sur une réalité qui est souvent négligée: le fait que dans le monde il n'y a pas simplement quelques langues dominantes, mais d'innombrables langues et dialectes régionaux, ces "langues de la terre" qui sont dans bien des cas supprimées, considérées comme inférieures, sans qu'une reconnaissance publique soit estimée nécessaire à l'établissement d'une "carte". "Notre langue perdue" est une expression que Spivak a apprise des habitants du Kimberley Oriental; le sentiment qu'elle exprime est une réalité aujourd'hui pour des millions de gens qui ne vivent plus dans leur propre idiome culturel. "La langue est utilisée ici comme un concept métaphorique plus vaste. Ils veulent dire qu'ils ne donnent plus de sens à leur vie en terme de leur idiome culturel. Foucault dirait que leur idiome culturel n'est plus leur pouvoir-savoir, leur compétence à savoir. "Spivak parle ici de sa relation avec les langues, ayant grandi avec une langue indienne hégémonique et l'anglais du colonisateur: "Que ma propre langue maternelle transportait avec elle une histoire de domination, nous ne le savions pas. Et si nous nous concentrons sur la domination de l'anglais alors nous regardons ma langue maternelle, par exemple, comme une sorte de langue-victime." Spivak ne se gêne même pas pour critiquer quelque travaux sociaux venus de la théorie post-coloniale: "Pour moi, le fait même de commencer avec l'idée de la domination de l'anglais fait partie du problème".

Lors d'une conférence à New York, Julia Kristeva a lu son texte, "L'autre langue ou la sensibilité linguistique", dans une langue qui lui est étrangère, l'anglais. Bien qu'étant citoyenne française, elle n'a pas fait sa contribution avec un accent français, mais avec celui du slave, sa langue maternelle. Le texte traduit du français débute presque directement avec le problème de "l'autre langue": "Immédiatement, mais aussi fondamentalement, l'étranger se différencie de celui qui ne l'est pas car il parle une autre langue. Observé de plus près, le fait est moins trivial qu'il n'en a l'air; il révèle une destinée extravagante: une tragédie aussi bien qu'un choix. Tragédie, car l'être humain est un être parlant, et il parle naturellement la langue de son peuple: la langue maternelle, la langue de son groupe, la langue nationale. Changer de langue équivaut à perdre quelque chose de naturel, à trahir sa langue maternelle, ou, du moins, à la traduire. Un étranger est, par essence, un traducteur." Kristeva développe une théorie de la traduction d'un point de vue psychanalytique, conscient des conditions d'échange qui produisent l'abject. Elle parle de Proust, d'autres auteurs, mais aussi d'elle-même.

Mon interview avec Sylvère Lotringer s'intitule "Agent de l'étranger (*Foreign Agent*)". J'ai été surpris par le chemin que la discussion a suivi. C'est son travail comme éditeur-fondateur de "Semiotext(e)", principal plate-forme de l'introduction de la théorie dite française aux États-Unis depuis les années 70, à une époque où personne ne s'intéressait à publier ces auteurs, qui m'a poussé à interviewer Lotringer. Il donne un compte rendu critique de l'université américaine et de ses organes de publication. Intéressé au départ par une "sémiotique 'matérialiste'", il est passé à une "sémiotique en ACTE", un activisme de signes qui crée un délire à travers la manipulation de textes et d'images, une "schizo-culture" plus proche du capitalisme que de l'université. Lotringer reflète non seulement les mouvements intellectuels et déplacements majeurs du post-structuralisme, mais aussi le désastre politique du fascisme qu'il a vécu en tant qu'enfant juif, caché pendant la seconde guerre mondiale. C'est, en fin de compte, une telle expérience qui lui a fait quitter la France: "un Vichy m'a suffi". Lotringer a depuis travaillé avec beaucoup d'attention sur le fascisme, qu'il voit à l'oeuvre dans nombre de productions littéraires, culturelles et religieuses de l'époque, et dont il analyse les sous-bassements.

La crise, le déplacement des identités collectives et leurs représentations sont le sujet de l'article de Sami Naïr, "Les identités aléatoires". Naïr est un intellectuel basé à Paris. Son arrière-fond ethnique est véritablement en crise, non seulement en Afrique du Nord mais aussi en France, à travers des politiques d'immigration racistes, ethnocentristes et répressives qui ont une place si importante dans toute l'Europe contemporaine. L'auteur les connaît bien, et il les analyse rigoureusement. Avec sa perspective culturelle et intellectuelle aux multiples facettes, Naïr développe une critique sociale qui vise aussi les institutions: "la norme égalitaire masque une réalité inégale", une inégalité structurelle qui ne se joue pas seulement au niveau individuel mais aussi entre différentes cultures. Naïr s'intéresse aussi aux effets négatifs que les crises sociales produisent dans la perception des différences culturelles et ethniques. Les conflits ne sont pas fondés sur des oppositions objectives mais sur une "mobilisation hautement fantasmatique concernant l'imaginaire collectif des populations locales dans leur relation avec celui qui est considéré comme étranger". Retournant au titre de son texte, Naïr voit les "identités aléatoires" non pas comme un simple terme descriptif pour l'individu en crise, mais aussi comme un complexe d'identifications qui gère la relation au changement, à l'ambiguïté, aux conflits, à la singula-rité et à l'Autre, sans souscrire à des concepts d'identité collective fixes, universels ou nationaux. Ce n'est pas un problème d'universalité ou de particularité, mais de singularités sujettes à la transformation et à la négociation. Il demande ce que veut dire être beur: "Être beur, c'est donc être entre-deux et c'est, par la force des choses, se choisir dans le présent, à défaut de choisir entre ces monstres froids que sont les appartenances collectives. C'est attendre, attendre que 'ça change'".

Le texte de Zeigam Azizov "La russification et le terrain de 'l'autodétermination'" montre comment le processus de construction d'un empire signifiait aussi la fabrication d'une langue. Entre autre, Azizov trace une histoire détaillée de la langue russe et de sa carrière impériale; l'effet de ce processus pendant l'ère soviétique avec sa *nomenclatura* particulière; la théorie de l'impérialisme de Lénine, son concept "d'autodétermination des nations" et sa réalité; la géo-linguistique de Staline et son livre "Marxisme et linguistique", ainsi que quelques histoires personnelles d'intérêt. Azizov – son nom a dû être "russifié"– est né en Azerbaïdjan, a étudié plus tard à Leningrad sous une pression raciste provenant à la fois d'institutions et d'individus. Puis, comme artiste et écrivain il a émigré à Londres où il habite aujourd'hui, muni d'une nouvelle langue et d'un nouveau passeport. Aujourd'hui, à l'heure de l'après-*perestroika*, l'indépendance des anciennes républiques soviétiques signifie aussi la fin de la langue russe jouant le rôle de *lingua franca* pour un tiers du monde géographique. Cette fonction est reprise par l'anglais. "Pour les 'républiques libres' la *perestroika* a tourné l'histoire à l'envers. En essayant de trouver leur indépendance, ces républiques ont dû reconsidérer leur histoire et véritablement réapprendre leur langue, ces langues qui avaient été interrompues par la révolution socialiste... le début d'une 'dé-russification totale'". Le texte se termine sur quelques critiques de la situation contemporaine: "Le 'rideau de fer' qui était autrefois tendu entre l'empire soviétique et le capitalisme occidental est aujourd'hui multiplié et provoque des discriminations entre langues, cultures, et relations dans les anciennes républiques de l'Union Soviétique. "

On pourrait traduire le titre de la contribution de Victor Tupitsyn par " 'Le corps sans nom': le héros de son temps ou de son espace?". Elle est écrite en russe, bien que l'auteur vive et travaille comme écrivain et universitaire à New York. Le "corps sans organes" deleuzien est transformé en un "corps sans nom". Ici, Tupitsyn fait référence à la scène artistique et aux intellectuels russes, dont certains, malgré cet argument, ont réussi a obtenir une reconnaissance internationale, et ceci, malheureusement par le biais d'actions terroristes destructives (par exemple: le 'tagage' d'une peinture de Malévitch dans un musée). Les relations intellectuelles entre l'ouest et la Russie sont étudiées et critiquées dans un langage à haute densité théorique – citations de Hegel, Kant à travers Freud, Brecht, Bakhtin, Deleuze, Derrida, etc. Cette relation est discutée comme prenant la forme d'une opposition centre-périphérie. Tupitsyn voit en elle une forme particulière d'orientalisme. L'auteur critique des intellectuels restés dans son pays. Librement traduit, il écrit: "Si dans leurs articles des auteurs moscovites font référence à Lacan, Foucault, Lyotard, Derrida et Deleuze, ces citations n'ont qu'un caractère décoratif, quand elles ne sont pas l'exemple du résidu d'une tradition bureaucratique de référant à des figures d'autorité. En d'autres termes, ces textes, ne présentent pas de modèles théoriques, de méthodologies, seulement des phrases de ces 'camarades autoritaires' arbitrairement choisis. (Autrefois, ces camarades étaient Staline, Zhdanov et Lisenko)."

Le texte de Karen Kelsky, "Flirt avec l'étranger: sex interracial dans l'âge 'international' japonais", est une étude de la dynamique sexuelle, raciale, économique et libidinale tant à l'intérieur qu'à l'extérieur du Japon contemporain. De jeunes femmes japonaises indépendantes – loin du stéréotype des soi-disant "office ladies"– découvrent et vivent leur mobilité matérielle et leurs désirs dans un décor touristique international où elles peuvent donner libre cours à leur imaginaire érotique, exotique, racial et matérialiste. Cette réalisation de désirs et de fantasmes féminins par la consommation de mâles étrangers exotiques est une réflexion de la rigidité des hiérarchies au Japon. Cet article ne conclut pas que l'économie hétérosexuelle des relations interraciales fournit une fin heureuse. Il examine plutôt comment de vieux stéréotypes sont réinscrits de tous côtés et comment sur "la carte sexuelle globale, le capital et les forces de réification peuvent dominer tout en libérant les désirs". Dito Kelsky: "Ce qui est 'recréé' dans le phénomène du taxi jaune [les femmes japonaises, stéréotypées par les hommes (japonais)] n'est pas un nouveau monde de gain de pouvoir féminin et d'intimité internationale, mais plutôt un vieux racisme dans un nouveau costume."

"Los Angeles 1965-1992: de la restructuration générée par la crise à la crise générée par la restructuration" d'Edward Soja dresse un profil qui comprend l'histoire urbaine, sociale, industrielle, technologique et démographique entre deux soulèvement violents, les rebellions de Watts et les émeutes de L.A. en 1992. Il recherche et relie rigoureusement déclin économique et restructuration, industrialisation et désindustrialisation, migrations de masse, oppression raciale et ethnique, pauvreté et richesse, soulèvements sociaux, ainsi qu' économie et productions migrantes. Son étude de la géographie urbaine touche aussi à l' "*anglofication obsessive*", au rôle de l'armée, à celui de la technologie, de la ségrégation et du racisme, pour nommer quelques questions. Soja décrit les développements urbains et suburbains de L.A. en relation avec les processus globaux de restructuration transnationale: "Le local devenait global ... La manufacture américaine ne quittait pas seulement ses concentrations métropolitaines, elle quittait complètement le pays" laissant derrière elle une banlieue urbanisée traumatisée sans production mais avec sa démographie conflictuelle. Soja essaye de "reconceptualiser la nature même des études urbaines, de considérer la forme urbaine comme une mosaïque régionale complexe et polycentrique de développements géographiques irréguliers affectant et affectés par des forces et des influences locales, nationales et globales." Étudier Los Angeles (ou Tokyo, ou Sao Paulo, ou Little Rock) ouvre ainsi une fenêtre sur un panorama de sujets plus large que ce qui a traditionnellement été considéré dans le cadre des études sur la ville."

L'interview avec Benjamin Buchloh est de bien des façons révélatrice. Buchloh a joué un rôle majeur en introduisant des théories (en tant que membre de la rédaction d'*October*) et des artistes (mâles pour la plupart – il commente principalement Broodthaers, Buren, Richter) européens aux États-Unis dans les vingt dernières années. Il critique les institutions culturelles, la réception culturelle et les politiques des États Européens. "La réception européenne de la praxis culturelle américaine tend à isoler les oeuvres de leur contexte... La praxis culturelle en Europe est encore intensivement construite sur la fiabilité des concepts culturels (*Kulturbegriffe*) et des institutions culturelles". Il mentionne aussi un exemple parisien signifiant: le jour où le corps d'André Malraux, un activiste de gauche à son époque, était transféré au Panthéon, le groupe français NTM était condamné à six mois de prison pour les paroles de leur rap. En discutant une grande variété de sujets – problèmes méthodologiques et histoire de l'art, sociologie de l'art, le musée, la *Frankfurter Schule*, la théorie post-coloniale, etc.– les politiques de l'identité deviennent centrales. Buchloh envisage l'identité de manière autobiographique en tant qu'immigré allemand aux ÉU et en termes de politique allemande contemporaine: il critique avec véhémence l'Allemagne pour la rénovation de Berlin en une capitale centrée sur un modèle traditionnel d'identité étatique à un moment où les métropoles sont interconnectées internationalement et globalement. En conséquence, nous avons appelé cette interview "Remarques méchantes entre Moscou et Los Angeles", un titre composé à partir de deux citations.

Wulf Schmidt-Wulfen est un géographe allemand qui, depuis plus de vingt ans, travaille sur les représentations de l'Afrique dans le contexte de l'éducation allemande. Peu familier avec la théorie anglo-américaine contemporaine, cet universitaire est arrivé à des conclusions comparables à celles de la critique "post-coloniale". "Cercles Vicieux – imaginations/représentations géographiques de la jeunesse allemande au sujet des 'pays en voie de développement' africains" est un texte qui donne la synthèse d'un projet de recherche empirique pour lequel il a demandé à plus de 1700 enfants et adolescents (de 10 à 17 ans) à travers toute l'Allemagne de remplir un questionnaire sur l'Afrique. Les résultats sont désastreux et confirment les versions les plus pessimistes de la déformation de l'Autre culturel. L'appellation 'cercle vicieux' ne décrit pas seulement l'imagination de l'Afrique qu'a l'étudiant moyen, "parce qu'il fait chaud et sec, ils sont noirs, pauvres, morts de faim et sous-développés et ont besoin d'aide" mais aussi la façon dont les médias, les livres scolaires et toutes autres représentations perpétuent une 'imagination géographique'[1] catastrophique et complice d'un *statu quo* idéologique (colonial) post- et néo-colonial qui infiltre la politique et les affaires au jour le jour. Il faut ajouter que par contraste avec l'université et les médias américains, la majorité des contextes intellectuels et médiatiques européens ne sont pas familiers avec les débats critiques sur le pouvoir et la problématique de la représentation. Le travail de Schmidt-Wulfen est pour cette raison une entreprise unique qui n'a eu qu'une réception limitée et sceptique dans un contexte purement universitaire.

Ma propre contribution s'intitule "Écrire, lire, apprendre, enseigner" (*"Sprechen, Lesen, Lernen, Lehren"*). Au moment où le contexte institutionnel est changé ou disparaît, ces pratiques quotidiennes d'apprentissage prennent une dimension inquiétante (*unheimlich*). Personne ne considère la lecture ou l'apprentissage comme un travail en dehors d'un contexte qui les justifie – école, université, profession, temps libre, etc. Derrière cette étrangeté se cache une dimension critique qui m'intéresse. J'ai commencé à apprendre les langues étrangères à l'âge de dix ans, et ceci principalement en dehors ou à l'encontre du système scolaire. Pour un grand nombre de raisons j'ai réfléchi moi-même à cette pratique, quant à ses implications critiques, sociales, psychanalytiques et spécifiquement identitaires. En tant qu'artiste j'utilise la parole, la lecture, l'apprentissage et l'enseignement au sein d'une stratégie d'exposition, afin de mettre l'accent sur les relations entre pouvoir, politique, institutions, savoirs et techniques du soi. De plus, j'ai "importé" ces pratiques culturelles de base – parole, lecture, apprentissage, enseignement – dans mon travail artistique, une juxtaposition institutionnelle qui mérite réflexion.

Le texte de Dana Leonard et Lisa Adkins sur le féminisme français m'a été proposé par Isabelle Graw à qui j'ai aussi demandé une contribution en tant qu'éditeur de "*Texte zur Kunst*", un journal qui traduit et produit principalement de la 'théorie culturelle' dans le contexte linguistique allemand. "*Texte zur Kunst*" était en train de traduire et de publier le texte de Leonard et d'Adkins sur les migrations de la théorie féministe française. La contribution de Graw à cette publication convient non seulement de façon idéale à ce livre, mais elle est aussi symptomatique de la situation de la consommation de théorie contemporaine en Allemagne et en Autriche: l'importation. Leonard et Adkins sont deux critiques basées au Royaume Uni et leur texte s'intitule "Reconstruire le féminisme français: réification, matérialisme et sexe". Le texte montre en détail comment la catégorie du "Féminisme français" a été constituée dans le contexte anglo-américain à travers une politique de traduction, d'édition et de publication limitée et réductrice. Je cite ici une de ces nombreuses raisons: "L'étrange 'réduction synecdotique' au travail d'auteurs influencés par la déconstruction et la psychanalyse est aussi crucialement connectée au bagage intellectuel de la majorité des spécialistes de la France en langue anglaise... Ces spécialistes ont généralement un bagage intellectuel en linguistique et en littérature, et ont donc une familiarité bien plus grande avec les féministes françaises écrivant de la fiction ou de la théorie littéraire qu'avec celles qui travaillent en sociologie, anthropologie ou psychologie". Il est intéressant de lire comment des travaux matérialistes et liés au social des théoriciennes françaises ont été négligés ou réduits à une réception limitée. En plus d'une analyse historique précise et rigoureusement recherchée de certains des pouvoirs qui ont défini le "féminisme", l'article présente, reprend, et développe aussi d'importants arguments quant à des débats orientés de façon plus sociale, matérialiste et sexualle, qui sont loin d'être épuisés.

Tout discours critique est dépendant de sa circulation, de son évaluation et de la réception de son contenu. Le climat des perceptions culturelles, des débats critiques et des productions artistiques qui y sont liés, doit être constamment réarticulé et réexaminé. Une des expériences qui m'a le plus profondément frappé a été, en traversant différentes langues et différents milieux de réception, d'observer comment les perceptions et les procédés d'évaluation sont changeants et hétérogènes. Ce volume de textes tente, de manière encore insuffisante, de rassembler quelques unes de ces voix différentes.

New York, avril 1997.

Traduite de l'anglais par Mai-Thu A. Perret.
1. See texts by Edward W. Said and others.

序文

本書は、私が世界六ヵ国で行なった「リーディング・セミナー」の総括としてまとめられている。この公共プロジェクトは "IMPORTED—A Reading Seminar in Relationship with my 'A Portable (Not So Ideal) Imported Library, Or How to Reinvent the Coffee Table: 25 Books for Instant Use (7 different National Versions)' (1993-96)"『輸入品（さして理想的ではない）手持ち輸入図書館、あるいはコーヒーテーブルを飾る方法、またはすぐに使える25冊、（7ヵ国語用）』と題されている。私は異なったセットのライブラリーを携えてアジア、ヨーロッパ、アメリカを巡った。各地の大学、美術館、アート・センターに「図書館」を設立し、1ヵ月か、2ヵ月にわたるセミナーを行なった。そのプロジェクトの延長として、本書は、「輸入」を共通のテーマにした文章を収めている。セミナーを開いた各地に因んだ作家に、さまざまな側面から文化交流について論じたテキストやインタヴューを依頼した。各テキストは、原文のままプリントされており、その結果、本書には英、日、露、独、仏語のテキストが収められている。作家のなかに、テキストが読まれるチャンスが、高いことから、あえて英語で書くことを選んだ人達もいたということは、切実な問題を含んでいる。作家を「国」別に分けているのは、ある意味で正しくないが、皮肉なかたちでテキストを分類するのに役立っている。そしてそのことが、さらにこのプロジェクトに必要だった迂回した手続きを示唆している。「リーディング・セミナー」で使った「輸入した」図書目録は、巻末にのせ、各セミナーで撮った写真が、各章のはじめを飾っている。オーストリアでは、セミナーを開くことが出来なかったため、この章には「図書館」をなす本の写真だけが載せられている。セミナーの開催地は、招待か以前からの繋がりによって選ばれた。資金は、ほとんどの場合オーガナイザーに援助してもらった。

本書に収められた文章と同じく、多角的な「リーディング・セミナー」は全体として、交換、グローバリゼーション、ナショナリズム、ツーリズム、言語、理論、欲望、アイデンティティ、政治といった問題に触れている。こういった問題に関して、すでに膨大な量の文献があるが、ここで教育、および文化政策に関連して指摘しておきたい点がいくつかある。数世紀の間、西洋の技術的、軍事的、経済的支配は、国内外の覇権と勢力を概念化し、実行し、正統化する主な手段として、その文化装置を利用し発展させてきた。文化的、イデオロギー的、宗教的傲慢は、国内外の人民やグループの集団虐殺や支配など極端な行為をもたらした。そして残念ながら、われわれは今まだポスト・コロニアルの新たな世界秩序の下部構造を造り出す、搾取と誤った表象に彩られた歴史と共にある。そういった「あたりまえの日常」が、権力や暴力に直接うったえることなく存続しえているわけだ。教育と言語のプログラムは、十九世紀における国民国家形成の主軸であり、人々を同質化し、地域の政治的統一を先取りした。特にドイツでは、イデオロギー的影響力をもつブルジョア教育制度として知られるBildungが、国民的統一が政治的事実となる前にそれを賛えるために発明された。国語が国民文学や演劇や国民史や国民芸術、さらに音楽、オペラを生産した。フランスでは、フランス革命の時点で、今でいうフランス語を話す市民は、全体の33パーセントしかおらず、状況はその後急速に変化したという事実が思いだされる。国民教育プログラムは、フィヒテが、主に国語とその文化のメタファーとして「内的国境」と呼んだものを積極的に造り出そうとした。人々を規制するためヨーロッパ同盟全体を、永久的な境界地区に今変えようとしているシェンゲン安全保障条約や、郵便局、病院、学校といった州施設において自動的に人々を取り締まろうとするカリフォルニア州議会での提案を考えると、このメタファーは今日いっそう重要である。「内的国境」は、人種的な、または階級的な偏見による、パノプティコン的な検査手段とは関係ない、むしろクレジットカードの所持や、教育や、職業における資格の取得といった日常的事例のなかに貫徹されている。現代情報化社会において、「教育」がもつ多大な影響力は、人々の大半を高等教育から排除する差別の歴史を反映している。教育規制は、つねに社会的ヒエラルキーを再生産してきた。たとえば合州国では、十九世紀末までアフリカ系アメリカ人の教育が、法的に禁止されてきたが、このことは今日の教育レベル上の統計と無関係ではない。

教育はたんに社会的再生産の言説ではない。それは政治的でもあるが、同時に投資でもある。ふつう、大学に行くのはとても費用がかかるため、排他的であり、批判的思考さえも商品に還元されてしまう企業となる。カントやフンボルトなどが、批判的自立性を保証する哲学的領域を考えることが出来たのに対し、今日どのような批評家もまずスポンサーを見つけなければならない。批判的言説は、それに付随する変動や流行があるにせよ、もう一つの市場として機能する傾向にある。また政治、イデオロギー、性差、人種、社会経済などの矛盾も、この論理のなかに含まれるものである。何を、だれに対して、どの言語で、どういった利益集団に教えるのか、といった問題は、全ての国民を教育するといった目的によっては、もはや自動的に保証されていない。むしろこの問題こそが論議の主題であり、陰にも陽にも、抑圧の歴史と権力をめぐる抗争について考えるうえで、不可欠な論点となるだろう。「クリティカル・スタディーズ」の範疇にある文献は、しばしばこういった偏見を持った教育原理の書き換えをめざし分析している。

旅行は、裕福で教養のある人々のみに与えられた特権であった。教育プログラムは、しばしば旅行を含むか、または旅行そのものによって構成されていた。世界へと広がりつつ、他者を支配し、搾取し、研究し、また表象することは、富や、権力そしてあらゆる支配の基盤であった。慈悲深い人道主義と無知や「より知っている」といった思い上がりの入り混じった文化的傲慢が、ほとんどの布教活動を特徴づけてきたが、この拡張は地球上の地理、言語、経済の再編という大きな枠組みのなかへと回収されていった。人身売買あるいは奴隷制度は、植民地の運営を経済的に基礎づけてきたが、さらにそれは工業化した資本主義の生産と交換に寄与してきた。今日の文脈では、人々の移動には新たな名称や、理由や、実践形態があてがわれている。性的奴隷は娼婦になり、経済活動のため搾取される不法移民と観光事業は、異なった見せかけのもとに重複する現実を示してる。ある場合には無理強いされ束縛され、または自らの自由意志で旅するのはなにも人々だけではない。

労働、生産、原料、情報、知識、テクノロジー、ごみ、病気、神、商品、イメージ、欲望、抗争、つまり消費されるものすべてが旅する。可動性と速度と適合性は、アーティストや学者をふくむ現代知識階級の目標となりつつある。

今日、国家間で、領土や植民地や資源を巡って争うことはあまりなくなっている。その代わりに、われわれはトランス・ナショナル・コーポレーション（TNC）の不透明な権力の網目に対処しなければならないのである。その権力構造をつかむのは容易なことではない。TNC の権力は、もはや特定の境界や権威に従属するように、ある場所を他の場所に優先したりはしない。TNC は、国家のレトリックで話しさえする。というのも、段々と国家自体が TNC の権力と独占権を司る単なる官僚制度へと変容しているからである。刑務所は、国営銀行や健康管理や教育システムと同じように私物化できるようになっている。国家権力の崩壊と腐敗が、その中心に設けられた教育や文化制度を破壊する。国家権力やナショナリズムと共犯関係にあった大学は、批判的機能を失うことはなかったが、いまではそれも消えかかっている。 TNC の力学は、国民国家と関係のない機能によって動かされているが、国家を超えた資本とその排他的な株主の論理に対してのみ責任をもち、かつ忠実なものである。またこの国家を超えるモデルは、文化産業が一層企業の協力と利益に依存するにつれ、そこにも採用されてきた。たとえばニューヨークのグッゲンハイム美術館の場合、外国の投資家が博をつけて、独占的な影響力を勝ちとるために美術館の運営を後援している。その代わりに美術館は、財政援助を保証され、拡張し、世界各地に支店を開くというように、それ自体小規模の TNC となっている。湾岸戦争時や、今日では NATO とその拡張主義に見られるように、軍隊自体も多数の国家から物資や兵隊を徴集し、TNC のように機能しようとしている。だが、このことはナショナリズムがもたらした植民地主義とそれによる不幸が終わりを告げることを意味しない。むしろ、状況はその逆である。支配と搾取は、地理的境界に沿っては起らなくなっただけで、機能的論理としてあらゆる大型の社会組織に浸透しつつある。

私の旅する「リーディング・セミナー」は、今日の国家を超える趨勢と結託しているわけではなくも、その徴候を充分示すものである。1970年代以後、747 現象とでも呼ぶことができるかもしれない芸術と文化の国際的移動の影響は、広く文化生産全体に見ることができるようになった。ある種の文化的な特権により結ばれた世界に位置する者として、このプロジェクトを進めるにあたり、私は、様々な施設の使用と資金をえることが出来た。大抵の場合、私はパブリック・リーディング・セミナーとディスカッションを、そういった議論に関心を寄せる時間をもてるだけの特権と自由を楽しむ人達に対して行なった。そして色々な問題を違った文脈と言語のなかで議論することから多くの経験をえた。セミナーは、すべてテープに収録され保存されているが、この序文では、私が遭遇した議論や抗争といった逸話を示すつもりはない。そういったことは主催者側の文脈における複雑な歴史の産物なのだから…。むしろ私の関心は、私が行った場所と何らかの関係のある意見や、われわれが議論した話題それ自身に語らせることにある。いうまでもなく、ここに集められたテキストは個人の意見であり、そのような意見から私はさまざまなことを驚くべき仕方で学んだ。

本書には翻訳が含まれていない。ここでは受け取ったテキストをそのまま出版しているため、外国語で書かれたテキストへの手引きとして、それぞれの寄稿論文の要約を以下に示そう。テキストの順序は、私のプロジェクトの行程と平行している。「思想の交通」と題されたサブ・コーソによる柄谷行人のインタヴューは、現代社会の相互依存的状況における思想の問題に濃厚かつ幅広く言及している。他のアジア諸国同様、日本は、西洋において生産された誤った表象と直面してきた。そしてそれに関連して、「オリジナルとコピー」といった偏ったレトリックが存在し、柄谷はそこに権力関係を見い出している。「日本関係の本は大抵、美学的、あるいは宗教的表象の要請関係を満たすように書かれており、さもなければ経済的かつ技術的関心をめぐり形成される。……そして知的かつ倫理的領域は排除されている。」柄谷によるモダニズムの分析と批判的アプローチが生産的なのは、彼がそれを地理的周縁から研究し分析しているからである。柄谷の音声中心主義批判は、言語の政治的／経済的側面を明らかにし、国民と人種の形成におけるそのイデオロギー的道具性に関して重要な指摘を行なっている。

柄谷作品の翻訳の一部を手がけてきたサブ・コーソは、英語による「二つのタイプの翻訳、あるいは太平洋上の行き違い」また、それとは微妙に異なる日本語のエッセイ「翻訳、満たされぬ愛、あるいは日本語を読むあなたへの手紙」を寄せている。日本生まれで長年ニューヨークで暮らしているコーソにとって翻訳は、実存的ビジネスとしてある。翻訳者にとって、日本語から英語へ、また英語から日本語へという両方向への翻訳は、「全く異なる思考とパフォーマンスと生産と存在の仕方が関与する交通であり、……二通りの翻訳は自分のなかに二人の違った人格を生み出す。」コーソは、独特のスタイルで、二重のアイデンティティの構築と翻訳という作業を関連づけるとともに、日本人の国民性一般と翻訳を結びつけている。「翻訳は常に国民を形づくる道具であった……」と論じるコーソは「外来文化を輸入することへの国民的オブセッション」をもつ自国への辛辣な文化批評としての翻訳論を展開している。彼の批判は単に日本の交換経済に向けられているのみではなく、日本語から何を輸入するかという翻訳のポリティックスにおける西洋の偏った姿勢にもまた向けられている。日本製の批判的思考が、日本国外で翻訳され、流通することはごく稀であると語りつつ、「批判的日本の対極にある美的日本が好まれ、……今日、最も人気のある日本の文化的輸出品は、ゲームソフトとアニメである。これらはまたしても日本の不均衡なプロフィールを反映している……」。ここで再び、コーソの的確な批判は、反対方向へと向けられ、いわゆる「オリエンタリズム」に焦点が当てられる。彼の中間的位置は、なぜ彼が自らの二重のアイデンティティに沿い、必ずしも翻訳を介さずに英語と日本語で書くのかを説明している。

キュレーター、ビル・アーニングは「だれしもゲイだ。（クルト・コーベインがそう言ったんだったら本当さ。）」のなかで、自分自身を「失業中のおかまキューレター」と称している。彼は「反男性」、「ストーンウォール25、あるいはゲイの過去をふりかえって」などの展覧会を企画しつつ、オープンかつ率直に現代ニューヨークのゲイ・アイデンティティを表現してきた。彼は同性愛恐怖の風潮を反映する個人的逸話として、海外に展覧会を「輸出」した際の興味深い遭遇について語っている。そのことは、「ニューヨークの視点で言えば、良いキューレターには、正直でないとなれないし、自分を隠していたんじゃダメだ。」という問題に集約されている。読み進むにつれて、「セクシュアリティには常に文化的な文脈がある」ということを、作者自らがどのように理解するようになったかを魅惑的なスタイルで教えてくれる。私自身、性と文化の文脈が常に変化しているという事実は、性とゲイ・ポリティックスに関するテキストを、さまざまな場所で、さまざまなオーディエンスとともに読んだ際、経験したことでもある。

フィリピン系アメリカ人、ダン・バカルゾは、劇作品「すみませんが、わかりません」を寄せてくれた。幸いにして、私はニューヨーク大学に設けられたステージでの、彼の一人芝居を観る機会をえた。そのなかで彼は、ゲイ、アジア系アメリカ人のアイデンティティというセクシュアリティと文化的文脈に言及している。バカルゾは、自らのヴァイオレントな初体験を取り上げて、文化的にまた人種的に偏った「新たな異国の故郷」を映し出す。そしていかに性的、言語学的、また人種的ステレオタイプが混ざり合い、暴力的な現実が成り立っているのかを、彼はこんなふうに巧みに語るのである。「彼にやられている間、ぼくは表象だとか、アジア人は、ゲイ・セックスでいつもほられ役だとか、白人の男はアジア人の上で植民地的ファンタジーを満喫しているだとか、……考えてはいなかった。」

地政学とセックスの問題は、ココ・フスコによる「ドルを求めての客引き、あるいはキューバにおける性労働と観光事業」と題されたテキストの主軸でもある。「普及するセックス産業における有色人女性への私の関心は、1993年以来キューバでの売春が著しく増加したことと結びついた。そして私は、売春に携わる女性に関する記事を書くことを思いついた。特に私の関心は、資本主義への困難な移行過程にある第三世界社会主義国において、売春がもたらす問題にある。」世界規模でのセックス産業という問題は、他の暗く、暴力的な「経済」と直接繋がりがあるにもかかわらず、残念ながら十分な検討や言及がされていない。ココ・フスコによるキューバの歴史的、時事的記述は、単にその事実ゆえに、豊富かつ挑発的だというのみでなく、不平等な交換関係に苦しむ多くの他国の状況に共通するシナリオでもある。

「思想や理論は、人々やさまざまな批判的学派と同様に、人から人へ、状況から状況へ、そして時代から別の時代へと旅する。通常文化的、知的生活は、こういった思想の流通により養われ、維持されている。そして思想と理論の場所から場所への移動は、自覚的な影響だろうと無意識の影響だろうと、想像的な引用だろうと無差別の盗用だろうと、生命的現実であり、それこそ知的活動をあらしめるものなのである。」このようにはじまるエドワード・サイードの 1984 年論文、「旅する理論」は、『歴史と階級意識』（1923 年）の著者として物象化論を発展させた G・ルカーチについて論じている。ルカーチの思考は、革命期のハンガリーから第二次世界大戦後のパリ（ルシアン・ゴールドマン）を経由し、ケンブリッジ（レイモンド・ウィリアムス）へと巡る。サイードは、文化表象に関する彼の他の論考に沿って、知的労働の問題、そして批判と批判的意識の機能について触れている。「批判的意識は、状況間に見られる差異への意識であり、いかなる体系や理論であっても、それらが生み出され、もたらされた状況を消し去ることはできない、という事実に気づくことでもある。そして何よりも批判的意識とは、理論への抵抗を意識することであり、理論が（それと対立関係にある）具体的経験や解釈によって導き出されたことを意識することである。批評家の仕事は、理論への抵抗をもたらすこと、つまり、歴史的現実や社会、人間の必要や関心に向かって理論を開くことであり、そういった解釈的領域の外部、またそのすぐ向こう側につねに先行している、日常の現実から引き出される具体的な例を、指摘することにあるとさえ言えるだろう。」

ガヤトリ・スピヴァックと筆者が「われわれの失われた言葉、言語学地図から見落とされた言葉」と名づけることにしたインタヴューは、見落とされがちなある現実を示している。世界には単に幾つかの支配的言語があるのではなく、無数の地域的言語や方言が存在し、そういった「土着語」は、多くの場合、言語学的「地図」をつくる際に、その存在を公認されることなく、劣ったものとみなされるという現実がある。「われわれの失われた言葉」という表現は、スピバックが東キンベリーの民衆から習ったもので、自分達の文化的イディオムを現在もはや所有しない多くの人々にとってのリアリティーを心情的に表わしたものである。「ここでは言葉は、より広い概念的メタファーとして使われている。彼等は、自分達の文化的イディオムによって自分達の生活を意味づけられないと言っているのです。フーコーだったら、彼等の文化的イディオムは、もはや彼等にとっての力／知、彼等の認識を可能にするものではないと言うでしょう。」スピヴァックは、インド語と植民地的言語である英語のもとで育った彼女自身の言葉との関係について語っている。「私の母国語は、それ自体の内部に私達の知らない強要の歴史を内包している。英語の刻印から入っていくかぎり、私たちは母国語を、例えば、犠牲になった言葉として見るでしょう。」ポスト・コロニアルの批評家、スピヴァックは、ポスト・コロニアル理論にもとずく社会福祉事業さえ批判する。「英語の刻印といった発想からはじめることにさえ、問題があると思う。」

ジュリア・クリステヴァは、ニューヨークでの会議で「他者の言語、あるいは感性を翻訳すること」と題された講演を、彼女にとって外国語である英語で発表した。フランス市民ではあるが、彼女はフランス語の訛ではなく、母国語であるスラヴ系の抑揚をもった英語でテキストを読み上げたのである。フランス語から翻訳されたそのテキストは、冒頭から「もう一つの言語」の問題を取り上げている。「直ちに、また根本的に、外国人がそうでない者と異なるのは、その人がもう一つ別の言語を話す時においてです。しかしよくみると、この事実はそれが示す以上に重大なことです。というのも、それは途方もない運命、つまり選択であると同時に悲劇でもある運命を露呈させるからです。人間は話す存在であり、その際に、人は、当然ながら自らの民衆の言葉である母国語、集団の言語、国語を話すがゆえに悲劇なのです。言語を変える行為は、何か自然なものを失うこと、自らの母国を裏切ること、また少なくともそれを翻訳することに相当するでしょう。」「アブジェクト」を生みだす交換の条件を示唆する心理学的見地から展開されるクリステヴァの翻訳論は、プルーストなどについて語ると同時に、自伝的要素を含んでいる。

シルヴェール・ロトランジェとのインタヴューは、「フォーリン・エージェント」と題されているが、それは全く予期せぬ行程を辿ることになった。これは、七十年代以来、アメリカにいわゆるフランス理論を（当時まだ誰もそういった著書の出版に関心を示す以前に）紹介してきた出版社である、「セミオテキスト」の設立エディターとしての彼の役割についてのインタヴューである。その中でロトランジェは、アメリカの大学とその出版組織を批判している。ロトランジェは「唯物論的記号論」から出発し、「行動的記号論」へと移行しつつ、テキストとイメージの錯綜体である「スキゾ文化」を作り出したが、それは大学組織よりは、むしろ資本主義そのものに共鳴するものである。ロトランジェは、単にポスト構造主義といった知的かつ「旅する」運動について言及するのみならず、隠れたユダヤ人の子供として彼が体験し、フランスを離れる理由ともなったファシズムの政治的悲劇についても語っている。「ペタン政権でたくさんだった。」と語るロトランジェは、それ以来、ファシズムを注意深く観察し、それを主要文学、文化そして、宗教的生産の中に見い出している。

集合的アイデンティティとその表象の危機は、「射幸的アイデンティティ」と題されるサミ・ナイールの論文のテーマである。ナイールは、パリ在住の学者である。人種差別、民族中心主義、抑圧的移民政策がヨーロッパ中に強く根づくなか、彼の民族的バックグラウンドである北アフリカやフランスは危機に瀕している。こういった事実に精通する作者は、それらを綿密に分析するとともに、さまざまな文化的、知的見地から、制度を告発する社会批判を展開している。「平等主義的規範が、現実の不平等性を被い隠している。それは個人個人の関係において、そして異なる文化間において行なわれている。」さらにナイールは、社会的危機が文化的、民族的差異の認識にもたらす否定的影響に焦点を当てる。抗争の根拠は、現実の客観的対立にあるのでなく、「他者との関係において仮想的に動員される地元の民衆という集合的幻想にある」と論じている。彼のテキストのタイトルに戻れば、ナイールは、「射幸的アイデンティティ」という言葉の中に、単に危機に瀕する個人を表わす以上の、「アイデンティティ・ポリティックス」が作り出す固定的、普遍的、国民概念に従属しない、変化や、曖昧さや、抗争や、単独性、また他者といった問題を受け入れる認識概念を見ている。変化と折衝に必要なのは、普遍性や特殊性ではなく、単独性に関わるものである。彼は、「ブール（北アフリカのアラブ人）」、またはアラブ人であるとは一体何なのかを問うている。「アラブ人であることは、中間的な存在を意味する。あれらの冷血な怪物や集合的所属性の間の、現時点における、選択を欠如させているがゆえに、物事の力に直にさらされている中間的存在である。それは待つことであり、その存在が変わるのは、待つことにおいてである。」

ゼガム・アジゾフのエッセイ、「ロシア化と自己決定の地勢」は、帝国を造り出すことが言語を作り出すことにおいてあったことを示している。アジゾフは、なによりもロシア語の詳細な歴史とその帝国的経歴について物語っている。たとえば、ソビエト時代特有の命名法の問題、レーニンの帝国主義論と「国民自決」の現実的背景について、スターリンの地勢言語学と『マルクス主義と言語学』という著作について、さらにいくつかの興味深い個人的エピソードなど、さまざまなかたちでこの言語史は語られている。自分の名前をロシア化しなければならなかったアジゾフは、アゼルバイジャンに生まれ、後に制度的にもまた個人的にも人種差別的な圧力下のレニングラードで学んが、新たな言語とパスポートを携え、アーティスト兼作家としてロンドンに移住した。ペレストロイカ以後の今日、かつてのソヴィエト共和国と衛星国の自立は、つい最近まで国際語として世界の三分の一以上の地域で機能したロシア語の終焉を意味している。そして今ではこの機能は、英語にとって代えられようとしている。「ペレストロイカは、もろもろの自由共和国にとって、歴史を逆行させたのである。これらの共和国は、独立を求め、自らの歴史を見つけ出し、自分達の言語や社会主義革命によって断続されたものを学び直す必要があったのである。それこそが脱ロシア化の出発点である。」このテキストは、現状に対する幾つかの批判をもって締めくくられている。「かつてソヴィエト帝国と西洋資本主義との間にそびえていた鉄の壁は、元ソヴィエト連邦共和国に属していたもろもろの共和国のあいだに分散し、文化間、言語間、そしてさまざまな関係における差別をもたらしている。」

ニューヨーク在住のライター兼学者であるヴィクトール・トピツィンは、ドゥルーズ的「器官なき身体」をもじった「名前なき身体、時代のヒーローあるいは地元のヒーロー」とでも訳されるであろうテキストをロシア語で寄せている。トピツィンはそのなかで、彼の反論にもかかわらず、一部の現代ロシア美術とロシア人知識人が国際的名声を得ていることに言及している。残念なことには、近年そういった名声が、美術館に展示されたマレーヴィッチの作品にスプレーするといった疑似テロリスト的行為により話題になっているという。ヘーゲル、フロイドを介したカント、ブレヒト、バフチンからドゥルーズ、デリダ等々に至る引用など、理論的ボキャブラリーを多用しつつ、1989年以後のロシアと西洋との知的関係性が検討され批判されている。この関係は、中心と周縁という対立関係として議論され、この関係をトピツィンはオリエンタリズムの特殊な例と見なしており、祖国ロシアに残る知識人に対し、非常に批判的である。「モスクワ在住のライターが、論文のなかでラカンやフーコーやリオタールやデリダやドゥルーズについて言及するのは、単に装飾的な意味か、あるいは、権威に頼るという官僚的伝統の名残りに等しい。言い換えれば、テキストには何の理論的モデルや方法論もない代わりに、無作為に、権威ある同志の名言が借用してあるだけなのである。むろんかつてのスターリン、ズダノフ、ライセンコ同志の延長として…。」

カレン・ケルスキーの「日本の国際化時代における人種間セックスとのたわむれ」と題されたエッセイは、現代日本国内外における性差、人種、経済、リビドーの力学についての研究である。若い自立した日本人女性は、いわゆるオフィスレディーといったステレオタイプを超えて、観光による国際的な場において物資的充足と欲動を発見し生きており、そこでエロティックで、エキゾチックに自らの、人種的、物資的想像力を試している。しかしこの論文は、人種間交際にハッピーエンドをもたらしてはいない。むしろそれは、従来のステレオタイプが、繰り返され、またいかに「地球的セックスマップにおいて、資本と商品化の諸力が、それらが欲望を解放するにせよ、いかに支配的でありえるのか」を検討している。「イエローキャブ現象のなかで、再び捏造されたのは、女性の権限といったすばらしき新世界や国際的交際などではなく、むしろ新しさを装った従来のレイシズムである。」とケルスキーは述べている。

エドワード・ソージャによる「ロスアンジェルス 1965-1992、危機が生みだした再構造化から再構造化が生みだした危機へ」は、ワッツ暴動および1992年のL.A.暴動間に観察された都市的、社会的、産業的、技術的、統計的歴史の様相を提示している。ソージャは、景気の落下と経済再構造化、工業化と脱工業化、大規模な人口移動、人種的/民族的抑圧、貧困と富有、社会変動、観光経済と生産などについて調査し、それらを綿密に関連づけている。また都市的地形についての彼の研究は、「強迫的アングロ系白人化」としての軍隊、テクノロジー、人種の分断、人種差別などの役割について触れている。ソージャは、L.A.の都市的、郊外的発展を、世界規模でのトランスナショナルな再構造化のプロセスとの関連性において論じている。「ローカルなものが、グローバルになりつつあった。.....アメリカの産業は都市集中を避けるのみならず、国家自体からも離れようとしていたのであり」その結果、都市化した郊外は、もはや生産をもたらすことがなくなると共に、人種的に対立する人口統計をともないつつ取り残されたのである。ソージャは、「都市研究の本質を再概念化しようと試みるが、それは地域的、国家的勢力や状況を影響しつつ、またそういったものに影響されつつ、地理的に不均一な発展を遂げた都市形態を、複雑かつ、複数の中心からなる地域的モザイクとして理解するためである。そういった意味で、ロスアンジェルス（または、東京、サンパウロ、やリトル・ロック）の研究は、都市研究の分野で従来扱われてきた主題よりも一層広範な視野を提供する。

ベンジャミン・ブクローとのインタヴューからは、じつに啓発される点が多かった。ブクローは、過去二十年にわたって、欧州のアーティスト（ブロートハース、ビュラン、リヒターなど、大半が男性アーティストであるが、このことについて、彼はコメントしている）および理論（『オクトーバー』誌の編集員として）をアメリカに紹介することにおいて重要な役割を演じてきた。彼は、欧州の文化制度や、文化的受容や、国家政策を厳しく批判する。「アメリカの文化実践一般に対する欧州の受け止め方は、作品を文脈から孤立させる傾向にある。欧州の文化実践は、いまだに、文化概念と文化制度への信頼の上に強く築かれている。」ブクローは、フランスからの興味深い挿話として、当時、急進的左翼であったアンドレ・マルローの亡骸が、文化的英雄を祭る共和党の講堂であるパンテオンに移された日に、フランスのラップグループNTM に歌詞の問題で6ヵ月の拘留の判決が言い渡されたことに触れている。美術史の方法論的問題について、社会芸術史について、美術館について、クリティカル・セオリーについて、ポスト・コロニアル理論について、等々、一連の広範かつ興味深い問題に触れている。なかでもアイデンティティ・ポリティックスは、インタヴューの焦点となっている。ブクローは、大都市が国際的にも、グローバルにも交叉する時代において、ドイツがベルリンを国民国家のアイデンティティにもとづいた都市として再変容しようとしていることを辛辣に批判している。「モスクワとロスアンジェルスの中間からの意地悪な意見」というタイトルは、本書にでてくる二つの都市を引きつつ、この文章を位置づけることを意図している。

ドイツ人地理学者、ヴォルフ・シュミット-ヴルフェンは、二十年以上にわたりドイツの教育における「アフリカの表象」の問題に取り組んできた。現代のアングロ・アメリカ系の理論的生産とはほとんど無縁であるにもかかわらず、この学者は、結果的にいわゆるポストコロニアル理論に匹敵する成果を上げている。「悪循環あるいはアフリカ的発展途上国に関するドイツ人の若者の地理的な想像力と表象」と題されたテキストは、経験的な調査をもとにして、ドイツ全土にわたる10歳から17歳までの千七百人以上の学生を対象にした質問調査とその分析をまとめたものである。その結果は、うんざりする程ひどく、文化的「他者」への誤った表象がはびこっているだろうという悲観的予測を再確認するものである。悪循環と呼ぶのは、単に「彼等は、暑く、乾いた土地に暮らすため、肌が黒く、貧しく、飢えていて、遅れているから、助けを必要としている。」といった平均的学生のアフリカのイメージのためではなく、悲劇的な「地理的想像力」（サイード）を延命させるため、メディアや教科書やその他の表象機能が、植民地主義、また新植民地主義のイデオロギーと結託し現状を維持しているからである。さらにつけ加えれば、アメリカの教育機関やメディアとは対照的に、主要なヨーロッパ知識人やメディアは、権力と表象の問題系に関する現代の批判的議論に馴染みがない。シュミット-ヴルフェンの仕事は、欧州の学術的領域内では、むしろ特殊な企てであり、そのために一部の懐疑的受容しか得ていない。

「話すこと、読むこと、習うこと、教えること」は私のエッセイである。一度、制度的文脈が変更されたり、あるいは全面的に削除されると、このような日常的な実践は、「不気味なもの」の様相を帯びる。学校、大学、職場、余暇、等々、それを正統化する文脈のなかで成されないかぎり、だれも「読むこと」「習うこと」を、「労働」とは見なさないにちがいない。私の関心はこういった「奇妙さ」を背後から形成するものにある。私は教科とかかわりなく、またむしろそれに逆らいつつ、10歳になった頃からさまざまな外国語を習ってきた。そしてさまざまな理由から、この実践の批判的、社会的、心理学的、またアイデンティティに関する問題を自覚するようになった。そして私は、長年の間アーティストとして「話すこと、読むこと、習うこと、教えること」を戦略的に利用しつつ、権力、政治、制度、テクノロジー、知などや「自己のテクノロジー」に関するディスカッションを開き、それを強調してきた。私は、話す、読む、習う、教えるといった基本的な文化的実践を自分の芸術作品のなかに「輸入」してきたが、そういった作品は、それら実践の制度的二重化として議論されるべきであろう。

ダナ・レオナードとリサ・アドキンスによるフランスのフェミニズムについての論文は、寄稿依頼者の一人に私が挙げたイザベラ・グラーフの薦めによって掲載することになったものである。グラーフは、ドイツの文脈において、いわゆる文化理論を翻訳、生産してきた理論系ジャーナル、「Texte zur Kunst」の創設メンバーである。「Texte zur Kunst」誌は、フランス産の「移動する」フェミニズム理論に関するレオナードとアドキンスのテキストを翻訳し、出版を目前にしていた。グラーフが、この出版に際して払ってくれた配慮は、本書にとって理想的なものであると同時に、ドイツ、オーストリアでの現代理論の消費及び輸入状況において重要である。「フランスのフェミニズムを再構築すること、あるいは商品化、唯物論、そして性」と名づけられたイギリス在住の作家ダナ・レオナードとリサ・アドキンスによるテキストは、いかに「フランスのフェミニズム」が英米において限定され、還元された翻訳、編集、出版体制によってでっち上げられたかを詳細に示している。その理由のひとつは以下のことにある。「フランス系フェミニズムが脱構築や精神分析的作品のみへと代喩的に還元されてしまったのは、英語圏の大抵のフランス専門家の学問的背景と決定的に関連している。通常、それらの専門家は、言語学と文学のバックグランドをもっているため、社会学、心理学、あるいは人類学におけるフェミニズムに比べて、フィクションや文学理論について論じるフランスのフェミニストとの繋がりが圧倒的に強い。」このように、唯物論的、社会学系統のフランス理論が、いかに取り残され、限定された受容へと縮小されたかという問題は実に興味深い。この論文は、フェミニズムと定義された諸力についての的確かつ注意深く調査された歴史的考察のみならず、社会的、唯物論的、性差的諸問題に比重を置いた論争をめぐる重要な議論を展開している。この論争はまだ始まったばかりである。

あらゆる批判的言説は、情報やテキストやその翻訳が、交通し評価され受容されることに依存している。異なった文化とその受容の場を移動していて最も啓発的だったのは、感性と評価の過程の変動性と多元性の発見にあった。本書は、そのほんの一部に自らを語らせるという不十分な試みにすぎない。

訳：桜本有三

IMPORTED – A READING SEMINAR in Relationship with my "A Portable (Not so Ideal) Imported Library, Or How to Reinvent the Coffee Table: 25 Books for Instant Use (Japanese-Version)," 1993/95
Haizuka Project, Hiroshima Prefecture, August, September 1995

INTERCOURSE OF IDEAS

KOJIN KARATANI — SABU KOHSO

ORIGINAL AND IMPORT

Sabu Kohso: I would like to talk with you about the starting point—the basic ground of your thinking and your ideas. Let's begin with Rainer's question: Is the idea of importation functional at all in the process of cultural formation?

Kojin Karatani: This question is highly relevant for Japanese thinkers, or more broadly, non-Western thinkers. It relates to the credibility of our epistemology. We are always faced with the question: Isn't your idea imported from the West? or, Is your idea really original? It is nevertheless easy, perhaps too easy, to answer by way of deconstructing the metaphysics of originality, namely, the precedence of origin to its derivative. Or you may say it is wrong to consider a culture as a whole that has been formed either by importation or by itself. Civilization is generally thought to have originated in places like Egypt, India, China, and Greece, with other civilizations all forming themselves by having imported from these places. Yet these so-called origins did not come into existence by themselves either. Greece was in fact the hub of the active space of traffic among Mediterranean cultures. Therefore, Greek philosophy came into existence through the intercourse between many thoughts and many languages. This intercourse is inscribed in the works of Plato and Aristotle. If Nietzsche was pointing to the space of traffic of the Mediterranean rather than to individual philosophers of the time when he advocated a "return to pre-Socratics," then I totally agree with him. What is original is produced not in the continuum of the identical, but in the intercourse between the manifold.

Yet the stereotypical question—whether original or copy—is still a knotty problem. In the face of this challenge, Japanese and non-Western thinkers tend to pose something original within their particular cultural domain. Of course there is nothing purely original in any culture. The construct of the original in the non-Western culture is simply to placate Westerners. On the other hand, what Westerners do not want to see is a foreign product that, appropriating what seems to be their own vocabulary, undermines the status of the West as the one and only. Being threatened by Japanese industrial capital, some Western voices tend to stress Japan the copycat.

In fact, something different from oneself is not really threatening because there are ways to deal with it: either foreclose it as strange, or do the reverse—worship and enshrine it on aesthetic terms. Rather, the real threat comes from something similar to oneself, that is, the other as opposed to the stranger. To the stranger, who is different from us, we can either foreclose or worship—the contradictory attitudes are often contained in one and the same relationality. The other is similar to ourselves, yet is an impenetrable existence. What Edward Said called "Orientalism" is a stance by which to see the other as the stranger.

S. K.: In the relationship with the other it seems that there is an irreconcilable crossing. What a culture wants to export or say to the foreigner is not always imported or appreciated by the other culture. Perhaps the other wants to import something that represents us as a stranger, and we, vice versa.

K. K.: Yes, for instance, there is a certain pat representation of Japan in foreign countries. Most of the books about Japan are written to fulfill the requirements of a representation which is formed around either aesthetic or religious realms, or economical and technological interests. After all, combinations of images such as Ukiyo-e [wood-blockprints] and high-tech products, or Shojo manga [girls' comics] and Akihabara ["Electric Town" in Tokyo] seem to be most favored. Omitted are the intellectual and ethical domains. That is to say that ordinary Japanese, who think and live their daily lives in the modern landscape just like people in the West, are not included in the representation. Furthermore, Japanese who talk about themselves to Westerners tend to cater to this representation. They take pleasure out of performing the Japanese of the

Westerners' mind's eye. One of my main concerns is this critique of the representation of Japan, formed by both Westerners and Japanese in their unconscious collaboration.

Modernity is identified with the West. Because it started there, this is correct in terms of historical fact. Yet in terms of critical thinking, the two should be separated, because modernity has been and continues to be a new event in the West too. Not only in Asia, the Islamic worlds, and Africa, but also in the West, the critique of modernity is often shaped as a return to the medieval or the Greek, or an orientation towards the non-West. This tendency, which was first established in Romanticism, is repeated in various forms today. And the representation of Japan, i.e., interest in Japonism or Zen Buddhism, is a form of both the Western and Japanese attempt to go beyond modernity. But modernity cannot be surpassed by resorting to non-Western representations. Overcoming modernity itself is the very consciousness immanent in modernity.[1] In the final analysis, modernity is a universal condition which happened to have begun in the West. This condition, this bind, cannot be dissolved either by undermining the political and economical domination of the West or by returning to the East.

It seems that to Westerners, Tanizaki Junichiro, Kawabata Kosei, and Mishima Yukio are the Japanese novelists who most represent traditional Japanese views. However, even from the moment of their debuts, they were all prominent modernists. Their Japonism or aestheticism derived from their modern consciousness. Whatever the contents represent, and whatever they maintain, their novels are modernist in "form". Fortunately, American Japanologists today no longer think of representing Japan in terms of so-called "Japanese things", but Japanese studies in Europe are the same as ever. It is because they seek "the stranger" in Japan, or the non-West, but not "the other". Long ago, a famous American Japanologist said that the Japanese can sense things well, but they cannot think. All that this means is that such a Japanologist can neither think nor sense. This impression persists in some sectors of Western academies.

Yes, modernity did emerge in the West, but it does not necessarily mean that Westerners are the only and the best ones to account for modernity. Because modernization occurred as a gradual change or an extended shift in the West, it is almost impossible to trace it there. I began to think that the mechanism of modernity could be analyzed more efficiently in a non-Western context—in Japan, for instance—where modernization occurred dramatically and over a short period of time. While Western modernization became naturalized and evident step by step as an accumulation of many changes, non-Western modernization tends to happen swiftly—as a concentration of changes. My book, *Origins of Modern Japanese Literature*, was an attempt to grasp an inversion of modernity—how the present produces the past—that appeared all at once during a ten year period in the late 19th century.[2] Although my example was Japan, my target was really an essence of modernity that could be applied to other contexts.

JOURNALISTIC AND ACADEMIC INTELLECTUALS

S. K.: You are one of a very few living Japanese intellectuals whose works have been published in America and Germany. Would you speak of what it means to be an intellectual who intervenes in both Asian and Western nations?

K. K.: The appearance of my books in America corresponded to a great change in terms of readership, that is, the emergence of "theory" in the 1980s. It is neither criticism nor philosophy but something that deconstructs distinctions between literature, philosophy, and science: They all share the domain of textuality, so long as they were written.

What I have been doing in Japan is similar to theory. For example, *Origins of Modern Japanese Literature* is not a book on the history of modern Japanese literature, even if it sounds that way. *Architecture as Metaphor* is not a book on architecture at all.[3] If it were not for the change in America, neither book would ever have been read there, much less published. I had been working this way independent of American theory. In Japan the way I work is called "criticism [*hihyo*]", and this practice has long existed outside academies. As a matter of fact I am a professor at a university, but I have never thought of myself as a scholar. Academies in Japan unfortunately are segmented, exclusive, and non-creative. I chose "criticism" not only because it goes beyond these segmented enclosures of knowledge, but also because it intervenes in the actual political discourse. It was Kobayashi Hideo who first cultivated this "criticism" in Japan. Last year, for the first time in America, a collection of his work was published. This was edited and translated by Paul Anderer of Columbia.[4]

Kobayashi started his career about 20 years before World War II. Although he was called a critic, to me he was really a philosopher. He was a contemporary of the celebrated Kyoto school philosophers.[5] In the philosophical studies in Japan that developed since the Meiji period, German idealism was so dominant that very few were engaged in French or Anglo-American philosophy. In order to study French philosophy, one had to go to the French literature department, which Kobayashi did. It was similar to what happened in the United States: French philosophy—the realm in which there is no clear distinction between philosophy, literature, and social sciences—was introduced to America through French literature departments, and later came to be called theory as distinct from criticism or philosophy as such.

Simply said, what Kobayashi did was to interject his critical gaze into the gap between the ideal, namely ideology, and the real state of being. This was around 1929. He was the first Japanese thinker who became aware of the discursive practice in writing, or the materiality of the text. Although he was considered an opponent of Marxists in Japan, then as now, his stance was really similar to Marx's, especially to his critique of *The German Ideology*—the book on the gap between the ideal and the real in the context of the Young Hegelians. Kobayashi's first essay was entitled "Multiple Designs," which meant multiple ideologies. That essay shows his critical consciousness of the gap between how one exists and how one thinks of one's existence in the context of other thinkers of the time—in this case, Marxists and philosophers in Japan right before the world financial crisis. Kobayashi then committed himself to the difficult conjunctures of the 1930s to 40s with his criticism, which itself can be read as creative work. When I began to write, I positioned myself along this line of criticism.

S. K.: Is it also related to the fact that in Japan there has been an active and popular kind of intellectual journalism, the equivalent of which does not exist at all in America? I mean that in the US the theorists and philosophers are academics, while Kobayashi was an intellectual who lived by selling his writing and not by teaching.

K. K.: Yes. But it is becoming more and more difficult for the "selling critics" to exist in the way they used to in Japan. They are going back to university campuses. Nearly 20 years ago, Paul de Man told me with a sigh that intellectuals independent of the university system had disappeared with Sartre. Maybe Edmund Wilson was the last in America. De Man said that he himself was a journalist by nature, and critics should be like that. I remember I was rather surprised that he praised Susan Sontag for writing prolifically—like a journalist. After his death de Man was criticized by American scholars for his involvement in anti-Semitic journalism in Belgium under the Nazi occupation. I cannot agree with dismissing his achievement entirely because of this involvement. It reminds me of the very complicated strategies of writing that certain Japanese writers employed under Fascism. It is unimaginable today, but what was not profascist in that context could sound totally so today. As I researched the various ways of resistance that they chose under Japanese Fascism, I realized that the ostensible message is not always what they were trying to address. Such intellectuals as Edward Said and Gayatri Spivak are not simply academicians since they are engaged in the actual situation. I would like to call them "critics" in the Japanese sense.

S. K.: How do you define your positionality in comparison with them?

K. K.: Despite my deep respect for them, I neither can nor would do the same thing they do. Comparing my own position with theirs, I see a clear difference. This comes from Japan's place in world history, to which I belong: though it is one of the non-Western nations, it has a history (which is still present in a certain sense) of dominating the non-Western world. I cannot ignore this ambiguity, or rather I want to deal with it. But it does not mean that Japan is a peculiar case. Any nation that escaped colonialization or achieved independence has the potential to behave the same way: we see this type in, among others, Israel, China, and America, which was the first case.

My criticism is oriented not only toward the discourses of the West that represent the non-West, but also toward Japanese discourses that construct Asian representations. While Said and Spivak, too, fight against feudalism in their own countries, in America at least they can behave as representatives of oppressed and forgotten people. I cannot do this with respect to the positionality of Japan. But Japanese intellectuals of the 19th century were not only able but compelled to do so. Okakura Tenshin, for instance, wrote everything in English and curated the Asian collection of the Boston Museum of Fine Arts in collaboration with the American scholar Ernest Fenollosa.[6] Before the advent of modernity, there was no "art" in the East. I do not mean that there were no important cultural products—there were many important things, but they were not considered to be aesthetic objects in today's sense. In Japan, many Buddhist statues were destroyed after the Meiji revolution as a way of expelling Buddhism in order to stress the importance of Shinto as the national religion.[7] It was Okakura and Fenollosa who gathered the abandoned artifacts, categorized them, and contextualized them as historically important art. Then they did the same thing more broadly with Asian art. Therefore, it might be said, the history of Asian art came into existence thanks to their efforts.

For Okakura it was not enough just to prove the existence of art in the East; he went so far as to stress that Eastern art was greater than Western art. Through the cultural-critical agenda, he represented the power of Asia to the West. He also collaborated with Rabindranath Tagore to establish a coalition of Asian nations to fight against Western domination. He proposed the concept, "Asia is one." This influenced Tagore and even some leaders in the Arabic world. But Okakura's revolutionary stance lasted only until 1904, around the time of the Russo-Japanese War. It was the time Japan turned into an imperialist power, let alone consolidate into a coalition with Asian nations. In despair, Okakura confined himself to the aesthetic world until his death. In the 1930s, his slogan, "Asia is one," was appropriated as an apologist ideology for marching into Asia. Because of this historical background, I cannot repeat what Okakura did. Engaged in the ambiguity of this historical experience which confronts Japanese intellectuals, I hope to place it in a more universal context and act upon it practically. My critical discourse in Japan deals with abstract issues on one hand, but it also tackles the political and practical issues in the public domain outside university campuses on the other.

NISHIDA KITARO AND THE KYOTO SCHOOL

S. K.: Would you speak about Nishida Kitaro? Although he did not actively intervene in the West like Okakura, he is still known outside Japan as a philosopher whose work is often thought to represent an esoteric Asian or Japanese essence. And this question may lead to some concerns about the Kyoto School and its role as an ideologue for the "Great East Asian Co-Prosperity Sphere."[8]

K. K.: Nishida himself, not to mention the Kyoto School which consisted of Nishida's students, was partly responsible for the commitment to the expansionist ideology. But still, Nishida was a true intellectual. He was a Zen disciple, but his Zen was never an Orientalism. Nishida's Zen was a serious struggle against Japanese feudalism, which actually existed as an obstacle to modernization at the early stage. For Nishida, Zen was an effort to achieve an interiority yet to be developed in Japan's modernization. In the context of modernization, religion often assumed a construction of the individual's internal space. For this reason, many in Japan turned to Christianity as something new, but Nishida chose Zen. It was a means to construct an autonomy of interiority, and not an excuse to escape to nostalgia. It functioned as a foundation for the struggle for modernity. More significantly, Nishida never spoke of Zen. He never said anything under the rubric of the East. When he wrote, he kept strictly to the terms of German Idealism: he thought in the words of Kant and Fichte. He counter-posed his reading of German Idealism against that of the official philosophy of Tokyo University, namely, the philosophy of the Japanese Empire. Nishida read Kant and Fichte as a rebellious drop-out, and it was a new, savage reading.

Nishida was a thinker who was placed into the most severe discrepancy between the ideal and the real. If the real could not be surpassed without a certain dosage of the ideal, Nishida's power of ideation in this sense was tremendous, even if it contained some perversion, as often is the case. On the other hand, the Kyoto School was just a group of scholars who tried to interpret anything required by the new situations in Nishida's terms; they were, in a sense, the equivalent of the Young Hegelians Marx criticized in *The German Ideology*. The process through which Nishida established his philosophy was also the process by which he conceived of the gap or contradiction in Japanese modernity. When some people talk about the Oriental *satya* in his philosophy, I have to say, wait a minute, it is not so easy. Even Nishida's later commitment to Japanese Imperialism came from the internal problematic of Japanese modernity itself, and not from the Oriental essence of his thinking that many expected from him. It is wrong to read Nishida apolitically.

Now, when we examine the commitment of the Kyoto School, we should not forget that it took the form of a critique of modernity—which they identified as the invasion of the West into their homes. They believed that the crux of going beyond modernity existed in the pre-modern East or pre-modern Japan. Needless to say, they forgot the conditions that made them invoke the East or Japan in the first place. That is to say that they did not realize that their East/Japan was a representation imaginarily composed within their own modernity.

Along with some literary critics, the scholars of the Kyoto School organized a symposium called "Overcoming Modernity" right after the outbreak of World War II. It was held in an attempt to contextualize "The Great East Asian Co-Prosperity Sphere" which had already been acknowledged as the official policy of the Japanese government to expand its territory in Asia. This ideology came into existence at a time when the Japanese national capital needed an imperialist war: the regionalism of "East Asia" was an ideological apparatus fabricated for this purpose. However, they should not be thought of so much as nationalists. Aside from them were the "literal" nationalists, who attacked Nishida aggressively. The role of Nishida and the Kyoto school was that they provided the theory—based upon Leibnitzian monadology—that accounted for the situation wherein nation-states were relativized under the globalization of economy, or transnational capitalism. This situation is similar to that of today in the sense that the movements to form regionalism beyond the nation-state are becoming active, including in Asia. And no wonder that some Asian thinkers are now saying similar things to what the Kyoto School espoused, but without knowing it. In this sense, even Japan's mistakes vis-à-vis theoretical construction might present a useful example for other nations to avoid the same trap.

I would like to bring up Islamic Fundamentalism at this point. Of course, its faith is not one of nationalism, but rather that which opposes nationalism. Certainly it has an old "origin," but at the same time, it is structurally very similar to Luther's Reformation, which advocated a return to the Bible. For that matter, early Protestantism was a kind of fundamentalism. Islamic Fundamentalism recurred only after an intense modernization took place in Iran. It follows that it is also a critique of modernity represented as anti-West and as a return to the origin. Both Japanese nationalism during World War II and Islamic Fundamentalism tend to identify modernization with the West. Thus Islamic Fundamentalism is essentially a modern phenomenon, with a significance similar to that of Protestantism in the West. Although it appears as anti-modern/anti-West, it represents the cry of modernization in the Islamic context. The "Overcoming Modernity" movement in Japan was similar. After all, it is my argument that if overcoming modernity was difficult in the West, it is difficult everywhere.

Today when we speak of Heidegger, we no longer ignore his commitment to Nazism. Although it is wrong to reduce everything in his text into this reading, it is also wrong to read Heidegger without considering this allegiance. On the other hand, Nishida's text is appreciated totally outside his commitment to Fascism. Though far less than his Kyoto School disciples—Keiji Nishitani, et al.—Nishida, too, played an active role in justifying Japan's expansionism.[9] Today both in the West and in Japan, Nishida as well as Nishitani are read either as thinkers who carry on an esoteric tradition of Eastern philosophy or as those whose philosophy is an useful example of deconstructing Western metaphysics.[10] But I would like to remind readers of the fact that their works were not politically innocent and are not exempted from deconstruction. I do not mean to blame Westerners for their interest in Japanese or Eastern thinking, or for trying to utilize it in their own context. Rather, I appreciate it and encourage them to do so. But it should be kept in mind that when a culture sees another culture, its own internal problematic is always projected into the observation; every national culture looks at the other with a transference of its own internal complexes. Therefore, what needs to be analyzed always exists in the cross-section of the transference.

KANTIAN CRITIQUE OF MARX AND UNO KOZO

S. K.: However, when you have examined prewar thinkers and critics in recent years, it is not simply because you want to criticize them, but because you think there is still something worthwhile there.

K. K.: Exactly. It is the same reason I still refer to the problems posed by the German thinkers, from Kant to Hegel. I still marvel at their ideational achievement. In a culture there is often a discrepancy between intellectual/theoretical development and the development of production. Sometimes it happens that a culture knows advanced things intellectually but the power and relation of production are behind; such a discrepancy can produce great thinking. For instance, German Idealism after Kant. Both Kant and Hegel were familiar with Adam Smith and knew the existence of industrial capital theoretically, though it did not exist in Germany. This discrepancy is precisely the idealist illusion that Marx criticized in *The German Ideology*—how their notion was separated from reality. But it is possible to see it another way: how far one's thinking can go away from reality. If not for this counter-perspective, we are bound to the empirical reality which itself is a production of ideational mediation on another level. One can even see a kind of two-sidedness in Marx. He, who used to attack Hegel, began to call himself "Hegel's disciple" when he went to Great Britain, where the empirical mode of thinking presided.

S. K.: You see some sort of inconsistency or flexibility in Marx's critical stance, which is overlooked.

K. K.: Yes. It seems to me that Marx constantly shifted between empiricist and rationalist stances. He emphasized empiricism in the rationalist dominant situation, while he became rationalist in empiricist circumstances. And this shift was never fixed as either/or. This is clearly the stance of the Kantian critique. I think that Marx criticized Hegel by returning to Kant. Hegel established his dialectics by criticizing Kant's. To subvert the Hegelian system, it is not enough to invert it materialistically, that is, by remaining in the same type, but to undo it by returning to Kant.

Marx had already begun to assume the stance of the Kantian critique in his doctoral dissertation, "Difference between the Democritean and Epicurean Philosophy of Nature," in which he criticizes both Democritus and Aristotle in the attempt to show the Epicurean dimension. In *Capital*, the double-edged posture is apparent in his manner of analyzing the value form by way of criticizing both empiricist/skepticist Baily and rationalist/dogmatist Ricardo.[11] In *Capital*, Marx proceeds in his analysis by performing a Kantian antinomy at every crucial phase. For instance, for commodity to be a value, it has to first be a use value, but at the same time, for commodity to be a use value, it has to first be a value. Also, surplus value cannot exist in the process of circulation, but at the same time it can be achieved only in the process of circulation.

In any event, the ideational power of German Idealism was so strong that we still have to contend with it. The same can be said about the cultural climate of Vienna in the early 20th century, and that of France in the 1960s—the time and place where information of the new was available, while the society was industrially or technologically underdeveloped. This gap brings forth the tremendous ideational power of production. Adorno said the same thing somewhere.

I presume that such a productive gap existed for the prewar Japanese thinkers. I mean not only Kobayashi and Nishida et al., but also various Marxists such as Uno Kozo and Tosaka Jun.[12] They presented a tremendous range of productive readings of Marx on the one hand, and refined analyses of Japanese ideology on the other hand. I learned much from their works, and I regret that they are not known outside Japan, except that Uno's work on Capital is available in English.[13]

S. K.: I know that your undergraduate degree was from the political economy department of Tokyo University, where the Uno School is dominant. Would you speak of the importance of Uno in Japan?

K. K.: What is interesting is that the basis of Uno's thinking was formed after the collapse of the Japanese Marxist front around 1935. The majority of the activists converted, not so much because of a crackdown, but because of their despair toward the policies of Comintern and conditions in the USSR. In the conjuncture, I suppose, Uno thought hard about how to persist in being a Marxist. In a manner similar to the Kantian categorization, he distinguished between theoretical stance and practical stance. *Capital* targets the nexus of human relations under the capitalist economy, in which an individual's subjectivity and free will become obsolete. No matter what you think and no matter how you behave, the capitalist law of value dominates. Capitalism based upon the commodity of labor power contains an irresolvable contradiction, but the basis and necessity of socialist revolution does not result from it. For communism belongs to the domain of the practical and the ideological. Uno acknowledged communism, again in Kantian terms, as a regulative idee, but denied it as a constitutive idee. Because of this stance, Uno could overtly research and teach Marxist economics even under the fascist regime during the War. There is no doubt that it was a form of conversion. Though Uno's thought later became influential to many new left factions, he himself was not committed to political activities. He simply scrutinized the capitalist economy and its fatal flaws.

Especially after communism collapsed, however, I came to believe that it was necessary to reconsider the problem Uno tackled. We should not think that Marxists committed the historically significant mistakes simply because of their misjudgment of the situations. It was because of the constitutive use of idee, the arrogation of reason. By claiming the dialectic synthesis of theory and practice, they diluted both. It is wrong, however, for the left to abandon the idee of communism entirely and affirm the bourgeois stance.

In any event, I hope I'll have more opportunity to introduce Japanese debates concerning Marxism.

PHONOCENTRISM AND THE FORMATION OF NATIONALISM

S. K.: I have the feeling that the critique of phonocentrism by Jacques Derrida is used too much as a critique of Western metaphysics per se, as if it resided only in the West. You have presented a new view of the sound-centered ideology of language in your essay entitled "*Écriture* and Nationalism."[14] Would you speak about it?

K. K.: In fact I talked about it with Derrida at a conference at Irvine, California, in 1995. In the paper I presented, I questioned his notion of phonocentrism, and after the presentation Derrida told me that what he had meant was the same as what I said. He said that he never claimed that phonocentrism belonged to the West, and he never claimed that it went back to Plato. I had misread his phrase in a way that was apparently counter to his intention. In any event, my point is that in the wake of modernity, phonocentrism came to be dominant in every nation.

With respect to Saussure, Derrida points out the existence of phonocentrism on the one hand, but on the other hand he claims that Saussure denied phonocentrism. This ambivalence is quite understandable to me. I believe that for Saussure, neither sounds nor letters matter in the end. What counts is only difference, therefore sound cannot be his main concern. When Saussure used the term "internal linguistics," this really meant "introspective linguistics." In his linguistics, the raw state of the language we speak—a sum of all the idioms we use—is the *langue*. At the same time, he apparently conceived of the sense of "external linguistics," in the context of which a language is violently deformed by the institutionalization of writing (*écriture*) by nation-states, and by all other external forces. Affected by extra-national situations, language is transformed. And, as often happens, when a nation-state is conquered, the language can die, or it can be considered just a dialect, as often happens in the modern educational system. Minor languages always disappear. That is to say, Saussure implied how language is transformed by the political climate, that is, by the writing of letters or *écriture*.

As exemplified in Herder's notion of *Volksgeist*, phonocentrism derived from Romanticism, which considered language as an expression of interiority. But when was the German language formed? There was no German language before Luther's translation of the Bible. The writing of German was made up through the translation of Latin and Greek. Because the German nation lacked a substantial political power center, the language itself became the core of the nation. In this situation, the nation could exist only as literature, and in this climate, the internal voice is essentialized, and the writing of that voice became the language. It is the essence of phonocentrism as expressed fully in Fichte's term "internal border."[15] But the phenomenon is not limited to Germany.

In the context of Japan, around the time of Herder, there was a philologist, Motoori Norinaga. He established a school called "National

Studies" [*Kokugaku*],[16] which was identified as the origin of nationalism in the Meiji Revolution. But at the time of Motoori, in the Edo period [1603-1867], Japan was almost like Germany, divided into territories each ruled by a feudal lord.

In Japanese, the main letters were Chinese characters [*kanji*], which inscribe concepts. In this structure, in which an alien element forms the core, what was required was a phonetic element that would vibrate inside the nation's heart. Similar to the situation of the fragmented power center in Germany, only language or literature could form the nation of Japan. Thus the classics written in *hiragana* (a phonetic syllabary that connects Chinese characters) were identified as the Volksgeist. The hiragana syllabary—i.e., sounds—was considered to contain an original sound/spirit, pre-Chinese influence. It is an equivalent of the Germans returning to pre-Latinized Greek to counter Latin, believing that German and Greek were close (even though it was in fact they who made them closer by way of translation).

My point is that the structure of phonocentrism becomes clear in a close analysis of either Japan or Germany, and the tendency to resort to a fabricated past is universal. Therefore, it was a modern tendency, rather than Plato's own inclination, that invoked the sound-centered ideology. To dare to consider one's own vernacular language as the national language inexorably occasions a sound-centered stance. This is nationalism through and through. Furthermore, this movement is not only an episode of the past, but an ongoing phenomenon everywhere on earth.

It is evident that the production of interiority in the context of nationalism is provoked by external pressure. Therefore, the critique of phonocentrism should be oriented towards an analysis of the political nature of language, and not the game of criticizing metaphysics.

The primary detonator of regional conflicts in the world is language rather than religion, because language is an economic power. In America, whether or not an immigrant speaks English drastically changes his/her labor value. When one dialect, as opposed to other dialects, is assigned to be an official national language, the whole internal power structure changes. This first provokes a change of the economic power structure, and immediately thereafter come religious conflicts; finally, race consciousness takes over. As a result, only the interiorized elements—religion and race—remain in the memory, and the real agents that have caused the conflict—economy and language—are forgotten. Social changes always happen first with economy and are then concretized as language—that which produces a national literature. Language should not be treated as neutral, because it is a measure of the value of labor. There is a famous episode of Marx needing work when he was in England. He applied for a job in a railroad company, but was rejected because his handwriting was so bad. (Laughter!)

In this manner, language is a political and social being, and I have a strong sense that Saussure's major interest was tacitly on this side. He was Swiss and he had to choose whether to become a French citizen in order to obtain a professorship in France or to go back to Geneva. He chose the latter. But can French, while it is used in Switzerland, be deemed the French national language? Saussure was keenly conscious of the trap of national language. He also clearly stated that linguistics itself makes nations. Imagine what a difference it makes if a vernacular language has a written grammar or not. Written grammar produces a national literature, while ethnic/racial ties are, despite their representations, just a transient element which disperses easily. The problem of racial identity is always fabricated according to the power relations formed by economic factors. A period of ten years or so can fabricate the memory of a nation's whole history by way of producing language/literature.

THE PROLIFERATION OF ENGLISH

S. K.: This interview is being conducted in Japanese, but is going to be translated/transcribed in English in order to be read widely. What do you think of the role of English in today's world? Is it a hopeful sign that English is expanding more and more and is seemingly unifying the world?

K. K.: To tell you the truth, I didn't imagine that English would become so dominant before the emergence of the internet. It is hard to believe for those who are in America, but all communication between Asian nations today is conducted in English, rather than any Asian language. In this climate, nations that used to be British or American colonies—the Philippines, Singapore, India—are growing. It is ironical, isn't it? Hong Kong was dominant, too, in the same sense, but is now shifting in a different direction.

S. K.: English may make humanity possible out of tribalism at the same time as expanding and becoming a more and more monstrously large entity.

K. K.: We should not forget that the expansion of English also indicates the global expansion of the capitalist economy into the world market. In *The German Ideology*, Marx used the expression "power of production and intercourse," which Engels later replaced with "power of production and relation of production."[17] Marx obviously stressed the expression "*Verkehr*." With this term he not only signified traffic in a narrow sense, but implied sexual exchange, too. In other words, he proposed a concept that covers the whole nexus of human exchanges.

In human history it was only after long distance navigation became possible that worldwide intercourse began. Without this, world history as we know it would not have come into existence. Since the age of sea voyages, the world has begun to come closer to itself. We should reconsider history in the Marxian term of "intercourse" because today the ongoing revolutions of the exchanges centered on traffic and communication are being more and more stressed. In terms of economy, the world is always/already interrelated by way of the expansion of circulation of commodity and capital. And the cyberspace that began with the worldwide network of the stock exchange is now coming down to the lives of the masses.

Affected by this tendency made possible by the development of electronic media, old divisions of labor are becoming obsolete, and many jobs are no longer in demand. The market economy has been formed in such a way that it always destroys the old divisions of labor and rewrites them. This current change has happened with a speed that no one could have imagined, and for better or worse, it will produce something totally new by dispensing with many old things.

In *The German Ideology* Marx wrote: "Empirically, communism is only possible as the act of the dominant peoples 'all at once' and simultaneously, which presupposes the universal development of productive forces and the world intercourse... The proletariat can thus only exist *world-historically*, just as communism, its activity, can only have a 'world-historical' existence. World-historical existence of individuals means existence of individuals which is directly linked up with world history."[18]

In retrospect, however, the period in which Marx wrote this, or even the late 20th century, could not yet be called "world-historical." World War I was not a world war, but a European war. Although it involved European colonies, and larger domains of the world, the fighting masters were Europeans. It might have been too early for him to talk about the world-market and world-history and so on. The fact is that the situation after the collapse of so-called communism became closer and closer to what Marx described in 1848.

Anyway, Marx's communism is not the kind of communism we saw in Russia or China—which was just another means of modernization. Hence it is time to think of communism again. Right after the above quote Marx wrote: "Communism is for us not a *state of affairs* which is to be established, an *ideal* to which reality [will] have to adjust itself. We call communism the *real* movement which abolishes the present state of things. The conditions of this movement result from the premises now in existence."[19]

I am not optimistic about the future, since the global class struggle may soon end up in a new type of Fascism. I intend to scrutinize *Capital* again under a new light.

S. K.: Thank you very much.

Note: Japanese names follow the Japanese order—surname first—except for living individuals.

1. As discussed later in the interview, "Overcoming Modernity [*Kindai no Chokoku*]" is also the name for a round table discussion held in 1942 between prominent Japanese intellectuals including Kobayashi Hideo, Nishitani Keiji, Kamei Katsuichi, Hayashi Fusao, Miyoshi Tatsuji, Kawakami Tetsutaro, and Nakamura Mitsuo. This was occasioned right after the outbreak of the Pacific War. See H.D. Harootunian, "Visible Discourses/Invisible Ideologies," in *Postmodernism and Japan*, 1989, Duke University Press.

2. Kojin Karatani, *Origins of Modern Japanese Literature,* translated by Brett de Bary et al., Duke University Press, 1993. And with respect to the critical function of the time gap, see Fredric Jameson's forward, "In the Mirror of Alternate Modernities."

3. Kojin Karatani, *Architecture as Metaphor*, translated by Sabu Kohso, edited by Michael Speaks, 1995, MIT Press.

4. *Literature of the Lost Home: Kobayashi Hideo—Literary Criticism, 1924-39*, trans. & intro. Paul Anderer, Stanford University Press, 1995. In the introduction, Paul Anderer speaks of Kobayashi as a figure who parallels Walter Benjamin and Roland Barthes.

5. During the 1920s and 1930s, the philosophy department of Kyoto University attracted many young intellectuals because of Nishida Kitaro. The Kyoto School is a vaguely defined group formed around Nishida mostly by his students.

6. Okakura Tenshin (1862-1913) was the leader of art and art education in the early stage of Japanese modernization after the Meiji Restoration, and later curator of the East Asian Art Department of the Boston Museum of Fine Arts. He was also an international activist. Going back and forth between Asian countries and America, he promoted Asian art in the West. Ernest Fenollosa (1853-1908) was an American philosopher who came to Japan in 1878 to teach at Tokyo University. He was Okakura's teacher and collaborator. His existence proves that Asian art in the Japanese context was produced with or thanks to Western intervention. See Kojin Karatani, "Japan as a Museum: Okakura Tenshin and Ernest Fenollosa," in *Japanese Art After 1945*, ed. Alexandra Munroe, a catalogue for a show held at Guggenheim Museum, Harry N. Abrams, New York, 1994.

7. Although it was influenced by the Buddhism that came from China, Shinto represents the original Japanese religion, as opposed to Buddhism. Throughout Japanese history, its rise in popularity has corresponded to periods of more active nationalist tendencies.

8. This term was coined as a slogan to justify the Japanese invasion into Asia during the Pacific War. It stressed a unified regionalism, led by Japan, involving Manchuria, China, Korea, and South-East Asia, to counter Western imperialist power.

9. Among Nishida's disciples, Nishitani is the most well-known in the West. See Keiji Nishitani, *Religion and Nothingness*, trans. with an introduction by Jan Van Bragt, University of California Press, 1982.

10. Perhaps the most productive and interesting example is Norman Bryson, "The Gaze in the Expanded Field," in *Vision and Visuality*, edited by Hal Foster, Dia Art Foundation, 1988.

11. Samuel Baily, *A Critical Dissertation on the Nature, Measures and Causes of Value: chiefly in reference to the Writings of Mr. Ricardo and his followers, by the Author of Essays on the Formation and Publication of Opinions, etc. etc.*, London 1825.

12. Tosaka Jun (1900-1945): beginning his philosophical career as a student of Nishida, Tosaka later became a Marxist. He led a group called Materialism Research Circle [Yuibutsuron Kenkyu Kai], but was arrested under the Maintenance of Public Order Act and died in prison. His works include: *Nippon Ideologii Ron* [Japanese Ideology].

13. Uno Kozo, *Principles of Political Economy: Theory of a pure capitalist society*, trans. by Thomas T. Sekine, Brighton, Sussex; Harvester; Atlantic Highlands,

N.J, 1980.
14. Kojin Karatani, "*Écriture* and Nationalism," in *Yuumoa to shiteno Yuibutsuron* [Materialism as Humor], Chikuma Shobo, 1993.
15. See also Etienne Balibar, "Fichte and the Internal Border," *Masses, Classes, Ideas*, Routledge, 1994, pp. 61-84.
16. "A general name for the textual and exegetical study of Japanese classical literature and ancient writings which began in the 17th century. [...] *Kokugaku* is [...] specifically defined as the philosophical study of Japanese classical literature and ancient writings with the aim of identifying peculiarly Japanese cultural elements or examples of a typical Japanese mentality." Koyasu Nobukuni, *Kodansha Encyclopedia of Japan*, vol. 6 (Tokyo: Kodansha, 1983)
17. Karl Marx and Frederick Engels, *The German Ideology*, International Publishers C., Inc., 1970. See the note on p. 42.
18. Ibid., p. 56.
19. Ibid., pp. 56-57.

TWO MODES OF TRANSLATION, OR A CROSSING OVER THE PACIFIC

SABU KOHSO

Translation is my business and daily practice. One would think I would feel comfortable with it, but the work never stops making me face the strange nature of language which produces monstrous fantasies in my thoughts. Its characteristics are perhaps similar to those of commodity that Marx expressed as "abounding in metaphysical subtleties and theological niceties."[1] Indeed both the commodity-ness of objects and the translatability of texts seem to exist in (and simultaneously reify) the gap from which all of my illogical spells tumble. In the gap between translation/*honyaku*, for instance, there is nothing that can be spoken of in postive terms. If I try, what comes to mind is at best an imaginative description of the invisible space between communities, or an anthropomorphization of the sum of forces at work in the merciless power relations. Epicurus called this space the *intermundia*—the place God exists.[2] Thinking of how commodity or the equivalent form arises out of mere objects leads me to confront the human nexus which I cannot fully grasp.

Although I practice translation *as the exchange of texts*, like the daily exchange of products for common business, it becomes a knotty thing, and perhaps the knottiest when I attempt to unravel it. Simply said, translation is like money that inscribes the events in the exchanges between different values. The relationship of translation to text is akin to that of money to commodity in the aspect that both translation and money are ghosts of these substances—which make them commensurable.[3] But, what is the ghost that makes the "equivalent meaning" in different textual realities? What is it that appears as the "common essence" in the act of translation? The strangeness abounding in its secularness compels me to turn back and forth between the very basic social analyses and my monstrous fantasies, fantasies about the invisible whole of the social network—Where is it going? How much is it expanding? In this manner, I try again and again to confront the mechanism of my own fantasy production.

I translate two ways: from my mother tongue, Japanese, into a foreign language, English, and the other way around. This two-way trafficking involves totally different ways of thinking, performing, producing, and being. It is not a going and returning along the same route; the difference between the two is not a simple dichotomy.[4] They are neither parallel nor symmetric, neither in accord nor contradictory. Abounding in one and the same place of myself, the difference seems to point to different ways of engaging in society, i.e., America or Japan. The two ways produce two different personae in me.

Translating from English to Japanese is business as usual for me as a Japanese. It has always been a part of my life—from wrangling Hershey's bars from American soldiers to watching every Peckinpah film at the movies. Translation has always been the main tool of shaping the nation, both before and after its modern revolution—the Meiji Restoration.[5] The stereotype of calling the Japanese a copycat culture might be justified partly by taking into account the national obsession of importing foreign cultures. Thus the first mode of translation for me is the importation of information, translation from a foreign language into my mother tongue. It is often said that the Japanese community is more solid than others. If so, it is not so much because Japanese culture is narcissistic as because the language has a built-in mechanism that makes Japanese culture resistant to fundamental change despite its massive, and perhaps unequaled, importation of anything and everything foreign. According to Kojin Karatani, the crux of the mechanism is manifest in one distinctive feature of Japanese, its three layers: *kanji* (Chinese ideograms), *hiragana* (a phonetic syllabary, simplified from the ideograms), and *katakana* (a second phonetic syllabary, further simplified, and used exclusively for transcribing foreign words).[6] The feature concretizes the strata of the history of introducing foreign cultures, and it is this stratification that makes Japan resistant to structural self-destruction or oversaturation by a flood of translated foreign elements. *Kanji*, imported from China, was the first introduction of writing into Japan.[7] But to fill the gap between speaking and writing or to democratize writing, *hiragana*, the simplified *Kanji*, began to be used in writing as a support. In terms of structure, *Kanji* inscribes concepts, while the *hiragana* syllabary "copulates" concepts/*kanji* with its sound-centered role. The relationship between *kanji* and *hiragana* is often spoken of in terms of structure and anti-structure, like architecture and the body, or rocks and streaming water. Or, perhaps *kanji* represents the authoritative father-figure, while *hiragana* represents a mother's warmth. Devised mainly after the Meiji Revolution, *katakana* offers a concession for foreign words which are semantically untranslated. Because of this function of *katakana*, it might be said, foreign languages introduced into Japanese can forever coexist there. This division itself between *kanji*, *hiragana*, and *katakana* functions, metaphorically speaking, as Japan's immune system—accepting, rejecting, altering, camouflaging. But what strikes me most is the fact that none of these systems originated in Japan. The national language called Japanese is like a colony of strong foreign forces dividing and coexisting in the capital of a weaker nation. However, while such a clear stratification of totally different scripts is idiosyncratic in Japanese, it does not necessarily mean that Japanese is the only language that is formed historically by different layers of foreign influences; nevertheless the strata is clearly exposed in Japanese, and as such it makes a good example to show that no language/culture is made by itself. What is unique in a language, then, is less the ingredients than the way the foreign elements are composed. And the composition is not totally a conscious program, but the accumulation of historical contingency.

Japanese is an example of a modern national language—one of many which appeared out of the languages of an empire, whether Han or Latin. Modern national languages share some affinities with each other (and when we use the term "language" today, it usually indicates modern national, instead of dialects and vernacular languages, which might be called "tongues"). These languages came into existence during the various efforts to achieve independence from the empires. Revering the oppressive power and authority of empires, that is, relying upon the concepts derived from the paternal imperial languages, they tried to essentialize the sound of their own mother tongues. In the long history of importing civilization and culture from the empires, the nations gradually developed the self-consciousness to describe the world to their people in their own languages. In fact it was by so doing that they were formed.

In the enclosure of national language, when we translate we take for granted that there is a solid entity of the language which is represented as a grammatical system. Materially, this belongs to the amalgam of nation-state-language. But it can also be said that it is the translation as the production of national identity that binds the unshakable amalgam. In the sense that Fichte, the German philosopher of the time of modern national formation, called national language an "internal border," it assumes the self-consciousness of a nation by way of forming the interiority of individuals.[8] It is like an invisible filter that articulates and rearticulates the space of inside and outside self. At the doom of the father/empire, when modern nations were formed to achieve an autonomy or isolate themselves from a chaotic state of power conflicts, it was the social/economical organ, backed by a common language, that formed the internal body of the nation. In this process, it is external pressure that motivates the formation of internal space; that is, interiority does not appear out of nowhere, it is not autotelic. Nonetheless, as soon as national language as a nation's consciousness comes into existence, it begins to exist as if it were *causa sui*. Usually the history of national literature assumes the role of representing the collective subject. Just like a living organism (if I am allowed to use my fantasy production here), the amalgam absorbs nutrition at the same time as expelling poisons by use of the principle of immunity. The body of the nation-state has a similar mechanism to select what and what not to introduce; this is the task of translation as importation.

In this manner, the monolingual life was naturalized in the modern nations formed with national languages. The subject is normally considered as a construct of one language in this system. It goes hand in hand with the canon that translation should always be done from the foreign language into the mother tongue. (One has to return to one's mother, after playing outside.) I cannot help thinking that the translator's act repeats the vector of the mythological itinerary. Fighting with various monsters and enemies, braving the hardships of a foreign land, the hero brings home the foreign value as the sign of his struggle and tells a story of the voyage—to those who share a common language. In this itinerary, there are two ambivalent values—familiar and unfamiliar—and the transference between them. The value of the familiar is always soothing and affectionate, but never good enough. Something really good must come from the unfamiliar. Although the space where the unfamiliar exists may be hostile, it is worthwhile to travel there in order to win the superior value. The more valuable, the harder the struggle to capture it. Upon return, the cost of the struggles are added onto the captured value. Using a psychoanalytic metaphor, the "translation drive" is provoked by the enigma of the encounter with the other—both fear and seduction of the undecodable messages that the other sends.[9] It is after the encounter with foreign value that the process of translation as decoding of the enigma begins. In this sense, translation might be seen as identical to the production of one's own interiority, that is, the production of national culture. The translation from foreign language to mother's tongue thus traces the mythological territorialization of a nation. That is the story of my translation from English to Japanese.

Of course for some, there is no homecoming. For those whose mother tongue does not have writing, or whose nation is crumbling, the itinerary does not include a return. In contrast to translation as import, there is translation as export. It seems to be a new, revolutionary mode of translation, especially for a person like myself, who comes from an enclosed space where the dominant mode is importation. Therefore when I translate into a foreign language, I feel I am facing the external world. It is an act of speaking *to* the other, instead of speaking *of* the other. In this discourse, one cannot rely on the familiar jargon of a shared paradigm. But one becomes the other as one writes in an unfamiliar system. Of course, this mode of translation is not new, but it has been invisible until recent written history. This translation has been practiced all over the planet by immigrants and traveling merchants. People whose languages do not have writing have to write (and often speak) in the more powerful language, and their practice produces a heterogeneous field of lingual production on the periphery of imperial and national languages: pidgins. Minorities can participate in business in the empire only by using the imperial language or translating from their minor languages to the imperial language. Or consider the language use of nomads—who even adopt foreign customs, religions and languages, wherever they go—an endless, one-way journey of translation away from the mother tongue. This translation is a challenge with unknown consequences—a fatal leap. There are more possibilities of miserable defeat than glorious victory. It is the struggle of minor voices to achieve their equivalent value in a powerful language. However, this translation or this use of language is also an index of the potential of the post-national subject to accelerate global intercourse.

But for now, in the case of Japan, there is a disequilibrium with respect to exports: technological and industrial products have become successful transnational commodities, while intellectual products have hardly realized any equivalent value. On the international map of cultural and intellectual exchanges, Japan is a very small community. Although the intellectual productions are abundant within the nation as the result of the massive importation and the reactions it prompts—for example, a book of theory can sell 200,000 copies—they are still waiting to be exported, uncertain if their intellectual commodity can be sold on the overseas markets. This disequilibrium determines Japan's tragi-comical representation in the world. Akira Asada analyzed Japan's post-industrial society and its representation as "infantile capitalism,"[10] and it can appear to be a playful development (decoding) without maturity. Although Japan, too, has been a colonial power, it has not proven that it has evolved a responsible, serious critical thinking like the Western imperial powers. The Western colonial powers have expanded on multiple levels: they expanded as military and economical forces, and rational thinkers who criticize their own expansion. Of course, these movements go hand in hand with the expansion of their languages. And translation from English to Japanese, rather than vice versa, is a part of the expansion of Western power/knowledge.

As a translator or an exporter of Japanese critical thinking, I believe (or want to believe) that good Japanese writing—including the immanent critique of Japanese colonialism—will make an "equivalent value" when translated into Western languages. But there is always an uncertainty before the event of exchange between different values. As Karatani's reading of Marx emphasizes, the "equivalent form of value" exists only as a result of exchanges. It does not exist as a "common essence" prior to the exchanges, even if it persistently makes us believe so.[11] What culture A wants to import from culture B is not necessarily the same as what culture B wants to export to culture A. Furthermore, in the world atlas of power/knowledge expansion, the hegemony is on the side of the expanding West. In this scheme, the Western subject of export is often the de facto subject of import. That is to say, small nations cannot decide what to export to/import from stronger nations by themselves, because what is in supply/demand in the larger market is predetermined in the intercourse. All in all, there is a wide range of crossings of interests and intents between different values. In the domain of Japanese modern thought, those writers who played the crucial role in criticizing the social formation have not necessarily attracted a Western readership. Their discourses, which often traverse both Japanese and Western paradigms, tend to appear to Westerners as Westernized, unoriginal thinking. Those writers whose works represent the fantastic Japan cast in the Westerners' mind—aesthetic Japan as opposed to critical Japan—are persistently sought out.[12] I think my role as a translator from Japanese to English is to insert the critical aspects fostered in modern Japanese language as much as possible into English, threading them through the background of the main stream of exportation—aesthetic Japan. Today, Japan's most powerful cultural exports are electronic game software and animation. They again reflect Japan's unbalanced profile: a high-tech superpower with an infantile mentality (and in a double sense: first the media themselves are originally made for kids; second, they represent less ethical thinking than a libidinal flow in the techno-social network). There is no doubt that some of them are worthy of praise not only for technique but also narrative. They spectacularly depict the world that we seem to be becoming: a high-tech future, multicultural metropoli, strong women warriors with machinic-eroticism, and mind and body dispersing into a network of which the totality is invisible, and of which ethical judgment is endlessly postponed. "The net is vast and infinite," (as Motoko Kusanagi, the super cyborg cop, says at the end of *Ghost in the Shell*, as she disappears into the vast city and cybernetwork.[13]) In a sense, these images of the unknown future, both utopic and dystopic, matches with what the deconstruction of the so-called Western subject has targetted. Marveling at this attraction, I feel the need to sprinkle the spice of critical intervention over the techno-fantastic libidinal body flowing out of Akihabara, even if it is less seductive, at least at this moment. That is my story of translation from Japanese to English.

It is a metaphysical hope and theological faith to expect the existence of universally common understanding outside the reality of power relations and before the act of communication/translation. There is no "universal money" (=God) to measure the equivalent value of reason inscribed in different languages. Yet the act of translation needs a projection of metaphysical hope and theological faith. That is to say, if one cannot assume the common measure of value in texts written in two languages, the act of translation cannot be motivated. Because of the hope that the result is going to be understood and liked, one translates. For this reason, it might be said, the analysis of translated text as a commodity calls for "metaphysical subtleties and theological niceties." For that matter, Walter Benjamin's concept of "pure language" hopes for a universal money that represents the values that belong to different languages.[14] But in the same essay, he also uses the metaphor of the "broken vessel," in which the original unity of the pure language is fragmented, and it is never possible to repair the whole as it is promised in the ideal. That is to say, if the process of translation is pursued to the *n*th degree of precision, minute local conflicts of values begin to appear all over the text and the micro fissures dominate the whole to the point that it disappears. (And if translation were not a business, and if there were no deadlines, it would literally be like that.) Like fragments of the broken vessel, it is only with patching that is always temporary, and never ultimate, that the imaginary communion of two languages can be constituted, while if no patching is done the common understanding will be dispersed into meaningless babel. (Or the return to the tribal struggles all over.)

Translation from and into English is the most dominant practice in world intercourse today. English rules at the same time as transforming itself by spawning pidgins all over. English, once the language of the empire, is now the language of technology and the cybernetwork. With the advent of the internet, its expansion seems to have achieved the definitive acknowledgment as an irreversible process of human history, at least where it is positively used. It is not "pure language," but it certainly does a good job of simulating it. It is not an imaginary but an actual monster which gives us a glimpse of the hope of universal communication at the same time as territorializing our mind and body to the fullest. Thus the translation from Japanese to English, that on the one hand appears to be liberating, also makes me face a huge network of a lingua-economico apparatuses, whose totality is invisible, and of which ethical judgment is for now endlessly postponed.

1. Karl Marx, *Capital*, Volume One, intro. by Ernest Mandel, trans. by Ben Fowkes, New York: Vintage Books Edition, 1977, p. 163.
2. Ibid. p. 172.
3. For further theoretical speculation about the affinity between money and language, i.e., "form," see Kojin Karatani, *Architecture as Metaphor—Language, Number, Money*, trans. by Sabu Kohso, ed. by Michael Speaks, Cambridge: MIT Press, 1995.
4. With respect to this asymmetry, Kojin Karatani presented an experiment using his own essay on Marx: when the English translation of the Japanese is translated back to Japanese, the result is two different works. See "*Dentatsu Geimu toshiteno Shiso*" ["Idea as 'Whispering Down the Alley'"] in *Inyu toshiteno Kenchiku* [Architecture as Metaphor], Tokyo: Kodansha, 1983.
5. For analyses of the mechanism of cultural formation by importation, see Arata Isozaki, "A Witness to Postwar Japanese Art," and Kojin Karatani, "Japan as Museum—Okakura Tenshin and Ernest Fenollosa," in *Japanese Art After 1945*, ed. by Alexandra Munroe, Harry N. Abrams, 1994.
6. For a discussion of the formation of Japanese as an effort to read Chinese, namely, a translation from Chinese, see the analysis of Kojin Karatani in "*Écriture* and Nationalism" in *Materialism as Humor* [Hyumoa toshiteno Yuibutsuron], Chukuma Shobo, 1993.
7. I have to note that there has been a recurring obsession among nationalists to attempt to "discover" a Japanese writing system from pre-Chinese influence.
8. For an extensive discussion on language and nation, along with the above essay by Karatani, see Etienne Balibar, "Fichte and the Internal Border," in *Masses, Classes, Ideas*, trans. by James Swenson, Routledge, 1994.
9. See Jean Laplanche, *Seduction, Translation, Drives*, Institute of Contemporary Arts London, 1992.
10. See Akira Asada, "Infantile Capitalism," in *Postmodernism and Japan*, Durham: Duke University Press, 1989.
11. For the analysis of Marx's *Capital* with respect to the event of exchange, see *Architecture as Metaphor*.
12. Ioannis Menzas made the following remarks concerning Natsume Soseki: "The surprising gap between Soseki's reputation in his own country and that overseas has multiple causes. Its continuation, among other things, involves the complicated relationship between Orientalism and poststructuralism. On the one hand, poststructuralism, in the form of discourse analysis, is interlaced with critiques of Orientalism (Said himself readily admits his debt to Foucault). On the other hand, however, the poststructuralist fetishization of fictional modes that "know their own fictionality" has allowed the continued valorization of those modern Japanese writers who have opted to portray a quasi-mythical traditional Japan. Soseki's mature novels fit far less into the anti-referential category compared to those of Kawabata and Tanizaki (whom

foreign audiences continue to prefer). This alliance between Orientalism and poststructuralism is so powerful that those of us who are interested in works that attempt to engage their social background, especially the hybridizing effects of Westernization, must still largely despair." From "Soseki in London, or Fetishism, Mimicry & De-nomination," 1997.

13. *Ghost in the Shell*, 1995, directed by Mamoru Oshii, is based upon the Manga by Masamune Shirow.

14. Walter Benjamin, "The Task of the Translator," *Illuminations*, edited and with an intro. by Hannah Arendt, trans. by Harry Zohn, Schoken Books, 1969.

翻訳、満たされぬ愛、あるいは日本語を読むあなたへの手紙

高祖岩三郎

自分自身が翻訳をしてきた体験から、かねがね疑問に思っていたことがある。翻訳者ははたして自分が書いたテキストを、ほんとうの意味で翻訳できるか、という問題である。たとえばこの本の日本語原稿のために、英語で書いた拙文 "Two Modes of Translation, or a Crossing over the Pacific" を日本語に訳し、それをあてようとしたが、どうもそれが最良でない気がして、このように別のエッセイを書いている。やってできないわけではないが、どうも不自然なものがあるのである。アメリカ人にむけて書きたいことと、日本人あるいは日本語で思考している人にむけて書いて意味があることには違いがあるということ。片方にとって自明なことも、他方にとっては新しいということがあるし、その逆もありえよう。それでは「普遍的」な知ではないのではないか、といわれるかもしれないが、逆に普遍性を目指す知が、そうなりえないところに現代の言語・共同体・世界の問題系が露呈しているのである。

さらにここには、心理的にどうも自分が書いた原稿を、不可変的な決定稿とはみなしがたいという事実もからんでいる。翻訳にとっては、すでに完成した原稿、つまり「原典」が必要なのである。そしてこの原典とは、他者のテキストに対してのみいえることではないか。この他者は、自分などにはおよびもつかぬ知をもつものでなければならず、そのテキスト＝原典には、変更など加えようもない絶対的価値がなければならない。あるいはこの他者のテキストが、訳し出される文脈に対して「あやまち」あるいは「齟齬」をはらんでいたとしても、それら自体が歴史的な価値を持つものでなければならないのだ。　まだ生きている未成熟な自分の書いたテキストにどうして「原典」の座など与えられよう。そこに自分が書いたものを「翻訳」する不

自然があるのである。ある言葉で書かれた自分の文章を別の言葉で「書く」行為は、「翻訳」を形成する様々なテキスト的な移送、転移、照応をふくみながらも、それ以前の段階にとどまる。それは精確には「翻訳」ではなく、テキストのもうひとつのヴァージョンと呼んだほうがよいだろう。ヴァルター・ベンヤミンが有名な「翻訳者の使命」でいっているように、翻訳はあくまでも原典の後にくるものである。それは原典の「死後の生」なのである。ということは、この「原典」とは、すでに発展をやめた死んだテキストの謂いである。いわば翻訳が、生きた不安なテキストを、一旦死んで不動となった決定稿にし、あくまでもその後で、そこから全てが始まる母型の位置にすえるのである。

こうした「翻訳」を成立させるのは、ある「関係」である。それはある決定的な不均衡をはらんだ二つの「価値」の関係である。翻訳には「他者のテキスト＝原典」を成立させる政治的関係が介在している。それはいわば、身近なものの親しんだ「価値」と、見知らぬ他者の良く分からないが魅惑的な「価値」の関係である。自分にとって親しみがあるものは大切ではあるが、どうももの足りない。絶対的にすぐれたものは、見知らぬ土地の見知らぬ人々にあるにちがいない。あるいはより露骨に、自分にとって親しみのあるものは弱く、親しみのない強力な文化につぶされてしまった。だからその強力な他者の文化をうけ入れる以外にない。そこにはその無慈悲な力関係にもかかわらず、あるいはそのためにこそ「魅惑」のような働きがあるのではないか。そしてそのようなアンビヴァレントな他者との関係のなかで、その価値に身近な価値との「等価」を発見し、それを転移させることが、外国語から母国語への翻訳の一つのモデルと考えられる。

精神分析学者で、フロイトの翻訳者としても知られているジャン・ラプランシュは、翻訳論と精神分析理論を相補的にかけ合わせた独自の理論を展開している。そこでは「自国語で書くこと」にとっての「翻訳」と「自我の形成」にとっての「無意識」が相補的メタファーを形成する。彼は無意識を形成する「衝動」を「翻訳」の第一の次元とする。そしてその衝動こそが、人間的時間（＝書くこと）を構成していくのだが、それを起動するのは、あくまでも他者の存在、そして他者との不均衡な関係なのである。つまり時間の動力となっているのは、「子供にとっての大人」との出会い、または「他者」一般との出会いである。他者あるいは対他関係こそが、人間主体を形成する自問＝自意識の起源に介在しているというのだ。彼はそのあたりを次のように表現する。「誘惑は非対称的な関係において発生する。その原形は、子供と大人の対である。たとえば子供が大人の世界に対面するやいなや、それは子供にメッセージを送りはじめるが、そのメッセージには性的意味や無意識の意味がふくまれている。そしてそれはメッセージの送り手にとってさえ無意識なのであるが、子供にとっては謎として受信され、翻訳されねばならないものとなる。」[1]

個人の内面の問題を、どこまで「国語」や「国民文化」の問題に敷衍させて語りえるかわからないし、そこには危険があるかもしれない。しかし翻訳という現象をとうして間文化的問題をみると、そこには子供と大人の間の非対称的関係から生まれるような謎＝魅惑の存在が否定できないような気がするのである。子供の意識形成にとって、大人の不可解な恐怖＝魅惑が不可欠だというように、強国の強力な文明・文化の恐怖＝魅力が弱国の文化の形成にとって必要であるということは、国民言語＝文化の自律性をおとしめることだろうか。しかしこうした関係こそが、近代と呼ばれるわれわれの世界の日常的光景ではなかったか。諸国民間の関係には、植民地主義や帝国主義の暴力と悪逆非道が介在してきただろう。しかしそこには同時にある種の刺激・魅惑・接種のようなエロティックな交通の糸もからまってきたのではないか。そうでなければどうして日本が、原爆を投下したアメリカの文化をかくも熱心に導入してくることができたのか。そうでなければどうして、ロックやハリウッド映画やマクドナルドやポスト・モダン建築が、第三世界にうけいれられるようなことが起こっているのか。

ラプランシュの比喩のように、他国語から自国語への翻訳、つまり輸入としての翻訳とはある種の内面化である。それは決して外国文化に向かって開かれているわけではなく、むしろ外の刺激を内に向かって折り込んでいく国語あるいは文化の自己形成と考えられよう。この文脈で考察されている「翻訳」とは、無意識的な言葉の形成運動（主体形成運動）そのものを指している。それはドイツロマン派の詩人、ノヴァーリスが「翻訳衝動」と呼んだような国民文学の形成である。もしわれわれにとって、それを「翻訳」せざるをえなくなるような「謎」がなければ、あるいはそこに不均衡関係からくる衝撃がなければ、そもそも書くという欲動など存在しないであろう。この意味での翻訳は、「自意識」や「書くこと」の問題そのものであり、内面と呼ばれるものの本質的他律性を示してはばからない。

くりかえすが、この運動は、あくまで「二つの価値の不均衡」を動力として動いている。たとえば後進国は先進国の文化や技術にほぼ全面的な関心をもち、それらを積極的に輸入／翻訳する。しかし先進国が後進国に関心をもつのは、資源かエキゾティズムからみられた伝統文化中心である。よくある恋愛関係ににて、この関係においても、人はけっして自分が相手に欲しているものをえることはできず、相手が自分に欲しているものを与えることはできない。そのうえ必ず二人は平等ではなく、どちらかが優勢な位置にあり、権力を行使し暴力さえふるいもするのである。翻訳における原典と訳書の関係には、どこかにこのような赤裸々な非対称性が記されているのではないだろうか。

「日本文化は輸入文化である」というよくいわれることは、ある意味で事実であろう。しかしそれはそこにオリジナルなものがないという意味ではないし、もの真似は良くないということでもない。逆にその大量輸入と独自の内面化のために高度な文化が生みだされてきた印であろう。そして何よりも輸入によって構成されていない文化は存在していない。しかし日本の輸出入のバランスの中に、移民としてアメリカで暮らす者として壁のように感じられるジレンマがあるのも事実である。日本近代の思想を糧として青少年時代を過ごしてきた者として、アメリカの知的パラダイムの中に日本近代が全く存在していないというのは、実に不便なことである。日本の車や寿司やゲームソフトはどこにでもあるが、日本の批判的知性はどこにもないのである。そしてそれを説明するためにはゼロから始める必要があり、会話のなかでは適当にごまかす以外ないのである。同時にアメリカ人の日本に対する一般的イメージにも根強い不均衡がある。どうも日本はその影響力にみあった理性や責任感がないのではないか、そういう印象がアメリカにはあるのである。それは日本が現実的に世界に輸出している商品の「種類」の不均衡と関係しているのではないか。テクノロジーと自動車産業の大国は、同時に現代の批判的な思考においては、ほとんど何も輸出していないのである。アメリカで知られる日本文化とは、美的伝統文化か現代の風俗表象文化がおもで、そこには批判的理性が完全に欠落している。「どうも日本は、その影響力に見合った理性や責任感がないのではないか」というのは、もちろん「嘘」である。しかしこの「表象」は現実の関係に決定され、またそれを決定していく主動因ともなってしまっているようだ。たとえば日本も西洋諸国と同じく、かつての「帝国主義」勢力であり、その力が弱まっているとはいえ、今も経済的な支配を継続している。しかし西洋諸国が世界に輸出・伝播した「批判的理性」のようなものが日本にはみられない、という印象がある。それもむろん「嘘」である。西洋勢力は帝国主義を世界に伝播してきたが、その影響力の一部分として自らの帝国主義を内から批判する「批判的理性」も広めてきた。この文脈において、日本の不均衡、そこには何とも絶望的な悪循環があるようだ。というのも、武器とテクノロジーをもった「幼児的資本主義」（浅田彰）という日本の表象的現実を、世界の通商関係の中で作りだしている当の西洋が、日本の批判的理性には関心をもたず、それを輸入しようとせず、日本側もそれに対してはどうしようもないという姿勢をとってきているからである。確かにこれはどうしようもない問題かもしれない。売れないものを売り、望まれない商品を輸出する馬鹿がどこの世界にいよう。まさにここにあるのは、柄谷行人が「交通空間」とよび、批判的思考の臨界として設定した、われわれを規定しているが、われわれにとって不可視な関係総体のダイナミズムという以外ない。

もちろん日本の新しい世代の文化が西洋の若者にうけている事実もある。最近世界で人気が高まっている日本のゲームやアニメのあるものが体現する世界像が、どうも西洋のポスト構造主義が目指してきたそれ（ことに西洋の男性中心的主体の脱構築）と符号する側面があるようなのだ。ハイテク未来社会、マルチ・カルチュラル・メトロポリス、女サイボーグの強力なエロティシズム、不可視な電脳知と一体化する自意識…。この世界像において、あらゆる欲動の流れと反秩序・構造的なものを肯定しようとするラディカリズムは、テクノロジーと合体していく。またこのテクノ・エロティシズムは、「絶対的な危険という形でしか想定しえない未来」（デリダ）を魅惑的なものにもしていくメカニズムをもっている。日本のアニメがさしだす大きな魅力の一つは、「人間」というものが解体する限界の表象である。戦争や汚染やテクノロジーによる環境再構成の果てにあられるその限界には、それでも何かまったく別の「価値」があらわれ、それによってわれわれは生き延びるという信仰のようなものがある。それは西洋が自己を拡張・解体しつつ確実に世界化してきた近代的な価値の徹底化を表象し、その果ての廃墟において、何か西洋的な理性によっては、あるいはどのような思考によっても捉えられない摂理のようなものが現れるという期待でもあろうか。私はアニメの多くが、くりかえし強調するユートピア＝ディストピア的崇高の中に「原爆以後の世界の表象」を視ないわけにはいかない。あらゆる未来のイメージは、危機的なものとしかみえないというのも事実であろうし、どのような破壊をへても都市＝文明は再生するというメタボリズムが（われわれの統制不能な所に）あるというのも事実かもしれない。そして原爆の後もあそこまで再生できたというのは、その証しでもあろう。アニメの魅力の中には、オタク達が強調するその技術の信じがたい高度な達成のみでなく、それが「日本」で作られたという記号がどこかに織り込まれ機能しているのではないか。つまりアニメが西洋で、そして世界ですぐれた「交換価値」として提示している記号総体の中には、交換しえない「原爆」の事実が刻まれているのではないか。とすれば、このアニメの成功も「日本という表象」の不均衡から自由ではないということである。日本の魅惑は、あるいは魅惑としての日本は、西洋人がいくらほしくてもその父の「否」のためにえられない不均衡そのものにあるのである。極端に高度な科学技術産業と幼児的表象世界の共存、見事に統制されたビジネスの世界と信じがたい程みだらな快楽の共存、人類の戦争史上の極限を示す原爆とその後の発展…。しかしわれわれ日本語を読むものは、この不均衡の表象をまといそれを売ることはできても、不均衡そのものを生きてはいないし、生きるわけにはいかない。

柄谷行人がマルクスから導いたの「交通空間」概念は、もっとも世俗的な公準である経済活動をもとに構築されている。そしてその交換の最小単位を形成する「売る・買う」という関係項は、最終的に理論化しえないような出来事性として記されている。つまりそれこそ人間が、宗教的な表象、そしてあらゆる妄想を生産する原基でもある。いわばエピクロスが intermundia と呼び、神の住処とした共同体の間の空間を形式化すると、まさにこの「売る・買う」という関係項に到達する。私は翻訳の問題を、技術論やテキスト論的形而上学批判としてでなく、まさに「売る・買う」の問題として考えるべきだと考える。そうでなければ、翻訳という事象もその一部である、あまりにも日常的で、あまりに奇怪な「交換」による「交通」の謎は解きあかせないだろう。端的にいって「翻訳されたテキスト」とは、「商品」である。あるいはそういった事実とは別に「商品のようなもの」である、といったほうがよいかもしれない。様々な生産物に「等価価値」をあたえ商品とするような出来事、あるいは異なった言語で書かれたテキストに「等価価値」をあたえ翻訳させるような現実の関係がなければ、「神」のみならず「イデア」などという「共通の本質」は思考されえないであろう。翻訳とは（貨幣のように）異なった価値の交換を物象化する出来事（物）である。ベンヤミンの「純粋言語」という概念には、そのような観念＝妄想の発生の問題がこめられている。そこには、われわれが捨てることのできない普遍的なものへの憧憬がある。そのような観念がなければ、どうして結果のわからない交換の賭にふみきれよう。しかしそれと同時に、同じテキストには「果てしないもの」、「底なしのもの」というニュアンスも宿っている。

ベンヤミンは、一方で、すぐれた翻訳によって、原典もその翻訳もともに、より大きい「本来の言語」の断片でしかないということを開示しえるのだという。すぐれた翻訳によってこそ、特定の言語の呪いに封印されていた「純粋言語」を、もう一つの言語のなかへと解き放つことができるのだという。しかし同時に、彼は「割れた壷」の隠喩を挿入している。こちらの視点からは、個々の国語で書かれた原典もその翻訳もともに純粋言語の壊れた断片でしかない、つまり純粋言語の本来あるべき統一が壊れてしまい、それを完全にもとに戻すことは不可能だというペシミズムが語りかける。この普遍性への希求とあきらめ、この二律背反には道理がある。その両面性は、ほとんど不可避である。それはわれわれ（一あるいは数ヶ）国語に閉じこめられた主体にとっての世界の有りようそのものだからである。世界の情報化・資本化がすすみ、一つの世界・人類・地球の「内在性」が、ますます実感として認知されればされるほど、同じ世界内部の「差異」が際だってくる。「差異」が際だてば際だつほど、一つの「内在性」を認知するしかたが、激しく問われるのである。われわれはこの「内在性」と「差異」の間で、右往左往するのみである。

翻訳にとって、インターネットによるコミュニケーションそしてハイパーテキストといわれるデジタル化されたテキストの流動体は、画期的な変換である。ここにおいては、厳密にはもはや不動の「原典」は存在しないのかもしれない。ハイパー・テクストにおいては、個々のテキストは自らを自由自在に切り刻み、はたまた接合しつつ、つまり果てしなく差異化しつつ、「純粋言語」にどこまでも近づいていくという感じを与える。ここでは「割れた壷」の破片を繋げて、全体の近似値に向かうのみならず、それらの破片をさらに細かく砕くことによって、つねに全体を差異化することもできるのである。しかし忘れてはならないのは、これが実際には、純粋言語ではなく、疑似純粋言語としての英語だということである。まず各国語が使われているにしても、構造的にコンピューター言語としての英語のテキスト・フォーマットにそれらが接ぎ木されたものである。したがってこれらは新しいタイプの「テクノ・ピジョン」とも呼べる事態であろう。したがってハイパー・テキストの拡張は、基本的にはコンピューター語・インターネット語である英語の世界化（＝帝国主義的拡張）と切り放して考えることはできない。しかしハイパー・テクストにおいてのみ、「純粋言語」の可能性に近いものを、つまり割れた壷の総体ににたものを垣間みることができるというのも事実である。この事態は基本的に各国語から英語への翻訳を強要していくであろう。それを拒絶する言語グループは、現実のテキスト的交換の輪からはずされていくだけである。そして日本語の内部で今まで醸成されてきた高度な知的文化、そして批判的理性が、英語になっていくか、それとも内的空間に埋もれたままでいるか、それはまだ未知である。

それにしても、この英語の現実的な支配＝純粋言語化、あるいはそれをフィールドとした世界的交換の実現は、非可逆のものなのであろうか。しかし歴史は閉じたわけではない。かりに英語が、このまま拡張し続けたとしても、みずからの他者を内在化していく過程で、自らも変形していくだろう。そして様々な次元でピジョンを形成していくであろう。ともかく英語＝ハイパー・テキストは「内在性」と「差異」がますます激しく衝突し、ますます激しく燃えさかるわれわれの地球＝世界の生成に限りなくにたシミュレーションとして、仮想世界を広げていくだろう。そして純粋言語という理想は、現実に広がっていく疑似純粋言語としてのハイパー・テキストに凌駕され忘却されていくのだろうか。

1. John Laplanche, *Seduction, Translation, Drives,* I CA, London, 1992

IMPORTED – A READING SEMINAR in Relationship with my A Portable (Not so Ideal) Imported Library, Or How to Reinvent the Coffee Table: 25 Books for Instant Use (US-Version)," 1993/95
Florida, Polk Museum of Art, November, December 1995

EVERYONE IS GAY (IF KURT COBAIN SAID IT, IT'S TRUE)

BILL ARNING

I exercise at the Gym downstairs from White Columns, where I was director and chief for eleven years. Because I was there so long I still receive much mail at the gallery. They keep a box for it. I still have my keys so I often stop in at night to pick it up. Recently there was a little package inscribed "A special present for Bill Arning." I unwrapped it to find an unflattering painting of me, almost a caricature, with the word "fag" hacked into the surface above my face. Oddly, it was numbered, 660, and signed "Garth Amundson," a name with which I am not familiar.

As I am totally out the closet, and have been since I was fourteen, and have never minced words about my sexuality and personal history in my writing, calling me "fag" is, at the very least, obvious. I am reminded of a story about Lari Pittman, the painter, whose studio was in a somewhat dicey section of L.A. When he would walk his not very butch dogs, and someone would yell "fag" out of a car window he would respond with a simple "thank you." Lari's response is perfect. Thank you, I am proud to be a fag, I have no remaining horror at the word, and other than the potential ill will of the person saying it, why should I care?

But what of Garth Amundson? If this is indeed a real person, (Garth as in "Wayne and Garth" from Wayne's World?) he did at least sign his piece and thereby claim responsibility, be it credit or guilt. He is perhaps some self-important and not very technically proficient grad-student trying to, as all students should, push people's limits. For all I know he has sent other art-world figures paintings with Nigger, Jew, Cunt or Chink appended as gouged captions. Perhaps, despite failing to capture my masculine pulchritude, he meant this as a tribute to my out-ness. Maybe he is painfully shy, and it was just his way of trying to ask me on a date. (Sorry Garth, I have a boyfriend.)

I grew strangely fond of this tiny painting, leaning it on the shelf over the computer where I write. I found myself showing the piece to friends, asking for their take. Is it flattering or threatening? Reaction has been mixed. But the whole experience has been a good gauge for how it feels to be an out-curator speaking to an international audience that has very different takes on identity politics and art as we careen toward the millennium. It is impossible for me to ever know if I am taken as seriously for my achievements in the field of curating exhibitions and writing on art as I would be if I were heterosexual, or god forbid, closeted.

> "What do you think cause I'm not sure
> whether I didn't get that job (we hired someone else)
> because my hair's parted on the wrong side
> or because I'm a flaming SM rubber dyke, whoa"
> TEAM DRESCH *I'm Illegal* 1996

Take one unemployed faggot-curator, me, who has spoken from a position of privilege for over a decade, all high and mighty, and stir with vermouth. As curator of White Columns, a New York alternative space since 1985, I knew incredible freedom. The U.S. alternative space system was and is a tremendous fortress in which difference is more than tolerated. It is no wonder smart queers are attracted to this world, and are a major force in the field. (It is also no surprise that conservatives, in trying to defund the National Endowment for the Arts, spent a disproportionate time attacking alternative space shows that barely received federal funding at all.)

Now it's fall 1996 and I have to wonder whether my employing that freedom to speak of gay and lesbian issues in contemporary visual arts has bitten me on the ass. Although I was with an institution for eleven years and am therefore reluctant to settle down at one position, I have applied for a few jobs (I need money, health insurance, etc.). In each case I was courted at first and than rejected. Would it be paranoid to think a more meticulous reading of my resume revealed a show I organized in Argentina called *Maricas* (*Faggots*), one in L.A. called *The Anti-Masculine* and one for White Columns called *Stonewall 25—Imagining the Gay Past* (which earned me the best press I ever received)?

My coming out as a person was easy. I had a liberal family, I was the baby of the family, my older sister was in acting school and had quite a number of flamboyant grand old-fashioned queenly visitors. Walking home from school when I was ten I saw two women swapping spit in the street. This was heaven for a intellectually precocious proto-homosexual.

Gaining some success as a curator I began to be invited to international shows and conferences. Clad in my new Big-Fag-Curator superhero clothes, not embarrassed to say anything out loud, I packed my bag and went, unaware that I could still be parochial in my knowledge of the ways of world art. I was unaware that much of the world saw North American confessions as just embarrassing and not at all heroic. Looking at what seemed to be homoerotic photos in Brazil, I asked the dealer if it was indeed from a queer perspective; I was subtly chastised that in Brazil it was not spoken of in those terms. In Germany, apart from Frank Wagner, who has done amazing shows with queer themes, and one or two others, no one I met was out professionally.

From my New York perspective, you can't be a good curator unless you're an honest curator, and you can't be honest if you're closeted. I must acknowledge that other perspectives exist. Some think curators, like good waiters, should be invisible, and speak from a universal, rather than a personal perspective, when they speak at all. The vogue for using "*ausstellungsmacher*" rather than curator in German-speaking countries, while a bit precious sounding, like art-worker, does indicate a helpful demythologizing of the role. Admitting that I am more prone to be enthusiastic about queer work because I like to suck dick seems a good starting place to humanize my work.

I have started asking foreign curators for the names of the great tortured closet case artists in their countries art-history. There is always at least one. If memory serves there was someone named GOM in Sweden. In Argentina, several. Only in Japan was the question rebuffed. Finally a nearly universal counter-narrative of modernism, an anti-hero with a thousand faces.

I was invited to organize *Faggots* at Centro Cultural Rojas in Argentina, at the invitation of director Jorge Gumier Meier, an very out curator. During an interview with the press I was repeatedly asked what gay art looked like. I said there was no look. What we have in North America is a moment when gay artists can for the first time in history invite their sexuality to be a part of the reading of their work without being dismissed as marginal. If we progress as a society there will no longer be a need to do a show called *Faggots*, as sexuality will be seen as one more element to be included in any reading of a work.

Constructions of sexuality are always fluid and diverse. The idea that you can have sex with people of the same sex and by not being penetrated still be straight is acceptable in some countries, and provokes howls of laughter in others. A heterosexual Argentine artist told me that it was a fact that every man in the country had been anally penetrated before they were forty, leaving me to envision a center to help out 39 year olds who had neglected their duty. An American artist living in Mexico told me that it was a fact that 80 percent of Mexican men were functionally bisexual. Whatever. Sexuality is endlessly slippery, thank God.

It is not surprising that no one wanted to be labeled a gay artist in the past because for most people the image conjured up was a conservative history of tasteful male nudes. Contrary to myth, fags are not known for our good taste in art, and Bruce Weber and David Hockney sadly dominate queer themed collections.

But in 1996, after Felix Gonzales Torres and Robert Gober, who I feel it is safe to say will be considered among the most significant artists of the century, there is actually a gay art tradition being reconstructed from shards, one that is worth caring about and protecting.

Is it colonial of me to wish to internationalize that history? Gay Australian artist Matthew Jones startled me when he said that ACT-UP's exportation was an example of US cultural colonialism. I always thought of ACT-UP as pure good, direct grass roots action to fight AIDS. He pointed out that in Australia, where the government was much more quickly responsive, ACT-UP arrived as a sexy look, a cruising outfit, lacking the needed enemy to fight against. Jones did open my eyes to the need to remember that sexuality always has a cultural context, and my urging a prominent queer Brazilian artist to be more out about the content of his work might make no sense, or different sense, in his country. If I construct a hierarchy around out-ness, it is automatically suspect, because in its construct, I am guaranteed to be on top.

There is no resolution possible. I will continue to look at art from a queer perspective. Maybe I will even get a job someday. Meanwhile, the achievements of today's artists will be continued, challenged and reinterpreted by younger artists. What the legacy of the last ten years of out artists is will only then be known.

P.S.: The story has a happy ending. Garth Amundson was a friend of a friend. It turns out I had juried a show at an alternative space in New Haven, Connecticut, and I had picked his piece *1000 Fags* for inclusion. As anyone who juries knows, the slides go by quickly, and your response is limited to thumbs up or thumbs down, so I had forgotten. That does account for the vague sense of familiarity I had upon seeing my personal *Fag* painting. It still hangs above my desk, but now it no longer scares me, and often triggers my re-telling the story I just shared with you. After several entertaining phone calls with Garth I am looking forward to meeting him. I have a new buddy—Thank you queer theory 1997.

I'M SORRY, BUT I DON'T SPEAK THE LANGUAGE
A Solo Performance

DAN BACALZO

[A young Filipino-American man stands alone on a bare stage.]

I'm told that I speak very good English.

People ask me where I'm from, and usually, I say, "Kansas." Sometimes, I'll tell them I'm Filipino. But since I've never actually been to the Phillippines, I find it harder to make that sort of claim. I was, however, at least exposed to some of its language when I was growing up.

I remember in particular three words or phrases that my grandmother would constantly say: "Esusmaoseph!" "Bunsit Assou!" "Sige." Raised as I was in the United States, the only language that I'm fluent in is English, and so it took me awhile to realize that my grandmother could speak several different languages at the same time.

The Phillippines has numerous native dialects—roughly 7,000—but the National language is Tagalog. "Sige" in Tagalog means "Okay" or "All Right" or "Go ahead." Depending on how its spoken, the particular nuance given, its a way of acknowledging someone, or ending a conversation.

"Bunsit assou!" is a phrase in Ilocano, my grandmother's regional dialect. It means "smelly dog." You see, my grandmother had one of those love/hate relationships with our dog, Bucky. She called him a "Bunsit assou" whenever she was in her hate phase, which was quite often.

"Esusmaoseph" is actually English, although not immediately recognizable as such. My grandmother is a very devout Catholic, and so she says this in lieu of swearing. "Esusmaoseph" is a shortened version of "Jesus, Mary, and Joseph." And so my grandmother never has to take the Lord's name in vain.

One of my deepest regrets is that when I was growing up, I never learned to speak Tagalog, or any other Asian language with anything resembling fluency. Even if the words look and sound, somehow very familiar, it's someone else's language. Not mine.

Whenever I meet new Filipinos, and they greet me, "Oy, Kumusta?" I have to tell them, "I'm sorry, but I don't speak the... I mean, I don't speak... I don't understand." And I feel like I'm failing a language proficiency exam. I need remedial lessons on being Asian in order to catch up, to fulfill my role, to play my part.

And so I jumped at the first opportunity that came along. Freshman year in high school, and my first role in the theatre. I played Ling in the musical, Anything Goes. To be honest, I never even auditioned. I was on the props crew. But the Chinese boy who had been playing Ling dropped out, and the director asked me to take over the part, since I was Asian.

I wore a loose fitting, light blue, pajama-like outfit and a field worker's hat. Ling, along with his fellow Oriental companion, Ching, was a rather minor character in the show. We weren't in most of the big musical numbers and we didn't get any solos or even duets.

In every scene that we were in, our director had us shuffle in with little baby steps. *[He shuffles.]* We also bowed a lot. *[He bows several times in rapid succession.]* And smiled. *[He smiles a cheesy grin.]*

Neither one of us in our real lives spoke with any kind of pronounced Asian accent. But my director thought it would be funnier if we would try to do one. Now, my parents Filipino accent had the wrong inflection for the role. It didn't sound right. It wasn't what the director wanted. And so I did what any other aspiring, teenage American actor does in these kind of situations—I turned on the television. I chose as my role model, a short Asian actor who appeared as a regular character on a popular television show. He sounded something like this: "De plane! De plane!"

My director approved of this accent. It sounded authentic. And so, I would say my lines in a voice imitating Mr. Roark's small-in-stature assistant on Fantasy Island. "I bet pants!" I boldly declared, secure in the knowledge that I had finally gotten the role down. It was my first role, and I felt that I had to do it properly. I had to do what was expected of me. And you know what? My director was right. It was funnier.

People laughed.

[He squats down into a "ready" stance, and throws a punch with a cry, "KI-YAA!!!" As he says the next section, he performs a "kata," a sequence of choreographed karate movements.]

I decided to take karate in order to further my lessons in being Asian. This was a more dynamic image of what an Asian should be like. And if I could learn the moves, then perhaps it wouldn't matter so much that I didn't speak an Asian language. I wasn't a tremendous success at karate. I mean, it did get me in shape, but it didn't make me more Asian. I briefly wondered if this had anything to do with the fact that both my karate instructors were white.

[He ends this sequence back in a "ready" stance.]

A couple of years after I stopped taking lessons, I ran into one of the guys from my class. He invited me over to his apartment to "practice our karate." I showed up. Without my karate gear. Without even so much as a change of clothes. And he became my first lover.

Now, adding a gay identity to this Asian connection which I never quite fully felt brought with it its own complications. After coming out, I went around buying anything with a pink triangle or a rainbow flag on it. Not only do I have a set of freedom rings, I have freedom triangles. I wanted to buy this gay identity. To have it. To own it.

[He relaxes into a "cruise" stance.]

But standing alone in a gay bar, I felt far from ownership. I saw men laughing, cruising. And they were predominantly white men. There were no other Asians in this bar. And I felt out of place. Like I didn't belong.

[He starts a slow, rhythmic movement sequence that repeats 3 times, with increasing speed.]

A man approached me. He wasn't particularly handsome. He had a roundish, pock-marked face, overgrown with stubble. The hair on his head was shaved close to the skin. He was taller than me. Broad chest. Stocky build. There was a roughness to him that excited me. Besides, he was the first man to express an interest in me that night, and I was beginning to feel desperate.

He smoked—which I don't—but I took a drag off of his cigarette, anyway. It made me feel older, like I knew what I was doing.

We had to wait for the bus. It wasn't due to arrive for awhile, so he asked me to go with him to the public toilet, which was around the corner. My first thought was, "Well, I don't really have to pee."

We stood side by side at adjacent urinals. "What's the procedure here?" I wondered. But, of course, I couldn't ask. He already had his dick out, which was starting to grow hard. I still hadn't undone my fly.

He reached his hand over and pulled out my cock. I glanced around, but we were the only ones there. "It'll do." he said. And I wondered if I had just passed some kind of test.

We got on the bus. He placed his hand between my legs, slowly rubbing the rough denim. The other passengers on the bus began to stare. I turned to him. I was about to say something. But then he kissed me, on the lips, his tongue sliding into my mouth as the other passengers watched, and as the bus continued slowly on its way.

When we arrived back at my place, he sat on my bed and told me to take off all my clothes. I slipped off my too tight T-shirt, my 28-inch waist Levi 501 blue jeans, and finally, my black briefs. "Should I keep my boots on?" he growled, his harsh stubble bruising my oh-so-ready lips.

And he fucked me. In every position imaginable. On my bed. On the floor. With me hanging upside down and him holding onto my legs. And while he was fucking me, I wasn't thinking about representation. I wasn't thinking that Asians are always playing the role of the bottom in gay male sexual encounters. I wasn't thinking that this white male was playing out his colonial fantasies on my Asian body. I was thinking, oh God, I was thinking, I was thinking, I was thinking, I was thinking, I was thinking, I was thinking, I was thinking, I was thinking, I was thinking, I was thinking, I was thinking, "Oh God!!!… this hurts."

[*He remains on the floor.*]

I was bleeding. When he realized this, he stopped. He had been wearing a condom. He hadn't even come. It was the first time that I had ever been fucked.

"Why didn't you say something?" he asked. "I would have taken it easier." But I hadn't known what to say. I hadn't wanted to disappoint him. I hadn't wanted to let him know how inexperienced I was. I knew… or maybe I just thought… he expected it of me.

"You're a stupid fucker," he whispered in my ear, holding close my trembling body. And as I lay against his warm, broad chest, I thought, "Yeah, he's right. I am a stupid fucker."

[He slowly begins to rise.]

I'm a stupid fucker because I'm trying to speak several different languages at the same time. But unlike my grandmother, I lack fluency.

I'm sorry, but I don't speak the…I mean, I don't speak… I don't understand.

Sige. Okay. All right. Go ahead. But am I acknowledging you, or ending a conversation?

[*As he says these last few lines, he slowly backs up. He stares out at the audience for quite some time, then slowly turns. When his back is to the audience, he shifts position, then speaks. His movement in this section is slow, sensuous, sort of like an erotic dancer.*]

"I like my Asians to look like Asians," a lover once told me. "You have a very feminine face," said another. What is it they expect from me? What fantasy do I fulfill? Feminine? Boyish? Oriental? Moving with grace and beauty.

My body is not the type you normally find in mainstream gay magazine ads. You know the ones I mean. Where the men are muscular, manly… white.

A friend of mine told me that there was a Japanese guy at his gym that has a body "just like a Caucasian." If I worked really hard, if I went to the gym every day, maybe I could have a body like that.

[*He shifts body position and tempo, building up to a frenzy.*]

In a crowded hallway I kissed him. The lights were dim, but I could see him well enough. And when the eyes failed, the sense of touch allowed me to navigate every curve and indentation of his chiseled Caucasian body.

I ran my fingers through his short blond hair, gently caressed his perfect cheekbones, stroked his muscular chest, his washboard stomach.

Parting my unbuttoned shirt, his hands wandered over my own slim Asian body. Did he like what he felt? Or did I not measure up? Did he have to lower his standards for me?

My lips traced their way down from his hardened nipple to his even harder cock. I wish my body looked like his. I couldn't help but think it. I wish my body looked like his. Why can't my body look like his?

If my body looked like his, would that be perfection, then? If my body looked like his, would I be more desirable? If my body looked like his, would I be happy?

[*He breaks from the position he is in (on the floor), turns around and starts the sensuous movement sequence over, with variations.*]

I put my body on display, dancing on the bar wearing nothing but a green thong and my Doc Marten boots. It felt good to have men look at me. To have my body completely objectified. But I wonder what they were thinking. Was my body too thin? Was my chest too narrow? Were they looking for perfection? Did they even know what perfection was? Did I?

[*The following two narratives are interlaced with a movement sequence which alternates between frenzy and stillness.*]

I stumbled home, a little drunk from a party. I brought someone with me. "Do you want to fuck me?" I asked him? Giggling, he said, "yes." I wondered if people usually asked him this. Maybe he was a bottom. He was wearing a dress before I took it off of him.

My parents, it seems to me, are probably the perfect immigrants. They arrived in the U.S. in 1966. They had with them my oldest brother, Michael, and the grand sum of $5.

I pulled out my KY jelly and handed him a condom. I began working my asshole with the lube. I'm always pretty tight.

They started out in New York, and slowly worked their way westward. My father is a psychiatrist. My Mom is one, too. Originally, she had wanted to be a pediatrician. But as she tells it, she decided to run her own nursery ward instead.

I had a hard time getting erect. This often happens to me when I've drunk too much. He had no such trouble. He slipped into me smoothly and I groaned with pleasure.

I am the youngest of five children. My Mother remained at home until we were old enough for her to complete her residency in an American hospital.

Afterwards, we lay together, bodies pressed close. Sticky. He whispered a word into my ear which I didn't understand. I wanted to remember that word. It was a Jewish word, he said. It meant "predestined."

They worked hard. Their children grew up. They now own a lovely home in Spokane, Washington. And I think that they're happy, but I'm not really sure.

We were predestined to be fucking, he said. But that wasn't really what he said. Because he didn't say "predestined." He used that word, instead. That Jewish word, which I can't remember.

I never asked my parents what they thought perfection was. I never asked them if perfection was living in a country where anti-Asian violence and discrimination is often labeled "not racially motivated." I never asked them if perfection was constantly being told "You have a funny accent, and where are you from again?" I never asked them if perfection was speaking words in a language that…

I don't understand… why my parents won't tell their friends that I'm gay. I don't understand why I've never asked them to.

It's not that they're ashamed of me. It's just that…there's no reason for their friends to know.

Especially not their Filipino friends.

I visit them in Spokane. I have dinner with their friends. We talk about the husbands, wives, fiances of my siblings. And inevitably, someone will ask me if I have a girlfriend. And it is so much easier to just say, "no."

And then change the subject.

I think about what it would be like to tell them I have a boyfriend, instead. I think about how my parents would react. Would they try to stop me? Would they be mortified? Would they mind? I don't know. I've never asked them.

My parents and I don't talk much about my boyfriends. The first time they met one, I didn't even tell them we were dating until afterwards—even though I was already out to them. His name was Martin, and I met him while vacationing in London. A couple weeks later, my parents joined me on this trip. To them, Martin was just a friend of mine… who was kind enough to act as our tour guide, and accompanied us wherever we went.

My friend, Kevan, who I was staying with in London, introduced me to Martin. And it was love at first sight. Or so the story goes.

Martin and I spent a number of hot, steamy summer nights together. In London and in New York. Always conscious of our immanent separation, we spent every moment together as if it was our first and our last.

And the moments multiplied into minutes, into hours, days, weeks. But they were all still moments. Still moments:

[*He performs a movement sequence which corresponds to each image.*]

The droplets of sweat on his face glistening in the morning sunlight.

Holding him close on the stairway of his apartment building the night that I left London, and saying the words, "I love you, Martin" for the first time.

Staring, wordless, into each others eyes in a dimly lit London pub.

Standing on a subway platform, not being able to touch, or to kiss.

Lying sleepless in the bed of a cheap New York hotel room, watching his chest rise and fall with each breath.

Still moments. Neither lost nor forgotten. But still…out of reach. He went back to London. I had already started making plans for a Christmas visit. But then, the letter. Early November.

[*He pulls out a very worn letter, that has apparently been read many, many times.*]

Dear Dan,

I really must apologize for not writing sooner. In fact I have been trying to write this letter for nearly a week. I'm afraid that its not going to be a letter that you want to read.

All I do have to say is that the time we spent together was very precious and special to me. I will always remember it fondly. I want you to do so as well. Since I returned from the States I made a lot of friends through the gang in the house, one guy in particular who has now become more than a friend.

It is my fault that I have to hurt you—I am the one who is weak but I am at least brave enough to admit it.

Dan, I want you to get on with your life—you have so much to give and I speak from great experience in that long distance relationships do go wrong: life is for living and you should take those opportunities that are in front of you. I want you to go on and be happy in what you do.

To say things so cliched as let's be friends—as I'm the instigator of all of this I cannot call the shots. I'm sorry to have hurt you. I think that if you can hate me it would be easier than anything else.

If you don't want to write/phone—that I can understand. I hope and I know you will find your way with someone who cares and can give you more than me.

Take care,

Martin

[He slowly folds the letter, and puts it back into his pocket.]

I wondered if I had imagined the perfect love I had found. Or is it perfect only in my memory?

You see, that's the problem with memory. It translates things into images, pictures, that are no longer quite real. Encrypted passages for deciphering. A language which you think you can read, but you're not sure if you understand.

Sort of like a fortune cookie.

I had a boyfriend once who had various cookie fortunes taped to his bathroom mirror, door, and other parts of his apartment. He told me that I should never underestimate the wisdom hidden in a fortune cookie.

But too often, it's not wisdom that I find. It seems to me that the fortunes are usually so generic. They don't really seem to mean anything in particular. The advice they dispense is aimed to apply to everyone. They're universal.

Or are they?

When I was studying theatre as an undergraduate in Wichita, Kansas, I was taught the concept of the "universal character." This is someone whose experience is applicable to everyone.

But have you ever noticed that universal characters are always white?

Back in Wichita, I would audition for roles that I identified with, that I viewed as universal. "This can reflect my experience," I thought. "It's not race specific." And time after time, I wouldn't get the part.

I used to think that this was because I was a bad actor.

And maybe I was.

But maybe it's also because while the *role* might be universal, *I* am too specific.

And when I did get cast in shows back in Wichita, people would almost inevitably comment about how it was "non-traditional casting." I was made to feel as if I got a part not because of my acting ability, but because the director felt pity for me. And I was grateful. But I was also always aware that non-traditional casting is not a universal practice.

The universe, you see, is a small place. And often, you don't belong in it if you're not white.

A while back, I was reading an article about how there are a bunch of (white) Americans who want to stem the tide of (Asian) immigration into the U.S. It seems they are particularly concerned about the Chinese. Their leader was quoted as saying, "Do we want a billion highly fertile people here?"

When my parents immigrated to the U.S., they were threatening the National borders—even if they aren't Chinese. After all, they arrived with one Asian child and then had four more. All of whom were born American citizens.

And you know what? They really want grandchildren.

Funnily enough, they don't ask me to provide them with one. I guess they figure that this particular duty belongs to one of my heterosexual siblings.

They drop them hints. One time they brought my sister, Mary Anne, a gift wrapped in a little baby bonnet. My parents are nothing, if not subtle. And I guess persuasive, since she's now pregnant.

When Mary Anne first told me that she was considering going off of the pill, so that she and her husband could have a baby, I remember feeling so very envious of her. Because she could do something that I can't.

And, I'm not talking about having a baby.

What became clear to me, was that not only was she going to have unprotected sex in order to reproduce, but she and her husband had apparently not used condoms while they were fucking, for quite some time.

Yet, no one thinks this is strange. No one thinks that unprotected sex between a married heterosexual couple is inherently dangerous and risky.

(pause)

I want to get fucked without a condom.

(pause)

I want to know what it feels like to have someone's unprotected dick sliding in and out of my asshole. I want to know what it feels like to have someone cum inside of me.

I'm scared because I think I'm never going to know what that feels like. I'm scared because I think that I will know what that feels like.

And immediately regret it.

[*He begins a movement sequence, accompanying the following section.*]

Because I remember how I felt when I went in for an HIV test.

And I remember how I felt at the first AIDS activism meeting I attended.

And I remember how I felt when my one and only female lover asked me to stick my condomless cock inside of her.

And I remember how I felt when I gagged on my first male lover's cum, not knowing whether I should spit or swallow.

And I remember how I felt when I got fucked on stage at a Safer Sex party.

And I remember how I felt when someone asked me if I've ever been a Top, and I had to say, "No."

And I remember how I felt that night when I would have consented to anything.

And I remember how I felt when my test result came back… negative.

I felt lucky.

"You will have a long and healthy life," read the fortune in my cookie. And I realized that didn't apply to a lot of the gay men that I know. And I wonder how they feel when they open up their fortune cookies and read the same message.

Even if the words look and sound, somehow very familiar, it's someone else's language. Not theirs.

[*He turns his head, slowly.*]

"God Hates Fags." The words were emblazoned upon the sign held by the Reverend Fred Phelps.

It was a Day of Remembrance. I watched Phelps lead a group of his followers in a protest outside the small Kansas church where people whose lives have been affected by AIDS had gathered. We were there to remember. To pay tribute to friends, lovers, family, and strangers that had been lost to the epidemic.

Looking out the window of the church. Looking at the protestors with their hate-filled signs. Looking at Fred Phelps, passing judgment upon all gay males and proclaiming AIDS as our punishment.

This is what I remember from that day. But I don't understand this hatred. It makes no sense to me. The words invade my mind and penetrate my body. God. Hates. Fags. God hates fags. God hates fags. God hates fags. God hates fags. God. Hates. Fags.

These are not the words I want to remember. This is not the language I want to speak. But my memory holds fast to these words.

You learn… you remember… through repetition… and through feeling. Language crawls up inside of you and you speak the words you've learned to remember.

I don't really understand the process. Which words stuck in my memory first, little by little forming a language. My parents tell me that I started to speak by the age of six months. You learn by doing, or so I'm told, and so I kept speaking. And I kept speaking. And I kept speaking. And eventually, someone told me that I spoke very good English.

But I don't remember when that first happened.

Most of my childhood memories are based on endlessly repeated family stories, or photographs which I'd see again and again. This way, I can remember things that happened before I was born, or immediately afterwards.

Like my first bath. My parents ruthlessly documented each and every one of their children's first baths. As the youngest in my family, I was no exception.

At some point or another, me and my four siblings have tried to hide, burn, or otherwise destroy these photographs, lest they fall into the wrong hands, or be used against us later. We lived in mortal terror that our parents would whip out these photographs for the scopic viewing pleasure of all of their friends. Or worse, all of ours.

I'm not sure why I find these photographs so embarrassing. Is it the nudity that bothers me? Am I somewhat disturbed by the full frontal shots...taken by my father? Do these depictions of my baby body somehow contribute to the cultural stereotype of the small dicked Asian?

[*He looks down at his crotch, then continues.*]

"I like men with small dicks. Do you have a small dick?"

The guy was adorable. Blond hair, cute smile, sexy body. But that was one of the weirdest pick up lines that anybody has ever said to me. It kind of caught me off guard.

"Um...What do you mean by small?"

He smiled at me, cutely, "I'm being stupid." He caressed my cheek, walked away and left me standing there, alone.

[*He sighs, shifts focus.*]

I don't know if I'll ever get used to cruising at bars. You learn by doing, or so I'm told. Several of my gay white male friends say that it's not easy for them, either. You don't always get who you want. You get used to being rejected. But I wonder if they ever get asked lines like that.

Sometimes, I'd rather just stay at home and masturbate to a good porn mag. Although that's not perfection, either.

When I first started looking at pornography, it was of the heterosexual variety. My brother, Roger, convinced me to help him raid our father's *Playboy* collection.

Naked women on display. Less frequently, naked men. On my own, I would go back and look at the issues which featured couples. I didn't want Roger to know that what I wanted to see the most…

Was such a forbidden pleasure. Shame mixed with the thrill of secrecy. Imagining the heaviness and warmth of these male bodies on top of mine, mine on top of theirs. I could do anything I wanted. And I…

did.

And being with my friend, Darren, flipping through his vast porno collection, wondering if he wanted to do more than just look at the pictures.

And sitting beside a nun, testifying to the City Council, "I am a gay man and I use pornography."

And making love to an Asian boyfriend as we watched a group of white Euroboys fucking on the small TV screen.

And trying to explain to a friend of mine that even though I am pro-porn, I am still critical of the stereotypical representations within it.

Take a leap with me.

[*He leaps.*]

I get excited. I get horny. I get hard. But most of what I see…

Is that white men are the ideal…

But most of what I see…

Is that Asian men are usually nowhere to be found…

But most of what I see…

Is that these images are very sexy…

But most of what I see…

Is that race is not normal, it's a fetish…

But most of what I see…

Is that I want to objectify these bodies…

But most of what I see…

Is that I want to be desired…

But most of what I see…

Is that I want…

But most of what I see…

I mean, I want…

But most of what I see…

I want to…

But most of what I see…

I want to be…

But most of what I see…

I want to be someone's…

But most of what I see…

I want to be someone's fetish!

[*He stops. Shifts position.*]

"I have ten One hundred dollar bills right here. They're all for you… if you come back to my hotel room with me."

Well, I'd never had an offer like that before. Most of the guys I date don't even buy me dinner.

Do you know what a rice bar is? It's a place where usually older white men go to pick up younger Asian… boys. He got my attention by grabbing my ass.

"You're very cute," he said.

"Thank you," I replied.

"I mean it," said he.

"A hundred dollars…" he said.

The alcohol hung heavy on his breath. His face was very close to mine.

"That's very… sweet of you, but I…" "Five hundred." "No, but…" "I'll give you a thousand dollars. All you have to do is lie on the bed." "I can't do that." "I'm not going to go any higher." "You're being very generous, already."

I mean, wasn't he? I was flattered. I…I…

I imagined going back to his hotel room with him. What should I do to earn a thousand dollars? Let him strip me? Run his hands all over my body? Let him fuck me? With a condom? Without one?

[*He begins moving, creating a rhythm between his words and his body.*]

I would be his lotus blossom. I would be his butterfly. His dragon lady, if he wanted it rough. If I was older, I'd be his Fu Manchu, scraping my fingernails across his naked body. But then, he probably wouldn't like me if I was older. I'd be his houseboy, at his beck and call. I'd tell his fortune, read the tea leaves, quote Chinese proverbs.

I know the art of making love. Tantric sex. Ancient Chinese secret. Even though I'm Filipino. Or Filipino-American.

What is it you want? Do you want me? For a thousand dollars, I'd...

Learn to speak the language. Which one would you like to hear? "Ichi, ni, san, wan, go." "Bui doi." "ts'ai ch'ao. "Nua nam mun hoy." "Esusmaoseph, bunsit assou, sige."

[*He stops. The KURATSA music plays. He repeats the movement sequence accompanying the above narration three times, with variations in mood. As he finishes, music fades.*]

I used to belong to a Filipino-American dance troupe. It only sounds impressive. In actuality, it consisted of the teenage sons and daughters of the Filipinos in Topeka, Kansas. We would dance at "ethnic festivals" or at the July 4th celebration at the local university which was trying to demonstrate that it actually gave a shit about people who weren't white. Diversity and all that.

Our parents convinced us to learn the dances so that we could perform our cultural authenticity. We would dress in "Native" costume. I wore a barong (a kind of shirt passing as Filipino formal wear) and a pair of bright red pants which I picked up at the local K-Mart. It was the only place I could find that actually sold bright red pants.

One of the dances we performed was called the tinikling. We introduced it to our audiences as being based on the movements of the Filipino tikling birds, which danced/flew lightly and quickly from branch to branch. We danced between two bamboo poles beating out a rhythm.

[TINIKLING music starts up. He beats out a rhythm with his hands, dances side to side. As he starts to spin, lights fade.]

END

HUSTLING FOR DOLLARS

COCO FUSCO

INTRODUCTION: In January, 1996, I traveled to Cuba to conduct interviews with *jineteras,* women who exchange a range of favors, including sexual ones, for money from foreigners. Having traveled to Cuba regularly over the past twelve years as a journalist and artist, I was already familiar with the *"jineterismo"* as a social phenomenon on the island. My interest in the special role that women of color are playing in the burgeoning sex tourism industry there, coupled with my awareness that since 1993, there had been a marked increase in prostitution in Cuba, prompted me to write an article about the women involved. I was also particularly interested in the issues that prostitution raises for a third world socialist country that is in the process of making a difficult transition to capitalism. The research I conducted for the following article also served as the sociological basis for a new performance of mine, which I have created with Chicana artist Nao Bustamante. The piece, entitled *STUFF,* deals with the role of Latin women in the peddling of spirituality and sex for first world consumers. The performance will premiere in November, 1996, in Glasgow, Scotland. I am also considering developing this essay into the basis for a documentary film, or a more extensive written work about *jineteras* in Cuba. A shorter, slightly different version of this piece appeared in the September/October issue of *Ms. Magazine.*

JINETERAS—PART ONE

In January, 1996, on a visit to Cuba, I was sitting one night in Havana's Cafe *Cantante,* a bohemian chic watering hole for the country's cultural elite. On the dance floor, a young woman with the tawny complexion, oval face and aquiline nose of a young Josephine Baker twists her hips and rib cage in opposite directions, her creamy yellow baby doll dress swinging from side to side. The way she gyrates her torso is called a mono, or knot. It's nothing short of a simulated sex act, and brings on erotically charged smiles as couples mime lovemaking to the music. But this girl, who can't be more than seventeen, is dancing alone. Her look, her age, her hip clothes and her foreign date are tell-tale signs that she's a *jinetera*, the popular term for Cubans who exchange a range of services, including sex, for money from foreigners.

A well-groomed *YUMMY* (Young Urban Marxist Manager) in *Benetton* sportswear struts over to the table where I'm sitting with a friend of his and kneels for a moment to light a cigarette. "I've read every manual about cross-cultural exchange that exists," he says to me, not yet realizing that I am not a resident Cuban but a visiting Cuban-American, "and I'll tell you one thing. No one comes to Cuba for ecotourism. What sells this place is right on the dance floor—rum, cigars and *la mulata*." My table mate Anita, a Cuban who now resides in Spain, gives me a weary look. "It's the foreigners who are out of control, not the *jineteras*," she says. "Everyone in Madrid thinks every Cuban woman is a *puta*. I keep asking them why they don't worry about prostitutes in their own country and leave us alone."

I don't tell her that I, too, have come to Cuba to engage in some *jinetera* watching. Magazines all over Europe have been running stories about Cuba as a sex tourist's paradise since 1993. The press in Miami has been accusing the Cuban government of being the country's number one pimp. A marathon meeting on women's rights was called by the *United Nations Committee on the Elimination of Discrimination against Women* in January, 1996, in which a *Federation of Cuban Women* spokesperson fielded questions for two hours about this "new wave" of *jineteras*. This renewed international scrutiny is due as much to the real explosion of sex work in Cuba as it reveals the particular irony that such a resurgence of prostitution represents for a third world socialist nation.

Prostitution is hardly new to Cuba. As early as the 18th century, a Spanish captain was dispatched to the island to suppress a scandal by closing down a string of brothels run by the local clergy. In a society that once adhered to a strong Latin Catholic tradition of separating men and women in the public sphere, brothels were among the few spaces available for casual exchanges, and particularly for encounters between white men and women of color, which accounts for the island's extensive mythology enshrouding the sexuality of mulatas. While there were always plenty of opportunities for exploitation of disenfranchised women, it is also true that the world of the brothel served as the well-spring for much of Cuba's popular culture.

By the 1920's, an extended network of brothels that was managed by Cuban pimps was operative primarily in Havana and Santiago, as well as around the U.S. military base in Guantanamo. Those pimps employed poor Cuban women (black and white), as well as many dancers and actresses. At the other end of the social spectrum were the many high-class Havana salons featuring French and Spanish hookers, which were run by Europeans. With tourism emerging as the island's second-largest industry in the 1940s, and the Mafia's takeover of major hotels and casinos in the capitol by the mid-1950s, prostitution connected with Havana's infamous night life was firmly entrenched. It was that demi-monde that gave Cuba an international reputation as a whorehouse for visiting Americans and former Cuban dictator Fulgencio Batista's cronies.

Fidel Castro had promised to change that—one of the first moves by the revolutionary government nearly forty years ago was to reeducate the hundreds of Cuban prostitutes who had serviced the island's foreign and home-grown elite. The government then provided them with jobs as clerks, bus drivers and waitresses. Their "liberation" from sex work was touted as evidence that the Revolution had eradicated the corruption and immorality associated with capitalism. Indeed, Fidel Castro's public image as a benevolent savior was substantially enhanced by the sympathy he expressed toward these supposedly "fallen" women. By the standards of today's pro-regulation sex work activists, such a position would be interpreted as extremely paternalistic. Nonetheless, for many supporters of the Revolution, as well as for the exiled opposition, the reemergence of prostitution is the ultimate sign of the system having failed Cuban women.

The truth, however, is that *jineteras* emerged in Cuba long before most of the Revolution's supporters suspect. When I started visiting the island over a decade ago, it wasn't unusual to find a few well-dressed young women circulating in hotel cabarets, at festivals and embassy functions. All my Cuban friends would warn me to be careful around them: they were sex workers operating with the approval of the Ministry of the Interior, who would report on exchanges with foreigners in exchange for immunity. The two men I was filming a documentary with in Havana in 1986, for example, were offered a package deal of two women and a gram of cocaine by a pimp hovering around our hotel bar. We took it as an indication that we were being followed by the state security. And before the current wave of prostitution that has made foreign men the main objects of desire, Cuba went through a phase called *titimania*, in which older men, usually high-ranking members of the military or the political machine, would play the role of sugar daddy to younger women who served as trophy mistresses.

Since the bottom fell out of the Cuban economy in the early '90s, however, the tourist industry has become the country's main source of hard currency. The Cuban Ministry of Tourism claims that 750,000 people visited the island in 1995, up from 640,000 the year before, and it projects 1,000,000 tourists for the year 2000. Among these visitors are planeloads of men from Spain, Italy, Germany, Canada and even the U.S., whose buying power and social status is multiplied tenfold upon arrival in a cash-starved country. "Pussy Paradise," as Cuba is now called over the internet, is a place where these men can act on their fantasies without any threat of police intervention—not unlike multinationals looking for cheap unregulated labor across the border. Once there, they meet up with Cuban women who are looking for dollars, a good time, and very often, a ticket out of the country. It's no secret that many Cubans see the *pepes* (foreign *johns*) as replacements for a paternalist government that can no longer provide for them. One of the top salsa hits on the island when I arrived in January, 1996, called on Cuban women to find a *papiriqui con mucho guaniquiqui,* a sugar daddy.

As the Cuban economy totters on the brink of ruin brought about by the withdrawal of Soviet subsidy and the U.S. trade embargo, the number of women offering themselves as temporary partners or potential wives to foreigners escalates. When this last wave began in 1993, a substantial number of the women were white, but as client demand has grown for Cubans whose appearance corresponds to the tropicalist cliche, women of color have become the majority, which is also attributable to their generally being poorer than the mostly *criollo* elite. A sizable number of the *jineteras* are minors, and the majority of them these days have no direct connection to any state enterprise. Some women work on their own while others, particularly the young ones from the provinces, are managed by *chulos*, or pimps. From the salsa singers, the cab drivers' quips and the bawdy folk art renderings of *jineteras* I encountered around Havana, I got the sense that on the street these women are perceived as heroic providers whose mythical sexual power is showing up the failures of an ailing macho regime. As Paco, a young hustler I met in La Habana Vieja explained, "Everything is upside down now. The men are at home with aprons cooking and taking care of the kids, while their wives are on the street working."

The more affluent Cubans tend to be outraged about the rising tide of *jineteras* for politically motivated reasons. In January, 1996, Miami pop star Willie Chirino pulled a music video produced for his hit number, "Eva *la Jinetera*," off the air, after being pressured by Brothers to the Rescue leader Jorge Basulto. Chirino removed scenes in which he appears to be touching *jineteras* while dancing with them. The official explanation given by Chirino and his producers at Sony was that flirtatious physical contact with *jineteras* might imply that the singer condoned the women's lifestyle, an attitude which the Miami right interpreted as too soft on Castro.

Some other Cubans, however, tend to be more concerned with the potential for exploitation, likening the *jineteras'* situation with that of prostitutes in other sex tourism hot spots such as Bangkok and Manila. Cuban friends exiled in Barcelona were indignant when they explained to me last spring that the latest Christmas bonus for Spanish executives was a trip to Varadero Beach with an "escort" waiting at the airport, a story made more credible by a Miami Herald report last year claiming that a Spanish businessman had set up an agency specializing in such matchmaking. Upon coming back from visits to the island, other Cuban friends had told me that some families were practically selling their daughters to prospective foreign husbands as a way either to insure a constant source of hard currency or to eventually get themselves out of the country.

To get to any sort of truth, though, about Cuban *jineteras*, you have to plow through the myths that make any discussion of mulatas, tourism and prostitution in Cuba so incredibly complicated. Throughout

Cuba's history the mulata has stood for illicit sex—stemming from the reality that from colonial times onward, many mixed-race women were the "love children" and mistresses of white men. According to the old adage of the Caribbean plantation, white women were for marrying, black women were for work, and mulatas were for sex. That legacy, told and retold through scores of songs, poems, and novels made the mulata a national symbol that the country's tourism campaigns simply take advantage of. Even though not all of today's *jineteras* are actually mulata (although demographics indicate that Cuba's youth are majority mixed race due to greater population growth among people of color and higher immigration rate among whites), the stereotype still carries enormous power, so much so that to engage in sex work practically means to assume a mulata identity by association.

The current wave of attention to *jineteras* also obscures the fact that Cubans aren't the only ones who've turned to sex work when their country's economy faltered—or when, as in certain Asian countries, as capitalism develops in some sectors, the need for dollars grows faster than there are legal jobs available to provide them. Sex tourism thrives in other parts of the Caribbean, but on other islands such as Jamaica, the sex workers are predominantly male. In Eastern Europe, economic crises similar to Cuba's have prompted many women to make drastic career changes, moving into exotic dancing and prostitution at home and abroad.

Images of Cuba's past flickered through my mind as I watched the current *jineteras* in action. Having something of an insider's perspective keeps me from jumping to easy conclusions. My mother is a tough as nails doctor, who is also, like many of the *jineteras* of the '90s, a mulata from the Southwestern province of Oriente. She set out for the capital in the 1940s, worked her way through school, then left the island in the '50s. Eventually she married a foreigner to stay out for good, sensing she could never have the life she wanted in her homeland. She also instilled in me a healthy degree of skepticism about what Cubans with power say about their country, wherever they might be. I thus acquired a special distaste for the hypocrisy of the Miami extremists who throughout my adolescence ranted about freedom from tyranny while thrusting repressive Catholic morality, complete with chaperones, virginity cults, and unquestioning acceptance of male dominance, on their daughters.

Because I was used to seeing such an extreme form of patriarchal control in Cuban exile households, I was duly impressed by the much more relaxed attitudes towards sexual assertiveness among women that I encountered when I first visited post-revolutionary Cuba. The stigmas attached to women having an active sex life before or outside marriage had diminished considerably among people of my generation. More than thirty years of free birth control, sex education, co-ed boarding schools and a social system that reduced parental control laid the groundwork for this increased permissiveness, and set the island apart from most other Latin American countries, not to mention most Cuban exile communities.

Not only had attitudes toward sex become somewhat more liberal. In a country where consumer pleasures were few and far between, casual sex had become the most desirable leisure activity for the younger generations on the island. In addition, Cuban intellectuals I have spoken to who are attempting to evaluate the meaning of the increasing openness about extra-marital sex—including gay, lesbian and bisexual activity—have interpreted it as an unspoken revolt against both the socialist emphasis on productive labor and the revolution's puritanical morality.

What Cuba's current situation brings into relief is the connection between sexual freedom and affluence. That a tropical socialist utopia that became famous as a site of sexual liberation in the 1980s would be transformed into a impoverished island ripe for sexual exploitation in the 1990's is just one of the more painful indicators of what it means for Cuba to be reentering a global post-industrial economy. At the heart of Cuba's current transition from state socialism to a mixed economy lie thorny questions about the state's authority to intervene in the private choices of adult women.

I decided to hit the streets in La Habana Vieja to get the perspective of prostitutes who were in the business long before the recent explosion. Nestled around the Havana port area, La Habana Vieja is the most heavily touristed neighborhood of the city, and also happens to be one of its poorest, famous for illegal activity. By the time I reached the *Plaza de la Catedral*, with its bustling craft market, a mischievous-looking street hustler had latched on to me. Paco was a thin, small framed 24 year old mulato with short hair, crisply ironed jeans and imitation Ray Bans. We strolled past the cathedral towards the Malecon, Havana's waterfront boulevard that wraps around half the city. Eventually, he agreed to introduce me to two women, Helen and Margarita, both in their late 20s, and both of whom had been working the streets of la Habana Vieja for over ten years. Margarita had a young son whom she supports, while Helen lived alone. When they first started, Margarita explained, their main clients were merchant marines and foreign technicians. At that time, dollar possession was illegal, so they would hide their money in their vaginas and get visiting African students to buy consumer goods for them in the dollar shops. They were careful not to be too ostentatious so as not to encourage envy that might lead someone to inform on them. They were lucky and had never been arrested, but they have friends in jail.

They said at least two thirds of the young women in the barrio are *jineteras*. When I ask what the men in the neighborhood think about it, they both laughed.

"They see the *gallego* (Spaniard) coming in with a girl, and they don't see him," says Helen. "They see a chicken, beans, rice—a full fridge." What did come across clearly in our conversation is these women's sense of what constitutes fairness in dealings with clients-and their willingness to defend their sense of their own rights as women providing a service. "The guys sometimes show up with bags of bras and underwear, thinking that's enough to get us into bed," says Helen with a smirk. "There are a lot more younger guys coming now, and they try to tell you it's for *amore, amore*. "Sensing that I was dealing with sophisticated traffickers in fantasy as much as sex, I asked them to classify their clientele according to tastes. Helen and Margarita leaned towards me, as if we are high schoolers engaging juicy gossip.

"Look, the Italians are the ones coming here most now, and they like *tortilleria* (lesbian sex)," they begin. "The Mexicans used to come a lot, but since the peso devaluation they don't show up that much anymore. They used to ask for marathon sessions of oral sex. It was awful!" exclaimed Margarita. "The Spaniards tend to be older, " Helen added. "Some of them just want to talk. Others want to come and live with us for a while. I used to bring guys home with me for a week at a time. They loved it, and didn't mind the blackouts and water shortages. They'd show me pictures of their wives. Now, though, most guys want a different girl every night."

I told them about the image of *jineteras* outside the island, that they are often described as brash tarts with bleached blond hair and stretch pants. Helen was wearing a white sweater, loose fitting white pants and a tan jacket, with a little white cap. Margarita had on jeans, a light blue pullover and plastic earrings. Neither of them have colored their hair. If anything, explained Margarita, "the natural look is back. Even the white girls are perming their hair so they look more like mulatas." Both acknowledged that styles cater to client tastes. "The Spaniards really like black girls with braids, so all the *negritas* are wearing their hair like that now. The Italians like mulatas with wild hair."

What about the possible dangers? The only case of violence they could think of was the 1993 case of a *jinetera* who was impaled on a mop by a European tourist who then threw her body from the balcony of one of the hotels in the Vedado. Of course, the murderer was out of the country before the *jinetera*'s body was found. Health risks? Helen and Margarita immediately answered that they insisted on condoms, and that health was the one thing that the government still had under control. Knowing about the declining conditions in Cuba's hospitals, and chronic shortages of medicine, I wondered if they were not just convincing themselves that the old revolutionary promises still work just to ward off fears. No one I spoke to throughout my entire trip wanted to accept the idea that an STD epidemic, including but not limited to AIDS, was in the making, which seemed to me an almost criminal oversight.

When I asked them if they ever think about getting out of the business, Helen told me a story that perfectly illustrated the dilemmas facing Cuban women who've been socialized to believe in their equality but who now faced an extremely polarized world that leaves them little room to maneuver in. "I got married once," she confessed with a wry smile. "But it didn't work. I thought I'd go to Spain and start a new life. I thought I would work, and that we would live together. But he was nuts, crazy," she continued. "He wanted to keep me at home all day. He wouldn't let me work or go out. I lasted two months, and then I realized that I had to get out. I sat him down with his mother and explained. I had no money, and no place to go, so I had to come back here. He's so mad that he won't even give me a divorce now because he says it's too expensive." Both Margarita and Helen knew that some *jineteras* triumphed in Europe, but that others were stuck in awful situations, some forced by pimps to work long hours seven days a week. At least in Cuba, they could survive working a few times a month.

JINETERAS—PART TWO

In search of more upscale *jinetera* action, I grabbed a cab one night with a Cuban journalist friend named Magaly and head out for the disco at *El Comodoro*, a hotel wedged between the embassies and Party officials' homes of the swanky Miramar district. The Havana Club disco at the Hotel *Comodoro* is the capital's most famous den of iniquity. Being there is like taking a trip out of Cuba to a teeny bopper club in Rome or Madrid. It's a labyrinth of chrome and vinyl, with Europop dance music blaring so loud I got hoarse from trying to have a conversation. We stood at the railing of the sunken round dance floor, while Magaly shows me how the girls position themselves in full view while they dance so they can attract a *pepe*. These are the five-star *jineteras*, Magaly explained—they could afford to pay their own way into the club.

The men tended to look a little older than those on the street, which I attributed to the high cost of entry and drinks, and the steeper prices charged by many of the *jineteras*. Magaly and I walked over to one of the bars where a dozen overweight, middle-aged men were having their heads massaged by teenagers.

I was wrestling with what I saw, asking myself what, if any, difference there was between this scene and the action inside any downtown chic club in New York, where dark-skinned girls are also all the rage. The fact that sex work was the best way for many young women to make a living in Cuba, I silently acknowledged, made the stakes quite different than in a place where other viable job options abound. On the other hand, the negative factors associated with working class prostitution in places like New York—its association with drugs and drug addiction, for example, or the stigmatization of the women involved—seemed to be less of a problem in the Cuban context.

What irks me as I discuss *jineteras* with many privileged Cubans, however, is the snobbery that too many Cubans indulge in over this issue. No one I talk to takes into account that most Cubans, *jineteras* or not, always expected foreigners to pay the bills when they were in dollars, a habit that comes from years of not having had legal access to them. And few Cubans seem willing to see a parallel between the *jineteras* and the many artists, musicians, and professionals with exportable skills who are also looking for opportunities to socialize with—and occasionally have sex with—foreigners to secure invitations abroad and even foreign jobs, not to mention to enjoy the best of Havana's nightlife. When Cuban men do it, or when the women involved were part of the elite, everyone looks the other way. It's the poorer, non-white women who always take the heat.

I'm convinced that much of the fuss over the *jineteras* reveals certain biases regarding race, class, and gender that Cubans have not shed. One of the most glaring aspects of Cuban's re-insertion into the capitalist orbit is the way in which racial divisions have become more apparent. Cuban blacks are far less likely than whites to have wealthy relatives sending dollars from abroad, a factor that has played heavily in their disproportionate involvement in illegal activity. Now that tourism is the main source of hard currency, the state is less invested in an image of itself as a modern industrial nation, and instead showcases "traditional" Afro-Cuban religious rituals and art, "traditional" Afro-Cuban music, and of course, Afro-Cuban women. Those are the sorts of tropicalist cliches that used to drive many upwardly mobile Cubans up the wall. The prospect of developing a modern society with a diversified economy was linked in the minds of many with no longer having to service first world desires for exotica. Ironically, Cuban economic decline has led to a situation in which those who represent marginality within the Cuban system are quickly becoming the island's *nouveau riche*.

The current obsession with controlling the *jineteras,* I believe, is linked to deeply rooted cultural attitudes about sex between black women and white men. Most of the black Cuban women I know who are involved with white men are with foreigners, whether they are *jineteras* or not. This not unrelated to the fact that white Cuban men would rarely even consider marrying black Cuban women, due in part to a colonial history that marked them "for sex only." It's also due to folk wisdom that has circulated for ages among black Cuban women that European men's fascination with us as exotic objects was a better, safer basis for a marriage than the options offered by black Cuban men. Liaisons with Europeans, whether they culminated in marriage or not, implied more economic security and social status than did relations with other Cubans.

The fact that black and mulata *jineteras* are succeeding in marrying Europeans at an unusually high rate also makes these women the objects of envy in a country where many people are using every means possible to emigrate. The more affluent, and mostly white sectors of the female population are not accustomed to such steep competition over foreigners, and often resort to moralizing rhetoric as a mask for their resentment. A black Cuban artist who married a white American years ago endured endless harassment from her compatriots, who simply wouldn't believe she wasn't a *jinetera*. The only Cuban mulata I know who is married to a white Cuban is an actress who was mistaken for a *jinetera* when they tried to rent a hotel room in Varadero last year. "The guards kept saying that they had seen me before," she told me. "I had to explain to them that they recognized me from TV, not police records."

Other Latinos reject the *jineteras* strictly out of Catholic-inflected prudery. In the summer of 1995, for example, The Miami Herald ran a hilarious report on touring troupes of Cuban nightclub dancers. According to journalist Andres Oppenheimer, the dancers' brazen sexual behavior was luring many of the wealthiest men in Merida, the capital of Yucatan, away from their wives. The ladies of Merida took to the streets to protest the disintegration of the Mexican family at the hands of the Cuban mulatas, who, they claimed, were turning tricks after every show.

In the months before I left for Cuba, I periodically picked up stories in the news about a Cuban "crusade" against *jineteras*. This signaled a drastic change in attitude. In 1992, Fidel had commented somewhat cynically that Cuban women were *jineteras* not out of need, but because they liked sex, and that they were among the healthiest and best educated hookers in the business. This famous speech was interpreted by many Cuba-watchers as a cynical invitation to male tourists to take advantage of the sexual prowess of the Revolution's children. Three years later I find Federation of Cuban Women leader Vilma Espin denouncing *jineteras* as decadent trash whose parents had lost control of them.

Seconding her position during a press conference last December, Deputy Tourism Minister Miguel Bruguera announced that Cuba "rejected" prostitution, and sought instead to promote "healthy, family tourism." These recent pronouncements spearhead an offensive that includes police sweeps of key areas, stiffer penalties for prostitutes, and a crackdown on hotel guards who had been accepting bribes from tourists. In Varadero, I heard rumors of work camps nearby where many jailed prostitutes were supposedly being sent, which reminded me somewhat chillingly of the camps that held homosexuals, hippies and other social outcasts in the mid-1960s. While these moves might suggest that the Cuban government is acting on the same revolutionary principles that informed its 1959 campaign to save prostitutes' souls, they seem to be more directly the result of accusations from exiled opposition leaders that the Cuban government has been encouraging prostitution for years to lure tourists. At the Havana Club nightclub, when I checked my bag, a guard had taken my camera, saying that picture-taking had been banned due to "negative publicity outside the country." I added that comment to my mental list of Cuban government moves that show how saving face means more than protecting the women involved.

Such inconsistencies in the Cuba's position on prostitution were also noted by international women's rights experts who gathered at the UN last January to discuss the situation of Cuban women with Ferrer Gomez, Secretary General of the Federation of Cuban Women and a member of the Cuban Communist Party's Central Committee. Ferrer Gomez referred back to the official line at the meeting, stating that prostitution had resurfaced due to a growth in tourism, that it involved a minority of young women who were healthy and highly educated, that the women involved were not doing it to survive but simply to buy luxury goods, but that their activity represented a health risk and that it was linked with crime and drugs.

Were I convinced that the Cuban government was seriously concerned about the well-being of teenagers engaging in sex work, I would actually be impressed. The government's exaggeratedly moralistic rhetoric masks more significant economic concerns as much in the case of the *jineteras* as it has for other freelancers in Cuba in the past. In the early 1980s, for example, Fidel Castro denounced peasant farmers when they started to prosper in private markets, and then a few years later lambasted artists who did well selling their work without state intermediaries. Whenever an authorized private practice gets big enough to threaten the state's control over the economy, the government launches a clean-up campaign, and many people land in jail, often stuck there even after laws change.

These days Cuba's emerging class of self-employed vendors, beauticians, cab drivers and private restauranteurs are having their profits taxed heavily by the Cuban government. Most of those newfangled petty capitalists, incidentally, used to be engineers, architects, and economists, but can no longer make a living in their professions; *jineteras* aren't the only Cubans who've switched careers. However, freelance *jineteras* don't pay dues to the state—they are part of an illegal economy that also includes *chulos* and the homeowners renting rooms to them. Thousands of dollars of bribes pass among *chulos, jineteras* and cops and hotel guards each day. That underground economy is hedging in on a tourist industry run primarily by the Cuban Armed Forces and the Ministry of the Interior.

"What bothers the government now isn't that women are selling themselves," explained political scientist Maria de los Angeles Torres, an expert on Cuban affairs at DePaul University. "It's that the business is now out of their hands. The state has been directly involved in promoting sex tourism for years." Torres recalls that in 1991, when Cubans were supposedly not allowed past hotel lobbies, the Comodoro Hotel offered male guests—for a price—special certificates authorizing those "with intent to marry" to take Cuban women to their rooms. "They are just repressing *jineteras* now while they try to figure out new ways to regulate prostitution and extract profit from it," she asserts.

Indeed, who can and who does profit is the key issue. What one's position is on adult women resorting to prostitution in Cuba hinges on the degree to which one can entertain the idea that sex work, even for a woman in a poor third world country, involves an exchange of benefits, and that it could be a viable option by comparison to other choices available for survival. That the range of profitable activities has dwindled since 1989 is obvious. When Cuba entered its Special Period in 1993 and the country faced the worst food shortages and highest black market rates it had experienced in decades, the choices for those who didn't have relatives abroad who could bail them out narrowed down to two—work in or around tourism and make dollars or make a pittance in pesos and watch your family suffer. Legitimate jobs in hotel construction, maintenance, tourist entertainment, and sales are not plentiful enough to satisfy the population's demand for dollars. I remember a conversation I had in '93 with the granddaughter of a respected but humble *santero* (priest of the Afro-Cuban religion *santeria*) in Regla. Walking me to a nearby bus stop, she burst into tears when she told me that all the female coworkers at her office were turning tricks after hours. "You see my daughter and my grandparents, how thin they are, Coco," she cried. "But I just can't do it. I think about it, but I can't."

While the hardship that led many women to take up sex work is real, the frequently invoked image of the *jinetera* who's selling herself for a pound of meat doesn't explain the range of motivations for the women—and men—involved. The desire among the populace for the kind of nonproductive leisure and pleasurable consumerism that the Revolutionary government had once linked with capitalist corruption is another extremely important—and explosive—factor. When the Cuban government began to stimulate tourism in the early 1980's, it created a world of consumer pleasures inside Cuba that was off-limits to most of the citizenry. Area Dolares, as it was called, reminded more than a few Cubans of de facto race and class segregation that restricted their use of clubs and beaches prior to 1959. It generated enormous resentment in a mostly working class populace who watched the same government that would pontificate to them about nationalism and the Socialist work ethic offer pleasure, leisure, and the finest resources of the country to visiting capitalists with bucks and the Party elite.

The Union of Communist Youth tried to stem the growing tide of disenchantment among Cuba's under-25 majority during the early 1990s with street parties and rock concerts. But those sporadic activities can't compare with the mobility and lifestyle many adolescent *jineteros* and *jineteras* can buy with the dollars they make. The legalization of dollars possession in 1994 further facilitated these youths' access to "el hi-life", offering them respite from power shortages, overcrowded housing, interminable lines, and lousy TV fare. "What would I do with a Cuban boyfriend on a Saturday night?" a *jinetera* asked me rhetorically while we shared a drink one afternoon. "Wait for a bus for two hours, and then go home to an apartment with no privacy. These guys might be old and gross, but at least when I'm with them, I sit in a nice place with air-conditioning, listen to good music, and have a real drink. That helps me forget about bad breath and a big belly."

All the adult pimps and *jineteras* I interviewed noted the marked rise in tourist demand for adolescents and even children, and most sex workers I spoke to agreed that this was alarming. When I first met Paco, I asked him about the rise in demand for child prostitutes. A recent client from the Dominican Republic, he said, offered $2000 for a girl under fourteen, "without a scratch," to work in a brothel there. He also mentioned that some arriving Europeans were using *lollipops* to bribe kids into performing oral sex.

On a windy Sunday night, I went out on my own looking for teenage *jineteras* and decided to pay a visit to the new and very pricey *Melia Cohiba Hotel.* It's a monstrously oversized high rise building dwarfing the old *Hotel Riviera* just next to it, full of marble and glass, too many indoor fountains and $400/night rooms. As I approached the door, a guard with a mysterious earphone in one ear gestured for me to stop. I knew what he was thinking, so I told him in my best imitation of gringo Spanglish that I was visiting from America, and he immediately looked embarrassed, whispered an apology and let me through.

At the bar in the lobby, I ran into a Chicano academic I had met on the plane the week before. "See those guys," he said to me, pointing at two middle-aged men at the other side of the bar. "They're from Canada. I asked them what kind of work they had come to do here. They laughed. 'Work?' they said. 'We're here for the women. The only thing that bugs us is that they have to go to school in the morning.'" He was visibly disgusted. "This is awful," he said. "I keep thinking about my own daughter."

I stepped outside and spotted two teenagers chatting up a short, 50-ish man in a gray suit. One girl had over-the-knee spike heeled leather boots and a peroxide blond afro. The other was wearing a smoky blue long dress, had long dark unstyled hair and a lot of acne. At one point in their exchange, the man stepped inside. In a flash, three cops descended on the girls, and pulled them over to the other side of the entrance. The ensuing exchange looked calm, and within minutes the cops had let the girls go. I approached them and invited them out to eat.

As we made our way through the parking lot, a wild-eyed blond Italian in a Hawaiian shirt and jeans hopped out of a *Havanauto rental* car. The faux blond, clearly the more assertive one, made plans to meet him—in flawless Italian. I asked her how she learned Italian. "Italian? I speak Italian, French, German, even some English—whatever you want," she exclaimed with pride.

Katy and Sussy told me they were eighteen, but they looked about fifteen. They said they had been in the business for four years. They claimed that the clampdown was so tight that most hotel guards wouldn't take the $25 bribes to let a girl upstairs anymore, since the penalty for doing so had been raised to two year's imprisonment. An old vagrancy law has been resurrected and was being used against the *jineteras*, who got three warnings before they faced up to eight years imprisonment, up from four years. Their being underage didn't protect them from such punishment.

Katy, the faux blond mulata, did most of the talking. I asked her if she was supporting anyone. "We're helping the country!" she told me, reiterating the most common line of those defending the *jineteras'* right to engage in sex work. "I'm too used to this life to give it up," she said. "I'm used to having money, and I love to go to the clubs."

How much does she charge, I asked. "I won't work for less than $50," she claimed adamantly. "Some girls are ruining things by taking $20 or $30." Katy said she had seen as many as three clients a day. And they both insisted that they went to school, though they didn't see any point to it.

I asked Katy if she'd like to get leave the country. She explained that regulations didn't permit someone her age to marry and leave. She had visited Italy, where her older sister lived with her Italian husband, and liked it, but decided not to overstay the three-month period her visa permitted. That sister got her started as a *jinetera*. "She told me that she didn't want me to 'become a woman' with a Cuban man who would mistreat me. She found me a nice Italian guy. He spent a month here with me, and then left me $500. He's waiting for me to be old enough for us to get married," she claimed. Between the lines of her story I heard old and new Cuban moralities converging: on the one hand, there was the post-revolutionary pragmatism of strategically planning how to lose one's virginity before marriage, and how to get around Cuban immigration restrictions; on the other, there were the older beliefs that white male foreigners protect women of color from the archetypally controlling, even abusive Caribbean male.

I asked the girls what they do with the really old men. Sussy blurted out, "We just have to suck 'em a long time," and then went back to munching on her French fries.

Listening to them, I felt I was watching the saddest part of Cuban socialism's last chapter—living proof of the island's own nihilistic version of a Generation X without any dreams of a future beyond the next purchase. But my conversation with Katy and Sussy came to an abrupt end as a Cuban who was clearly an illegal cab driver pulled up nearby and waved to them to get in the car. That the girls interacted with everyone in the environs of the hotel with an easy familiarity—the guards, the cops, the drivers, and waiters—was yet another indication of the popular sympathy for the *jineteras*, and of a bond among struggling Cubans in many sectors of that society that comes from their shared weariness of excessive state intervention in their lives, as well as of spartan living. I'm not trying to suggest that there isn't something fundamentally wrong with a society in which sex work is the best paying job for women, but that the current moves to repress jineteras are misguided, wrongheaded, and nothing if not hypocritical. That doesn't mean I want to forget about the abuses and inequities that are built into sex tourism. It just means that Cuban women deserve more culturally acceptable ways to express their sexuality than a still harshly patriarchal society permits, and that the moralizing of the power brokers—be they prudish liberals, fanatic Catholics or Communist bureaucrats—would concede.

TRAVELING THEORY

EDWARD W. SAID

Like people and schools of criticism, ideas and theories travel—from person to person, from situation to situation, from one period to another. Cultural and intellectual life are usually nourished and often sustained by this circulation of ideas, and whether it takes the form of acknowledged or unconscious influence, creative borrowing, or wholesale appropriation, the movement of ideas and theories from one place to another is both a fact of life and a usefully enabling condition of intellectual activity. Having said that, however, one should go on to specify the kinds of movement that are possible, in order to ask whether by virtue of having moved from one place and time to another an idea or a theory gains or loses in strength, and whether a theory in one historical period and national culture becomes altogether different for another period or situation. There are particularly interesting cases of ideas and theories that move from one culture to another, as when so-called Eastern ideas about transcendence were imported into Europe during the early nineteenth century, or when certain European ideas about society were translated into traditional Eastern societies during the later nineteenth century. Such movement into a new environment is never unimpeded. It necessarily involves processes of representation and institutionalization different from those at the point of origin. This complicates any account of the translation, transference, circulation, and commerce of theories and ideas.

There is, however, a discernible and recurrent pattern to the movement itself, three or four stages common to the way any theory or idea travels.

First, there is a point of origin, or what seems like one, a set of initial circumstances in which the idea came to birth or entered discourse. Second, there is a distance transferred, a passage through the pressure of various contexts as the idea moves from an earlier point to another time and place where it will come into a new prominence. Third, there is a set of conditions—call them conditions of acceptance or, as an inevitable part of acceptance, resistances—which then confronts the transplanted theory or idea, making possible its introduction or toleration, however alien it might appear to be. Fourth, the now full (or partly) accommodated (or incorporated) idea is to some extent transformed by its new uses, its new position in a new time and place.

It is obvious that any satisfactorily full account of these stages would be an enormous task. But though I have neither the intention or the capacity to undertake it, it seemed worthwhile to describe the problem in a sketchy and general way so that I might at length and in detail address a particularly topical, highly limited aspect of it. Of course the discrepancy between the general problem and any particular analysis is itself deserving of comment. To prefer a local, detailed analysis of how one theory travels from one situation to another is also to betray some fundamental uncertainty about specifying or delimiting the field to which any one theory or idea might belong. Notice, for example, that when professional students of literature now use words like "theory" and "criticism", it is not assumed that they must or should confine their interests to literary theory or literary criticism. The distinction between one discipline and another has been blurred precisely because fields like literature and literary study are not longer considered to be as all-compassing or as synoptic as, until recently, they once were. Although some polemical scholars of literature can still, nonetheless, attack others for not being literary enough, or for not understanding (as who should not?) that literature, unlike other forms of writing, is essentially mimetic, essentially moral, and essentially humanistic, the resultant controversies are themselves evidence of the fact that no consensus exists on how the outer limits of the word "literature" or the word "criticism" are to be determined. Several decades ago, literary history and systematic theory, of the kind pioneered by Northrop Frye, promised an orderly, inhabitable, and hospitable structure in which, for instance, it might be demonstrated that the mythos of summer could be transformed definably into the mythos of autumn. "The primal human act in Frye's system," writes Frank Lentricchia in *After the New Criticism*, quoting Frye's *The Educated Imagination*, "and a model for all human acts, is an 'informative,' creative act which transforms a world that is merely objective, set over against us, in which we 'feel lonely and frightened and unwanted' into a home."[1] But most literary scholars find themselves now, once again, out in the cold. Similarly, the history of ideas and comparative literature, two disciplines closely associated with the study of literature and literary criticism, do not routinely authorize in their practitioners quite the same Goethean sense of a concert of all literatures and ideas.

In all these instances the specific situation or locality of a particular intellectual task seems uneasily distant from, and only rhetorically assisted by, the legendary wholeness, coherence, and integrity of the general field to which one professionally belongs. There seem to be too many interruptions, too many distractions, too many irregularities interfering with the homogenous space supposedly holding scholars together. The division of intellectual labor, which has meant increasing specialization, further erodes any direct apprehension one might have of a whole field of literature and literary study; conversely, the invasion of literary discourse by the *outré* jargons of semiotics, post/structuralism, and Lacanian psychoanalysis has distended the literary critical universe almost beyond recognition. In short, there seems nothing inherently literary about the study of what have traditionally been considered literary texts, no literariness that might prevent a contemporary literary critic from having recourse to psychoanalysis, sociology, or linguistics. Convention, historical custom, and appeals to the protocols of humanism and traditional scholarship are of course regularly introduced as evidence of the field's enduring integrity, but more and more these seem to be rhetorical strategies in a debate about what literature and literary criticism ought to be rather than convincing definitions of what in fact they are.

Geoffrey Hartmann has nicely dramatized the predicament by analyzing the tensions and vacillations governing contemporary critical activity. Today's criticism, he says, is radically revisionist. "Freed from a neoclassical decorum that, over the space of three centuries, created an enlightened but also over-accommodated prose," criticism is undergoing what he calls "an *extraordinary language* movement."[2] At times this language movement is so eccentric as to approach, even challenge, literature itself; at others it obsesses the critics who are borne along its currents toward the ideal of a completely "pure" language. At still others, the critic discovers that "writing is a labyrinth, a topological puzzle and textual crossword; the reader, for his part, must lose himself for a while in a hermeneutic 'infinitizing' that makes all rules of closure appear arbitrary."[3] Whether these alternatives for critical discourse are called terrorist or "a new type of sublimity or an emerging transcendentalism," [4] there remains the need for the humanist critic both to define more clearly "the special province of the humanities" and to materialize (rather than spiritualize) the culture in which we live.[5] Nevertheless, Hartmann concludes, we are in transition, which is perhaps another way of saying (as he does in his title *Criticism in the Wilderness*) that criticism today is alone, at loose ends, unlucky, pathetic, and playful because its realm defies closure and certainty.

Hartmann's exuberance—for his attitude is at bottom exuberant—ought to be qualified by Richard Ohmann's devastating observation in *English in America* that English departments represent "a moderately successful effort by professors to obtain some benefits of capitalism while avoiding its risks and, yet, a reluctance to acknowledge any link between how we do our work and the way the larger society is run."[6] This is not to say that literary academics present a united ideological front, even though Ohmann is right *grosso modo*. The divisions within cannot be reduced simply to a conflict between old and new critics or to a monolithically dominant antimimetic ideology, as Gerald Graff very misleadingly argues. Consider that, if we restrict the number of debated issues to four, many of those in the vanguard on one issue are very conservative on another:

(1) Criticism as scholarship, humanism, a "servant" to the text, mimetic in its bias, versus criticism as revisionism and as itself a form of literature.

(2) The role of critic as teacher and good reader: safeguarding the canon versus subverting it or creating a new one. Most Yale critics are revisionist with respect to (1), conservative with respect to (2).

(3) Criticism as detached from the political/social world versus criticism as a form of philosophical metaphysics, psychoanalysis, linguistics, or any of these, versus criticism as actually having to do with such "contaminated" fields as history, the media, and economy systems. Here the distributional spread is much wider than in (1) or (2).

(4) Criticism as a criticism of language (language as negative theology, as private dogma, as ahistorical metaphysics) versus criticism as an

analysis of the language of institutions versus criticism as a study of relationships between language and nonlinguistic things.

In the absence of an enclosing domain called literature, with clear outer boundaries, there is no longer an authorized or official position for the literary critic. But neither is there some new sovereign method, some new critical technology compelling allegiance and intellectual loyalty. Instead there is a babel of arguments for the limitlessness of all interpretation; of ideologies that proclaim the eternal yet determinate value of literature or "the humanities"; for all systems that in asserting their capacity to perform essentially self-confirming tasks allow for no counterfactual evidence. You can call such a situation pluralist if you like or, if you have a taste for the melodramatic, you can call it desperate. For my part, I prefer to see it as an opportunity for remaining skeptical and critical, succumbing neither to dogmatism not to sulky gloom.

Hence, the specific problem of what happens to a theory when it moves from one place to another proposes itself as an interesting topic of investigation. For if fields like literature or the history of ideas have no intrinsically enclosing limits, and if, conversely, no one methodology is imposable upon what is an essentially heterogeneous and open area of activity—the writing and interpretation of texts—it is wise to raise the questions of theory and of criticism in ways suitable to the situation in which we find ourselves. At the outset, this means an historical approach. Assume therefore that, as a result of specific historical circumstances, a theory or idea pertaining to those circumstances arises. What happens to it when, in different circumstances and for new reasons, it is used again and, in still more different circumstances, again? What can this tell us about theory itself—its limits, its possibilities, its inherent problems—and what can it suggest to us about the relationship between theory and criticism, on the one hand, and society and culture on the other? The pertinence of these questions will be apparent at a time when theoretical activity seems both intense and eclectic, when the relationship between social reality and a dominant yet hermetic critical discourse seems hard to determine, and when, for all of these reasons and some of the one I have just referred to, it is futile to prescribe theoretical programs for contemporary criticism.

Lukács' *History and Class Consciousness* (1923) is justly famous for its analysis of the phenomenon of reification, a universal fate afflicting all aspects of life in an era dominated by commodity fetishism. Since, as Lukács argues, capitalism is the most articulated and quantitatively detailed of all economic systems, what it imposes upon human life and labor under its rule has the consequence of radically transforming everything human, flowing, processual, organic, and connected into disconnected and "alienated" objects, items, lifeless atoms. In such a situation, then, time sheds its qualitative, variable, flowing nature; it freezes into an exactly delimited, quantifiable continuum filled with quantifiable "thing" (the reified, mechanically objectified "performance" of the worker, wholly separated from his total human personality): in short, it becomes space. In this environment where time is transformed into abstract, exactly measurable, physical space, an environment at once the cause and effect of the scientifically and mechanically fragmented and specialized production of the object of labor, the subjects of labor must likewise be rationally fragmented. On the one hand, the objectification of their labor-power into something opposed to their total personality (a process already accomplished with the sale of that labor-power as a commodity) is now made into the permanent ineluctable reality of their daily life. Here, too, the personality can do no more than look on helplessly while its own existence is reduced to an isolated particle and fed into an alien system. On the other hand, the mechanical disintegration of the process of production into its components also destroys those bonds that had bound individuals to a community in the days when production was still "organic." In this respect, too, mechanization makes of them isolated abstract atoms whose work no longer brings them together directly and organically; it becomes mediated to an increasing extent exclusively by the abstract laws of the mechanism which imprisons them.[7] If this picture of the public world is bleak, it is matched by Lukács' description of what happens to intellect, "the subject" as he calls it. After an astonishingly brilliant account of the antinomies of classical philosophy from Descartes to Kant to Fichte, Hegel, and Marx, in which he shows the increasing retreat of the subject into passive, privatized contemplation, gradually more and more divorced from the overwhelmingly fragmented realities of modern industrial life, Lukács then depicts modern bourgeois thought as being at an impasse, transfixed and paralyzed into terminal passivity. The science that it produces is based on mere fact gathering; the rational forms of understanding therefore cannot cope with the irrationality of physical *données,* and when efforts are made to compel "the facts" to submit to "system", their fragmentation and endlessly atomized *thereness* either destroy the system or turn the mind into a passive register of discrete objects.

There is, however, one form of experience that concretely represents the essence of reification as well as its limitation: crisis. If capitalism is the embodiment in economic terms of reification, then everything, including human beings, ought to be quantified and given a market value. This of course is what Lukács means when he speaks of articulation under capitalism, which he sometimes characterizes as if it were a gigantic itemized list. In principle nothing—no object, person, place, or time—is left out, since everything can be calculated. But there are moments when "the qualitative existence of the 'things' that lead their lives beyond the purview of economics as misunderstood and neglected things-in-themselves, as use-value [Lukács here refers to such "irrational" things as sentiment, passions, chance] suddenly becomes the decisive factor (suddenly, that is, for reified, rational thought). Or rather: these 'laws' fail to function and the reified mind is unable to perceive a pattern in this 'chaos.'"[8] At such a moment, then, mind or "subject" has its one opportunity to escape reification: by thinking through what it is that causes reality to appear to be only a collection of objects and economic *données.* And the very act of looking for process behind what appears to be eternally given and objectified makes it possible for the mind to know itself as subject and not as a lifeless object, then to go beyond empirical reality into a putative realm of possibility. When instead of inexplicable shortage of bread you can imagine the human work and, subsequently, the human beings who produced the bread but are no longer doing so because there is a bakers' strike, you are well on your way to knowing that crisis is comprehensible because process is comprehensible; and if process is comprehensible, so too is some sense of the social whole created by human labor. Crisis, in short, is converted into criticism of the status quo: the bakers are on strike for a reason, the crisis can be explained, the system does not work infallibly, the subject has just demonstrated its victory over ossified objective forms.

Lukács puts all of this in terms of subject-object relationship, and proper justice to his argument requires that it be followed to the point where he shows that reconciliation between subject and object will be possible. Yet even he admits that such an eventuality is very far into the future. Nevertheless, he is certain that no such future is attainable without the transformation of passive, contemplative consciousness into active, critical consciousness. In positing a world of human agency outside the reach of reification, the critical consciousness (the consciousness that is given rise to be crisis) becomes genuinely aware of its power "unceasingly to overthrow the objective forms that shape the life of man."[9] Consciousness goes beyond empirical givens and comprehends, without actually experiencing, history, totality, and society as a whole—precisely those unities that reification had both concealed and denied. At bottom, class consciousness is thought thinking its way through fragmentation to unity; it is also thought aware of its own subjectivity as something active, energetic, and, in a profound sense, poetic. (Here we should note that several years before *History and Class Consciousness* Lukács had argued that only in the realm of the aesthetic could the limitations of pure theory and of pure ethics be overcome: by the former he meant a scientific theory whose very objectivity symbolized its own reification, its thralldom to objects; by the latter a Kantian subjectivity out of touch with everything except its own selfhood. Only the Aesthetic rendered the meaning of experience as lived experience—*der Sinn des Erlebnisses*—in an autonomous form: subject and object are thereby made one.[10])

Now because it rises above objects, consciousness enters a realm of potentiality, that is, of theoretical possibility. The special urgency of Lukács' account of this is that he is describing something rather far from a mere escape into fantasy. Consciousness attaining self-consciousness is no Emma Bovary pretending to be a lady in Yonville. The direct pressures of capitalist quantification, that relentless cataloguing of everything on earth, continue to be felt, according to Lukács; the only thing that changes is that the mind recognizes a class of beings like itself who have the power to think generally, to take in facts but to organize them in groups, to recognize processes and tendencies where reification only allows evidence of lifeless atoms. Class consciousness therefore begins in critical consciousness. Classes are not real the way trees and houses are real: they are imputable by consciousness, using its powers to posit ideal types in which with other beings it finds itself. Classes are the result of an insurrectionary act by which consciousness refuses to be confined to the world of objects, which is where it had been confined in the capitalist scheme of things.

Consciousness has moved from the world of objects into the world of theory. Although Lukács describes it as only a young German philosopher could describe it—in language bristling with more metaphysics and abstractions than even I have been using—we must not forget that he is performing an act of poetical insurgency. To attain to theory is to threaten reification, as well as the entire bourgeois system on which reification depends, with destruction. But, he assures his readers, this destruction "is no single unrepeatable tearing of the veil that masks the process [of reification] but the unbroken alternation of ossification, contradiction and movement."[11] Theory, *in fine,* is won as the result of a process that begins when consciousness first experiences its own terrible ossification in the general reification of all things under capitalism; then when consciousness generalizes (or classes) itself as something opposed to other objects, and feels itself as a contradiction to (or crisis within) objectification, there emerges a consciousness of change in the status quo; finally, moving toward freedom and fulfillment, consciousness looks ahead to complete self-realization, which is of course the revolutionary process stretching forward in time, perceivable now only as theory or projection.

This is very heady stuff indeed. I have summarized it in order to set down some small indication of how powerfully responsive Lukács' ideas about theory were to the political order he described with such formidable gravity and dread. Theory for him was what consciousness produced, not as an avoidance of reality but as a revolutionary will completely committed to worldliness and change. According to Lukács, the proletariat's consciousness represented the theoretical antithesis to capitalism; as Merleau-Ponty and others have said, Lukács' proletariat can by no means be identified with a ragged collection of grimy-faced Hungarian laborers. The proletariat was his figure for consciousness defying reification, mind asserting its powers over mere matter, consciousness claiming its theoretic right to posit a better world outside the world of simple objects. And since class consciousness derives from workers working and being aware of themselves that way, theory must never lose touch with its origins in politics, society, and economics.

This, then, is Lukács describing his ideas about theory—and of course his theory of sociohistorical change—in the early twenties. Consider now Lukács' disciple and student, Lucien Goldmann, whose *Le Dieu caché* (1955) was one of the first and certainly among the most impressive attempts to put Lukács' theories to practical scholarly use. In Goldmann's study of Pascal and Racine, class consciousness had been changed to "*vision du monde*", something that is not an immediate, but a collective consciousness expressed in the work of certain highly gifted writers.[12] But this is not all. Goldmann says that these writers derive their world vision from determinate political and economic circumstances common to members of their group; yet the world vision itself is premised not so much on empirical details as on a human faith that a reality exists "which goes beyond them as individuals and finds its expression in their work."[13] Writing as a politically committed scholar (and like Lukács as a directly involved militant), Goldmann then argues that because Pascal and Racine were privileged writers, their work can be constituted into a significant whole by a process of dialectical theorizing, in which part is related to assumed whole, assumed whole verified empirically by empirical evidence. Thus individual texts are seen to express a world vision; second, the world vision constitutes the whole intellectual and social life of a group (the Port-Royal Jansenists); third, the thoughts and feelings of the group are an expression of their economic and social life.[14] In all this—and Goldmann argues with exemplary brilliance and subtlety—the theoretical enterprise, an interpretive circle, is a demonstration of coherence: between part and whole, between world vision and texts in their smallest detail, between a determinate social reality and the writings of particularly gifted members of a group. In other words, theory is the researcher's domain, the place in which disparate, apparently disconnected things are brought together in perfect correspondence: economics, political process, the individual writer, a series of texts.

Goldmann's indebtedness to Lukács is clear, although it has not been noted that what in Lukács is an ironic discrepancy between theoretical consciousness and reified reality is transformed and localized by Goldmann into a tragic correspondence between world vision and the unfortunate class situation of the *noblesse de robe* in late seventeenth-century France. Whereas Lukács' class consciousness defies, indeed is an insurgent against, the capitalist order, Goldmann's tragic vision is perfectly, absolutely expressed by the works of Pascal and Racine. True, the tragic vision is not directly expressed by those writers, and true also that it requires an extraordinarily complex dialectical style of research for the modern researcher to draw forth the correspondence between world vision and empirical detail; the fact nevertheless is that Goldmann's adaptation of Lukács removes from theory its insurrectionary role. The sheer existence of class, or theoretical, consciousness for Lukács is enough to suggest to him the projected overthrow of objective forms. For Goldmann an awareness of class or group consciousness is first of all a scholarly imperative, and then—in the works of highly privileged writers—the expression of a tragically limited social situation. Lukács' *zugerechnetes Bewusstsein* (imputed consciousness) is an unverifiable, yet absolutely prior theoretical necessity if one is to effect a change in social reality; in Goldmann's version of it, admittedly limited to an acutely circumscribed situation, theory and consciousness are expressed in the Pascalian wager upon an unseen and silent god, the *deus absconditus*; they are also expressed for Goldmann the scientific researcher, as he calls himself, in the theoretical correspondence between text and political reality. Or to put the matter in another way, for Lukács theory originates as a kind of irreducible dissonance between mind and object, whereas for Goldmann theory is the homological relationship that can be seen to exist between individual part and coherent whole.

The difference between the two versions of Lukács' theory of theory is evident enough: Lukács writes as a participant in a struggle (the Hungarian Soviet Republic of 1919), Goldmann as an expatriate historian at the Sorbonne. From one point of view we can say that Goldmann's adaptation of Lukács degrades theory, lowers it in importance, domesticates it somewhat to the exigencies of a doctoral dissertation in Paris. I do not think, however, that degradation here has a moral implication, but rather (as one of its secondary meanings suggests) that degradation conveys the lowering of color, the greater degree of distance, the loss of immediate force that occurs when Goldmann's notions of consciousness and theory are compared with the meaning and role intended by Lukács for theory. Nor do I want to suggest that there is something inherently wrong about Goldmann's conversion of insurrectionary, radically adversarial consciousness into an accommodating consciousness of correspondence and homology. It is just that the situation has changed sufficiently for the degradation to have occurred, although there is no doubt that Goldmann's reading of Lukács mutes the latter's almost apocalyptic version of consciousness.

We have become so accustomed to hearing that all borrowings, readings, and interpretations are misreadings and misinterpretations that we are likely to consider the Lukács-Goldmann episode as just another bit of evidence that everyone, even Marxists, misreads and misinterprets. I find such a conclusion completely unsatisfying. It implies, first of all, that the only possible alternative to slavish copying is creative misreading and that no intermediate possibility exists. Second, when it is elevated to a general principle, the idea that all reading is misreading is fundamentally an abrogation of the critic's responsibility. It is never enough for a critic taking the idea of criticism seriously simply to say that interpretation is misinterpretation or that borrowings inevitably involve misreadings. Quite the contrary: it seems to me perfectly possible to judge misreadings (as they occur) as part of a historical transfer of ideas and theories from one setting to another. Lukács wrote *for* as well as *in* a situation that produced ideas about consciousness and theory that are very different from the ideas produced by Goldmann in his situation. To call Goldmann's work a misreading of Lukács', and then to go on immediately to relate that misreading to a general theory of interpretation as misinterpretation, is to pay no critical attention to history and to situation, both of which play an important determining role in changing Lukács' ideas into Goldmann's. The Hungary of 1919 and post-World War II Paris are two quite different environments. To the degree that Lukács and Goldmann are read carefully, then, to that precise degree we can understand the critical change—in time and in place—that occurs between one writer and another, both of whom depend on theory to accomplish a particular job of intellectual work. I see no need here to resort to the theory of limitless intertextuality as an Archimedean point outside the two situations. The particular voyage from Hungary to Paris, with all that entails, seems compelling enough, adequate enough for critical scrutiny, unless we want to give up critical consciousness for critical hermeticism.

In measuring Lukács and Goldmann against each other, then, we are also recognizing the extent to which theory is a response to a specific social and historical situation of which an intellectual occasion is a part. Thus what is insurrectionary consciousness in one instance becomes tragic vision in another, for reason that are elucidated when the situations in Budapest and Paris are seriously compared. I do not wish to suggest that Budapest and Paris determined the kinds of theories produced by Lukács and Goldmann. I do mean that "Budapest" and "Paris" are irreducibly first conditions, and they provide limits and apply pressures to which each writer, given his own gifts, predilections, and interests, responds.

Let us now take Lukács, or rather Lukács as used by Goldmann, a step further: the use made of Goldmann by Raymond Williams. Brought up in the tradition of Cambridge English studies, trained in the techniques of Leavis and Richards, Williams was formed as a literary scholar who had no use whatever for theory. He speaks rather poignantly of how intellectuals educated as he was could use "a separate and self-defining language" that made a fetish of minute, concrete particular; this meant that the intellectuals could approach power but speak antiseptically only of microcosm, profess not to understand reification, and to speak instead of the objective correlative, not to know mediation although they knew catharsis.[15] Williams tells us that Goldmann came to Cambridge in 1970 and gave two lectures there. This visit, according to Williams in the moving commemorative essay he wrote about Goldmann after his death, was a major event. It introduced Cambridge to theory, Williams claims, understood and employed as it had been by thinkers trained in the major Continental tradition. Goldmann induced in Williams an appreciation of Lukács' contribution to our understanding of how, in an era of "the dominance of economic activity over all other forms of human activity," reification was both a false objectivity so far as knowledge was concerned and a deformation thoroughly penetrating life and consciousness more than any other form. Williams continues:

> The idea of totality was then a critical weapon against this precise deformation; indeed, against capitalism itself. And yet this was not idealism—an assertion of the primacy of other values. On the contrary, just as the deformation could be understood, at its roots, only by historical analysis of a particular kind of economy, so the attempt to overcome and surpass it lay not in isolated witness or in

> separated activity but in practical work to find, assert and to establish more human social ends in more human and political and economic means.[16]

Once again Lukács' thought—in this instance the avowedly revolutionary idea of totality—has been tamed somewhat. Without wishing in any way to belittle the importance of what Lukács' ideas (via Goldmann) did for the moribund state of English studies in late twentieth-century Cambridge, I think it needs to be said that those ideas were originally formulated in order to do more than shake up a few professors of literature. This is an obvious, not to say easy, point. What is more interesting, however, is that because Cambridge is not revolutionary Budapest, because Williams is not the militant Lukács, because Williams is a reflective critic—this is crucial—rather than a committed reflective critic—this is crucial—rather than a committed revolutionary, he can see the limits of a theory that begins as a liberating idea but can become a trap of its own.

> At the most practical level it was easy for me to agree [with Lukács' theory of totality as a response to reification]. But then the whole point of thinking in terms of a totality is the realization that we are part of it; that our own consciousness, our work, our methods, are then critically at stake. And in the particular field of literary analysis there was this obvious difficulty: that most of the work we had to look at was the product of just this work of reified consciousness, so that *what looked like the methodological breakthrough might become, quite quickly, the methodological trap.* I cannot yet say this finally about Lukács, since I still don't have access to all his work; but in some of it, at least, *the major insights of History and Class-Consciousness,* which he has now partly disavowed, *do not get translated into critical practice* [Williams refers here to Lukács' later, much cruder work on European realism] and certain cruder operations-essentially still those of base and superstructure—keep reappearing. *I still read Goldmann collaboratively and critically asking the same question,* for I am sure the practice of totality is still for any of us, at any time, profoundly and even obviously difficult.[17]

This is an admirable passage. Even though Williams says nothing about the lamentable repetitiveness of Goldmann's later work, it is important that as a critic who has learned from someone else's theory he should be able to see the theory's limitations, especially the fact that a breakthrough can become a trap, if it is used uncritically, repetitively, limitlessly. What he means, I think, is that once an idea gains currency because it is clearly effective and powerful, there is every likelihood that during its peregrinations it will be reduced, codified, and institutionalized. Lukács' remarkably complex exposition of the phenomenon of reification indeed did turn into a simple reflection theory; to a degree of course, and Williams is too decently elegaic to say it about a recently dead old friend, it did become this sort of idea in Goldmann's hands. Homology is, after all, a refined version of the old Second International base-and-superstructure model.

Beyond the specific reminder of what could happen to a vanguard theory, Williams' ruminations enable us to make another observation about theory as it develops out of a situation, begins to be used, travels, and gains wide acceptance. For if reification-and-totality (to turn Lukács' theory now into a shorthand phrase for easy reference) can become a reductionist implement, there is no reason why it could become too inclusive, too ceaselessly active and expanding a habit of mind. That is, if a theory can move down, so to speak, become a dogmatic reduction of its original version, it can also move up into a sort of bad infinity, which—in the case of reification-and-totality—is the direction intended by Lukács himself. To speak of the unceasing overthrow of objective forms, and to speak as he does in the essay on class consciousness, of how the logical end of overcoming reification is the self-annihilation of the revolutionary class itself, means that Lukács had pushed his theory farther forward and upward, unacceptably (in my opinion). The contradiction inherent in this theory—and perhaps in most theories that develop as responses to the need for movement and change—is that it risks becoming a theoretical overstatement, a theoretical parody of the situation it was formulated originally to remedy or overcome. To prescribe "an *unbroken* alternation of ossification, contradiction, and movement" toward totality as a theoretical remedy for reification is in a sense to substitute one unchanging formula for another. To say of theory and theoretical consciousness, as Lukács does, that they intervene in reification and introduce process is not careful enough to calculate and allow for the details and the resistances offered by an intransigent, reified reality to theoretical consciousness. For all the brilliance of his account of reification, for all the care he takes with it, Lukács is unable to see how even under capitalism reification itself cannot be totally dominant—unless, of course, he is prepared to allow something that theoretical totality (his insurrectional instrument for overcoming reification) says is impossible, namely, that totality in the form of totally dominant reification is theoretically possible under capitalism. For if reification is totally dominant, how then can Lukács explain his own work as an alternative form of thought under the sway of reification?

Perhaps all this is too fussy and hermetic. Nevertheless, it seems to me that however far away in time and place Williams may be from the fiery rebelliousness of the early Lukács, there is an extraordinary virtue to the distance, even the coldness of his critical reflections on Lukács and Goldmann, to both of whom he is otherwise so intellectually cordial. He takes from both men a sophisticated theoretical awareness of the issues involved in connecting literature to society, as he puts it in his best single theoretical essay, "Base and Superstructure in Marxist Cultural Theory." The terminology provided by Marxist aesthetic theory for mapping the peculiarly uneven and complicated field lying between base and superstructure is generally inadequate, and then Williams goes on to do work that embodies *his* critical version of the original theory. He puts this version very well, I think, in *Politics and Letters*: "However dominant a social system may be, the very meaning of its domination involves a limitation or selection of the activities it covers, so that by definition it cannot exhaust all social experience, which therefore always potentially contains space for alternative acts and alternative intentions which are not yet articulated as a social institution or even project."[18] *The Country and the City* records both the limits and the reactive alternatives to dominance, as in the case of John Clare, whose work "marks the end of pastoral poetry (as a systematic convention for describing the English countryside) in the very shock of its collision with actual country experience." Clare's very existence as a poet was threatened by the removal of an acceptable social order from the customary landscape idealized by Jonson and Thomson; hence Clare's turning—

as an alternative not yet fully realized and not yet completely subdued by the inhuman relationship that obtained under the system of market exploitation—to "the green language of the new Nature," that is, the Nature to be celebrated in a new way by the great Romantics.[19]

There is no minimizing the fact that Williams is an important critic because of his gifts and his insights. But I am convinced it would be wrong to underestimate the role in his mature writings played by what I have been alluding to as borrowed, or traveling, theory. For borrow we certainly must if we are to elude the constraints of our immediate intellectual environment. Theory we certainly need, for all sorts of reasons that would be too tedious to rehearse here. What we also need over and above theory, however, is the critical recognition that there is no theory capable of covering, closing off, predicting all the situations in which it might be useful. This is another way of saying, as Williams does, that no social or intellectual system can be so dominant as to be unlimited in its strength. Williams therefore has the critical recognition, and uses it consciously to qualify, shape, and refine his borrowings from Lukács and Goldmann, although we should hasten to add that it does not make him infallible or any less liable to exaggeration and error for having it. But unless theory is unanswerable, either through its successes or its failure, to the essential untidiness, the essential unmasterable presence that constitutes a large part of historical and social situations (and this applies equally to theory that derives from somewhere else and theory that is "original"), then theory becomes an ideological trap. It transfixes both its users and what it is used on. Criticism would no longer be possible.

Theory, in short, can never be complete, just as one's interest in everyday life is never exhausted by simulacra, models, or theoretical abstracts of it. Of course one derives pleasure from actually making evidence fit or work in a theoretical scheme, and of course it is ridiculously foolish to argue that "the facts" or "the great texts" do not require any theoretical framework or methodology to be appreciated or read properly. No reading is neutral or innocent, and by the same token every text and every reader is to some extent the product of a theoretical standpoint, however implicit or unconscious such a standpoint may be. I am arguing, however, that we distinguish theory from critical consciousness by saying that the latter is a sort of spatial sense, a sort of measuring faculty for locating or situating theory, and this means that theory has to be grasped in the place and the time out of which it emerges as a part of that time, working in and for it, responding to it; then, consequently, that first place can be measured against subsequent places where the theory turns up for use. The critical consciousness is awareness of the differences between situations, awareness too of the fact that no system or theory exhausts the situation out of which it emerges or to which it is transported. And, above all, critical consciousness is awareness of the resistances to theory, reactions to it elicited by those concrete experiences or interpretations with which it is in conflict. Indeed I would go as far as saying that it is the critic's job to provide resistances to theory, to open it up towards historical reality, toward society, toward human needs and interests, to point up those concrete instances drawn from everyday reality that lie outside or jut beyond the interpretive area necessarily designated in advance and thereafter circumscribed by every theory.

Much of this is illustrated if we compare Lukács and Williams on the one hand with Goldmann on the other. I have already said that Williams is conscious of what he calls a methodological trap. Lukács, for his part, shows in his career as a theorist (if not in the fully fledged theory itself) a profound awareness of the necessity to move from hermetic aestheticism (*Die Seele und die Formen, Die Theorie des Romans*) toward the actual world of power and institutions. By contrast, Goldmann is enmeshed in the homological finality that his writing, brilliantly and persuasively in the case of *Le Dieu caché*, demonstrates. Theoretical closure, like social convention or cultural dogma, is anathema to critical consciousness, which loses its profession when it loses its active sense of an open world in which its faculties must be exercised. One of the best lessons of that is to be found in Lentricchia's powerful *After the New Criticism*, a wholly persuasive account of what he calls "the currently paralyzed debates" of contemporary literary theory.[20] In instance after instance he demonstrates the impoverishment and rarefication that overtake any theory relatively untested by and unexposed to the complex enfolding of the social world which is never a merely complaisant context to be used for the enactment of theoretical situations. (As an antidote to the bareness afflicting the American situation, there is in Fredric Jameson's *The Political Unconscious* an extremely useful account of three "semantic horizons" to be figured in dialectically by the interpreter as parts of the decoding process, which he also calls "the cultural mode of production."[21]

Yet we must be aware that the social reality I have been alluding to is no less susceptible to theoretical overtotalization, even when, as I shall be showing in the case of Foucault, extremely powerful historical scholarship moves itself out from the archive toward the world of power and institutions, toward precisely those resistances to theory ignored and elided by most formalistic theory—deconstruction, semiotics, Lacanian psychoanalysis, the Althusserian Marxism attacked by E. P. Thompson.[22] Foucault's work is most challenging because he is rightly considered to be an exemplary opponent of ahistorical, asocial formalism. But he too, I believe, falls victim to the systematic degradation of theory in ways that his newest disciples consider to be evidence that he has not succumbed to hermeticism.

Foucault is a paradox. His career presents his contemporary audience with an extraordinarily compelling trajectory whose culmination, most recently, has been the announcement made by him, and on his behalf by his disciples, that his real theme is the relationship between knowledge and power. Thanks to the brilliance of his theoretical and practical performances, *pouvoir* and *savoir* have provided his readers (it would be churlish not to mention myself, but see also Jacques Donzelot's *La Police des familles*) with a conceptual apparatus for the analysis of instrumental discourses that stands in stark contrast to the fairly arid metaphysics produced habitually by the students of his major philosophical competitors. Yet Foucault's earliest work was in many ways remarkably unconscious of its own theoretical force. Reread *Histoire de la folie* after *Surveiller et punir* and you will be struck with how uncannily prescient the early work is of the later; and yet you will also be struck that even when Foucault deals with *renfermement* (confinement), his obsessive theme, in discussing asylums and hospitals, power is never referred to explicitly. Neither for that matter is *volonté* (will). *Les Mots et les choses* might be excused for the same neglect of power, on the grounds that the subject of Foucault's inquiry was intellectual, not institutional history. In *The Archeology of Knowledge* there are intimations here and there that Foucault is beginning to approach power through a number of abstractions, surrogates for it: thus he refers to such things as acceptability, accumulation, preservation, and formation that are ascribed to the making and the functioning of statements, discourses, and archives; yet he does so without spending any time on what might be the common source of their strength within institutions or fields of knowledge or society itself.

Foucault's theory of power—to which I shall restrict myself here—derives from his attempt to analyze working systems of confinement from the inside, systems whose functioning depends equally on the continuity of institutions as on the proliferation of justifying technical ideologies for the institutions. These ideologies are his discourses and disciplines. In his concrete presentation of local situations in which such power and such knowledge are deployed, Foucault has no peer, and what he has done is remarkably interesting by any standard. As he says in *Surveiller et punir*, for power to work it must be able to manage, control, and even create detail: the more detail, the more real power, management breeding manageable units, which in turn breed a more detailed, a more finely controlling knowledge. Prisons, he says in that memorable passage, are factories for producing delinquency, and delinquency is the raw material for disciplinary discourses.

With descriptions and particularized observations of this sort I have no trouble. It is when Foucault's own language becomes general (when he moves his analyses of power from the detail to society as a whole) that the methodological breakthrough becomes the theoretical trap. Interestingly, this is slightly more evident when Foucault's theory is transported from France and planted in the work of his overseas disciples. Recently, for example, he has been celebrated by Ian Hacking as a kind of hard-headed alternative to the too backward-and-forward-looking "Romantic" Marxists (which Marxists? all Marxists?), and as a ruthlessly anarchistic opponent of Noam Chomsky, who is described inappropriately as "a marvelously sane liberal reformer."[23] Other writers, who quite rightly see Foucault's discussions of power as a refreshing window opened onto the real world of politics and society, uncritically misread his pronouncements as the latest thing about social reality.[24] There is no doubt that Foucault's work is indeed an important alternative to the ahistorical formalism with which he has been conducting an implicit debate, and there is great merit to his view that as a specialized intellectual (as opposed to a universal intellectual)[25] he and others like him can wage small-scale guerrilla warfare against some repressive institutions, and against "silence" and "secrecy".

But all that is quite another thing from accepting Foucault's view in *History of Sexuality* that "power is everywhere" along with all that such a vastly simplified view entails.[26] For one, as I have said, Foucault's eagerness not to fall into Marxist economism causes him to obliterate the role of classes, the role of economics, the role of insurgency and rebellion in the societies he discusses. Let us suppose that prisons, schools, armies, and factories were, as he says, disciplinary factories in nineteenth-century France (since he talks almost exclusively about France), and that panoptic rule dominated them all. What resistances were there to the disciplinary order and why, as Nicos Poulantzas has so trenchantly argued in *State, Power, and Socialism*, does Foucault never discuss the resistances that always end up dominated by the system he describes? The facts are more complicated of course, as any good historian of the rise of the modern state can demonstrate. Moreover, Poulantzas continues, even if we accept the view that power is essentially rational, that it is not held by anyone but is strategic, dispositional, effective, that, as *Discipline and Punish* claims, it invests all areas of society, is it correct to conclude, as Foucault does, that power is exhausted in its use?[27] Is it not simply wrong, Poulantzas asks, to say that power is not *based* anywhere and that struggles and exploitation—both terms left out of Foucault's analyses—do not occur?[28] The problem is that Foucault's use of the term *pouvoir* moves around too much, swallowing up every obstacle in its path (resistances to it, the class and economic bases that refresh and fuel it, the reserves it builds up), obliterating change and mystifying its microphysical sovereignty.[29] A symptom of how overblown Foucault's conception of power can become when it travels too far is Hacking's statement that "nobody knows this knowledge; no one yields this power." Surely this is going to extremes in order to prove that Foucault is not a simple-minded follower of Marx.

In fact, Foucault's theory of power is a Spinozist conception, which has captivated not only Foucault himself but many of his readers who wish to go beyond Left optimism and Right pessimism so as to justify political quietism with sophisticated intellectualism, at the same time wishing to appear realistic, in touch with the world of power and reality, as well as historical and antiformalistic in their bias. The trouble is that Foucault's theory has drawn a circle around itself, constituting a unique territory in which Foucault has imprisoned himself and others with him. It is certainly wrong to say, with Hacking, that hope, optimism, and pessimism are shown by Foucault to be mere satellites of the idea of a transcendental, enduring subject, since empirically we experience and act according to those things daily without reference to any such irrelevant "subject". There is after all a sensible difference between Hope and hope, just as there is between the Logos and words: we must not let Foucault get away with confusing them with each other, nor with letting us forget that history does not get made without work, intention, resistance, effort, or conflict, and that none of these things is silently absorbable into micronetworks of power.

There is a more important criticism to be made of Foucault's theory of power, and it has been made most tellingly by Chomsky. Unfortunately most of Foucault's new readers in the United States seem not to know of the exchange that took place between them several years ago on Dutch television,[30] nor of Chomsky's succinct critique of Foucault contained in *Language and Responsibility.* Both men agreed on the necessity of opposing repression, a position Foucault has since found it more difficult to take unequivocally. Yet for Chomsky the sociopolitical battle had to be waged with two tasks in mind: one, "to imagine a future society that conforms to the exigencies of human nature as best we understand them; the other to analyze the nature of power and oppression in our present societies."[31] Foucault assented to the second without in any way accepting the first. According to him, any future societies that we might imagine now "are only the invention of our civilization and result from our class system." Not only would imagining a future society ruled according to justice be limited by false consciousness, it would also be too utopian a project for anyone like Foucault who believes that "the idea of justice in itself is an idea which in effect has been invented and put to work in different societies as an instrument of a certain political and economic power or as a weapon against that power."[32] This is a perfect instance of Foucault's unwillingness to take seriously his own ideas about resistances to power. If power oppresses and controls and manipulates, then everything that resists it is not morally equal to power, is not neutrally and simply a weapon against that power. Resistance cannot equally be an adversarial alternative to power and a dependent function of it, except in some metaphysical, ultimately trivial sense. Even if the distinction is hard to draw, there is a distinction to be made—as, for example, Chomsky does when he says that he would give his support to an oppressed proletariat if as a class it made justice the goal of its struggle.

The disturbing circularity of Foucault's theory of power is a form of theoretical overtotalization superficially more difficult to resist because, unlike many others, it is formulated, reformulated, and borrowed for use in what seem to be historically documented situations. But note that Foucault's history is ultimately textual, or rather textualized; its mode is one for which Borges would have an affinity. Gramsci, on the other hand, would find it uncongenial. He would certainly appreciate the fineness of Foucault's archeologies, but would find it odd that they make not even nominal allowance for emergent movements, and none for revolutions, counterhegemony, or historical blocks. In human history there is always something beyond the reach of dominating systems, no matter how deeply they saturate society, and this is obviously what makes change possible, limits power in Foucault's sense, and hobbles the theory of that power. One could not imagine Foucault undertaking a sustained analysis of powerfully contested political issues, nor, like Chomsky himself and writers like John Berger, would Foucault commit himself to descriptions of power and oppression with some intention of alleviating human suffering, pain, or betrayed hope.

It may seem an abrupt conclusion to reach, but the kinds of theory I have been discussing can quite easily become cultural dogma. Appropriated to schools or institutions, they quickly acquire the status of authority within the cultural group, guild, or affiliative family. Though of course they are to be distinguished from grosser forms of cultural dogma like racism and nationalism, they are insidious in that their original provenance—their history of adversarial, oppositional derivation—dulls the critical consciousness, convincing it that a once insurgent theory is still insurgent, lively, responsive to history. Left to its own specialists and acolytes, so to speak, theory tends to have walls erected around itself, but this does not mean that critics should either ignore theory or look despairingly around for newer varieties. To measure the distance between theory then and now, there and here, to record the encounter of theory with resistances to it, to move skeptically in the broader political world where such things as the humanities or the great classics ought to be seen as small provinces of the human venture, to map the territory covered by all the techniques of dissemination, communication, and interpretation, to preserve some modest (perhaps shrinking) belief in noncoercive human community: if these are not imperatives, they do at least seem to be attractive alternatives. And what is critical consciousness at bottom if not an unstoppable predilection for alternatives?

This text is reprinted with permission. Published in Edward W. Said, *The World, the Text, and the Critic*, Cambridge, Harvard University Press, 1983.

1. Frank Lentricchia, *After the New Criticism* (Chicago: University of Chicago Press, 1980), p. 24.
2. Geoffrey H. Hartmann, *Criticism in the Wilderness: The Study of Literature Today* (New Haven: Yale University Press, 1980), p. 85.
3. Ibid., p. 244.
4. Ibid., p. 151.
5. Ibid., p. 301.
6. Richard Ohmann, *English in America: A Radical View of the Profession* (New York and London: Oxford University Press, 1976), p. 304.
7. Georg Lukács, *History and Class Consciousness: Studies in Marxist Dialectics*, trans. Rodney Livingstone (London: Merlin Press, 1971), p. 90.
8. Ibid., p. 105.
9. Ibid., p. 186.
10. Lukács, "Die Subjekt-Objekt-Beziehung in der Ästhetik," originally published in *Logos*, 7 (1917-18), republished in Lukács, *Heidelberger-Ästhetik, 1916-18* (Darmstadt: Luchterhand, 1974); see pp. 96-97.
11. Lukács, *History and Class Consciousness*, p. 199.
12. Lucien Goldmann, *The Hidden God: A Study of Tragic Vision in the "Pensée" of Pascal and the Tragedies of Racine*, trans. Philip Thody (London: Routledge and Kegan Paul, 1964), p. 15.
13. Ibid., p. 15.
14. Ibid., p. 99.
15. Raymond Williams, *Problems in Materialism and Culture* (London: Verso, 1980), p. 13.
16. Ibid., p. 21.
17. Ibid., p. 21; emphasis added.
18. Williams, *Politics and Letters: Interviews with New Left Review* (London: New Left Books, 1979), p. 252.
19. Williams, *The Country and the City* (1973; rprt. New York: Oxford University Press, 1975), p. 141.
20. Lentricchia, *After the New Criticism*, p. 351.

21. Fredric Jameson, *The Political Unconscious: Narrative as a Socially Symbolic Act* (Ithaca: Cornell University Press, 1981), pp. 74, 102.
22. E. P. Thompson, *The Poverty of Theory and Other Essays* (London: Merlin Press, 1978).
23. Ian Hacking, "The Archaeology of Foucault," *New York Review of Books*, 28 (May 14, 1981), p. 36.
24. There is much evidence of this in the Winter 1980 issue of *Humanities in Society*, vol. 3, entirely devoted to Foucault.
25. The distinction is made by Foucault in *Radical Philosophy*, 17 (Summer 1977).
26. Michel Foucault, *The History of Sexuality, I: An Introduction*, trans. Robert Hurley (New York: Pantheon, 1978), p. 93.
27. Foucault, *Discipline and Punish: The Birth of the Prison*, trans. Alan Sheridan (New York: Pantheon, 1977), pp. 26-27.
28. Nicos Poulantzas, *State, Power, and Socialism*, trans. Patrick Camiller (London: Verso, 1980), p. 148.
29. Ibid., pp. 150ff.
30. A transcript is to be found in *Reflexive Water: The Basic Concerns of Mankind*, ed. Fons Elders (London: Souvenir Press, 1974). The curious thing about this book and the program—"the Basic concerns of mankind"—is that "mankind" is spoken for entirely by white European-American males. No one seems bothered by the claims for universality.
31. Noam Chomsky, *Language and Responsibility* (New York: Pantheon, 1979), p. 80.
32. *Reflexive Water*, pp. 184-185.

LOST OUR LANGUAGE – UNDERNEATH THE LINGUISTIC MAP

GAYATRI CHAKRAVORTY SPIVAK – RAINER GANAHL

> There are countless languages in which women all over the world have grown up and been female or feminist, and yet the languages we keep on learning by rote are the powerful European ones, sometimes the powerful Asian ones, least often the chief African ones. We are quite at home, and helpful, when large migrant populations are doing badly in the dominant countries, our own. The "other" languages are learned only by anthropologists who must produce knowledge across an epistemic divide.
> — Gayatri Chakravorty Spivak, *The Politics of Translation*

Rainer Ganahl: Could you please speak a little bit about the languages and the linguistic identities you grew up with and the languages you then have chosen to learn and still are in the process of learning?

Gayatri Chakravorty Spivak: The language I grew up with already reflects a problem which the essay that your quote comes from touches upon. The area of the world where I am from, West Bengal, a state in India, there are many so-called aboriginal ethnic groups who have many languages that are not Indo-European. This is the case in nearly every Indian state. There are 73 plus million so-called aboriginals in India. When I was growing up I had no idea that these languages were also languages of the soil. So I grew up with the hegemonic language: Calcutta Bengali. And of course there was English which was the imperial language. Given my class, my field of study, and my long residence in the US, I am bilingual in English and Bengali. This bilingualism completely obliterates the fact that any demand for a practice of bilingualism cannot recognize the hundreds of the world's so–called aboriginal languages which have been suppressed in every area in order for the map to be established. This critique of bilingualism which I was not able to appreciate as I was growing up is extremely well put by a man called Merwan Hassan, a Lebanese-Canadian, criticizing the French-English bilingualism demand in Quebec in terms of the hundreds of languages of the First Nations which cannot be acknowledged in the public sphere. It's an experience of the impossible, to quote Derrida. I have discussed an expression which I learned from the peoples of the Eastern Kimberley region in Australia who are also aboriginal folks, so-called, who use an expression that can be translated into mainstream Australian as "lost our language," by which they mean that they no longer compute with their cultural idiom. When they say that they have lost their language they do not mean that they have forgotten how to speak their language. Language is here being used as a broader concept metaphor. They mean that they no longer make sense of their lives in terms of their cultural idiom. Foucault would say that their cultural idiom is no longer their *pouvoir savoir*, their ability to know. It seems to me that this concept is so very different from the idea of bilingualism or language learning. To describe my growing up I would therefore say that I grew up like all of my companions and, I would say 100% of West Bengalis today, unless you count the aboriginals in as well and even they themselves perhaps are not clearly aware that their languages are part of, specifically, the language problem of the state, the country. So I grew up thinking that the language problem was divided into English and Bengali, mother tongue and imperial language. And then, as I began to grow into an adult, the mother tongue-imperial language and the national language which is Hindi. Today I know that it was a bad growing up in that sense. As a child I was not in touch with this much more mysterious and important problem of the languages of the first peoples of the earth that have become a non-part of the problem. I was not aware that there was a problem within Bengali of hegemonic Bengali nationalism-Hindu Nationalism-Indian Nationalism. At the beginning of the 19th century the planned disappearance of the Arabic Farsi part of the Bengali kept alive the Sanskrit-origin parts alone. Islamic Bengali, it's horrible to use a religious adjective but what else to say—disappeared from the language of Calcutta, which I thought was just natural Bengali. There is a tendency in my western interviewers to see some kind of victimized authenticity in my mother tongue but what I am trying to make clear here, is that already the situation of the mother tongue in India was marked by the fact that it was a dominant language that was based on the forgetability of the original languages and that it was a hinduized language which had chosen to suppress and silence its Islamic elements. So that was my mother tongue. And then, of course, over against that was English and then a bit later, after Independence, Hindi as the problem of the national language. And what I have chosen to learn? Well, I guess French is the one I have learned best, I mean, I didn't really choose to learn it, I am not quite sure yet how on earth I got to know as much French as I do. My French is far from perfect but nonetheless I do know it quite well. And to learn German, and I read 19th century German with a certain degree of ease. I can't really say that I know German. I can always manage on streets. That's because of the way I am. I mean I can manage quite well with Spanish, for example. But quite well, even have political discussions, but academic Spanish, I am not that good at but I can read with the dictionary. Italian the same, and so you know, it is really... well Latin, I can stumble along and classical Greek stumble along, somewhat more slowly. Sanskrit I have chosen to learn somewhat; I don't know it well but I know it better then many post-colonial critics, let's put it that way, and, what else, I think what you are talking about is my learning colloquial Arabic for the last 6 years. Yes, I am stumbling along in that as well because I started going to Algeria and I would like to be able to go again when the present situation clears a little.

R. G.: I think language is a concentrated form of history and reflects transformations, exchanges, encounters, war activities, and all sorts of impositions over time, but obviously, in the case of the imposition of English on this large scale in relationship with colonialism something else enters.

G. S.: I don't think you heard me because what I was trying to say is that if one focuses on English as the beginning item then one doesn't see that the languages on which English was imposed already imposed themselves on this other language structure, much more multiple, which in fact we don't even consider a part of the problem. We can't just begin with the imposition of English. That is what I was trying to say. That my own mother tongue was itself carrying within itself a history of imposition which we didn't know. And when we begin with the imposition of English then we look at my mother tongue for example as a kind of victim language. And in a certain way I resent that. To an extent what has happened is that those languages which are perceived as having been imposed on have themselves imposed on this earlier structure, which on the other hand is not itself without its subterranean traffic with English. Let's take the example of the 300 odd languages of the so-called Western Kimberley region of Australia. The do-gooding social workers, mainstream Australians who are, like you, mourning the fact of the imposition of English, they do not know any of these 300 languages. But they are still mourning that English was imposed and in order to show how politically correct they are, I mean the social worker, not the aboriginals, they are transcribing what is called Australian Creole, that is to say the way in which the aboriginals use English. And the social workers say that in Australian Creole the word "culture" is K-O-L-I-J-A. Your "normal" mainstream Australians would think that just a mispronunciation in the aboriginal accent because the aboriginals can't get their tongues around the word "culture" so they say "kolija," or something like this. But these politically correct social workers who are very happy to have found a problem in the imposition of English and who have not wanted to learn the many, many languages of the people to whom they are being benevolent are actually being politically correct by spelling out this word, by saying that this is the Australian Creole spelling. For me, even to begin with the idea of the imposition of English is part of the problem. Do you see what I am saying?

R. G.: Yes.

G. S.: OK, I want to go on even further. Still on the first question. Sometimes I lecture in my mother tongue in Calcutta. I publish in my mother tongue. When I lecture academically in my mother tongue I speak a Bengali which is without English words. Since Bengali is an Indo-European language it's quite possible, if you know it well enough, to construct translations of the most complicated deconstructive terminology and so on. And that is what I read, write, and speak when I am lecturing and publishing. On the other hand real Bengali as it is spoken in the street has, over the last 250 years, taken in English and many words have been lexicalized in Bengali. That is not an imposition. Therefore when one speaks Bengali, street Bengali or even middle class Bengali at home there are these lexicalized loan words which are like any normal loan words in

English. To see that as an imposition is really not to see how, like you say, how language grows. This is not imposed, in fact. The so-called pure Bengali is a kind of confection, faintly ridiculous.

R. G.: How do you account for the problems, privileges, and importance of foreign language acquisition? How has this shaped your personal and professional life?

G. S.: Well, accounting for the problem of foreign language acquisition disappears when we are in an imperialist or colonial or neo-colonial situation. If it is the language of the master then you learn it much more easily. And therefore it is not surprising that the United States, the English dominated part of the United States, is often spoken of as the least capable of learning languages. It is not some essentialist US character—and anyway how could there be, because, I mean, we are made up of migrant groups. It is just that unless someone's foot is on your neck you do not learn language easily. That's why we learned English so well, and the world is learning English so well. That is, I think, the main problem in foreign language acquisition in general. That it is learned best when it comes tied to power, legitimacy, capital, domination, exploitation, or a culture of imperialism. Anthropologists hardly ever learn a language in its spectrality. The privileges of foreign language acquisitions that it reflects what class one belongs to. And anthropological foreign language acquisition, about which I have spoke in the epigraph that you have chosen, is part of academic expertise—so it is not learned for survival. It is learned for academic transcoding, where the essence of knowledge is knowledge about knowledge. Anthropologists do not learn the languages in such a way that the history of the languages begins to show itself like a skeleton in their use. They attach words to concepts. When I speak English I can in fact see the history of the language as a skeleton in each sentence that I am using. But that is not how anthropologists learn the language of the object of their investigation. I think the question of the privilege and the importance of foreign language acquisition has been answered in my first answer. It is important to try to learn languages which are not the language of the person or of the figure whose boot is on your neck. I think it is extremely important to learn languages but to learn the languages of the so-called "others" in whose name you are attitudinizing. The first requirement that I have is not just to learn colloquial Arabic but also to learn a bit more of the many languages of the so-called aboriginals with whom I try to do a little bit of my work. Language learning has shaped my personal and professional life greatly because I was good in English. As far as French and German, I had to acquire them—I was a graduate student before multiculturalism. In my day if you were not a native speaker you did not really get a fellowship in English literature too easily. I was asked if I would go for a fellowship in comp-lit by de Man who had just become chair of comp-lit and therefore was trying to hold down a financial aid slot, and when I asked what would be the minimum requirements, it was French and German. So the absence of multiculti let me read Derrida and Marx and has shaped my personal and professional life.

R. G.: In one preface, you say, "Translation is the most intimate act of reading. I surrender to the text when I translate.... To surrender in translation is more erotic than ethical." Couldn't we say that there is also a surrender to another world when changing and shifting between different languages?

G. S.: Yes, but that is not completely like another world because, you know, you are making the shift. Whereas in translation somebody else tells you what to say. Sometimes you may feel that it would have been better if the person hadn't written this. But you can't change it. I said "erotic" rather then "ethical" but today I have a different sense of the word "ethical" and I would probably say it somewhat differently. But you don't want to hear that now; that is all right.

R. G.: Linguistic spaces, as you mentioned, are ethnocentric and class organized. They relate us back to questions of the public sphere. Could you please elaborate on these issues some more?

G. S.: Yes. I think in that essay that you read, part of the point I was trying to make was that some languages are seen as private because they are not the instrument of the structures of civil society. I was taking the example of Ngugi wa Thiong'o and Gikuyu. Gikuyu is private only insofar as the public is defined in terms of the structure of civil society. As much as notions of the public sphere are important, in this particular arena I don't think one could define "public" and "private" in this way and get anything useful. I am not saying that Gikuyu or all the aboriginal languages should become languages that are used in civil society. I am just saying that the distinction between public and private that is predicated on the existence of a civil society is not useful in the case of languages. When the body is medicalized, the body becomes public and any distinction between public and private which inexorably defines the body as private is not going to be much use if you are going to look for equitable medical practice. We cannot say public and private the same way for equitable language practice as we do for equitable practice in the civil society.

R. G.: So this doesn't have anything to do with what Wittgenstein said about private language?

G. S.: No, and that is why your example of Wolfson is not one that I can deal with. It seems too difficult when the diagnosis of schizophrenia is made outside of your use of Wolfson's practice. When one bases one's description upon a diagnosis made within another system of "public and private", then the legitimization of "outsider" in...

R. G.: Outsider art...

G. S.: ...is as scary as its delegitimization. On the other hand, outsider art is another thing when it is made from the Mississippi delta. I just saw such an exhibition. That too, on the class rather than the psyche register, is an art where the diagnosis precedes the discovery. For me they never become really useful for a description of the problems and the solutions of the situation of language. Deleuze and Guattari in the old days were not talking about clinical schizophrenia. They were very careful about that. The moment there is room for "diagnosis" you can't really use that for emancipatory purposes because the system which diagnoses is relied upon and the system which diagnoses is part of what you want to emancipate.

R. G.: You already answered this question but it has a second part: The American Luis Wolfson tried to acquire foreign languages in order to "kill" his mother-tongue, which was English.

G. S.: OK, carry on, ...

R. G.: Contrary to this voluntary schizophrenic obliterating of a mother-tongue, there are also all the forced abandonments of native languages for political, geographical, social and other imposed reasons that people have to surrender to. How do you see this?

G. S.: I began with that, didn't I? The aboriginals surrendered to my mother tongue. And how do you think I see this? I see this as a calamity obviously, how else would I see this. On the other hand I don't think you can really "remedy" it.... The language part of it is not the disease, it is the symptom. You can't "remedy" it by just saying "be nice to languages," you know. One has to see how much of this is surrender, how much of this so-called "forcing" is willed. Language grows in violence and violation, we are helpless in front of this. Eurocentric economic migration is the largest reason why languages are obliterated. On the other hand Eurocentric European migration is seen by the ones who leave as a liberation. One just has to look at the sort of visa lines outside of the embassies and consulates in the mother countries. One always has this romantic picture of crossing over illegally or coming with boats etc., those are the exceptions. The real bulk of it is people who are actually waiting for months and months and months and months to get visas and sometimes illegally paying for visas and stuff like this. The way it was in colonialism and the way it is under neo-colonialism is not at all the same as the way it is under Eurocentric economic migration or labor export. I would rather take our lesson from those Australian aboriginals who knew that the power to compute with that cultural system was lost and therefore they wanted mainstream education and they wanted their own cultural information integrated into the curriculum so that they could in fact "do" their culture as theater. It is not nothing. The year after the defeat at Wounded Knee Sitting Bull's cabin was taken to the Exposition in Chicago and the year after that Buffalo Bill Cody, freed some of the native Americans of the struggle on condition that they would perform Wounded Knee in his show. It is as if these Australian aboriginals are saying: don't take us into your shows. Let us organize our own shows with our own cultural material. Make cultural information available on the curriculum the way you teach European history. The question of the *mise en scène* becomes a question of *ins Werke setzen* to posit in the work. It is quite often translated simply as "setting to work" and that is not quite right. Maybe what the aboriginals are asking is a more profoundly theoretical demand, against which just saying "please use all the languages" is not very sophisticated.

R. G.: How do you then see the problem of multi-lingual education here in the United States?

G. S.: Well I must say that I am unable to think it through. I really have to know a great deal more: where, why, what group, what opportunities, etc. I am not able to give a generalizable answer to this question. I guess that I am always against the imposition of a national language on education. In India, of course, the national language is taught, English is taught and the local vernacular is taught. But you were asking about western situations. This I think is not a bad solution. In my own life time I find that Hindi has become much more possible all over India than I could imagine when I was growing up.

R. G.: Looking at the functioning of different languages in competition to each other one is immediately confronted with international power structures and class, gender, and race divisions. Do you think we can speak of linguistic imperialism in regard to the hegemonic status the English language has acquired in this contemporary world? And how do you see the long-term consequences for subordinate linguistic cultures?

G. S.: I am bad at looking at long-term consequences but sometimes I wonder if English will be the only language. I don't know. I don't know, because I am just coming back from the global South. It is true that English is understood a lot all over the place but there are many many people who still don't understand English. Are these people all going to be obliterated? I don't think so, unless these international population control programs just succeed beyond their wildest plans. I think the subaltern will continue to multiply. For me the situation of the migrant is not typical—it is one situation among many—so for the short run, at least, I don't see English as taking those areas which I will not define as only private, but rather those areas that do not belong to the functioning of civil society. I can only hope that linguistic differences will not disappear. I see this as a site of struggle. I don't think the problem will be solved by the fantasia of required bilingualism or multilingualism. I have the same problem with western multilingual education as I do with liberal multi-culturalism. But that is a very big issue. My question to an extent is what will a minority person in the west gain by having a multilingual institutional education? Stalin had said to the old multinational empires just before 1917 when he was trying to inaugurate the possibilities of a Russia-headed Soviet Union: What do you want? Cultural independence within your old imperial structure? That is not going to give you anything. You should want national self-determination. Of course, the moment the Bolshevik revolution "succeeded" Stalin changed his tune. But that was the earlier promise. It is Stalin's question that one puts to these people who want multilingual education. There were multinational empires before with the Ottoman, the Russians, and the Habsburg. So now one wants new multinational empires. When you ask for multilingual education within a dominant civil society, you gain some kind of cultural subspace within dominant capital, which you will find much easier to museumize if you become upwardly class mobile. Is that what you are gaining? I think it is a good gain. But it won't keep me awake at night.

R. G.: You wrote a beautiful article entitled "The Politics of Translations" from which I took the sentences I use here as an epigraph. How is translating from and into different languages, as you say, a political exercise?

G. S.: When diasporics translate irresponsibly from languages which nobody will check, the politics are more than questionable. When I translated Derrida, a million people criticized me in detail; they are still criticizing me. But when I translate Mahasweta Devi nobody knows about the quality of the translation. They just believe that the translation is OK, you know what I mean. And not only do they believe that the translation is OK they believe that the translated text is the text. I know how idiotic I sound when even very politically correct places like the Feminist Press doesn't care. I mean things that they take to their bosom as producing material for teaching constitute the global South as an object. They let go of a poor translation of Rokeya Sakhawat Hussein's *Abarodhbasini*, an incredible text by an Indian Muslim who wrote in the teens of the present century upon the veil. I'd rather patronize high rolling anthologizers of other people's translations, periodically visiting the United States to stash up some more money. This is how even the politically correct presses go to construct subject material for political teaching. I sound like an idiot when I say this. You have to hypercathect what you translate. That is the politics of translation. That is all, good bye.

R. G.: Thank you.

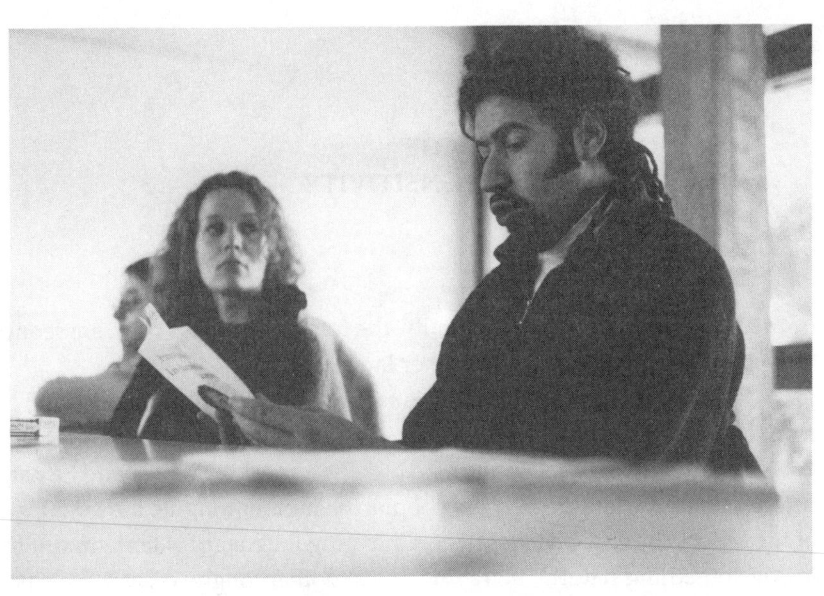

IMPORTED – A READING SEMINAR in Relationship with my "A Portable (Not so Ideal) Imported Library, Or How to Reinvent the Coffee Table: 25 Books for Instant Use (French Version)," 1994/96
Villa Arson, Nice, March, April 1996

THE OTHER LANGUAGE OR TRANSLATING SENSITIVITY

JULIA KRISTEVA

Immediately, but also fundamentally, the foreigner differs from someone who isn't, because he speaks another language.

Looked at more closely, this fact is less trivial than it appears; it reveals an extravagant destiny: a tragedy as much as a choice.

Tragedy, because the human being is a speaking being, and he naturally speaks the language of his people: the mother tongue, the language of his group, the national language. Changing languages is tantamount to losing something natural, betraying one's mother tongue or, at very least, translating it. A foreigner is, in essence, a translator. He may reach a point where he blends in perfectly with his host language, without forgetting his source language, or only partially. In most cases, however, he is regarded as foreign precisely because his translation, however perfect it may be, betrays a melody or a mentality that is not entirely in tune with the identity of the host. This non-indigenous trace—strange, amusing, exciting—irritates the native speakers: "So, there goes another language," they say to themselves, "Just 'another'—a translator—who's talking, he's not one of us, he doesn't belong here, what does he want, we don't want to have anything to do with him...." Fortunately, this kind of reasoning isn't always fully expressed. But it does underlie even the most tolerant attitudes and, in times of crisis, it invariably produces the worst consequences that people are capable of: the man/woman-hunt and murder.

However, the translator, intrinsically damaged and painfully conscious of his marginal position, knows very well that the suspicion that he gives rise to is also his salvation. He has left the source of his mother tongue either out of necessity or because a choice has irrevocably driven him towards the host language. A lucid yet nonetheless passionate love object, the new language serves as a pretext for rebirth: a new identity, new hope. The translator aspires to absolute assimilation, all the while breathing into his new identity, more or less unconsciously, the archaic rhythms and the underlying cadences of his native idiom. From now on, a divided subject, he can only live through sharpening his critical faculty. From this split, the old and new, the original family and the new community both appear to him as simultaneously binding and problematic: an inconsolable questioning, an ever-present anxiety. Is there a better choice than the insomniac lucidity of a translator?

Indeed, according to current norms, the ideal translator is not supposed to let the slightest sign of the source language appear. Although this conception of translation is debatable, it is largely accepted and seems satisfactory. From this point of view, a foreigner is not an ideal translator: one can always find "something or other" that points to his difference, while he, both wounded and proud of this discovery, has a tendency to be surprised that his alarming foreignness is not regarded straight-away as good fortune, enrichment, evolution, a new life for the spirit, language, nation, humanity.... For, falsely modest, our translator has an open mind that can't help wishing all minds were open, and is eager to build the utopia of a cosmopolitan paradise in which he would be the prophet.

Occasionally, our foreigner-translator is unable to choose a homeland other than that of language makers—writers. Didn't Mallarmé write that all literature provides "a total, new expression *foreign to the language*"? Style is indeed a vision, but one which modifies the original pleats and folds of language, to create a surprising, unrecognizable construction that initially disturbs the group's habits. And for that very reason, hasn't the writer, since the beginning of time, been the mirror image on the law maker—the one who modifies language as a jurist modifies laws?

This ambition does not allow for the identity needs of groups. In fact, what is the ultimate sign of group identity? Some nations define their identity through belonging to that land, others through blood ties. Most, however, rather than blood and soil, attribute their identification image to language. This is particularly true of France. The history of the monarchy and the republic, their administrative culture, their verbal code, their rhetorical and educational institutions have led to an unprecedented fusion between national identity and linguistic identity.

The result is that avant-garde literary figures must be even more subversive and radical in France than elsewhere in order to throw off this protective blanket of rhetoric. But at a time of national depression, which is always accompanied by an identity retrenchment, the avant-garde is brutally marginalized or eliminated, and the cult of traditional speech and "French good taste" acts as a balm for an injured, if unattainable identity.

In this context, our foreigner-translator is not very lucky. Of course, there have always been court Jews, just as there will always be foreigners in the French Academy. But these alibis of good national conscience should not let us forget the basic tendency: similarly to avant-garde audacity, those who dare to express themselves in the "other language" are considered suspicious and are quickly ostracized. In light of this, it can be understood that in France, the most clearly nationalist and insidiously xenophobic groups have established themselves and are able shamelessly and without any resistance to exercise their power in institutions that determine the fate of letters. Our foreigner-translator who speaks the "other language" is invited to be silent, unless he is willing to side with one of the local clans or adopt one of the current forms of rhetoric. Naturally he can also translate abroad, and be translated abroad. In fact, the fate of the translator is by definition open, interminable, undefined. Perhaps that is his salvation.

Let's look at things concretely. Suppose that I am this translator.

WHICH LANGUAGE?

I haven't forgotten my mother tongue. It comes back to me—with more and more difficulty, I admit—in dreams. Or when I hear my mother talking: then, after twenty-four hours' immersion in that now distant sea, I find I can swim in it quite well. Or again, when I'm speaking a foreign language—Russian or English, for example, if I'm at a loss for a word or can't remember the grammar, I clutch at the old life-belt, suddenly swept my way by the original source: it wasn't so deeply buried after all. So it's not French that comes to the rescue when I flounder in what amounts to an artificial code, any more than when I'm suddenly too tired to add or multiply properly; no, the language that rises to the surface, and shows me beginnings, is Bulgarian.

And yet Bulgarian is already almost a dead language as far as I'm concerned. A part of me was gradually extinguished as I learned French, first with the Dominican nuns, then at the Alliance Française, and later at the university. Lastly, exile turned the old corpus into a corpse, which it replaced with another body altogether, at first frail and artificial, then more and more indispensable; and now, the sole survivor, my only living language, is French. Yet I'm almost prepared to believe in the Christian myth of resurrection when I listen, as through a stethoscope, to my own dual body and mind. For I don't definitively mourn the language of my childhood: that would imply decease, detachment, a scar, a forgetting. Instead, over that underground crypt, by that stagnant and decaying reservoir I've built a new home: I live in it, it lives in me, and it's here that unfolds what I make bold to call "*la vraie vie*," the true life of the mind and of the flesh.

I feel the indescribable impact of the pearly mist that skims the Atlantic marshes, absorbing as if into swirls of Chinese silk the shrieks of the laughing gulls and the nonchalant siesta of the mallard. I dream of a spring when motor cars will be scented and the poor horses will eat flowers: Apollinaire. From the vagueness which is my own immersion in being, which no swift word can sum up, for which "joy" is too ordinary and "ecstasy" too solemn, there emerges a serenity punctuated with French words. From the frontiers of my perceptions an almost imperceptible tremor reaches out to search for the French word, from somewhere high up, at the same time but in the opposite direction, a bright mass of accumulated lava, a hoard of French reading and conversation, sends down a luminous thread that may be scented out to give life to my serenity. In the alchemy of naming, I'm alone with the French language. To name "being" makes me be: and I live, body and soul, in French.

But whenever it comes to narrative, whenever, in other words, being presents itself as a story, a story perhaps about that pearly mist or those mallard ducks, or of course about a dream, a passion or a murder—a great swell not made up of words, but with its own special music, forces upon me a more ungainly syntax, together with metaphors from the ocean depths which have nothing to do with French clarity and politeness, but which suffuse my serenity with Byzantine unease. And then I'm trespassing against French taste. French taste is an act of politeness between people who share the same rhetoric—the same accumulation of images and phrases, the same background of reading and conversation—within a stable society. But despite the fact that I've found new life in French—and I've been doing so for nearly fifty years now—my own French taste can't always withstand the beat of an ancient music coiled around a still vigilant memory. My two communicating vessels bring forth a strange speech alien to itself, belonging neither here nor there, at once foreign and intimate. Like the characters in *Time Regained* whose long years of voluntary and involuntary memory Proust sees as embodied in vast tracts of space, I am a monster of the crossroads, a freak of the forum.

At the intersection of two languages and of at least two time dimensions, I fashion a language that seeks out facts and then inserts emotional references into them, and beneath the smooth appearances of French words, as highly polished as the stone of holy-water stoups, reveals glimpses of the blackened gilt of Orthodox icons. Well, at least the resulting freak—whether giant or dwarf—is never self-satisfied, though it does annoy the natives. Those of the country I came from *and* those of the country I came to.

Whenever this anxiety—it's like an air pocket, a shortness of breath, the effects of an amphetamine—calms down enough to explain itself, I might tell you what such creatures of the frontiers are like, these unclassifiable cosmopolitans among whom I count myself. For one thing, they're the heartbeat of a modern world which, because or in spite of the pressures of immigration and interbreeding, has managed to survive its famous lost values. As a result of this, they also personify a new positive attitude that is taking shape in opposition to national conformisms and international nihilisms. More precisely, in relation to history as told by the newspapers, there are two ways of facing up to Sarajevo and the Crimea. One is to promote national languages and cultures. The other is to encourage certain species which, though still rare, are in the process of proliferating; to protect such hybrid monsters as ourselves, migrant writers who run the obvious risk of falling between two stools. Why? In order to engender new creatures of language and blood who are rooted in no one language and no one blood; diplomats of the dictionary, genetic negotiators, wandering Jews of being who challenge all true and therefore belligerent citizens in the name of a nomadic humanity that will no longer sit still and keep quiet.

And where does suffering come in, among all these noble projects? I was expecting that question, but my answer is only half ready. There's an element of matricide in abandoning one's mother tongue, but if it has been painful for me to lose that Thracian bee-hive, the honey of my dreams, I've also been able to enjoy a kind of revenge, and above all take some pride in realizing an ideal first cherished by my native bees. To fly higher than one's parents did—higher, swifter, stronger. It's not for nothing that we're the heirs of the Greeks: our children will have Russian, English, French—the whole world—at their disposal. Exile, painful though it must always be, is the only way left to us, since Rabelais and the fall of the Berlin Wall, of looking for what the Fifth Book of *Pantagruel* calls the "divine bottle." This vessel is never found except by self-conscious searching, or in an exile exiling itself from the exile's certainty, the exile's arrogance. The loss is never-ending, and though a French transplant has given language and body new life, I go on listening to another pulse—that of the still corpse of my maternal memory, of what I might call my mother or native memory, as one talks of one's mother or native tongue. I speak deliberately of maternal rather than involuntary or unconscious memory, because, hovering at the edge both of musicked words and of inexpressible urges, close to the meaning as well as to the biological existence which my imagination is lucky enough to conjure up in French, is a remembrance of suffering. Bulgaria, my suffering: my sufferance.

It isn't me, it's my maternal memory, a warm, still-vocal corpse, a body within my body, that throbs in time with infra-sound and news items; with stifled loves and open conflicts; with Gregorian chant and commercial slogans; with childlike affections and awful mob violence; with political, economic, and ideological inanities; with puzzled citizens and ambitious brutes; with profiteers and slackers; with speculators in a hurry, with individualists devoid of either shame or object and with all of you who've been left behind by history but are trying to catch up without quite knowing how; you, invisible and undesirable Bulgarians, a white blot on the light; you sombre Balkan people, transfixed by the indifference of the Western world. To which I belong. Your compliments are reproaches; your thanks are like demands; your hopes start out depressed and fall asleep before they're even expressed; your songs weep, your laughter anticipates sorrow; you're not happy, you're not part of the game. Although you set out too soon you arrive too late, in a world too old but always pretending to be younger, a world that dislikes latecomers. For some unknown reason, or none, you think the world owes you a living: you want everything, but you also want to doze, to laze, to avoid the issue, to beat around the bush and cheat, and maybe sometimes work yourselves to death, though why on earth should you? You hurt me, *mes semblables, mes frères.* Bulgaria, my sufferance.

FRANCE, MY SUFFERING

I maintain a dialogue with Bulgaria in this experience of the "other language", but it is clear that in "suffering" or more freely "suff(e)rance" there is the word "France". In fact, my dialogue is addressed as much if not more to the chosen language as to the given language.

The logical clarity of French, the impeccable precision of the vocabulary, and the exactness of the grammar appeal to my rigorous mind and provides—not without suffering—an exactitude to my bond with the dark sea of passion. I regret having abandoned the often undecidable lexical ambiguities and the multiple meanings of the Bulgarian idiom—so foreign to Cartesianism—resonating with heartfelt passions and hidden sentiments. But I love the Latin rule of the concept, the obligation to choose in order to follow that classic unfolding of an argument, and the impossibility of equivocating in judgment which, when all is said and done, turns out to be more political than moral in French. I am enchanted by Mallarmé's ellipses: so many contradictions in the apparent blankness of an insignificant content gives each word the hardness of diamond, the unpredictability of the fall of dice. But rather than this monitored music of meaning, I prefer the metaphoric profusion and the syntactic hyperbole of Proust and the pagan flavor of the prolix Colette. They teach me that even the writer writing in his native language never stops being a translator of his concealed passions, that the basic language he enjoys translating is the language of sensitivity. And that this nameless foundation, this hint of our innermost being and dreams never entirely fades, and is never diminished, in the codes of schools, clans, institutions, or the media.

My adjustment to this other language, which I have been speaking for fifty years now, has been such that I am almost ready to believe those Americans who consider me to be a French intellectual and writer. And yet, sometimes, when I return from a trip in the east, the west, the north or south, I feel out of place in these French discourses which turn their back on the evil and the misery of the world and which glorify the tradition of aloofness—when it's not nationalism—as a solution to our century which, alas, is neither the "great century" nor that of "the Enlightenment."

There's nothing more tedious, after a day of psychoanalytic sessions, than to talk with or to read some journalist, some worthy successor of Verdurin, dishing up the stereotypes of stylistic and philosophical protectionism. The French outdo themselves in false praise, shallow enthusiasms and extravagant acclaim of those who "belong". The rhetoric of ceremonial optimism beyond a melancholy that is more feigned than felt, and this penchant for values and a conventional turn of phrase, are not the signs of an ancient culture that respects itself, and wants to escape passing modernist fads. Rather, they reveal the private foundations of what some people—more numerous than one might think—turn into a nationalist and racist ideology. This foundation is nothing less than a fascination with an identity that celebrates itself through the family, of course, as well as through blood and soil, but also, and often above all, through the rhythms of language, as our parents, teachers and ancestors have passed it on to us. More reluctant to intermarry than the English, less adaptable to change than the youthful Americans and, despite everything, the Russians, the French today tend to indulge in their untranslatable authenticity. In short, a temple that certain institutions and press organs—more than writers themselves who are, by definition, sensitive and nomadic—use to perpetuate close-mindedness.

The foreigner-translator of the other language is required to fit in: distance disturbs, no one needs a night watchman. If he becomes concerned, engages in discussion or criticizes, he is accused of passing judgment on France; French national hackles rise; as in the times of Aeschylus, foreigners are only allowed one form of expression—that of "supplicants."

And yet I love returning to France. I wrote this in *Possessions*, and will repeat it: I love returning to France. No more opacity, no dramas, no enigmas. The clarity of the language and of the crisp, chill sky. Each tree along the road makes a sweeping bow. Here, scandals are always sexual, sometimes violently so; however, when they are really erotic, the fury evaporates. Fields are divided into evenly-shaped rectangles, the ancient geometry of the Romans, Gauls and other self-confident, yet gracious owners. I know very well that there is France and France, and that all French people are not as limpidly clear as they would like to believe. But when I return from Santa Barbara, this is how I see things. There is not an inch of landscape that is not studied; here, to be is immediately to be logical. Those delicate young elms, those sculpted gardens, those managed marshes mix with people who *are* because they *think*. But here effort dissolves; argumentation, however interminable, turns toward seduction and irony.

Many people love Italy, and I am one of them: a profusion of surprising beauty, creating an excitement that melts into serenity. Others prefer Spain: haughty because it's unreasonable, mystical, nonchalant. I, myself, have taken refuge in France, for good.

I used to know someone who only began enjoying life again once he had put his hand in the hollow made by millions of pilgrims in the stone at Santiago de Compostella: time embodied in this void with a human shape helped him learn to live with the present—and eternity. Twenty-five thousand years before him, on the wall of a deep rocky inlet at Marseilles, a Cro-Magnon laid his hand and breathed all around the black paint. Two hundred and forty hands in the Gargas cave, at the foot of the Pyrenees. The species was looking for shelter; but already proud of itself, it left its imprint on time that extends through to us.

All the same, I house my body in the logical landscape of France; I take shelter in the gentle, charming, relaxed streets of Paris, brush past strangers who deny themselves—quite deliberately—any intimacy, however inscrutable and, on the whole, polite. They built Notre-Dame and the Louvre, conquered Europe and a large part of the world, and then returned home because they prefer pleasures that are close to reality. But because they also prefer pleasure to reality, they continue to believe that they are the masters of the world, or at least a great power. A world—irritated, condescending, fascinated—that seems ready to follow them. To follow us. Often grudgingly, but all the same, for the time being. Here, human violence has given way to a liking for laughter, while a discreet accumulation of pleasures now makes it clear that the future is synonymous with leisure. Consequently, crime fiction barely exists in France, unless it's redolent with nonsense. I have already forgotten the death that prevails in Santa Barbara.

In sum, I would say that when all is said and done, everything in me adores the French language, the "other language", because one of the greatest writers, perhaps the greatest of the 20th century, was a translator. I am, of course, referring to Proust.

PROUST THE TRANSLATOR

This tormented man, half Jew and a homosexual who didn't want to be "one of them"—either a Jew, or a Frenchman, or a homosexual — chose only one country: writing as translation. Many critics have emphasized the fact that while translating Ruskin with the help of his mother and his friend, Marie Nordlinger, Proust had found in the translation, strictly speaking, the model of his poetic creed.[1] "I still have two Ruskins to do, and after that I will try to translate my poor soul, if it hasn't perished in the meantime," he wrote to Barrès in March 1904. The metaphor of translation punctuates his writing in *Remembrance of Things Past* and it is found in crucial passages where the narrator describes his aesthetics. For example, in reference to Elstir, he says "...if God the Father had created things by naming them, then by taking their names away or by giving them another one, Elstir recreates them."[2] Elstir, that is Proust. The author of what he himself defines as "this essential book, the only true book, [that] a great writer doesn't have to invent, in the current sense, since it already exists in each of us, but to translate. The duty and the task of a writer are those of a translator."[3]

But what people forget to mention, however, is that the language Proust translated into French wasn't another idiom that already existed, as in the case of English for instance, or Bulgarian for me. What Proust the writer—and the foreigner, this translator—transfers into the language of his community is the singular language of his "involuntary memory" and his "sensations." Does this mean that what is to be translated is the unconscious personal, alien to the community and irreducible? Certainly, provided that the unconscious is freed from the linguistic influence of which it has all too easily become a prisoner, and is given back its passionate, impulsive and sensory secrets, which Proust himself found necessary.

This sensitive "language" is not a language of signs: it is a "language" in inverted commas, a chaos and an order of rhythms, impressions, agonies and ecstasies at the boundaries of unformulable biology. This "language" is the true "foreignness"—more foreign than any idiom that already exists—that the foreigner hopes to express.

Throughout my presentation, I have used the metaphor of the foreigner as a translator and a writer. Now, I would like to invert the movement to enable you to appreciate the role of the writer who, in a single language, translates an insurgent sensory foreignness. As a translator in this sense, the writer is radically other—the most scandalous of foreigners. Proust knew this. Let's listen to him.

Before actually "translating", one must first "decipher": deciphering a "truth that cannot be seen", but that we "feel inside" and whose climatic pleasure (*jouissance*) can only be reached provided that "it be created": "So, there is nothing more precious—no matter how stunted this kind of impression my appear, the matter to which it refers—than those impressions which guide us from the stabs of truth that we feel inside. They are what is most precious in the world, because they can create truth—the pleasure of which is the only thing that leads our mind to greater perfection and pure joy. Not the truth that, with almost the same words, some call the humble truth that is observed and noted, that adorns the outside of things like a humble and characteristic branch that is planted there, but a truth that is not seen, which is expected, that has gone into hiding and that can only be attained provided that it is created, by so completely reviving the impression that contains it that, along with it its innermost heart is revived: truth. And this, its reality, passes by our doorstep and leaves us a note about it written in cryptographic characters that we don't even take the effort to deciphers."[4]

Clearly exposed in the Library of the Guermantes, a glimpse of this truth to be deciphered and translated is already announced in *Contre Saint-Beuve* like an osmosis between "mother language" and "our sensitivity", and takes on the Baudelairian aspect of the "perfume of the native land": "The symbolists will certainly be the first to admit that what each word retains, in its figure or in its harmony, of the charm of its origin or of the grandeur of its past, has an evocative power on our imagination and our sensitivity at least as great as its power of strict meaning. These are old and mysterious affinities between our mother language and our sensitivity which, instead of a conventional language, as with foreign languages, make it a kind of latent music that the poet can make resonate within us with incomparable sensitivity. He can give a word new life by using an old meaning, he can conjure up between two unrelated images forgotten harmonies; at any time, he lets us smell with delight the perfume of the native land."[5]

Later, Proust is careful to emphasize the fact that this deciphering is not an intellectual operation and is not one of the "intellectual truths" but rather "an impression" and "a personal effort": "The truths that intelligence understands directly and clearly in full daylight are less profound, less essential than those which, despite ourselves, life has communicated to us as an impression."[6] "What we did not have to decipher, to clarify with our personal effort, what was clear before us, is not ours."[7]

We are confronted with a depth of psyche distinct from the exterior superficial ego, and which Proust calls an "intermediate region," "material" however coiled within the body, which thought, like a "probe," proposes to bring out into the light, and translate. "So, that which is obscurely present deep down in the depths of consciousness, before it is made into a finished work, before it is brought out, must cross an intermediate region between the obscure self and the outside, our intelligence; but how can it be brought out, how can it be grasped?"[8] "The great difficulty is that the truth is hidden under something material, a simple form. How would I bring it out? I have felt I could do so by touching with thought this image in my mind; that under it, there is something; but what? Once again, I'm driving my thoughts like a probe and I am looking for the precise point of the image, where I have felt something, until I have found it; my thought has come up against something small that brings it to a halt—what I mean is a hitherto unencountered thought within me."[9]

UNCONSCIOUS DRAFT OR THE DRAFTED UNCONSCIOUS: LITERARY EXPERIENCE

Along the path of this translating probe lies the experience of writing in stages: an experience in which I cannot avoid the question of drafts. Indeed, if there is an undefined and perhaps undefinable meaning, then how can it lead to verbalized signification?

So, you see that the draft can acquire the dignity of placing us at the heart of phenomenology, if not theology.

For too long, a small group of people (Jakobson, Barthes, Kristeva) has been asserting against the salons, ideologues and functionaries who have been appropriating literature—that it is a *text*. A rescue operation, though a limited one. Drafts *can* lift this veil from experience underlying the text. Proust and the literary experience suggests just that: recreating experience in the text. An appeal to the reader's reason, imagination and unconscious.

Experience *Erlebnis* or *Erfahrung*? In this religious, hermeneutic and philosophical tradition, experience (read Hegel and Heidegger) implies a co-presence with the fullness of Being when it is not a fusion with God. Experience enables a new object to burst forth: immediate seizure, sudden appearance, inspiration *(Erlebnis)*. From this bursting forth, it later becomes knowledge, patient learning *(Erfahrung)*. From confused apparition, experience extracts a vision, a perspective, finally knowledge.

Opening onto the other which exalts or unsettles me, experience finds its anthropological foundations in my ties with the primary object: the mother, the archaic pole of needs, desires, love and repulsion *(Powers of Horror + Stories of Love)*. Whether we experienced it in the cosmos or with a paternal god, or through the critical control of sounds, colors, and language, experience unveils the narcissistic incompleteness of the subject and the dramas of his or her individuation. There reside depressions, hallucinations, desires and all the graces and joys created through understanding, reunion, or independence.

Thus, deriving from my most inaccessible memories, experience leads my *infantilism* to the most developed spheres of my culture and, conversely, it irradiates my culture from the most secret traumas engraved in my psyche and in my body.

Whether it be a felt emotion or an active synthesis, or both at once, experience traverses the social and verbal events of the subject and completely modifies its psychic makeup. It is also inseparable from desire and love. In and through these, experience is lived as a *conversion*. Both psychology *and* representation, experience marks a fragile, painful and jubilant link between body and thought, thereby making these distinctions obsolete.

I understand why Proust spoke of literary experience as "transsubstantiation."[10]

I call *literature* that which testifies from experience. When I write *The Samurai* or *The Old Man and the Wolves* or *Possessions*, I am on a journey, a crossing—to the end of the night; to the exhilaration of a pregnancy that I carry in the marshes of the Atlantic; to the impossible tears brought on by my father's murder in Bulgaria; to the deadly passions that a woman experiences but also inflicts in the experience of this feminine condition that many people speak of but are reluctant to see as a savage crime story.

This disturbance, this plunge, this "I as other" gives me access to the *dark continents* of my unconscious, but as well to the regions prior to meaning, sensation, perception that should be of interest to analytic theory but unfortunately are not (except in a few of Julia Kristeva's papers when she reads Merleau-Ponty). Add to this the rhythms, melodies, scansions—so many pre-syntactic and "semiotic" approaches, which in my view underlie "language"; forms of music that, for me, join up with French and Slav singing exercises, and produce a strange sound, that some people find disagreeable or in not very good taste—not French, in fact. In any case, it is a matter of sound, and therefore of a monstrous intimacy, perhaps even more monstrous than that of the giants at the end of *Time Regained*. For, not content simply to convert time into resonant, semantic, linguistic space, my own intimacy (my own experience) adds to French language another time of another language.

In short, experience mobilizes the unconscious, perception, prelanguage and language. The dynamic of experience is *in large part secret*. I mean that it winds its way through my nights or in opaque awakenings, and is realized in figures without words, in heavy sensations of pleasure and anxiety, and sometimes reaches words or even throws up sparkling ideas—and, by the next morning, I can't even recall why they appealed to me anyway. *But this development precedes the draft; its fluidity slips away. I am in a state of writing, a state of mind outside of the draft*: a sort of timelessness (since the draft places me in a temporality of work). That state of writing can be accompanied by *notes*: a pre-draft, fleeting trace, a word, a metaphor, flashes of wit, thoughts, always fragments, captures of the unusual, a glimpse of the writing state.

The stage of the draft is already a second stage. The experience slides with increasing precision from seizure to its patient *clarification,* to its *knowledge.* It's a matter of finding a fluid trace, what "will have happened", a "future perfect" as Mallarmé so well put it; and by writing it, by materializing it in language on the page, enriching it, modifying it and bringing it into final and definitive existence. Given that the final version is rarely definitively satisfying, it only becomes so when a coherent and cadenced piece of work encounters unconscious desire and yields a degree of *pleasure;* but also by a kind of *economy of effort,* when pleasure renounces the pursuit of perfection, when perfection becomes tedious, and one decides to leave it at that—the cusp of indifference.

During this factual writing, draft writing, feeling continues to surface, and the unconscious to astound; but the essence (or at least the specificities) of the draft lies in the *putting into language*—which comprises, when I think about it afterwards, two strategies:

— the choice of words (where I am under the influence of primary processes and music);

— the construction of phrasing, which is dominated by logic and, again, by music memory.

In the draft, one can discern this level of passing from experience to text. An *intermediate stage*. A stage of *craftsmanship.* A *crossroads* between:

1. Dream states where, conscious censorship being weakened, dazzling access to the Unconscious, to feeling, to Being is acquired.
2. Putting it into final form.

If we consider the draft as a transition (neither an origin, nor a completion): then the draft of the unconscious is, in reality, an unconscious already drafted, or rather scrambled, *une sorte de brouillon brouillé,* but certainly more exposed than the final form.

IS THE WRITER A FOREIGNER?

From the foreigner whom I have defined as a translator to the writer whom I have accompanied translating the world of feeling in its singularity: are we all foreigners?

I know how this emotive cry of the humanist conscience concerned about fighting against "exclusion" may appear demagogic and irritating. We are not all foreigners, and many writers have not been zealous ideologues of national nationalist, or Fascist identity, but have very sincerely, and without these excesses, regarded themselves as linked by the umbilical cord of codes!

It hasn't even entered the minds of many of them that the expression "foreign to the language" that Mallarmé wanted to write, or the "translation" of "feeling" that Proust envisaged, far from being extravagantly exceptional, are the very essence of creativity.

I would here like to emphasize this intrinsic and often unsuspected relation between the foreigner and the writer, to bring the two of them together in the shared yet still singular experience of translation.

I shall even go further. If we weren't all translators, if we didn't ceaselessly expose the foreignness of our private life, its infringements of the stereotyped codes known as national languages, in order to transpose it again into other signs, would we have a psychic life? Would we be living beings? "To be foreign" to oneself and to be the conveyer of this continuously rediscovered foreignness: isn't this how we combat our latent psychoses and succeed where the psychotic or autistic fail? That is, in going from time lost, through time regained, to time sensitive. Which is to tell you that, in my opinion, speaking "another language" is quite simply the minimal and primary condition of being alive.

Translated from French by Barbara Bray, Granville Fields and Mike Westlake. Presented by Julia Kristeva in November 1996 as Visiting Gildersleene Professor for French and English at Barnard College, New York.

1. Bizub, Edward. *La Venise inférieure*, La Baconnière, Neuchâtel, 1991.

2. *A la recherche du temps perdu*, I,JFF, Bibliothèque de la Pléiade, Gallimard, Paris, 19??, p. 835.

3. *A la recherche du temps perdu*, IV, TR, p. 469.

4. Bonnet, Henri and Bernard Brun. *Matinée chez la princesse de Guermantes*, Gallimard, 1982, p. 337.

5. CSB, Bibliothèque de la Pliade, Gallimard, p. 392-393.
6. *A la recherche du temps perdu*, IV, TR, p. 457.
7. Ibid., p. 459.
8 *Le Carnet de 1908*, Etudes proustiennes n' 8, Cahiers Marcel Proust, Gallimard, Paris, 19??, p. 102.
9. *Ibid*, note 6, p. 22.
10. Letter to Lucien Daudet, 1913, November 27. Transvertébration CS I 10, Transvertébration.

AGENT DE L'ETRANGER (FOREIGN AGENT)

SYLVÈRE LOTRINGER- RAINER GANAHL

Rainer Ganahl: Vous avez créé la revue "Semiotext(e)" et une maison d'édition du même nom qui a traduit et introduit la pensée française contemporaine aux Etats-Unis. J'aimerais savoir quand votre revue a commencé à paraître, quels sont les auteurs et les premiers textes que vous avez publiés?

Sylvère Lotringer: "Semiotext(e)" a commencé à paraître en 1974 et les volumes de la désormais fameuse collection *Foreign Agents* ont été introduits neuf ans plus tard, à l'arrivée de mon co-editeur, Jim Fleming, quand il m'a semblé que l'audience de la revue, tirée à 5.000 exemplaires, était devenue suffisante pour assurer leur réception. (Le titre *Foreign Agents* était un pied de nez à tous ceux qui, aux États-Unis, auraient pu nous accuser d'être des agents de l'étranger, autrement dit des espions à la solde de l'ennemi. "Ne vous en donnez pas la peine, nous le faisons nous-mêmes!" L'ennemi, c'était en fait toute réappropriation institutionnelle, université, monde artistique, ou idéologie de parade). Il y avait une autre raison majeure: aucune des maisons d'édition que j'avais contactées à l'époque pour les publier n'avait manifesté le moindre intérêt. C'était trop spécialisé, m'a-t-on dit, ça n'intéressera personne. Alors j'ai décidé de les publier moi-même. C'est comme cela que je suis devenu éditeur, malgré moi. Ces maisons d'édition qui faisaient la fine bouche sont les mêmes qui, quinze ans plus tard, se sont précipitées sur ces mêmes auteurs pour les acheter à prix d'or, et les recouvrir de commentaires critiques, analytiques, parasitaires, déconstructivistes, de gloses académiques à n'en plus finir, bref les pompes funèbres de l'industrie culturelle américaine.

Au fil des années la revue a publié tous ceux qu'à l'époque j'avais déjà appelés *post-structuralistes*, Félix Guattari, Julia Kristeva, Luce Irigaray, Gilles Deleuze, Jacques Lacan, Michel Foucault, Jacques

Derrida, Jean-François Lyotard, Toni Negri, et bien d'autres. Tous ceux qui cherchaient à échapper au modèle linguistique et aux universaux logiques construits par Ferdinand de Saussure et ses émules. Jean Baudrillard et Paul Virilio, les extrémistes de la théorie, anges exterminateurs et "extrapolationnistes", sont venus dans un second temps. "Simulations" de Baudrillard et "Pure War", que j'ai écrit en collaboration avec Paul Virilio, ont été parmi les premiers textes théoriques publiés en volume. Le troisième était un recueil de textes de Deleuze et Guattari que j'avais également édité pour l'occasion en 1983: "On The Line".

R. G.: Comment avez-vous fondé la revue "Semiotext(e)"?

S. L.: Pour fonder une revue il faut un groupe, un projet et des contacts précis. Rien de cela n'existait au départ, et il a fallu deux ans pour que ces conditions se trouvent réunies, par hasard ou délibérément. Je suis arrivé à New York en 1972 pour occuper un poste de professeur de littérature française à l'Université de Columbia. Il y avait là un petit nombre d'étudiants et de jeunes chercheurs formés à la linguistique, ce qui était assez exceptionnel à l'époque. Nous avons immédiatement constitué un groupe de travail dont le but était d'étudier, en termes un peu pompeux, "les fondements épistémologiques de la sémiotique". Nous nous inspirions des travaux de Gaston Bachelard, de Louis Althusser et de Jacques Lacan dans une perspective néo-marxiste en fin de compte assez inoffensive puisque typiquement académique. Notre but était de définir une sémiotique *matérialiste* et cela m'a amené à m'intéresser aux recherches de Félix Guattari sur les flux de signes et à celles de Julia Kristeva sur ce qu'elle appelait la *chora*, le stade pré-verbal qui prélude à l'instauration du signe (tous deux ont été publiés dans le no 1 de la revue). Je suis ensuite allé moi-même à Genève consulter les manuscrits de Ferdinand de Saussure. Il y a en effet un tout autre aspect de son travail, une folie des signes qui allait tout à fait à rebours de cette science linguistique qu'il avait contribué à fonder. Comme vous le savez, Saussure était obsédé par l'idée qu'il existait une pratique occulte, des mots sacrés cachés sous les mots selon des procédés "anagrammatiques" précis. C'était, en somme, le retour du délire dans la science. Je me suis toujours intéressé au délire, qui est en quelque sorte au plus près de la réalité capitaliste. C'est ce qui m'a intéressé chez Dali, Céline, Simone Weil, Artaud, et c'est ce qui m'a rapproché des analyses de Deleuze et Guattari. Un délire est toujours politique, au sens large, et tout ce que j'ai fait avec "Semiotext(e)" est toujours allé dans ce sens. Rien à voir avec les petits jeux binaires de la sémiotique classique.

En fait, l'aspect sémiotique proprement dit de "Semiotext(e)" – y compris son bilinguisme initial, signalé par le (e) entre parenthèses – a été rapidement abandonné, ou plutôt, il s'est radicalement transformé. Du jour au lendemain, la revue a cessé d'être une réflexion *sur* la sémiotique pour devenir une sorte de sémiotique *en acte*, un activisme des signes, une manipulation de textes et d'images fondée sur le refus de toute médiation. S'y est substituée la pratique du collage, des juxtapositions intempestives, des changements de contextes et autres dérapages calculés. Rien de cela n'était gratuit: il s'agissait de multiplier les contrastes et de complexifier les points de vue au moyen d'un humour imperceptible capable de suggérer les idées plus qu'il ne les énonçait. C'était, en quelque sorte, la pensée à l'état pur, sans introduction ni commentaire parasite, une réflexion capable de garder sa puissance de conviction et de métamorphose. La philosophie elle-même y était présentée comme "document" au même titre que les autres, sans explication ou argument d'autorité. C'était sortir de l'université pour entrer – par une porte étroite – dans le monde de l'art.

C'est à partir de ce moment que le groupe d'origine a commencé à se désagréger. De jeunes artistes se sont proposés à y participer. Le format de la revue a changé. De nouvelles stratégies ont été inventées. "Semiotext(e)" est devenu une présence "étrangère", mais familière, dans le monde artistique américain. Il n'en a jamais fait partie, puisqu'il s'est toujours refusé à en faire le commentaire. Nous avons rarement reçu de financement officiel, et les rares fois où cela s'est produit, cette aide nous a rapidement été retirée – par exemple après la parution d'un numéro jugé "scandaleux" en hauts lieux sur la *Polysexuality*. Je n'ai jamais recherché le scandale, mais les aspects controversés sont évidemment les plus problématiques, ceux qui demandent un effort de réflexion, et je n'ai jamais hésité à en traiter, qu'il s'agisse de pédophilie, de "terrorisme" (ce dont les autonomes italiens, des philosophes politiques à leur manière, ont été accusés à l'époque), ou des *black panthers*.

L'élément décisif a été la rencontre que j'ai faite personnellement, entre 1972 et 1974, d'un certain nombre de penseurs français. On m'avait en effet confié pendant deux ans la direction de l'école d'été de Columbia à Paris et j'en ai profité pour y inviter tous ceux dont je découvrais alors les recherches et avec qui j'avais le désir de travailler: Gilles Deleuze, Félix Guattari, Julia Kristeva, Jacques Lacan, entre d'autres. C'était en même temps établir, en France même, un premier contact entre des philosophes français et de jeunes intellectuels américains.

R. G.: Est-ce à ce moment que la théorie française a commencé à pénétrer aux Etats-Unis?

S. L.: Pas exactement. On peut en fait dater avec précision le moment où la théorie française a fait son entrée massive aux États-Unis. Cela s'est produit au cours du colloque *Schizo-culture* que *Semiotext(e)* a organisé en 1975 dans les locaux de *Columbia University.* Près de deux mille new-yorkais y ont participé, radicaux, artistes, intellectuels de tous ordres. Inutile de le dire, ce n'était pas un colloque ordinaire et il y eut des confrontations parfois violentes provoquées tant par des désaccords tactiques entre les clans français et américains que par des attaques montées par des "agitateurs" politiques prétendument de gauche, en fait venus semer le trouble à la faveur de ce que Michel Foucault avait appelé sarcastiquement, "le dernier événement contre-culturel des années soixante." R.D. Laing et Michel Foucault, entre autres, ont été publiquement pris à partie et accusés d'être des espions à la solde de la *CIA*, ce qui a jeté pas mal de confusion dans les esprits.

R. G.: *Schizo-culture* était, je crois, une référence aux théories de Deleuze et Guattari.

S. L.: Effectivement. Je venais de passer une année en France et je m'étais passionné pour *L'Anti-Oedipe*, qui venait tout juste de paraître. Cette année-là j'avais participé de près aux réunions du groupe *Recherches* de Guattari à Paris et le premier numéro de "Semiotext(e)" sur "Les Deux Saussure" avait en fait d'abord été publié en France, et en français, dans sa revue. J'avais beaucoup d'amitié pour Felix et grâce à lui j'ai eu également l'occasion d'observer l'impact de ses théories "anti-psychiatriques" à la Clinique de La Borde, à 100 km au Sud de Paris. Le colloque *Schizo-culture* de New York cristallisait donc toutes mes préoccupations du moment, jusqu'à mon désir d'établir un pont entre la France et les Etats-Unis, ce qui voulait essentiellement dire New York, que j'aimais alors (et que j'aime toujours) avec passion. *Schizo-culture* a donc traité de la folie et de la prison, ces deux aspects développés par Michel Foucault, Deleuze et Guattari et Jean-François Lyotard, que j'avais tous invités à venir à New York pour participer à ce colloque. Au dernier moment j'avais réussi à adjoindre à ce groupe l'anti-psychiatre anglais Ronald D. Laing, qui se trouvait être de passage à Boston, ainsi que des représentants des ex-psychiatrisés et des ex-prisonniers. Plus que l'audience universitaire proprement dite (l'université suit toujours, comme l'intendance) j'espérais pouvoir faire la jonction entre des forces réelles de la société américaine et des éléments de la réflexion françaisequi les anticipaient sans toujours en avoir conscience.

R. G.: Et vous croyez que cela s'est fait?

S. L.: En partie du moins. On ne sait jamais très bien ce qu'une idée (ou n'importe quoi d'ailleurs) va devenir en Amérique, et s'il est préférable qu'elle échoue ou qu'elle réussisse. En fin de compte, cela revient un peu au même, le "produit" finit toujours par vous échapper et suivre la pente du système. Ce qui m'avait frappé précisément dans "L'Anti-Oedipe", c'est la description originale qu'ils donnaient du capitalisme comme un processus anarchique, créateur et schizophrénique. Cela correspondait exactement à la réalité new-yorkaise dont je faisais alors l'expérience. D'où l'idée qui m'est venue de donner à l'Amérique les instruments théoriques dont elle avait besoin pour comprendre le fonctionnement effectif de sa propre société. En fait, les choses se sont passées autrement, car ce qui fait la force de la société américaine, justement, c'est son aveuglement systématique à sa propre réalité. La théorie française a fini par devenir une marchandise comme tout le reste, soumise aux fluctuations et saturations du marché intellectuel. Ce n'était pas exactement ce que j'espérais, mais cela a confirmé paradoxalement mon analyse. J'étais conscient qu'une fois transportées de l'autre côté de l'Atlantique, ces idées pouvaient prendre une portée pragmatique. C'est d'ailleurs ce côté pragmatique (et politique) qui m'avait tout de suite attiré dans les théories de Foucault, Deleuze et Guattari. J'entrevoyais alors la possibilité d'un *pragmatisme théorique* nourri à la fois par l'Europe et l'Amérique. Les Américains se trouvant avant être à l'époque terriblement anti-intellectuels, j'ai vite appris à laisser les concepts se déposer au fond de la tasse, comme le marc de café. A bien des égards, je suis devenu plus Américain que les Américains eux-mêmes, puisqu'ils ont fini, eux, par adopter la théorie française avec autant de furie qu'ils la refusaient au départ. Je ne me rendais pas compte, évidemment, que ce pragmatisme américain allait exactement en sens inverse: la transformation de la théorie française en *lingua franca*, en produit intellectuel de luxe, en capital d'exclusivité, en mode de promotion (carrières) et de production (l'industrie "critique") selon les lois de gravité de la culture américaine. C'est ce qui était arrivé à la psychanalyse. Freud avait craint d'apporter la peste aux Etats-Unis; en réalité il a fini par lui procurer un puissant instrument de normalisation. Et pour des raisons que Freud lui-même n'avait pas soupçonnées. Car la société américaine n'est pas particulièrement névrosée, bien au contraire: elle est même foncièrement *psychotique*. Lacan ne l'a pas compris qui était pourtant un spécialiste de la psychose: la société américaine a besoin de *produire de la névrose* (et non pas de la guérir) afin de se protéger de sa propre folie. D'où le succès de l'*ego psychology*, qui n'est pas une trahison de Freud, comme Lacan le pensait, mais une adaptation judicieuse de la tradition analytique européenne aux besoins pratiques de la culture américaine. Car ce n'est jamais la vérité qui est en question dans une théorie, mais son usage effectif dans un contexte bien circonscrit.

D'emblée, donc, ce qui m'a intéressé, ça n'a pas été d'importer la théorie française "en général" aux États-Unis, mais de mettre en circulation dans des secteurs particuliers de la réalité américaine des concepts précis selon des modes d'insertion spécifiques (par la revue, par des événements publics, conférences, concerts, performances, par des livres conçus en vue de toucher un certain public). Et c'est ce qui s'est effectivement passé. La *Schizo-culture*, en somme, ce n'était pas du tout la France, ou la pensée française, c'était la réalité new-yorkaise, le *heart of darkness* du capitalisme contemporain, et c'est cela que j'ai toujours cherché à cerner dans mon travail.

R. G.: Vous avez invité un certain nombre d'artistes à participer au colloque *Schizo-culture*. Qu'attendiez-vous d'eux?

S. L.: C'était une autre idée-force de ce colloque. Dès mon arrivée à New York je me suis rendu compte qu'à la différence des penseurs français, les véritables intellectuels américains ne se trouvaient pas dans l'université, ou ne maniaient pas forcément des concepts: ils faisaient partie du monde artistique. C'étaient des créateurs de formes, des inventeurs d'idées, des expérimentateurs dans le domaine de la musique, de la danse, de la peinture, de la littérature. C'est pourquoi, même si des philosophes et psychiatres américains ont été invités au colloque *Schizo-culture*, j'avais surtout en tête de faire se rencontrer pour la première fois à New York des penseurs français et ceux qui m'apparaissent comme leurs exacts répondants américains: William Burroughs, John Cage, Merce Cunningham, Richard Foreman, etc.. Je crois que c'est cela qui a été l'aspect le plus prometteur de cette rencontre, la jonction de la pensée théorique avec la pratique artistique. L'université, aux États-Unis, c'est l'industrie lourde. Cela met du temps à se mettre en branle, mais à partir de là c'est le rouleau compresseur du commentaire, de l'analyse, de la paraphrase. C'est l'extermination des idées par saturation du commentaire. Ce qui est arrivé à Freud est en train de se produire avec Foucault, Derrida, Baudrillard, etc. La réification de la pensée française par la machine académique. Le monde artistique, surtout au départ (il a bien changé depuis) m'est toujours apparu plus aventureux, plus risqué, puisqu'au plus près des flux du capital. Ce sont les artistes que j'ai essentiellement visés avec "Semiotext(e)" – les artistes, pas le monde artistique; les étudiants, pas l'université. Les artistes, les jeunes de tous bords, les punks de l'époque, les jeunes universitaires, les activistes politiques ont toujours été notre public. C'est pourquoi le prix de la revue ou des volumes a toujours été maintenu extrêmement bas. Ma première grande expérience new-yorkaise, cela a été les concerts de Patti Smith, des Ramones et de Television à ce petit club miteux sur la Bowery, CBGB, et à Max Kansas City, près d'Union Square, en 1973, quand leur public ne comportait encore qu'une poignée de fans. Du jour au lendemain cela a changé ma vision des choses. En un sens, je n'en suis jamais revenu.

R. G.: Pour terminer cette interview j'aimerais bien revenir sur une question qui concerne une autre sorte d'importation: c'est celle du fascisme en France. Vous vous êtes intéressé de très près au fascisme et aux intellectuels française impliqués dans cette sombre histoire.

S. L.: Oui, et cette seconde importation n'est pas étrangère à la première. Après tout, ce n'est pas par hasard si j'ai fini par m'installer aux États-Unis plutôt que de rester en France. Un Vichy m'a suffi. J'appartiens à une génération qui a grandi à l'ombre de la guerre et des camps de concentration sans en avoir pourtant souffert directement. Bien sûr, comme beaucoup d'autres enfants juifs, j'ai passé la guerre sous une fausse identité, caché dans une famille française, transbahuté d'un à l'autre endroit selon les dangers du moment. Et si moi et mes proches en sommes sortis vivants, c'est dû au hasard, à la chance, et à la générosité de certaines gens. Mais je mentirais si je disais que cette période ne m'a pas marqué profondément. Elle a imprégné ma vie de bien des façons, sans que j'en aie toujours eu conscience. J'ai passé une grande partie de ma jeunesse dans des mouvements sionistes en réaction contre l'humiliation que nous avions ressentie. Et c'est bien plus tard, en regardant le film de Jacques Lanzmann, *Shoah,* que j'ai finalement accepté qu'on puisse avoir été une victime sans jamais avoir eu la possibilité de résister. Pendant longtemps j'ai tiré de cette expérience une exigence morale qui était peut-être trop absolue et j'en ai beaucoup voulu à ceux que la mémoire des atrocités ne portait pas naturellement du côté de toutes les victimes. A cet égard, la guerre d'Algérie a été une révélation et une libération. J'ai milité dans le mouvement étudiant français en faveur des algériens rebelles alors que la communauté juive française était divisée entre ses convictions de gauche et sa solidarité avec Israël. Je me suis senti floué quand je me suis rendu compte que certain juifs pouvaient trahir leur histoire tout comme les autres et abandonner les victimes d'une répression politique au nom d'une solidarité étroite avec leur propre communauté. Il m'a fallu longtemps pour me rendre compte que la volonté n'est pas suffisante pour se débarrasser d'une telle expérience. C'était comme un voile qui n'en finissait pas de se lever, comme si, physiquement, j'avais perdu ma voix. Pendant longtemps je ne me suis senti le droit de parler qu'en empruntant la voix des autres. C'est cette sorte de dépossession qui, au départ, m'a attiré chez Antonin Artaud. C'est aussi ce qui, pendant toute une période de ma vie, m'a attiré vers l'interview comme une nouvelle forme d'écriture. Le volume "New Yorker Gespräche" ou mes interviews sur l'art ainsi que mes dialogues avec Paul Virilio et Jean Baudrillard sont venus de là. Il a aussi fallu des années pour que l'anglais devienne pour moi une langue de travail alors que le français, parallèlement avait cessé d'être une langue vivante. Je me trouvais entre deux langues, entre deux cultures et donc étranger aux deux, mais aussi, paradoxalement, libre de choisir dans les deux ce qui me paraissait convenir le mieux à ma situation présente. Sans doute mon rapport à la pensée française a été de cet ordre, une sorte de ventriloquie par défaut dont j'ai fini par tirer parti en faisant parler aux Américains une langue étrangère.

C'est un peu le hasard qui m'a fait participer en 1972 au colloque sur Artaud et Bataille organisé par la revue "Tel Quel" au château de Cerisy en Normandie. Ce qu'ils y célébraient, c'était l'avant-garde transgressive littéraire et pendant quelques années je m'en suis tenu là. Ce n'est que petit à petit que je me suis rendu compte que ce qui me fascinait chez ces écrivains, et chez quelques autres, c'était le rapport direct qu'ils avaient établi avec la violence et implicitement avec le fascisme.

R. G.: Vous voulez dire que ces écrivains étaient fascistes?

S. L.: Non, bien sûr, mais j'ai senti qu'ils pouvaient détenir la clé du fascisme, ou du moins une certaine clé qui avait échappé aux historiens traditionnels. Je n'ai pas de sympathie particulière pour les gens de "Tel Quel" issus pour l'essentiel de la bonne bourgeoisie catholique française. Et pourtant leur insistance sur le fait religieux m'apparaît assez judicieuse. Artaud, Bataille, Simone Weil – elle ne les a jamais intéressée d'ailleurs – et même Céline, qui était plus religieux qu'il n'en avait l'air, étaient l'aboutissement de toute une tradition qu'eux-mêmes reniaient, mais dont ils permettaient d'examiner les fondements. J'ai toujours eu une certaine répulsion pour tout ce qui relevait du Christianisme, et ces transfuges de la spiritualité chrétienne me donnaient l'occasion de sonder de l'intérieur ce qui, dans le fascisme, dérivait de toute une formation religieuse dont il avait hérité un antisémitisme virulent. En somme, travaillant sur les mêmes affects que le fascisme, ces écrivains permettaient en quelque sorte à leur corps défendant de définir ce qui pouvait y mener directement.

R. G.: J'ai été très étonné par le fait que Julia Kristeva qui faisait partie du groupe *Tel Quel,* s'intéresse aujourd'hui aux "nouvelles formes du sacré", ce qui ne peut être qu'une métaphysique spirituelle. Qu'est ce que vous en pensez?

S. L.: Je m'intéresse plutôt aux nouvelles formes du fascisme qui viennent se retremper dans le sacré. Les "hauts modernistes" français étaient portés par les mêmes mouvements de fond qui venaient bouleverser l'armature sociale de leur temps, c'est pourquoi ils m'ont paru être de meilleurs guides de l'irrationalisme fasciste que toutes les tentatives pour l'expliquer rationnellement. Ce qui ne veut pas dire pour autant que leur spiritualité m'intéresse en tant que telle. Emmanuel Lévinas parle quelque part du danger que représente la dimension païenne, terrienne, que l'Eglise n'a fait qu'utiliser à ses propres fins sans jamais l'annuler. C'est cette dimension païenne réappropriée par Bataille ou Artaud – les "nouvelles formes du sacré" – qui a pris avec le fascisme les formes catastrophiques que nous leur connaissons. Ce qui m'attire donc chez ces écrivains, c'est qu'ils ont pris le risque – ils n'ont pas toujours réussi à y échapper – d'explorer de l'intérieur les pratiques et les affects mobilisés par le fascisme. Et avec eux, c'est son vieux fond chrétien que j'entends faire ressurgir là où on s'y attend le moins.

LES IDENTIFICATIONS ALÉATOIRES

SAMI NAÏR

Nous vivons manifestement, sinon une crise radicale, du moins un très fort déplacement des identités collectives. Nous vivons une remise en question de ce que nous sommes. Cela s'est fait, au fond, assez vite: depuis une dizaine d'années, ce ne sont pas seulement les statuts sociaux, les identifications culturelles, les représentations individuelles qui subissent des mutations décisives – mais aussi les grands récits organisateurs de l'avenir qui s'affaissent brutalement: impasse des idéologies de la modernité sous leur aspect bourgeois; déconfiture des idéologies de l'émancipation (marxisme institutionnel, socialisme assistanciel, socialisme réellement existant) – retour brusque de l'individualisme farouchement concurrentiel (libéralisme carnassier et inégalitaire), déferlement des thérapies collectives radicales (fondamentalisme religieux). Régression, pour le dire avec les mots de Emile Durkheim, des solidarités mécaniques vers les solidarités organiques. Déplacement donc des statuts, dissipation des représentations de l'avenir. Nous vivons chacun pour soi et notre avenir est la nostalgie de notre passé. Opacité du futur, déficience de l'espoir.

Pourtant la vérité est que, écrit Claude Lévi-Strauss, "réduite à ses aspects subjectifs, une crise d'identité n'offre pas d'intérêt intrinsèque". Cette affirmation qui paraît à première vue choquante, présente cependant un profond contenu de vérité. Car les représentations, les catégories mentales, la structure des volitions réduites à leurs dimensions subjectives et strictement individuelles sont très relatives et souvent non significatives. Autrement plus intéressante, en revanche apparaît la crise qui touche les fondements profonds sur lesquels reposent ces représentations, ces catégories, ces volitions. Car ce sont alors les structures des identités collectives qui sont affectées et, par suite, les mécanismes mêmes de la cohésion sociale qui sont déstructurés.

Une crise d'identité individuelle peut être passible de diverses lectures: pathologique (sous l'espèce de la psychopathologie clinique), psychanalytique (par le biais de l'introspection freudienne), antipsychiatrique (par l'analyse critique des mécanismes de coercitions institués: famille, école, hôpitaux, etc.) ou parfois, encore, directement normative (voir la manière dont le comportement délinquant est saisi par la justice). Ce pluralisme méthodologique repose sur un postulat explicite et terriblement opératoire: le postulat de la cure. Le système des normes, des valeurs, ainsi que le mécanisme de leur articulation propre, étant structurellement stable, il ne reste plus qu'à réintroduire dans cette universalité normative et consciente d'elle-même les particularités individuelles en déréliction. La cure a précisément cette fonction. Et elle implique l'existence d'un curateur – c'est-à-dire, au fond, d'une référence originelle, et pour certains d'une source de lumière à revivifier.

Rien de tel dans les crises d'identité collectives: là, ce qui s'estompe, c'est en vérité le postulat, le sol stable sur lequel repose le vaste édifice des représentations admises et de l'entremêlement collectif. La cure existe bien, ici aussi, mais elle est souvent sauvage et d'intensité plus ou moins dramatique selon le degré de délitescence des solidarités de groupe: des apprentis sorciers peuvent alors se lever, qui entraînent dans leur délire des sociétés entières. Ce qui est cependant significatif de ces crises d'identité collectives, c'est qu'elles fonctionnent principalement à l'exclusion, et parfois à l'annihilation.

Il serait bien sûr trop facile de croire à une nette séparation entre ces deux formes de crise. Et si l'on a bien saisi le sens de la proposition de Claude Lévi-Strauss, il est nécessaire de tenter de repérer ce qui, dans la crise de l'individualité, participe d'un remaniement des structures profondes et des références identitaires collectives.

Le déplacement des identités collectives affleure d'abord à la surface de notre temps comme une réaffirmation exacerbée des identités spécifiques. Dans sa signification, cette réaffirmation est réactionnelle; dans son contenu, elle implique un comportement collectif logique bien que paradoxal: il est impérial et protectionniste. Impérial, car pour ne pas dépareiller l'identité menacée, ce comportement vise à rendre semblable, à pourchasser la différence, protectionniste, car cette quête de l'identique à soi est en vérité une forme spécifique de confirmation de la différence. Mouvement non dialectique par excellence, qui vise donc à hypostasier la particularité du soi menacée en universalité, en référence dominante. Mouvement en somme de réaffirmation de la domination. Ce mécanisme agit tout autour de soi: face à l'étranger, face au sexe différent, face au chômeur, face au jeune, face à tout ce qui implique un possible remaniement du soi. La crise des grands récits unificateurs, crise non des représentations transcendantales (la religion, le mysticisme), mais bien celle des conceptions laïques, rationalisatrices, temporelles, – la crise en somme de la réussite humaine collective ici-bas a libéré non pas le désespoir , non pas le pessimisme, non pas le renoncement, mais bien comme l'avait déjà perçu Max Weber au début de ce siècle, le désenchantement du monde, la réduction du monde des valeurs au système des moyens en vue d'une fin particulière (*Zweckrationalität*), le retour répétitif des individualismes anté et anticollectifs: valorisation de l'égoïsme, exacerbation de la xénophobie, du racisme, de l'ethnocentrisme.

Ce retour de l'individualisme caparaçonné est significatif: il présuppose en vérité un très profond décentrement de l'individualité elle-même. C'est parce que celle-ci, l'individualité moderne, ne se reconnaît plus dans la collectivité qu'elle débouche sur l'individualisme. En soi, l'individualisme comme représentation du monde n'est pas passible d'un jugement abstrait de valeur: il n'est ni bon, ni mauvais; il est, sans plus. Il correspond à une possibilité consubstantielle de l'espèce, enracinée dans la formation historico-sociale de l'individualité. Déjà Kant avait mis en évidence le dualisme qui commande ce processus: c'est le caractère, dit-il, d'*insociable sociabilité* de l'homme qui est le noeud fondateur de l'ordre humain. Le passage à la communauté, le dépassement de l'individualisme instinctif vers l'individualité raisonnable, non immédiatement instinctuelle, procède des contenus et des formes de socialisation soit donnés soit à constituer.

L'individualité débouchant sur l'individualisme instinctuel est, dans l'esprit de Kant, une manière de régression, une sorte de réduction inadmissible de l'individu à son soi, une rupture en somme du contrat de société. Voilà pourquoi Kant a besoin, pour fonder sa conception de la sociabilité, pour opérer le passage du particulier à l'universel, de l'individu à la communauté, voilà pourquoi il a besoin de la morale et de la table des impératifs catégoriques. Voilà pourquoi, en somme, il a besoin de ce qu'il nomme lui-même la *légalité universelle*, et de la définition de ses contenus dans la "Doctrine du droit" et dans la "Doctrine de la vertu". Toute cette métaphysique des moeurs repose cependant sur la contrainte, donc sur une vision radicalement affirmative de l'ordre social. La loi y est la Norme, et celle-ci est impérative. Le théoricien du normativisme juridique comme fondement de l'ordre social, Kelsen, avait donc raison de clamer sa filiation à Kant. Mais c'est là une stratégie artificielle: les normes ne tiennent que si les valeurs qui les sous-tendent sont stables. Or le décentrement contemporain de l'individualité, sa fuite vers l'individualisme, exprime peut-être une déstabilisation des valeurs fondatrices de la civilisation bourgeoise et capitaliste dans une époque où les valeurs temporelles alternatives (surtout socialisme réellement existant) n'apparaissent plus comme réellement alternatives et praticables. D'où le flottement de l'individualité, la polysémie de ses comportements, le caractère entropique de son parcours. La condition postmoderne est une aventure imprévisible, la condition identitaire contemporaine est aléatoire.

On pourrait à partir de là envisager une série de problèmes. Tenter par exemple de réfléchir sur les raisons historico-sociales qui rendent possible ce décentrement de l'individualité. L'analyse de la répartition des richesses, la structure de l'organisation des rapports de production, la formation des modes de domination, les stratégies d'exploitation, l'articulation des rapports de force, les mécanismes de légitimation et les formes de délégitimation, les objectivations enfin de l'ordre social (les idéologies, les cultures, les institutions etc.) – chacune de ces sphères permettrait de voir à l'oeuvre ce décentrement. Et chacune porterait sans doute une explication.

On peut aussi se limiter à une approche plus réductrice en repérant la caractéristique centrale de cette crise par ailleurs à l'oeuvre dans toutes les sphères du social: c'est ainsi que le décentrement de l'individualité apparaît, au-delà de la variété de ses figures, comme déployé sur le fond propre de la cohésion sociale: le parcours va ici de la déstructuration des groupes, de la redistribution des rôles, de la permutation des fonctions assignées, à la mutation des formes de l'individualité. Délitescence des groupes sociaux, déstabilisation de la cohésion interobjective et subjective, reformulation du lien social. Façon classique, en somme, de reconsidérer un vieux problème de sens commun: qu'en est-il des rapports de l'individualité et de la communauté dans une situation de crise

des solidarités collectives? De Emile Durkheim à Talcott Parsons, les grandes réponses, on le sait, ne manquent pas.

Deux perspectives doivent cependant être relevées ici. Dans la première, il est clair que la crise implique un redéploiement du rapport des normes et des valeurs: ces dernières, en tant qu'elles sont fondatrices de l'identité socio-culturelle des groupes, deviennent inadéquates par rapport au système dominant des normes. Envisageons par exemple le problème de l'égalité: on peut voir jouer aujourd'hui cette inadéquation d'abord sur le plan de l'affirmation normative de l'égalité des droits, laquelle est, sur le fond, directement démentie par l'inégalité originelle de condition sociale – mais ce premier aspect des choses est d'une certaine façon occulté et subsumé sous l'égalité formelle de la loi. La philosophie profonde de ce mécanisme peut se définir à peu près comme suit: la condition sociale dépend de l'individu et de sa puissance d'objectivation par rapport à d'autres individus tandis que la dimension publique de l'individu est déterminée par le principe de l'égalité devant la loi. Égaux devant la loi, les individus sont chacun pour soi dans la société. Autrement dit, la norme égalitaire est sous-tendue par le principe de la valorisation individuelle, virtuellement inégalitaire; l'écart entre la position normative et la position valorielle est ici structurel et inapparent.

Disons-le autrement: la norme égalitaire masque la réalité inégalitaire. Ensuite, sur le plan de la compétition sociale: celle-ci est devenue, dans l'actuelle situation de crise tellement exacerbée que le principe d'égalité devant la loi s'en trouve lui-même affecté; les valeurs liées à l'affirmation de soi dans l'ordre social (égoïsme, individualisme aversif, concurrence économico-sociale) prennent le pas sur les normes d'égalité et de justice telles qu'elles sont objectivées dans la loi: ce sont alors celles-ci qui changent: on le voit à l'oeil nu aujourd'hui dans le statut octroyé à l'étranger, à l'immigré, au chômeur en "fin de droits", aux femmes et aux jeunes. Cela signifie d'abord et surtout une réadaptation de la norme formellement égalitaire aux valeurs structurellement inégalitaires propres à l'ordre social contemporain.

La deuxième perspective tient au statut de la diversité dans la communauté. On l'a dit: la crise des identités collectives fonctionne principalement à l'exclusion; la diversité y est perçue comme une menace, elle devient intolérable parce qu'*incommunicable*. Il est intéressant de voir comment cette bipolarité de l'inclusion-exclusion est tout à la fois épistémologiquement critiquée, mais normativement légitimée par un auteur aussi solide que Claude Lévi-Strauss. Dans l'avant-propos du séminaire sur l'*Identité*, il écrit: "Ceux qui prétendent que l'expérience de l'autre individuel ou collectif est par essence incommunicable et qu'il est à jamais impossible, coupable même, de vouloir élaborer un langage dans lequel les expériences humaines les plus éloignées dans le temps et dans l'espace deviendraient, au moins pour partie, mutuellement intelligibles, ceux-là ne font rien d'autre que se réfugier dans un nouvel obscurantisme". Dans le *Regard éloigné*, il soutient en revanche qu'"il n'est nullement coupable de placer une manière de vivre et de penser au-dessus de toutes les autres, et d'éprouver peu d'attirance envers tel ou tel dont le genre de vie, respectable en lui-même, s'éloigne par trop de celui auquel on est traditionnellement attaché. Cette incommunicabilité relative n'autorise certes pas à opprimer ou détruire les valeurs qu'on rejette ou leurs représentants, mais maintenue dans ces limites, elle n'a rien de révoltant. Elle peut même représenter le prix à payer pour que les systèmes de valeurs de chaque famille spirituelle ou de chaque communauté se conservent, et trouvent dans leur propre fonds les ressources nécessaires à leur renouvellement. Si, comme je l'écrivais dans "Race et Histoire", il existe entre les sociétés humaines un certain optimum de diversité au-delà duquel elles ne sauraient aller, mais en dessous duquel elles ne peuvent non plus descendre sans danger, on doit reconnaître que cette diversité résulte pour une grande part du désir de chaque culture de s'opposer à celles qui l'environnent, de se distinguer d'elles, en un mot d'être soi; elles ne s'ignorent pas, s'empruntent à l'occasion, mais pour ne pas périr, il faut que sous d'autres rapports, persiste entre elles une certaine imperméabilité".

Ces deux positions ne sont pas contradictoires; on constate néanmoins que la seconde, non seulement atténue, mais réduit brutalement la première à une pétition de principe. Lévi-Strauss affirme certes que la communicabilité est relative, et qu'il suffit de vouloir pour pouvoir dresser des passerelles entre des cultures diverses. Cependant, en affirmant l'existence d'un noyau culturel irréductible au groupe et incommunicable, il rend légitime une sorte de différence ontologique entre les humains que rien dans la pratique, surtout dans la société moderne, ne justifie.

Qui, d'autre part, définit le *seuil* "en dessous ou au delà" duquel une société ne doit pas aller?

Or force est de constater que ces questions ne peuvent recevoir de réponse métaphysique ou de sens commun; elles ressortissent plutôt à la logique des rapports de force réels dans la société, et des positions qui y sont occupées par tel ou tel groupe social. De façon radicale encore, qu'est-ce que le contenu du concept de seuil lui-même? Se porte-t-il aux normes, aux valeurs, ou aux deux à la fois? Dans tous les cas de figure, l'accord sur le contenu du concept de seuil est indécidable puisque, excepté la situation d'agression violente, chaque groupe social, à peu près comme chaque individu, aura tendance à réagir différemment face à l'altérité humaine et culturelle. Il est en revanche manifeste que, dans des situations de crises sociales exacerbées, le rapport à la diversité devient plus problématique et des traits culturels ou ethniques distincts peuvent apparaître comme des points de fixation et de confrontation entre groupes et individus. Mais cela relève moins de critères *objectifs* d'opposition que d'une mobilisation, fortement fantasmatique, de l'imaginaire collectif de l'indigène par rapport à ce qui est perçu comme allogène. De là toute une série d'attitudes injonctives: injonctions d'assimilation, réaction différentialiste, et ainsi de suite – tant il est vrai, pour reprendre l'expression de Theodor Adorno, que "la violence du rendre semblable reproduit la contradiction qu'elle élimine".

Crise de l'individualité, déplacement du rapport des normes et des valeurs, ambiguïté de la diversité, inconfort de la différence: autant de signes favorisant l'émergence des identifications aléatoires. Il n'y a pas de panacée pour résoudre les redoutables problèmes inhérents à cette situation. Il n'y a au fond que deux attitudes réellement porteuses de sens. L'une consiste à se replier sur les références originaires, à s'opposer à l'ambiguïté et à la labilité des identifications, à fixer en somme dans des cadres mentaux et conceptuels précis l'identité personnelle, sociale, nationale, culturelle et religieuse – attitude dont Hegel a très lucidement mis en évidence l'équation tautologique dans la formule du *Ich bin Ich* – je suis je –, et qui rencontre, semble-t-il, aujourd'hui la faveur d'une grande partie de l'opinion française et l'assentiment d'intellectuels de renom. L'autre attitude en revanche retourne sur elle-même la crise de l'identité: et si, au fond, l'émergence des identifications aléatoires, changeantes, mutantes, était une bonne chose? Pourquoi devrait on concevoir *a priori* comme dangereuse la nouveauté, l'originalité, la singularité? Dans la crainte de l'Autre, c'est la position dogmatique et adversive du Je qui transparaît. La question réelle n'est pas d'accepter ou de refuser l'avènement de nouvelles identités; celles-ci apparaissent et sont de toute façon irréductibles, incontournables. La question est de savoir comment éviter socialement et culturellement de les soumettre à l'universalité abstraite ou de les réduire à des particularités folkloriques. Autrement dit, il importe de se demander quel peut être aujourd'hui le statut non de l'universalité (celle-ci est en crise, c'est une abstraction métaphysique), non de la particularité (celle-ci est narcissique et souvent bêtement réactionnelle), mais bien de la singularité. Comment peut-on être arabe en France, noir ou tout simplement de "souche" non européenne, – comment ces singularités peuvent-elles se négocier, se transformer, devenir des aspects culturels et humains intériorisés et assumés par la société française?

La tradition française dominante en ce qui concerne les valeurs est sur ce plan très inquiétante; si l'on prend le cas du rapport au monde arabe et africain, l'attitude qui a historiquement prévalu est celle de l'exclusion: celle-ci était précisément rendue possible par le fait que les Maghrébins comme les Africains étaient territorialisés dans leurs pays d'origine, donc situés en dehors de l'Hexagone. Le colonialisme français n'était assimilationniste que sur le plan idéologique; dans les faits il était une forme *d'apartheid*: en Algérie même, par exemple, la population européenne colonisatrice était séparée (par la loi, par les droits, par le savoir et par le pouvoir) de la population juive jusqu'au décret Crémieux (1870) et de la population musulmane jusqu'à la fin de la Seconde guerre mondiale. C'est cette séparation même qui détruisit ce qu'elle prétendait préserver, à savoir le système colonial. Vis-à-vis du Juif, en France, ou même du Polonais ou de l'Italien, le problème était différent, car l'intrus vivait au coeur du pays: la stratégie d'assimilation joua pleinement. La singularité du Juif, du Polonais ou de l'Italien n'a pu se maintenir ici que sur le fil étroit du repli communautaire. Même si l'exemple du judaïsme français prouve de façon éclatante que le statut de minorité peut se concilier avec une grande ouverture, rien ne permet de penser que le repli auquel sont acculées des communautés soit par ailleurs le meilleur garant de la singularité; tout démontre au contraire que, repliées sur elles-mêmes, les communautés risquent de se figer et de perdre le sens de l'ouverture aux autres. On retrouve aujourd'hui ce problème à propos des populations immigrées: pourront-elles s'intégrer sans se renier? L'identité culturelle française, aujourd'hui en crise, permettra-t-elle l'expression de cette singularité, ou au contraire, par son refus, rendra-t-elle inévitable l'émergence d'un sentiment communautaire stigmatisé, affligé, recroquevillé enfin dans le repli et le culte de la spécificité? Va-t-on vers un renforcement de la différence adversive, vers une sorte de solidification d'un individualisme communautaire ou permettra-t-on plutôt l'intégration libre de l'individualité singulière dans le système des valeurs et des normes actuellement en transformation? Car ces populations sont incontestablement aujourd'hui en situation de mutation; leurs identités sont incertaines, leurs identifications tout aussi aléatoires.

Que signifie par exemple être *beur* en France aujourd'hui? Est-ce une identité? Est-ce une identification? Est-ce un avenir? Etre *beur*, c'est être objectivé dans une représentation donnée: c'est avoir une généalogie arabe dont le statut est déprécié en France, mais c'est également être suspect aux yeux du monde arabe parce que trop occidentalisé. Etre *beur*, c'est donc être entre-deux et c'est, par la force des choses, se choisir dans le présent, à défaut de choisir entre ces monstres froids que sont les appartenances collectives. C'est attendre, attendre que "ça change". Espérer, consciemment ou inconsciemment que les déplacements d'identité en cours achèvent leur mouvement, réalisent leur révolution peut-être. Et vivre une vie incertaine, subir une identification sans concept, assumer une désignation objective sans renier ce qui la rend possible (la généalogie arabo-berbère) mais sans la survaloriser non plus.

On pourrait montrer d'autres mécanismes à l'oeuvre, pour fournir une idée plus concrète de ces procès d'identifications aléatoires dans une situation de crise d'identité collective: ainsi en est-il des modifications de l'identité collective; ainsi en est-il des modifications de l'identité sexuelle, des mutations de l'identité professionnelle, des tranformations de l'identité morale, etc. Tous ces processus sont certes relatifs, et ils ne peuvent en aucune manière apparaître comme une structure identitaire nouvelle: ils sont des passages, des voies d'accès vers autre chose. Mais, libérés, ils peuvent fournir, sinon l'image précise de ce que sera la société de demain, du moins l'air – l'air vital – que veulent respirer, simplement pour vivre, tous ceux sur qui la grâce d'une vie tranquille ne s'est pas posée.

IMPORTED – A READING SEMINAR in Relationship with my "A Portable (Not so Ideal) Imported Library, Or How to Reinvent the Coffee Table: 25 Books for Instant Use (Russian-Version)," 1994/95
Contemporary Art Center, Moscow, January – March 1995

RUSSIFICATION AND THE TERRAIN OF 'SELF-DETERMINATION'

ZEIGAM AZIZOV

Perhaps the most abused word in Soviet society before *perestroika* was "multinational". After perestroika the abuse of this word developed into the open abuse of the rights of peoples from different nations. During 75 years of Soviet history "multinationalism" was a policy bringing together huge "families" of "free" republics joined together through the Russian language and praying to the Mecca of the Soviet: Moscow.[1]

For the "free republics" *perestroika* turned history backwards; in trying to find their independence these republics had to look at their history and to learn their own languages properly, that which had been cut off by the socialist revolution. It soon became clear that the roots had been laid deeper than 75 years, the roots in "russification" on which the Russian empire had been successfully raised and through which it consequently failed. This *perestroika* gave rise to, among other things,the starting point of a complicated "de-russification". And the "union of inviolable free republics"[2] started to fall away from its russified nucleus. "De-russification" involved these republic's desire to establish their right of communication in their own ways. The Russian language, as an instrument of the manipulation of power, was rejected.

What does all this mean? Is it a realization of Lenin's notion of "self determination of nations" or is it complete ignorance of the whole history of the Russian revolution and a return to previous formations? Or maybe it is the "nationalism and fundamentalism of these nations" — as this situation has been labeled. An inquiry into some details of the history of "russification" would go some way towards explaining this most complicated question in today's Russia and its former colonies.

Colonial experience in Russia is a dramatic one; very unlike other empires who colonized far-off lands, Russia colonized countries around itself making one very compact land. Colonization, which started from expansion into Siberian lands with small ethnic groups in the middle ages, ended up in Trans-Caucasia in the 19th century. Russian thus permeated into these populations and gradually became the most influential language. Traces of this popular influence can be seen as early as the 11th century. The end of the 14th century, when the center of learning was transferred from Kiev (Ukraine) to Moscow, marks a new phase in the development of the Moscow district and in the influence on business language used in offices (*prikazi*). In the 18th century with Lomonosov (1711 - 1765) the Russian literary language falls more into line with the spoken language in order to popularize language for the people. In his "Russian Grammar" (*Rossiskaya Grammatica*) he reveals the true sources of the national language. In the first half of the 19th century Pushkin and Gogol, with whom modern literature begins, finally rejected the literary tongue of its pedantic tendencies and identified it with popular speech. The common language which Pushkin and Gogol transferred from everyday life into literature was subsequently used by powers to colonize other literary cultures, despite the fact that Gogol and Pushkin themselves were absolutely not colonialists. The Russian philologist Shakmatov held that the modern literary language was originally old Bulgarian transplanted to Russia as church Slavonic. First in the southwest, then in the northeast, it underwent a process of permeation by the spoken Russian of the people, became russified and as a result became almost identical to the present spoken language of central Russia. Up to the date of the October revolution in 1917 Russian was a language of administration and cultural contact between ethnic groups and nationalities living in the territory of the empire. A large variety of schools and universities in major cities of the empire taught almost all subjects in Russian, and the study of Russian culture was compulsory.

The Soviet state was founded by Lenin as a "free union of the free nations." He stressed that this union unquestionably had to be voluntary and that no nation should use violence against one another. Such a union was necessary to combat both the threat of internal counterrevolution and external intervention but the Bolshevik party made it clear that the right to self determination was subordinate to the needs of socialist construction. The Russian language, along with the military power of the red army has been used as a major force in the "self determination" of "free nations" which differed in ethnic character, language, religion, culture, and level of economic development. The Soviet state "provided" for the "needs" of these nations by sending to their lands thousands of teachers, scientists, and other specialists. "Russification" spread across all of the country transforming 400 nationalities speaking in, apart from Russian, 36 Iberian-Caucasian, 25 Turkic, 24 Indo European, 22 Mongolian, Tungus-Manchu and Paleoasiatic and 20 Finno-Ugric languages (this list is incomplete). These languages have been regarded as secondary in relation to Russian.

The Nationality question has been regarded by Lenin as one of utmost importance in many of his works. An attempt to promote world revolution on the one hand and a desire, on the other, to establish normal diplomatic relations with capitalist governments was decisive in the formulation of the multinational policy of the Soviet revolution. Russia's geographical position as both a European and Asian power should be noted at this point. Lenin, in his book *Imperialism as the highest stage of capitalism: a popular outline* (1917), depicts the acquisition and exploitation of colonies by process of profitable investment as the essence of capitalism in its final phase. One source of inspiration for this book was Joseph Chamberlain's speech on the international political program of imperialism which Lenin heard during his stay in London in 1903. Lenin could see that contemporary imperialism, by strengthening the urge to subjugate weak peoples, was a factor in intensifying national oppression. Therefore the Socialist's prevention of the Russian proletariat from influences by national chauvinism was a particular idea among Lenin's national and colonial questions. This idea led him to his theory of imperialism. He observed the formation of international capitalist monopolies who shared the world among themselves which changed the rules of international politics. If, earlier, Lenin had insisted on the struggle between "advanced" and "backward" nations, now he emphasized the importance of the struggle between oppressor and oppressed nations.[3] Rejecting the abstract presentation of the question of nationalism, Lenin distinguished between the struggle of the nationalism of big (oppressor) nations and that of small (oppressed) nations. Chauvinism could have been opposed by the international proletariat movement or proletarian internationalism. The eventual amalgamation of different nations into one single community would provide self determination of oppressed nations. Lenin did not see that this view could be reactionary. The Third International held onto Lenin's position until 1935 when, in reaction to Hitler's rise to power, the 7th Congress (under Stalin) took a nationalist turn. This brought about the politics of the "popular front" and coincided with Russia's revindication of its national heroes from Alexander Nevsky to Peter the Great, while the Soviet Union was identified with the traditions of the Russian empire.

Under Stalin this Leninist nationalities policy encouraged even stronger trends towards assimilation, rejection of the specifics of national development, the political accusation of all nations, and the resulting arbitrariness and lawlessness with regard to certain peoples. Stalin specifically engaged in the enlargement of Soviet influence first in Eastern Europe while planning the victory of the October revolution throughout the world. The internal policy was strengthened by the bureaucratization, collectivization and an administrative command system. Stalin's administrative command system completely ignored the requirements of national development. Repressions, including the infringement on the rights of all peoples and their enforced resettlement in other republics, played their part in the undermining of inter-ethnic relations. Stalin was dealing with these questions "scientifically". Following the Leninist idea of the "revolution in one country" Stalin strengthened control over science in order to encourage the notion of Marxism-Leninism as a triumph of science rather than politics. Stalin's approach to communism's heritage was important for his methods of testing it as a science. By keeping Lenin's body hostage in a mausoleum he was promoting his own policies and the Soviet Union which engaged popular consciousness in the immortality of communist ideas. Thus scientific Stalinism went on reworking Marxist ideas in a new way. Stalin went on to the point of altering theory itself if necessary in order to justify his claims on authority. On the other hand, Stalin's task was the foundation of history, and "the science of the history of society, despite all the complexity of the phenomena of social life, can become as precise a science as, let us say, biology."[5]

In the same way, Stalin's involvement in language policy as a dominant force resulted in his theory of linguistics. His book *Marxism and Linguistics* is paradoxical, maybe even the most paradoxical book ever written on language. Altering the Marxist theory of base and superstructure, Stalin turns this theory upside down (Lenin said something similar about Marx in his relation to Hegel's negative dialectics). In investigating this phenomenon as a fact of the unconscious, Lacan noticed "that we may recall that the discussion of the necessity for a new language in the communist society did in fact take place, and Stalin, much to the relief of those depending on his philosophy, cut off the discussions with the decision: language is not superstructure."[5]

This cutting-off of the discussions was based on Stalin's belief that language is superstructure "for a society divided into hostile classes; it is not compulsory for a society not divided into hostile classes."[6] For Stalin "this was revolution which eliminated the old bourgeois economic system, but this revolution did not take place by means of explosion, that is, by the overthrow of the existing power and the creation of a new power, but by a gradual transition from the old bourgeois system of the countryside to a new system."[7] "The old base and the old classes were eliminated," so there was not superstructure but a new base, a new language, a new society, a new power which replaced the old: "the transition of a language from an old quality to a new one does not take place by way of an explosion, by the destruction of an existing language and the creation of a new one, but by the gradual accumulation of the elements of their new quality."[8] It was the revolutionary Russian language which had these qualities. Stalin's book was considered an irreplaceable guide, which existed in order to prevent all arbitrary interpretations. For this reason authority was given to Stalin's "cadres", dealing with "cleanisation" of bourgeois elements. One of the victims of this cleanisation was, for example, V. N. Volosinov and his book *Marxism and the Philosophy of Language,* which was occluded for its insistence on the "class struggle at the level of the sign," contradicting Stalin's ideas quoted above, as well as his notion of a strictly economic causality in the links between base and superstructure. Repressions followed of others, like Marr, Propp, Bahktin (to name but a few) for similar reasons which also exposed the full meaning of Stalin's aggression.

The ferocity against Jewish intellectuals and other minorities continued Stalin's policy. His suspicion of anything "cosmopolitan" combined with atavistic anti-Semitism resulted in massive repressions. Another side to Stalinist "sterile reductionism" (Edward W. Soja) relates to his spatial policy and finds its culmination in resettlements. Enforced resettlements of Kalmyks, Karachais, Balkars, Chechenes, Ingushes, Crimean Tatars, Meskhetien Turks, Germans who lived in the Volga area, Koreans, Greeks, and Kurds were also scientific "in testings" of the national solidarity of Soviet people. That was one reason why Einstein's theory of relativity and Niels Bohr's complementarity have been regarded as doubtful, "subjective and idealistic," and spatial science (in its radical form) was rejected even after Stalin's death until Soviet cosmonauts invaded space. Genetics, as it was dealing with genes and chromosomes, has likewise been regarded as "cosmopolitan" and prohibited.

Thus rectification found "scientific" foundations in the form of Stalin's linguistic and geopolitical policy, controlled by a centralized command system which effected a passport regime (*propiska*), still existing in Russia, as well as the rectification of names. Many Jews and some other minorities were forced to be nationalized as Russians, others had Russian endings added to their names (like mine: Aziz + ov).

After Stalin's death the situation remained unaltered and the leaders of the Communist party, Krushchev, Brezhnev, and finally Gorbachev continued this tradition. The crucial question of inter-ethnic relationships is intertwined in such a way as to enable one to see it in all areas of activity.

The education system which was allowed to function in people's own languages was made up of nothing but "russified" subjects. Soviet students found themselves studying in a country which was the most free in the world and speaking in a language in which "Lenin himself spoke and wrote his books." Access to higher degrees at universities was outrageously controlled, specifically in relation to Jews and Caucasians, whose education has been limited in humanitarian departments of universities under the famous "Article 5" of the education program of the ministry of the USSR. I myself was a victim of this (I am from Azerbaijan).

Art and literature were not excluded from the existing rules which were imposed by the Communist party. These rules were formulated by Lenin in his famous article "Party organization and party literature" written in 1905. In his article Lenin writes about two cultures within one: Bourgeoisie and Proletariat. He insisted on the struggle of the one against the other. The congress of Soviet writers (1934) approved the doctrine of Socialist Realism as the only art appropriate to the building of communism. Works by artists and intellectuals from all over the country along with Russians themselves had been recognized only in accordance to principles set out in these documents. Socialist Realism dominated the atmosphere throughout the whole Soviet Empire as a means of propaganda promoting freedom and happiness as offered by a multi-national state. Each republic had their own established artists depicting Lenin during his talks to representatives of different nations about their destiny. Art forms invented at the beginning of this century were either regarded as "politically useless" (specifically by Lenin whose favorite artist was Shishkin, who painted Russian *beriozkas*) or transformed into means of propaganda, like Tatlin's *Third International*. After the 1930s even writing on the art which was invented at the beginning of the century could be left uncensored. Regardless of whether they were Russian or non-Russian, artists were connected to Socialist Realism. To think, however, that no other art existed would be a great mistake. The same is also true of the Sovietized countries of Eastern Europe, Asia, and Latin America. The exhibition of abstract art from Poland in 1958 remains one of the biggest events which was not dominated by Socialist Realism.

Total isolation from the rest of the world left serious traces on Soviet culture's limitedness. Russian intellectuals were trying to isolate themselves from the existing regime inside the Soviet Union. But sources of information were very limited ; they had to draw on information from the conservative local past. One of the sources of information was, of course, Russian culture of the 19th century which itself was paradoxical with regard to the question of the other. In order to feel strong, Russian culture imported cultures from other colonial empires while ignoring cultures in colonized lands of Russia. Russian intellectuals engaged in the adoption of imported cultures and made little effort to contact cultures dying out under pressure of russification. Thus one may find very peculiar attitudes towards Asians in political documents of the time as well as literary works. Influence from notorious figures of enlightenment, for example in Voltaire's letter to Catherine the Great, is obvious. "It is not enough to humiliate them, they should be destroyed. Beat the Turks and I'll die content," he wrote to the Russian Empress who exploited Asians because they seemed undeveloped in her eyes. While reading Russian literature of the 19th century one comes across the use of Asiatism as a metaphor for barbarism. It is particularly impressive when one finds Chekhov's positive hero in his "Cherry Orchard" using this metaphor endlessly. So, cultural nationalism which began to emerge in Russia during the Brezhnev period has been strongly influenced by these factors. The emergence of orthodox-Slavophile traditions in Solzhenitsyn's work is only one example among many. Another thing was the idealization of the Russian soul in the shape of the Russian peasant who no longer existed. The dissolution of the intellectual atmosphere turned from creation to agitation. This agitation was again based on collaborative work manipulated in collective forms in multi-national societies.

The years of great stagnation were "challenged" by the Jewish question in the 1970s when Brezhnev allowed the emigration of Jewish people from the Soviet Union as "non-loyal citizens of a communist state." The Soviet regime continued its aggression in the multinational question which found its most dramatic form during the invasion of Afghanistan. After Brezhnev's death in 1981 power was controlled by the KGB and its loyal leader Andropov who replaced Brezhnev. Sending non-Russians to their "homes", specifically those who came from Caucasia, and even stronger control by the Militia are the only cases which can be remembered from these times.

Perestroika has been marked by bloody conflicts in Nagarno-Karabach, Georgia, Middle Asia, Moldovia, and the Baltic Republics. Actions taken by special armed forces in these places resulted in huge tragedies which continue today. After the new Union treaty of 1992 many republics decided to become independent in order to develop possibilities of communication with the contemporary world—a possibility which they had not had before. This also meant rejecting their economic relationship with Russia in many ways.But many of these republics were main sources of economic developments for Russia. This is one of the reasons for the economic disaster in today's Russia.

Conflict between former Soviet republics and Russia also included a language policy when many minorities decided to start to speak their own languages. These minorities were particularly unhappy that many Russians living and working in their republics for many years did not want to learn their languages. After perestroika this policy seemed completely unchanged and remained as formulated in Stalin's "Marxism and Linguistics" which urged absolute homogeneity, loyalty, and slavery through the domination of one major language. When this question came into existence labels such as "nationalistic"and "fundamentalist" were given to the peoples of the Baltic Republics, Central Asia and Caucasia.

Meanwhile, in the new Russia utterly nationalistic-fascistic tendencies are emerging with enormous success. Fascist *"pamyat"*, *"volga"*, "fatherland" movements connected a number of parties such as the national Bolshevik party, the national democratic party and the campaign against Jews and other minorities. The de-zionization of Russia and the legal ban of Jews holding government posts and the restoration of the Tzar stands at the heart of this movement. Internationally some of these movements have formed links with extreme right individuals in London.[9]

In the beginning the perspectives which perestroika opened up for cultural developments seemed very large. Artists and intellectuals saw a chance for freedom of creativity and an ability for direct communication under this new regime. The suspension of authoritarian control over the culture industry was at the same time the end of censorship of so called non-official (i.e., other than socialist realist) art. Many emigrants returned to Russia in the hope of realizing their ideas freely—which they had not been able to do during the Soviet period and had caused them to emigrate in the first place. The translation of modern literature, philosophy, the publication of earlier banned books and exhibitions of contemporary art were signs of democracy. Cultural exchange with the countries of western Europe was the start of a new dialogue. Interest in the new Russia was encouraged by the visits of western artists and intellectuals. The visits of Rauschenburg, John Cage, Derrida, Habermas and many other previously ignored people were great events. There was a strong impression that "the curtain is down and will never be raised again."[10] The emergence and the success of some Russian artists in western Europe brought the promise of a definite turn to a new phase in questions of multiculturalism. However the question has remained outside the discussion and has not found its real critical circumstances. Artists engaged in redevelopments of culture which had emerged at the beginning of the century, and many attempts were made to promote Russian culture abroad.

This was also partly based on the idea of rebuilding a culture. It was interesting to believe that this beginning would lead to criticism of institutions, racial prejudices and other related questions as it had with many western European artists. The comprehensive nature of cultural encounter of this kind sometimes resulted in unexpectedly strange consequences. For example in St. Petersburg a group of young artists who desired to be noticed in the art world decided to combine the culture of Russian futurism with the art of the Stalinist period in an utterly ironic way. After having a brief success these ironic attitudes grew into dangerous games. These games are played within the institution of the New Academy of Fine Arts based in St. Petersburg. The New Academy is developing a movement of "neo-academism" consisting of interpretations of Stalinistic and fascistic art for a new Russia. One of the leaders of this group is Timur Novikov, officially registered as a member of the National Bolshevik party (led by writer Eduard Limonov, Zhirinovsky's ex-minister). Fascinated by the beauty of Stalinistic and fascistic art, these young artists are posing against western modernism because this modernism, in their eyes, destroyed beauty. "Ecologists of culture," how Timur Novikov defines this movement, stands against contemporary culture also because it imported "shamanism and africanism" and by doing so destroyed and betrayed the ideals of beauty.[11]

What has been written here are only some examples from a complicated multi-national policy exercised in Russia. Unfortunately these are facts that constitute the reality which exists and continues to prove itself today. The "iron curtain" which once hung between the Soviet empire and western capitalism is today multiplied and causes discrimination between cultures, languages, and relationships in the former republics of the Soviet Union.

1. I remember very well a story that my father told me about one of his visits to Moscow when he saw an old Muslim man from a Central Asian Soviet republic kissing Lenin's mausoleum stone. In Islamic societies such rituals are allowed only in Mecca in Mohammed's mausoleum (Kaaba).
2. From the hymn of the Societ Union of Socialist Republics.
3. V. I. Lenin, "Imperialism as highest stage of capitalism" and "Backward Europe and Advanced Asia," both quoted in C. Wright Mills "The Marx-

ists."Penguin Books, London 1977, pp. 199 -212
4. *Dialectical and Historical Materialism*, London 1941, "Little Stalin Library," no. 4, pp. 14-15, quoted in Paolo Spriano "Stalin Spriano "Stalin and European Communists." Verso, London 1985, p. 88
5. Lacan, J. "The Insistence of the Letter in the Unconscious" in *Modern Criticism and Theory*, Ed. David Lodge, Longman, London and New York 1988, pp. 105
6. See Stalin's "Marxism and Linguistics" in C. Wright Mills, *The Marxists*, Penguin Books, London, 1977, p. 292
7. ibid, p. 291
8. ibid, p. 292
9. Glynn Ford, *Fascist Europe—The Rise of Racism and Xenophobia*. Pluto Press, London 1992, p. 41
10. E. Hobsbawm, Foreward to the catalogue of the exhibition "Art and Power," Hayward Gallery, London 1996, p. 15
11. The Guardian, Londay, 17 February 1996

ТЕЛО-БЕЗ-ИМЕНИ (ТЕРМИДОР ТЕЛЕСНОСТИ)[1]

ВИКТОР ТУПИЦЫН

Прочтение Маркса, предпринятое Луисом Альтюссером в 1960-х годах, убеждает в том, что экономическое "я" общества организуется по принципу, сходному с организацией психического субъекта у Фрейда или Жака Лакана. Альтюссер проводит аналогию между уровнями развития производительных сил и стадиями развития либидо. Переход с одного уровня на другой описывается им в терминах ***displacement*, *Verschiebung***[2], из чего, впрочем, не следует, что либидо экономически детерминировано. Экономика -- всего лишь поставщик определенной части референтного "сырья", проецируемого на внутренний мир субъекта в виде бессознательных репрезентаций ***(imagoes)***. Таким образом, речь идет не о конвертировании, а о (многократно опосредованной) корреляции, учитывая, что, в то время как у Лакана бессознательное -- это дискурс ***другого***, марксизм эксплицирует сходный подтекст во взаимоотношениях между базисом и надстройкой. В период хрущевской оттепели базис и надстройка альтернативной художественной продукции были разведены. Надстроечные (суперструктурные) референты импортировались с Запада, тогда как инфраструктура (художественные материалы, мастерские и прочее) сохраняла свой прежний адрес. Вакуум между базисом культуры и ее надстройкой или, как сказал бы Альтюссер, между соматикой и ментальной жизнью, флексиями и рефлексиями, способствовал образованию дополнительных (вдобавок к уже имеющимся) пустот в художественной психике. Зияющие пустоты заполнялись инкарнациями отчужденных надстроечных референтов (иконические галлюцинации). Благодаря этим зияниям несоцреалистическое искусство отличалось от соцреалистического не только своими творческими установками, но и своим диагнозом.

Знакомство с западным изобразительным каноном послевоенного времени стало возможным благодаря нескольким выставкам американской и европейской живописи в Москве[3], а также благодаря потоку иллюстрированных книг и каталогов, изданных за границей. Любопытно, что отечественный модернизм 10-х, 20-х и 30-х годов повлиял на формальные опыты шестидесятников в значительно меньшей степени, чем западный, пригревший невостребованный у себя на родине призрак русского авангарда. Сведения об этой "тени отца Гамлета" были вытеснены из памяти индивидов и институций, что в равной степени касалось как культурного сознания, так и культурного бессознательного. В психоанализе (Лакан и его школа) такой вид радикального вытеснения носит название ***foreclosure (forclusion, Verwerfung). Foreclosure*** приводит к образованию параноидальных пустот в глубинах памяти и языка. В основном это имеет отношение к пациентам, которые в раннем детстве оказались свидетелями, соучастниками или жертвами преступления. Вызывающие дискомфорт (ужас, стыд и т.д.) воспоминания о подобных вещах подлежат искоренению, оставляя на месте себя невосполнимые бреши, зазоры, "пустые центры". И хотя опорожнение памяти принято анализировать в терминах индивидуальной (а не коллективной) психической защиты, аналогия с ***foreclosure*** работает и в случаях массовой, то есть общественной каталепсии. Последствия ***foreclosure*** прослеживаются на примере соцмодернистов, чье возвращение из утраченного времени если и состоялось, то только отчасти. Не угодный ни ревнителям чистого авангарда, ни ценителям сталинского искусства, социалистический модернизм 30-х годов, сокращенно -- соцмодернизм, существовал одновременно с соцреализмом, но, в отличие от него, сумел создать стиль. Архитектура первой линии московского метро, книжный и журнальный дизайн, плакаты, фотография и фотомонтаж, оформление выставочных павильонов и рабочих клубов -- вот тот неполный перечень жанров, в которых работали соцмодернисты (такие, как поздний Клуцис, поздний Лисицкий, поздние Родченко и Степанова, Сенькин, Кулагина, Теленгатор, Петрусов, Грюнталь и многие другие). Трансгрессивность их позиции -- в сравнении с традиционным авангардом -- в диалектическом преодолении (снятии) отрицания, то есть в переходе от негации к аффирмации. Отдавая должное этому обстоятельству, соцмодернизм можно считать аффирмативным авангардом.

За время, проистекшее после успеха аукциона Сотбис в Москве (1988г.), русские художники регулярно бывали на Западе, устраивая там выставки и продавая работы как известным собирателям, так и безымянным приобретателям. В музеях и выставочных пространствах несхожих калибров и разной степени важности они вешали на стены неразговорчивые (то есть не склонные к контакту с иностранцами) картины и воздвигали инсталляции, свидетельствовавшие о непроницаемости их контекста. Трудно припомнить случай, чтобы кто-нибудь из выставлявшихся за границей когда-либо пытался всерьез способствовать переводимости “своего закона” на язык “чужого монастыря”. Что касается западных ценителей и сопереживателей, то их (мимолетный) альянс с русским искусством заслуживает особого психотерапевтического внимания. Во времена перестройки это было проявлением любопытства центра в отношении периферии. Подопечные из России заранее втискивались в роль тех, кого нельзя обделить покровительством и душевным участием. Их ревеляции могли рассчитывать на понимание только в случае соблюдения правил игры, не позволяющих им прибегать к обобщениям или теоретизировать. ***Пятнице*** вменялась роль поставщика событийного сырья, дискурсивная обработка (огранка) которого лицензирована ***Робинзоном***. Но самое парадоксальное -- это отсутствие взаимного интереса к контексту искусства со стороны гастролеров -- гастролеров с Запада на Восток и с Востока на Запад. Даже те, кого трудно заподозрить в очарованности "чистой" формой, при ознакомлении с зарубежными выставочными экспозициями или журнальными разворотами неизменно довольствовались сугубо формальным, эстетическим ракурсом художественной репрезентации. И это при том, что для многих из них "визуальность -- это кожа, натянутая на скелет слов".

Жанр пишущих о русском искусстве у себя дома -- не критицизм, а аффирмация, что неудивительно, поскольку политическая и социокультурная структуры в России еще не вполне сложились. Разговоры о функциональности или полезности искусства воспринимаются сегодня скептически на родине конструктивизма и производственничества; отсутствие энтузиазма наблюдается и в случаях обсуждения проблемы ответственности. "Ответственность за что? Искусство -- вещь абсолютно бесполезная," -- заявил в беседе со мной один московский художник. По мнению другого, главное в любом ("настоящем") произведении искусства -- это "невозможность использовать его как-либо иначе".

Инфантилизм подобных заявлений объясняется безнадежной детскостью современного российского (коммунального) сознания. "Будьте как дети, -- призывал Христос, -- ибо таковых есть Царство Небесное. Истинно говорю вам: кто не примет Царствия Божия, как дитя, тот не войдет в него". Лицезрение самого себя в образе вечного дитяти (феномен, демонстрирующий сходство советских традиций не только с христианскими, но и с дзенскими) восходит к тем временам, когда бремя взрослости возлагалось на государственную бюрократию. Всем остальным с ранних лет внушали, что "единственный привилегированный класс в

СССР -- это дети". Следовательно, перспектива утраты подобных (классовых) привилегий, предвосхищаемая коммунальным бессознательным, обуславливала замедленность темпов взросления. И это при том, что возраст пребывающих в состоянии "институционального" детства отсчитывается не так, как у "взрослых". К числу наиболее разительных примеров относится несоответствие статуса современных русских художников их возрастным характеристикам. Так как на Западе работы пожилых классиков висят в национальных и частных собраниях, открытых для публичного обозрения, у них нет необходимости отвоевывать у молодежи места и позиции в галерейном мире. Неучастие Кунеллиса или Раушенберга в сегодняшней художественной хронике компенсируется для них иными (пенсионными) формами присутствия в культурной жизни. Каждый понимает, что музеи и хрестоматии -- эквивалент пенсии, без которой старость нелегитимна, ее нет. В глазах общества старик, не заслуживший пенсии, -- ребенок. Советское альтернативное искусство 50-х, 60-х и 70-х годов еще не обрело покой под сводами музеев, и его финансовая ситуация оставляет желать лучшего. Вот почему шестидесятилетние художники нередко впрягаются в одну упряжку с двадцатилетними, то есть продолжают оставаться "ровесниками" своих более молодых коллег.

Детская модель коммунальной субъективности покоится на презумпции единства мира, на вере в тотальность и непрерывность бытия, являясь в то же са́мое время примером крайнего эгоцентризма. Отсюда -- представление об "общемировом" культурном контексте как о квазисинтагматическом событийном поле, открытом для любого незапланированного происшествия, в сочетании с наивной апологетикой инцидента (***accident***) как нормативного события[4]. К числу парадигм детскости относится карнавальное (праздничное) восприятие актов насилия: убежденность в том, что "на миру и смерть красна", наилучшая тому иллюстрация. В переводе на язык городской проблематики несовершеннолетие --гетто, чей вклад в культуру -- не что иное, как китч (а не авангард -- вопреки мнению Клемента Гринберга). Выходцы из гетто нередко оказывались наиболее ревностными оберегателями конвенций и ортодоксий, тем ангельским воинством, которому поручена охрана власти или, точнее, тéла власти. Именно из их числа вербуются телохранители, -- наемная гвардия сильных мира сего. С этой точки зрения постсоветская мафия, несмотря на вершимые ею беззакония, законный наследник советских традиций.

Сопоставление происходящего в России с метаморфозами культурной жизни за океаном убеждает, что подмостки, предназначенные для осуществления творческих "отправлений", становятся все менее и менее приспособленными для текстуальных медитаций, для дискурса. Искусство перестает быть укромным местом, откуда можно дистанцированно, ничем не рискуя, вглядываться в ужасы позлащенного прошлого или парфюмерно вздыхать, предвосхищая события "грядущего" апокалипсиса. Мир художественных репрезентаций стал столь же телесным, токсичным и дискомфортным, как и сама реальность. Частичной иллюстрацией к сказанному можно считать фотографии ***Nan Goldin***, ***Jack Pierson*** и ***Mark Morrisroe***, а также видеоперформансы Мэтью Барни (***Whitney Biennial***, 1993). Еще одним опытом телесного ваимодействия с "референтным пространством" (***referential space***) являются инсталляции молодого афро-американского художника ***Nari Ward*** (***Whitney Biennial***, 1995), использующего автохтонность как материал для акцентации социальной проблематики. Из этого и других (приведенных выше) примеров отнюдь не вытекает, что к позиции американцев следует относиться как к жене Цезаря, которая вне подозрений... Меня в данном случае настораживает то, что, будучи в курсе умонастроений и политических программ западных художников, критиков и теоретиков, я до сих пор не знаю, каковы позиции их русских коллег и есть ли они у них вообще.

Телесность отнюдь не безобидная фигура идентичности. В свете не столь давних пертурбаций, постигших российскую действительность, представители арт-мира, отстаивающие право искусства на автохтонность, выдерживают сравнение со столпами аффирмации -- кариатидами и атлантами, поддерживающими статус-кво. Хотя "телесное" прочитывается теперь как "национальное по форме", это качество (то есть телесность) почти полностью отсутствовало в соцреализме, который не имел также ничего общего с социальным искусством. Последнее утверждение распространяется и на сегодняшних телесников, которых в Москве по недоразумению называют "социальными художниками". Если американские телесники олицетворяют сопротивление меньшинства большинству (объекта репрессии ее субъекту), то применительно к "новым русским" этого не скажешь. Захлестнутая волной преступности и меркантилизма, вся страна вовлечена теперь в процесс физического (телесного) выживания. Однако, "термидор" телесности не может обойтись без сопротивления, без апелляции (рано или поздно) к этическому самосознанию, дефицит которого -- отчасти -- объясняется той безмятежностью, с которой "московский коммунальный концептуализм" на протяжении двух декад заигрывал с телесными импликациями речевых практик. И хотя концептуалисты ограничивали себя сухим пайком "речеложства" и "текстурбации", они тем не менее способствовали "непорочному зачатию" генерации телесников. Подобный акт "благовещения", приведший к триумфу телесничества, я бы определил как психолексический гетерогенез -- продуцирование ***другого*** путем заимствования у текста его пластики и основанное на использовании его телесных ресурсов ("психомиметическое событие", в терминологии В. Подороги).

Автохтонность может иметь как "левую", так и "правую" ориентацию. В сегодняшней России, где телесность и ортодоксия стали синонимами, художественные акции – такие, как, например, публичное мастурбирование или скотоложство -- носят аффирмативный характер. В условиях, когда брутальная стадия победившего капитализма усугубляется повсеместным физическим насилием, автохтонный жест прочитывается как идентитарный, то есть как желание не отличаться от тех, кто "командует парадом". Наиболее последовательными из всех телесников, возросших на российской почве, следует считать Олега Кулика и Александра Бренера. Кулик прославился симуляцией половых актов с домашними и дикими животными, закланием свиньи в московской галерее Риджина, а также публичными акциями, в которых их автор позировал голый, изображая бешеную собаку, норовившую укусить прохожих и зрителей. Учитывая нравы недавно разбогатевшей российской публики, а также то, что большие деньги в России делаются в основном теми, кто задействован в криминальные структуры и для кого насилие -- стиль жизни, перформансы Кулика вполне отражают "текущий момент". Проблема в том, что они отражают его не критически. Стараясь быть более скотским, чем окружающий мир, Кулик -- в лучшем случае -- осуществляет его деконструкцию. Но деконструктивные коннотации не прочитываются "новыми русскими". Скорее, это их развлекает, не говоря о том, что некритическая адаптация их поведения, их стиля и их манер представителями художественной среды воспринимается ими как знак одобрения, свидетельство признания их власти, влияния и значимости.

Что касается Бренера, то разговор о нем мог бы ограничиться упоминанием о его мастурбировании на глазах у многочисленных купальщиков бассейна "Москва", о куче говна, которую он пытался наложить у картины Ван Гога в Пушкинском музее изобразительных искусств, и о попытке вызвать президента Ельцина на кулачный бой (в стиле Артура Кравана). На этом можно было бы поставить точку, когда бы не последняя "акция" Бренера в амстердамском музее Стедлик и связанный с ней судебный процесс. Поздней осенью 1996 года Бренер нарисовал зеленый знак доллара на картине Малевича, за что был арестован и (в феврале 1997 года) приговорен к пяти месяцам тюрьмы. То, что выбор пал на Стедлик, связано с мягкостью нидерландских законов: акция сначала планировалась в музее Метрополитэн в Нью-Йорке, однако адвокат, у которого Бренер заблаговременно проконсультировался, посоветовал ему выбрать другое, более "подходящее" место. "В Америке за это могут дать десять лет", -- сообщил он Бренеру. На суде Бренер сказал следующее: "В культуре наступил кризис, сравнимый с крупнейшей катастрофой XX века, Второй Мировой Войной. Мы различаем только голоса людей, производящих машины, и голоса тех, у кого власть. Я выступаю от лица культуры, сохранившей человеческий голос". Согласно Бренеру, современная художественная элита захлопнула дверь в новые миры, отрытые для нас Малевичем. Вопреки тому, что акция в Стедлике -- проявление "хорошо темперированного" фанатизма, фанатизма право-радикального толка, прикрывающего себя риторикой демократизации культуры, "инициатива" Бренера заслуживает комментария. Дело в том, что ценность произведений современного искусства -- достаточно условное понятие, связанное с модернистским "мифом об оригинальности" и -- в частности -- с тем, как он (этот миф) конвертируется в денежные знаки. В ситуациях подобной этой, то есть когда речь идет о взаимоотношениях между ценностями и ценами, Марсель Мосс (***Mauss***) и Жорж Батай могли бы употребить термин "потлач" (***potlach***), определяемый как модус операнди символического обмена. Но меня в данном случае интересует другое. Понятно, что, переходя из рук в руки и становясь собственностью индивида или секулярной (не жреческой) институции, символическая ценность зачастую перестает быть таковой. Что касается нашего отношения к музею, то здесь имеются две возможности: либо мы признаем его жреческой институцией и -- соответственно -- верим в сохранение в его стенах символического ингредиента искусства, либо мы считаем его светской институцией и -- до какой-то степени -- инструментом упразднения символического. Это упразднение или, как сказал бы Бренер, "узурпация" символического -- как раз то, что его больше всего беспокоит. Стараясь этому помешать, он действует от лица кланово-племенных, тотемных традиций, в духе того, что некоторые из его единомышленников определяют как "сакральный путь". Но "сакральный путь" Бренера -- путь индивида (сингулярная трансгрессия), тогда как символический порядок (***symbolic order***) опосредован психосоматикой коллективного тела. Поэтому всякий, кто выступает против конвертируемости символических ценностей в знаковые (например, денежные), должен согласовывать свои акции с себе подобными, действовать с их согласия, в соответствии с кланово-племенным консенсусом и т.п. Действия Бренера не были санкционированы коллективным телом, поэтому их следует квалифицировать как индивидуалистические, а значит -- противоречащие символу веры символического порядка. Единственные "тела", которые могли бы проявить солидарность с акцией в Амстердаме, это "тела насилия", произросшие на руинах тоталитаризма и предпочитающие экономический террор политическому. Многим ясно, что музей -- это хорошо освещенный сейф, что в число его функций -- помимо презервации культуры -- входит и ее подавление, и что именно в музее, несмотря на "свободный" доступ к произведениям искусства, мы ощущаем всю бездну отчуждения от них. Непонятно одно: неужели без

Бренера и ему подобных мы не в состоянии осознать серьезность и неотложность всех этих проблем?

В начале апреля этого года, возвращаясь из Неаполя, я решил переночевать в Венеции. Утром, прогуливаясь по полупустому городу, остановился у журнального стенда. На глаза попалась обложка итальянского издания журнала Флэш Арт. На ней красовался Александр Бренер, застывший в романтической позе у картины Малевича. Автор обложки, разумеется, не знал, как выглядит герой его произведения, и поэтому изобразил его похожим на молодого Тони Шафрази, прославившегося много лет назад скандальной порчей пикассовской "Герники". На вокзале во Франкфурте меня встречал художник Эдуард Гороховский. Он размахивал свежим номером англоязычного Флэш Арта, на страницах которого издатель Джанкарло Полити объяснялся в любви к Бренеру. По его словам Бренер намного "живее статичного Малевича", и на этом основании должен быть выпущен из тюрьмы. Что касается Полити, то в лице Бренера он обрел, наконец, идеал, напоминающий ему самого себя. Прежде, то есть до Бренера, это в основном были антиподы, такие как, например, Тони Негри, Феликс Гваттари или автор этих строк. Однако, флирт с интеллектуалами ни к чему "хорошему" не приводил. Восторженный интерес к ним неизменно сменялся у Полити неприязнью, неприязнь -- вероломством и т.д. Судя по всему, идентифицируясь с физическим (телесным) актом "творческого насилия" в исполнении Бренера, Полити тем самым рукоплещет термидору телесности в России, приветствуя "хозяев жизни", к числу которых принадлежит и он сам.

В случае Кулика и Бренера телесность сопряжена с выбором формы, фактуры жеста, системы опосредований и филиаций. Сходство этой "политики означающего" с поведенческими нормами новой буржуазии настолько велико, что "тонкие" мотивы или различия -- если таковые и существуют -- оказываются неразличимыми. Это как комариный писк в сравнении с хоровым пением. Одним из таких "тонких" мотивов повидимому является вполне оправданное недовольство российских художников и кураторов тем, как с ними обходятся за границей. Но разве неблагосклонность ***другого*** -- не повод для того, чтобы предпринять усилия, необходимые для реанимации культуры внутри страны? В качестве возможного ответа на этот вопрос приведу отрывок из диалога между мной и Маргаритой Тупицыной:

> В.Т.: На Западе мы часто ругаем музеи современного искусства, и они этого заслуживают Но когда их нет, то начинаешь с особой остротой чувствовать дефицит энергии, необходимой для воспроизводства культуры. От того, что альтернативное русское искусство трех предыдущих декад не висит в музеях, плохо в первую очередь художникам девяностых годов.
>
> М.Т.: Да, это как дом, в котором пропущено несколько этажей.[5]

Сегодня мы видим как прозрачные (то есть подчиненные глазомеру ***рацио***) утопические сверхтела начинают распадаться с тем, чтобы соединиться вновь, но уже на основе иной, автохтонной логики, в соответствии с которой "термидор" телесности в странах бывшего советского блока сопровождается ожесточением парциальности. Туловище восточной Европы номадически, как лимбургский сыр, расползается в разные стороны. В ряде случаев (Босния, Чечня) отторжение республик и регионов выдерживает сравнение с хирургическим вмешательством. И в этом смысле операция, перенесенная президентом России (перерезание артерий, замена одних сосудов другими и т.п.), вполне подстать происходящему. Если в США прагматизм межрегиональных отношений обусловлен контролем со стороны бюрократов с гарвардским образованием, то в России процесс увязания в автохтонности идет параллельно телесным корчам и судорогам территориально-земельного раздела. Так, укрепляя позиции в культуре, телесность становится протагонистом и на геополитической арене.

Если согласиться с тем, что в девяностые годы "все русское" на Западе вышло или выходит из моды, то придется признать и другой, не менее очевидный факт: оскудение интереса к современной русской культуре за пределами ее территориальных границ -- печальная кульминация затянувшегося романа между советским режимом и его поклонниками в Европе и США. Достаточно ознакомиться с воспоминаниями опьяненных Россией интеллектуалов (от Беньямина до Альтюссера[6] и др.), чтобы понять, до какой степени западная интеллигенция до– и послевоенного времени была загипнотизирована не только хроникой, но и художественной репрезентацией советской жизни, каждым триумфом социалистического строительства, каждым разоблачением врагов народа, каждым нюансом идеологической борьбы. Теперь, когда всем стало ясно, что Россия -- это затонувший Титаник (Титаник утопии), от нее бегут как черт от ладана. Холод и высокомерие, пришедшие на смену пылкой заинтересованности, -- расплата за семьдесят лет беззаветных душевных и умственных инвестиций в лопнувший банк советского утопического проекта. Если прежде к Москве были обращены взоры, устремленные в будущее, то с тех пор, как жизнь в ней стала напоминать американцам и европейцам их собственное прошлое, ею начали интересоваться ревнители утраченного времени, то есть, в сущности, ретрограды. Вот почему произведения литературы и искусства ностальгической масти продолжают пользоваться некоторым (ограниченным) спросом за границей. Сложность ситуации в том, что ретроградов, увы, не так много среди западных критиков, кураторов и активно выставляющихся художников.

В Европе и в первую очередь в Америке "искусство для искусства" и сопутствующие ему мифы в достаточной степени амортизированы. Их апологеты утратили репутацию ниспровергателей; адвокатируемые ими художественные программы стали общим местом, а сами они оказались интегрированными в то, что можно назвать эстетическим сервисом (для) большинства. Однако все, кто исповедовал сходные убеждения в СССР, акцентируя принцип "автономности эстетики", самим фактом своего существования и, чаще всего, помимо собственной воли вовлекались в противостояние гигантской машине обезличивания. И хотя в сравнении с сонмами ревнителей "социально неангажированного" искусства на Западе число их советских единомышленников было ничтожным, идиоматизм культивируемого ими художественного языка являлся камнем преткновения на пути к тотальной стереотипизации культуры. Словом, обитатели "башни из слоновой кости" парадоксальным образом врачевали мир, пытавшийся их коррумпировать.

В постперестроечные годы положение в корне изменилось. Извинительные мотивации, примиряющие нас с "политикой аполитичности" (***politics of nonpoliticality***) художественного андерграунда 60-х, 70-х и 80-х годов, не распространяются на нынешнюю генерацию творчески озабоченных людей. Дефицит реальности, компенсируемый в прежние времена переизбытком символических ценностей, уступил место ее метастазу. Именно в этих исключительно сложных условиях художественная культура утрачивает "буферную зону", предохраняющую от соударений с внешним миром, от инстантивного (с ним) контакта. Являясь "вторичной моделирующей системой", искусство распространяет идею вторичности на все, что его окружает. Отсюда --

необходимость взаимоотношений через вторые руки, каковыми обычно являются, с одной стороны, федеральные, муниципальные и частные спонсирующие инстанции, а с другой -- сонмы ревнителей, сопереживателей, комментаторов и толкователей, осуществляющих связь с обществом и формирующих изоляционный пояс вокруг художественной среды. В зажиточных буржуазных странах подобный изоляционный пояс, предохраняющий как авангард, так и его ***другое*** от взаимной агрессии, воспринимается как данность, как нечто само собой разумеющееся. В России это сейчас невозможно. Представители научно-технической интеллигенции, которые в хрущевские и брежневские времена сочувствовали диссидентам, составляли также основной процент зрительской аудитории, симпатизировавшей альтернативному творчеству. Их нынешнее обнищание лишило художников околотворческой среды. В силу этих и других причин мир рефлексий обнаружил себя приплюснутым к миру флексий, оказавшись лицом к лицу с бедствующим населением и нуворишами. Создавшаяся ситуация ставит под сомнение не только актуальность экспериментальных художественных практик в России, но и статус искусства вообще. Во всяком случае, она (эта ситуация) требует переопределения основных функций визуальной культуры.

[1] В эту статью включены фрагменты из недавней книги автора. См. В. Тупицын, *"Другое" искусства, Ad Marginen, Москва, 1997*.

[2] См. Louis Althusser and Etienne Balibar, Reading Capital (London/New York: Verso, 1979), pp. 243-247.

[3] Эти выставки происходили с 1956 по 1962 год.

[4] Апологетикой инцидента можно считать открытое письмо В. Мизиано в ответ на реакцию участников и организаторов проекта "Интерпол" в Стокгольме (февраль 1996 г.) по поводу разрушения А. Бренером работ других участников выставки. См. Flash Art, no. 188, May/June 1996, p. 46.

[5] Виктор Тупицын, "*Другое*" искусства, Ad Marginem, 1997, стр. 278.

[6] См. Walter Benjamin, Moscow Diary (Cambridge: Harvard University Press, 1986), а также Louis Althusser, L'avenir dure longtemps, suivi de ***Les faits***, Editions STOCK/IMEC, 1992.

IMPORTED – A READING SEMINAR in Relationship with my "A Portable (Not so Ideal) Imported Library, Or How to Reinvent the Coffee Table: 25 Books for Instant Use (Californian Version)," 1995
Otis School of Art, Los Angeles, April, May 1995

FLIRTING WITH THE FOREIGN—INTERRACIAL SEX IN JAPAN'S "INTERNATIONAL" AGE

KAREN KELSKY

INTRODUCTION

Since the late 1980s, a small population of young Japanese women has become the subject of intense controversy within Japan and abroad for its allegedly aggressive sexual pursuit of white, black, Balinese, and other non-Japanese (or *gaijin*) males.[1] The activities of these women—labeled "yellow cabs" (*iero kyabu*) in a racist, sexist slur coined by their foreign male conquests and appropriated by the Japanese mass media—have inspired best-selling novels, television documentaries, films, and, in the early 1990s, a heated debate in the major popular magazines. Anthropologist John Russell has observed of the phenomenon (which has tended to particularly sensationalize the role of black males), "what was once a taboo subject—the relations between black [men] and Japanese women—[has] suddenly become a topic fit for open discussion, sensational serials in Japanese magazines, late–night television debate, and underground cinema."[2] These women are interesting not only for the controversy that they have engendered in Japan, but also because they defy standard Western Orientalist understandings of the Asian-Western encounter, typically based on the *Madame Butterfly* trope of Western male power over and victimization of the Oriental women. In the standard yellow cab narrative, it is wealthy and leisured Japanese women who travel to exotic locales to pursue these sexual liaisons: it is the Japanese women who themselves pay for the expenses of initiating and maintaining the liaisons; and it is Japanese women who, along with Japanese men, have developed a thriving industry at home devoted to commentary upon and evaluation of the *gaijin* male as lover—a commentary entirely independent of the foreigner himself.

The term "yellow cab" is a slur that implies that Japanese women are "yellow," and that, like a New York taxi, "they can be ridden any time."[3] The persistent use of the term encapsulates the hysterical response of the male–dominated Japanese media (as well as of the foreign men who originally coined the term) to the specter of sexually aggressive and transgressive Japanese females. However, within the Japanese media there are competing voices, as the "yellow cabs" themselves, as well as female commentators and writers, proffer their own interpretations of the women's behavior. In fact, the graphic, semi-pornographic novels on the topic of black male-Japanese female sex which have comprised perhaps the most important element in this sensational media discussion have been written by two young women writers, Yamada Eimi and Ieda Shoko,[4] who are notorious for flaunting their preference for black men and black culture. These novels are not only best–sellers, but Yamada's work has been nominated for the Naoki and Akutagawa literary prizes—the most prestigious in the Japanese literary world.

In this essay I will examine the contradictions and negations which accompany the yellow cab phenomenon. I will show that critical Japanese male representations are countered and resisted by the women, who demonstrate their own active goals in choosing *gaijin* lovers. I argue that the goals and behavior of the so-called yellow cabs are in fact of considerable theoretical significance for a Western audience, for they constitute not only a coherent, although indirect, critique of Japanese patriarchy, but also an instance of the increasingly shifting and contested grounds of encounter between Japan and the West and, finally, the emerging local/global continuum along which both people and theories must now be tracked.

The intersections of race, gender, nationalism, and sexuality have come under increasing interrogation by Western scholars who are seeking to problematize the dark and obscure associations between "love of country," imperial will, and erotic longing. Much of this work has been concerned to show the extent to which "Oriental" and other nonwhite women have suffered from a unique brand of sexual colonization at the hands of Western men, not shared by their male counterparts. This line of research is necessary and valuable, and the various planes of continuing Western male power over the non-Western woman—particularly in the still-obscure areas of sexual encounters and sex tourism—must be further explored. However, just as Appadurai and Breckenridge have argued that "old images that we associate with neo-colonialism" do not exhaust all that is happening within "new forms of transnational, cosmopolitan cultural traffic,"[5] so, it must be kept in mind, old images of the victimized native woman do not exhaust all the possibilities of contemporary Asian female-Western male sexual encounters. In the age of M. Butterfly, things are not so simple. Japan refuses to be contained by Western tropes and academic theories, and Japanese women (although this point seems scarcely recognized) in many ways defy the Western-set gender dichotomy between public powerlessness and private influence. For one thing, they refuse to be, echoing Appadurai, "incarcerated" in the native land. Japanese women—particularly young, single, "pink-collar" women—are perhaps the most enthusiastic and committed travelers of any demographic group in the world; they are also, arguably, one of the wealthiest, with an expendable income over twice that of the typical Japanese male and with an expenditure in a vacation locale like Hawaii almost three times that of any other individual tourist. Thus Japanese women embody to a large degree what Clifford has called the new global "cosmopolitanism", which is marked, more than anything else, by the postmodern idiom of "travel" and the crossing (and inhabiting) of borders.

This essay begins with the notion of culture as travel (as well as its inverse, "travel as culture") to interrogate the meanings of a population of young Japanese women which enacts and resists, defies and maintains, Japanese cultural norms of gender, race, and sexuality. My goal, however, is not thereby to draw conclusions about a timeless, bounded, and coherent entity called "the Japanese culture," but rather to set these local discourses against a global backdrop of increasingly complicated and interconnected transnational flows of people and power in order to show the circumstances of flux, confrontation, resistance, and displacement that mediate the global/local nexus of Japan in the world.

Without question "yellow cabs" are a small, marginal group, and the term itself is highly contested. Even the women who engage in such behavior would certainly not apply the term to themselves, for it has become a rhetorical weapon used by Japanese men to discredit a form of female behavior that they find threatening and disturbing and by foreign men to maintain hierarchies of power over Asian women. There are many Japanese women, including a group founded in New York City by Japanese professional writers called the Association to Think About Yellow Cabs (*iero kyaby wo kangaeru kai*), who reject the term outright, alleging that no such women exist, and that the whole media phenomenon is the invention of Japanese men to undermine the activities of all Japanese women abroad.[6] Indeed, as time has passed, the yellow cab controversy has begun to have a deleterious influence on the reputations of Japanese women living abroad for any reason, first in Japan, but later even in the United States, where the term and its meaning has slowly dispersed to parts of the American male population. The anguish and humiliation at being labeled "yellow cabs" experienced by serious professional women residing overseas to pursue careers is undoubtedly great, and their consternation is understandable; however, to censor and/or deny yellow cab reality is not an adequate solution. Any such efforts to negate their existence and experience run the risk of reinscribing patriarchal systems' hostility toward and rejection of women as sexual actors.

CONNOISSEUR OF THE WEST

However few their numbers, the women come in large part from the ranks of "office ladies" (OLS); young, unmarried clerical office workers who, through the strategy of living with their parents, enjoy a large expendable income than any other group of people in Japan.[7] The OL has virtually no chance for upward mobility within the company, and for this reason has been almost universally branded, by Western observers, as a victim of oppressive gender discrimination. What is little recognized, however, is the degree to which the OLS have employed their considerable financial resources to construct a vital, vibrant subculture of their own in the interstices of the male-dominated Japanese business world. The very circumstances that are marks of the OLS' inferior professional status—lack of serious responsibilities, shorter working hours, flexibility to quit uncongenial jobs—are the same circumstances which leave these women free to pursue a substantially, independent lifestyle devoted to shopping, hobbies, gourmet dining, overseas travel and the satisfaction of purely personal leisure desires.[8] Many observers have remarked that only the OL truly enjoy the fruits of the Japanese economic miracle.

The OL lifestyle and subculture depend more than anything upon complicated and sophisticated patterns of consumption and demand a single-minded commitment to commodity ethics and aesthetics that goes beyond mere purchasing or appreciation, but instead enters the realm of connoisseurship. While this consumption has undoubtedly declined since the bursting of the 1980s "bubble economy" and extended recession, it still outpaces anything seen in Western countries in many years. In fact, OL connoisseurship has long since exhausted the resources of native or Japanese products and has in the last ten years expanded to encompass the goods, services, experiences, and opportunities of the entire globe—in particular, the West. Many OLs have traveled so widely, and shopped so extensively, that they are satisfied with nothing less the finest the West has to offer, including diamonds and gemstones, haute couture fashion, Club Med vacations, French perfumes and designer goods of all types. Things Western are not merely coveted, however; that was the case for earlier generations for whom foreign goods were seductively exotic. Now, Western goods are contained as signifiers within a largely self-sufficient OL universe of style and status; the West has been "domesticated", to the extent that it is Japan itself that is now, for this generation, exotic and alien.

As Tobin has noted, Japan "now has the desire, wealth and power to import and consume passion in many forms from the West."[9] Thus the stage is set for a few of these cosmopolitan young women—these connoisseurs of the West and citizens of the (late capitalist) world—to cross Japan's borders in search of the "*gaijin* lover", the exotic sexual experience that represents the final frontier of the foreign left to consume.

POSTCARDS FROM THE EDGE

The locations in which young women so inclined may seek out men are many and varied, but are concentrated, within Japan, in the fashionable districts of Tokyo, Yokohama, Kobe, and the U.S. military bases of Yokosuka, Yokota, Misawa, Iwakuni, Sasebo, and Okinawa. Outside of Japan, they include Hawaii, Bali, Saipan, New York, and the U.S. West Coast. Not coincidentally, each of these locations is a border region, inhabited by a highly transient ethnically, racially, and culturally mixed population. Even the regions within Japan are really not of Japan. The American military bases are of course, U.S. real estate; Yokohama and Kobe are historically the centers of foreign presence in Japan; and the Roppongi district—commonly known as the "*gaijin* ghetto" of Tokyo—is a kind of dreamlike (or nightmarish) liminal region of bars and nightclubs in which Japanese and non-Japanese mingle freely. Each of these locations is geographically ambiguous, caught within the post/neocolonialist regimes of U.S. military presence abroad, Japanese investment, mass tourism, international labor flows, and commodification of the "native". As such, they are obvious places to seek out the foreign erotic, for the foreign men in these locations are themselves often wanderers from Europe and the mainland United States, gravitating to the borderlands of Asia and the West in search of the "erotic Orient."[10] In Hawaii these men are known locally as "playboys"; they form a bounded and mutually recognizable population which roams the streets of Waikiki daily, seeking out and accosting Japanese female tourists for money and sex. Likewise, every weekend night in Roppongi, the clubs are packed with foreign men hoping to encounter their "Roppongi girl" for the evening.

Once in these locations, the young women, extending the consumer patterns that dominate their lives elsewhere, pay for the company of foreign males. This is not an institutionalized prostitution, but rather falls within the rubric of *mitsugu*, an old Japanese word—defined in the dictionary to mean "to give financial aid to one's lover"—that has taken on new life in this transnational context. The practice of *mitsugu* of foreign males includes the male's rent, upkeep, and outstanding debts, payment of all costs associated with the affair, and finally, material gifts including cars, designer goods, watches, and jewelry. It is understood by both parties that both inside and outside of Japan, Japanese women, as possessors of the strong yen, are likely to be in the financially superior position. As one "playboy" in Waikiki told me, "they know if they want us they have to pay for everything." Women have here usurped the traditionally male prerogative of purchasing sex in pleasure districts at home and abroad. Some women, in fact, assert that "it was Japanese men, with their sex tours, who taught us how to behave like this." As we shall see, however, Japanese men disclaim all responsibility for yellow cab behavior.

The intensity of the public outcry surrounding this yellow cab behavior suggests that it has indeed struck a nerve, particularly among Japanese men. The response of Japanese male journalists to the specter of the yellow cab can be described very simply: it is reactionary, conservative, and prurient. Devoted to the reassertion and reinscription of all elements of Japanese national/racial/sexual identity, and of traditional power hierarchies between Japanese men and women, men's representations derive their primary rhetorical force from the use of derogatory labels: not just yellow cab, but also "*burasagarizoku*" (armhangers), referring to the sight of diminutive Japanese women hanging on the arms of tall foreign men; "*sebun-irebun*" (seven-eleven), meaning that the women, like the stores, are "open twenty-four hours"; and "*eseburakku*" (fake blacks), referring to those who imitate "black" hairstyles, fashion, and mannerisms. Each of these labels draws attention to the ways in which "proper" racial/gender boundaries have been violated. Yellow cab and *sebun-irebun* imply that the women's sexuality has become abandoned, out of control; *burasagarizoku* and *eseburakku* suggest that critical racial distinctions—tall foreigner/short Japanese, blackness/Japaneseness—are threatened. That is, historically, Japanese women are always already deeply associated with the foreign, and foreign men are always already highly sexualized. Thus, the foreign men also imperil sexual boundaries, and Japanese women also jeopardize national/racial ones. These two themes, then, combine together into one hypersexualized, hostile and prurient male discourse that depends upon master narratives of oversexed foreign men and duplicitous Japanese women. "It's the Japanese girls who can be found dancing on the tables at discos, with their underpants showing for all to see.... They live in Waikiki hi-rises...that their daddies pay for."[11] "The temperature of Narita Airport goes up each time a planeload of girls return from their trips overseas...and on outbound flights, they all may pretend to be little ladies, but actually, in their hearts, each one want to be the first to get a *gaijin* to bed."[12]

Even the prose of highly regarded novelist and columnist Tanaka Yasuo (author of the popular cult novel *Nantonaku Kurisutaru*), degenerates into a hostile diatribe on the subject of yellow cabs: "Of course, they have no use for Japanese men, and this shows on their faces.... They try to pretend that they're intellectuals [but] people who know laugh at them.... These girls may seem delicate, but they're actually tough nails."[13] Tanaka is clearly as disturbed by the women's deceptiveness as by their sexual transgressions. This fear of the "traitor in disguise" reveals the male linking of female sexual duplicity and national honor. This linking is most explicitly achieved in popular writer Ishikawa Miyoshi's recent suggestion that "Japanese women spread their legs a little wider for the sake of U.S.-Japan relations."[14]

With this male rhetoric, AIDS takes on a dire significance. Through the specter of AIDS, Japanese men may at once paint the foreign male as not just an oversexed animal, but a diseased oversexed animal; the Japanese women as treacherous and dirty; and themselves as innocent victims whose lives and heath are endangered because of female duplicity. Again and again in the Japanese media, yellow cabs are targeted as the most high-risk group in Japan for HIV infection, while the men's sex tours to Thailand, Korea, and the Philippines go unmentioned. In fact, only a fraction of Japanese female heterosexual HIV-positive individuals contracted the disease overseas, compared to heterosexual Japanese males. However, statistics cannot compete against a self-righteous male hysteria which culminated in one man plastering the walls and sidewalks of Waikiki with small, xeroxed notes that read: "Aloha Japanese girls…all men in Hawaii have AIDS. If YOU go with them, they will give you liquor and drugged cigarettes, and while you are sleeping, you will be raped, and have everthing taken."[15] Writers such as Yamada Eimi and Ieda Shoko cannily feed into this hypersexualized hysteria by dwelling ostentatiously and obsessively in their novels on themes of black male sexual appetites and genital size. The works themselves are nothing more than soft-core pornographic novels which capitalize on the very worst racist notions of black male sexuality and racial inferiority:

"Nuzzling his chest hair with my lips, I inhaled his body odor. I recognized the smell as the sweetish stink of rotten cocoa butter.... His smell seemed to assault me, like some filthy thing. But it also made me feel, by comparison, clean and pure. His smell made me feel so superior. It was like the smell of musk that a dog in heat sends out to attract his bitch."[16]

"Jean stood over me as I lay naked on the bed, holding his heavy dick in his left hand and swinging it back and forth. I'm not usually so eager, but all I could think about was being wrapped in Jean's powerful body.... I was crazy with lust. While he toyed with it, his copper-colored "thing," which had been dangling in his left hand, swelled. It seemed as if it reached to his navel. I can only say, it was a wonderful sight."[17]

Yet by taking this line, Yamada and Ieda are guaranteed not just good sales, but critical acclaim and accolades from Japanese male reviewers.

GOOD GAIJINS/GAIJIN GOODS

Women other then Yamada and Ieda, however, offer an entirely independent interpretation of the foreign male as lover—one that is, compared to the monotonous rantings of male commentators, varied, subtle, and complex. On one level, women's accounts are concerned with issues not of identity and morality but of commodity and value. For what distinguishes the rhetoric of women is its shrewd and insistent contrast between Japanese and *gaijin* men—a kind of "comparison shopping" that carefully weighs the advantages of individual men on the basis of race and nationality.

The comparative advantages of the foreign male range widely, but include foremost an alleged "kindness" (*yasashisa*). It is in fact a virtual stereotype that foreign men are kind (*yasashii*), with many women offering contrasts like this one: "American men have been trained by their mothers since childhood to respect women—in a 'ladies first' kind of atmosphere.... But in Japan, women are always below men" (graduate student, University of Hawaii). "Other women swell up to look good, but a *gaijin* looks good even when he looks bad." Foreign males' native English ability is often mentioned as an attraction. As one source stated, succinctly, "It's faster, cheaper, and more fun than going to English classes." Finally, of course, there is the allegedly superior sexual skill of the foreign male:

"Americans know how to enjoy sex! It's fun, natural, wonderful. Japanese men treat it like something dirty or bad."

"The thing that black guys have in bed that other guys don't is a strong thrusting motion and a sense of rhythm."[18]

This sexual dimension is de-emphasized, however, by others who claim that in the sexual act itself foreign men are the same as or inferior to Japanese men in skill. Such women argue that it is *yasashisa*, both in and out of bed, that sets *gaijin* males apart. The glibly racist novels of Yamada Eimi and Shoko have, of course, made foreign male sexuality—in particular black male sexuality—a *cause célèbre* in Japan today.

The praise that is heaped upon the foreign male, however, is in most respects the praise given to a serviceable commodity object. Ieda states, "Girls know what they want! Chanel, Louis Vuitton bags, Hermes scarves, and *gaijin* men!"[19] Another woman, a habitué of Roppongi, suggests: "Gaijins are fun...but not if you fall in love...so it's better to just keep him around for a while, to show off, like a pet."[20] Once again turning to the works of Yamada Eimi, we can see that the *gaijin* male is, in many ways, merely a "stand-in" for his penis. "[Spoon's] dick was not at all similar to the reddish, disgusting cocks of white guys. It was also different from the sad and pathetic organs of Japanese men.... Spoon's dick shone before my eyes like a living thing. It reminded me of the sweet chocolate candy bars I love."[21] Here it is the male genitals that are made into marketable commodities, and rated, by race, according to their serviceability.

When it comes to the question of marriage, some women are blunt: "I'll never marry a hairy barbarian [*keto*]. I'll marry a Japanese even if he's terrible in bed and ugly. At least he's stable." A young woman interviewed on a television special entitled, "The Real Truth About 'Resort Lovers'" informed an aghast male interviewer that "In a few years I'll wash hands of this whole *gaijin* business, and return to Japanese men." An English student I spoke with was even more direct: "For marriage we want a Japanese guy; for playing around we want *gaijins*." The *gaijin* male's serviceability, then, is only in the capacity of escort/lover, and the reason lies in his rarity—or "*mezurashisa*."

"I have to admit we have a weakness for *gaijins*.The reason is, there aren't too many of them in Japan, so they're rare [*mezurashii*]." (English student, Hawaii)

"Why do we like blacks? 'Cause there aren't any in Japan [*Nihon ni nai deshol*]. (Tourist in Hawaii)

Apparently racial preferences shifted toward black men in the late 1980s based on the relative rarity of different racial types: "Two years ago everybody was going out with whites...but then, white guys weren't rare [*mezurashii*] anymore, so, right now everybody is going out with black guys." (English student) The commodity cycle continues to evolve as tastes more recently move toward Asian immigrant laborers. In men, as in other things, rarity brings status. This status is coveted, and its effect calculated. As *Cosmopolitan Japan* gushed in 1988, "We'd all like to be seen walking down the street arm in arm with a *gaijin* boyfriend, wouldn't we, girls?" A tourist in Hawaii explained, "We can walk a little taller. We think 'you go out with men from the same country, but I go out with men from a different country.'" Complete objectification has been achieved: "Being with a *gaijin* feels good.... When another Japanese comes up and asks me 'what language is that?' I feel pretty proud, you know? So, he's an accessory. From that point of view, any *gaijin* will do, even Sankhon."[22]

RACE AND REFLEXIVITY[23]

The primary characteristic of women's discourse on the foreign male is its insistent contrast between Japanese and *gaijin* men. The attractions of the foreigner are attractive precisely because those qualities—kindness, sexiness, English ability—are claimed to be lacking in the Japanese male. It is clear, then, that the Japanese male is the invisible but central point of reference in this female discussion. Intricately interwoven into the discourse of the "attraction of the *gaijin*" is a parallel discourse of frustration against the Japanese male. This discourse, althought indirect, amounts to a coherent gender critique of Japanese society and Japanese. Nearly every female statement from the previous two sections depends for its rhetorical force upon a critical contrast with the Japanese male: "But in Japan, women are always below men." "A Japanese guy would never do that." "Japanese men treat sex like something dirty."

Perhaps nowhere so much as in the realm of kindness (*yasashisa*) is the Japanese male felt to be deficient. As one source writes, poignantly, "[My black boyfriend] treated me like a lady after I'd been treated like trash by Japanese men." Another offers, "When I go to visit a British or Italian guy's place, he tries to make me clean his room and cook his dinner!"[24] Some women disparage the appearance of Japanese men: a tourist in Hawaii told me, "*Gaijins* are more masculine than skinny, unhealthy-looking Japanese men." And with exceptional virulence women can be heard criticizing the sexual behavior of their male counterparts: "Even in sex, I mean, if a *gaijin* is really telling you 'I want you, I need you, I want you', you get in a mood, right? Not like with some stone-faced Japanese guy who tries to push you into a hotel all of a sudden."[25] As mentioned above, however, other women contest this emphasis on sexuality, arguing in some cases that Japanese men are actually better at technique but lack "emotional availability" or "the ability to create a romantic atmosphere."

Perhaps the most explicit summarization comes from the pen of journalist Kudo Akiko in the women's magazine *Fujin Koron*:

"The reasons Japanese women reject Japanese men are *not just physical....* Women evaluate them badly in all areas—'they are childish and disgusting,' 'they have a bad attitude toward women,' 'they are fake and dishonest,' 'they are narrow-minded,' 'they are bad-mannered,' 'they can't take care of themselves,' 'they can't do housework.' Japanese men are the opposite of the Japanese GNP—they are the lowest in the world!"[26]

In this passage the writer confronts the sexualized focus of the yellow cab controversy in order to deny that the attractions of the foreign male are "just physical." To the contrary, I would argue that the attractions of the foreign male are whatever the female speakers and writers feel is lacking in the Japanese male. For Kudo and others clearly imply that the *gaijin* male is *not* childish and disgusting, is *not* fake and dishonest, is not narrow-minded, and loves to do housework. Yet, do they truly believe this?[27] I argue that, rather, they attribute these traits to the *gaijin* for exclusively rhetorical purposes. The foreign male becomes a reflexive symbol in an indirect discourse of complaint; a mirror against which the Japanese women can reflect back the deficiencies of Japanese men as lovers, husbands, and friends. He enables a coherent, albeit indirect, gendered critique. We can interpret the yellow cab encounters, then, not, as the Association to Think About Yellow Cabs seeks to claim, as a conspiracy perpetrated by Japanese men, but rather as a locus of potent and influential negotiations between some Japanese women and men over present-day and future gender relations in Japan.

As we have seen, the foreign male in reality may not be remotely kind, good-looking, or sexy; these facts are irrelevant. What is important is merely that he is not-Japanese. He is seen as an inert and harmless object, inherently *yasashii*, infinitely separate, entirely Other, by virtue of Japanese racial ideologies, and therefore endlessly malleable to the pursuit of female aims and agendas. That the *gaijin* may have any agendas of his own, in the pursuit of which the Japanese (or other Asian woman) is merely a tool, is not recognized or perhaps even imagined. The consequences of this ignorance can, however, be serious. Time and again young Japanese women in Waikiki are raped, impregnated, or, at the very least, taken advantage of financially and physically by the local population of "playboys." My playboy informants were blissfully convinced of their power over Japanese women, bragging about the sums of money they had extracted from them, and the abusive, humiliating, and degrading sexual acts they had compelled the women to perform. The Western men, then, are hardly passive and inert.[28]

However, circumstances conspire against women's recognition of the real nature of the Western male partner, The fantasy of *yasashisa*, Japanese racial ideologies of separateness and "alien"-ation, commodity aesthetics and commodity ethics, Japanese consumer power over the West—all these lead to the *gaijin* male being objectified and commodified, seen and treated in a manner that fails to recognize his agency and power.[29] Women have appropriated the gaijin males as reflexive symbols by which they construct an image of Japanese men as they are, and as they wish them to be. Yet for all his deficiencies, it is the Japanese man who, in the end, retains the status of legitimate marital partner. These "flirtatious commodities" (in a stunning illustration of Haug's argument) are, and must be, described in terms that communicate to Japanese women peers, and to Japanese men, that they are no more than discursive symbols through which genuine matters of power and status are discussed and negotiated.

CONCLUSION—GENDER AND (TRANS)NATIONAL SEXUALITIES

Yellow cabs challenge prevailing stereotypes of many things: of the passive and victimized Japanese woman, of the Madame Butterfly trope, of the "proper" relations between Japan and the West. In conclusion I will trace the meanings of their challenge to understandings of Japan and the transnational moment.

The yellow cabs challenge us to consider the new meanings that cultural marginality takes on in a transnational world. Ivy writes that in the cultural imaginary of Japan, men are associated with the native/authentic and women with the foreign: "images of fictionality and authenticity waver between the poles of the feminine and the masculine—the non-native and the native."[30] Women's impurity, derived from menstruation, childbirth, and household "dirty work", puts them forever at odds with the purity of blood and body required by Japanese racial ideologies. In the past, this marginality put Japanese women at a grave disadvantage, rendering them "inauthentic", unreliable, and unqualified to participate in many ritual and institutional practices. In the transnational world, however, such hierarchies are increasingly destabilized, even reversed. It is precisely because young Japanese women are marginalized professionally and culturally that they have both the leisure and the inclination to travel or reside abroad, to intensively study foreign languages, and consequently to enjoy ever more intimate relations with the foreign(er). And it is precisely because they enjoy an intimate association with the foreign/global that women gain discursive leverage in their domestic gender struggles and in their local dialogues with Japanese men.[31]

Thus Japanese women, through their very marginality, possess knowledge of gender alternatives and options, without which they could not criticize and challenge Japanese male norms and values so consistently and effectively. The benefits for women of foreign associations are clearly parallel to the changing status of the *kikokushijo* (returnee children) in Japan. Once viewed as contaminated from "too much" foreign experience, the *kikokushijo* are now often seen as possessors of an "elite 'cultural' or 'symbolic' capital" which guarantees them entry into some of the finest universities and most prestigious jobs.[32]

We can find, then, in these and other examples in Japan, ways that the transnational "refracts and shapes 'the local.'"[33] The yellow cabs demonstrate the necessity of taking a transnational perspective in ethnographic analysis; their behavior is simply not comprehensible within the confines of a bounded and essentialistic notion of "Japanese culture." The yellow cabs are who and what they are precisely because they negotiate the borders between cultures, races, nations, browsing among the wares of the (masculine) world. The yellow cabs act and speak in the places of "betweenness," of "hybridity and struggle, policing and transgression,"[34] in which flows of people and power meet and interact, creating new forms of encounter and behavior. The degree of policing and struggle that characterize such locations (both spatial and cultural) is revealed in the insulting labels with which this group of women has been branded by Japanese and foreign men. The price of transgression is condemnation. Eluding the "border police", however, women continue to flirt with the foreign in their desire to disturb and recreate the Japanese.

But what is recreated? Are the discursive strategies employed by the yellow cabs effective in changing male nativist behavior? Japanese men's response has not been to embrace women's demands but to exaggerate the threat they represent: to precipitate a crisis. An example of male inability to cope constructively with the challenge of the yellow cabs and of women's demands can be found in a "Public Debate" on the subject of kissing in public, staged by a popular magazine between feminist Kajiwara Hazuki and male columnist Ikushima Jiro. Kajiwara begins by arguing passionately that Japanese males' ability to express affection is "the worst in the world." She continues, "Because of that, recently the women whose desires for physical warmth and affection are not being satisfied find what they're looking for overseas, and end up being called 'yellow cabs.'"[35] Ikushima, however, responds in this way: "Japanese people are fundamentally poor at [public displays of affection]. They are a shy race. As proof, Japanese males may say 'I like you,' or 'I'm crazy about you,' but they find it difficult to say 'I love you.'... Women may say that easily, and demand that men say it too, but Japanese men will not say it if they can avoid it."[36] Kajiwara concludes her side of the debate by asserting, "I think the time has come for busy Japanese men to start changing.... [A]ny country that will go as far as 'exporting' women's frustration is just not right."[37] But Ikushima, it is clear, cares only to avoid confronting Japanese women's call for change; to reiterate essentialistic, nativist, and male-centered representations of "Japanese culture"; and to compel Japanese women to conform to such representations. It is as though Japanese men, confronted with an unflattering reflection in the mirror held out by women, have responded by turning away their eyes, to gaze instead upon women themselves as examples of female treachery, unbound sexuality and cultural inauthenticity. The men co-opt the women's voices, and in their higly influential media accounts, twist this discourse on gender into a discourse on sex and nation.

The dialogue between Kajiwara and Ikushima represents in microcosm the growing tensions between the much-touted boom in internationalization (*kokusaika*) and the equally conspicuous rise of neonationalist sentiments. Some believe that the two sides do in fact represent opposing opinions and desires, that there is a faction in Japan that seeks genuine internationalization. Others are not so sanguine. Yoshimoto argues instead that neonationalism and internationalization in Japan are merely two sides of the same coin and that "both are necessary to construct a model of the world at the center of which Japan is situated."[38] Similarly, I suggest that what is "recreated" within the yellow cab pheneomenon is not a brave new world of female empowerment and international intimacy, but rather old racism in a new guise. Women transform the foreigner into a signifier whose primary purpose is to further their domestic agendas. Japanese men respond to the challenge by reinscribing inalienable boundaries of race and nation. And foreign males permit themselves to be "bought" only to recreate, indeed relive, ancient Western male fantasies of sexual access to and manipulation of the Oriental woman.

For these reasons, the example of the yellow cabs finally challenges us to be unfailingly alert to the shifting, cross-cutting, and mutually contradictory—indeed incommensurate—claims of race, gender, desire, and sexual fetish in the transcultural border regions.[39] Too eager an embrace of the Bakhtinian carnivalesque, too gleeful a celebration of titillating possibilities of sexual "inversion", will result in our overlooking the local negotiations made of and through these sexual encounters and the way in which these encounters may obscure persistent inequalities, exploitations, and separations on a number of different planes simultaneously. Torgovnik has observed that "the essence of carnivalesque is that one cannot tell male from female, rich from poor, black from white… everything is possible."[40] But as we have seen everything is not possible, and the contact with the Other can just as easily depend on maintaining those differences between male and female, rich and poor, Japanese and black and white. Furthermore, an irresponsible fetishization of, for example, a highly marginal case of Japanese women's sexual objectification of the white male runs the risks of furthering the historical eroticization of the Oriental female ("she can never get enough") and inadvertently serving as "justification" for continued Western male sexual exploitation of Asian women.[41]

This failure of the carnivalesque should be kept in mind when evaluating other interracial sexual encounters, such as those increasingly glorified within the Bennetton-esque multicultural carnival of the contemporary United States. White America's eagerness to appropriate "lovers of color" simultaneously enacts and masks efforts to employ them as signifiers within a self-serving agenda of white liberalism and/or postmodern chic. Regarding this trend, bell hooks has written, "Getting a bit of the Other, in this case engaging in sexual encounters with non-white females, [is now] considered a ritual of transcendence.... White males claim the body of the colored Other instrumentally, as unexplored terrain, a symbolic frontier.... They see their willingness to openly name their sexual desire for the Other as affirmation of cultural plurality."[42] The increasingly common construction of the Asian woman as appropriate, even ideal, partner for white men must always be considered in light of a sexual economy which still permits (encourages?) the publication of essays such as: "Oriental Girls: The Ultimate Accessory."[43] We have entered a new era of race relations, in which sexual contact is often constructed as "a progressive change in white attitudes toward non-whites."[44] But in the age of *M. Butterfly*, things are not so simple. All too often the white men and women who see their foreign, non-white lovers as evidence that they are nonracist, liberal, sensitive, and culturally aware are "not at all attuned to those aspects of their sexual fantasies that irrevocably link them to collective white racist domination."[45] It behooves us to remember that on all points of the global sex map, capital and the forces of commodification can dominate even as they liberate desire. We must recognize this domination, and acknowledge the overdetermined agendas that underlie the exhilarating encounters (sexual and otherwise) of the transnational borderlands.

Credit for reprinting this text: Karen Kelsky, "Flirting with the Foreign," in Rob Wilson and Wimal Dissanayake, eds., *Global/Local: Cultural Production and the Trasnational Imaginary*. Copyright 1996, Duke University Press, Durham, N. C. Reprinted with permission.

1. In the interests of economy, throughout this paper the term *gaijin* will be used to refer to all non-Japanese men, although in actual Japanese usage the term (literally meaning "outsider") is sometimes restricted to Caucasian foreigners.
2. John Russell, "Race and Reflexivity: The Black Other in Contemporary Mass Culture," *Cultural Anthropology* 6, no. 1 (February 1991): 21.
3. The etymology of the term "yellow cab" is itself a remarkable example of the ebb and flow of transnational cultural tides. Ieda claims that the term originated in the United States, among certain black and white men in New York City and Hawaii who coined it to refer to Japanese women who were, from their perspective, "easy." Ieda made the term the focus of controversy by claiming that it is well-known in the United States as a slur on "loose Japanese women." When her work grew popular in Japan, the male-dominated Japanese media took it up as a catchall insult for "disreputable" Japanese women abroad. Women (including the New York-based Association to Think About Yellow Cabs) objected, claiming, rightly, that for the vast majority of Americans the term "yellow cab" has no meaning other than the name of a New York taxi company. Eventually, however, foreigners living in Japan and American journalists got involved in the fray, and as the controversy grew, the term and the debate around it did indeed flow back to the United States, where more men have now begun to use it. Since 1993, however, a new trend has emerged in which some young Japanese women have reappropriated the term in a gesture of pride and defiance against Japanese men. In 1993 a young female writer Iizuka Makiko published a book entitled *The Guys Who Can't Even Ride Yellow Cabs*, in which she argues that as low as some women's standards may be, they are still too high for "selfish, ugly, sexist" Japanese men to reach.
4. All Japanese names are written surname first, given name last.
5. Appadurai and Carol Breckenridge, "Editors' Comments," *Public Culture: Bulletin of the Project for Transnational Cultural Studies* 1, no. 1 (Fall 1988): 2.
6. This association has pursued a vigorous media campaign against the work of Ieda Shoko, so fierce that it has earned the name "Ieda Bashing" and has left Ieda's reputation seriously damaged. While Ieda's work is certainly of questionable reliability, it appears that she was also used as a scapegoat to bear women's rage over the yellow cab controversy.
7. This research is based on ethnographic fieldwork conducted over an eighteen-month period (January 1991-July 1992) in Honolulu, Hawaii. For an ethnographic account of the data, please see Karen Kelsky, "Sex and the Gaijin Male: Contending Discourses of Race and Gender in Contemporary Japan," ASPAC Occasional Papers No. 5 (1993). All translations, unless otherwise noted, are my own.

8. There is no question that many OLS experience real victimization in the form of thwarted career goals, demeaning work, sexual harassment, and corporate paternalism. Nevertheless, I feel it is important to respect the voices of those OLS who assert that equality with men is not a particularily appealing prospect and that they have no desire to compete -with or emulate "male corporate drones."

9. Joseph Tobin, "Introduction: Domesticating the West," in *Re-Made in Japan: Everyday Life and Consumer Taste in a Changing Society*, ed. Joseph Tobin (New Haven: Yale University Press, 1992), p. 11. The most recent form this imported passion takes is J-Club, a wildly popular male strip club in Tokyo, in which eight muscular foreign male dancers, dressed variously as American hillbillies, fifties rockers, cowboys, and trenchcoated film noir P.I.'s, gyrate and disrobe to a background of American rock music before a screaming female audience. As the climax of the performance women may tuck fake U.S. dollar bills (¥1000 for three bills) into the fluorescent G-strings of the foreigner of their choice in exchange for a kiss.

10. An exception are the "beachboys" of Bali, Indonesian men, often from poverty-stricken regions of Java, who look upon Japanese women less as "exotic Oriental women" than as economic benefactors.

11. Anonymous, "Hawaii Nihon ryugakusei no gcka naru benkyoburi" (Japanese overseas students extravagant 'pretend study' abroad), *Shukan Gendai* (August 1989): 151.

12. Anonymous, "OL, Joshidaisei kaigairyoko no seika hokoku" (OL, girl college students overseas travel sex report), *Shukan Hoseki* (August 1988): 218.

13. Tanaka Yasuo, "Otoko ni sukareru kao, kenkyu repoto" (Research report on the kind of face men like), *An An* (September 1988): 81.

14. John Russell, personal communication.

15. Japan is of course not the only country in which AIDS stands in as a metaphor for a host of other social ills. See Susan Sontag, *AIDS and Its Metaphors* (New York: Farrar, Straus and Giroux, 1989). Also, drugging and raping as described in the note is, according to the local police, actually one consistent pattern of Japanese female abuse in Waikiki.

16. Yamada Eimi, *Beddotaimu Aizu* (Bedtime eyes) (Tokyo: Kawade Shobo Shinsha, 1985), p. 13.

17. Ieda Shoko, *Ore no hada ni muragatta onnatachi* (The women who flocked to my skin) (Tokyo: Shodensha, 1991), p. 14.

18. Both quotes from Kudo Akiko, "Gaijin no otoko denakereba sekkusu dekinai onna" (The women who can only have sex with foreigners), *Fujin Koron* (June 20, 1990): 409, 410.

19. Ieda, *Ore no hada ni muragatta onnatachi*, p. 5.

20. Quoted in Katsuhira Ruika, "*Roppongi gyaru*" (Roppongi gals), in *Sekkusu to iu oshigoto* (The job of sex), ed. Ito Shinji (Tokyo: JICC, 1990), p. 215.

21. Yamada, *Beddotaimu Aizu*, p. 15.

22. Quoted in Katsuhira, "Roppongi gyaru," p. 215. Ousemann Sankhon is a Senegalese businessman turned Japanese TV personality; he is noted in the Japanese media for his "peculiar" and "amusing" African looks.

23. This phrase is borrowed from Russell, "Race and Reflexivity," p. 3.
24. Quoted in Kudo, "Gaijin no otoko denakereba sekkusu dekiinai onna," p. 408.
25. Quoted in Murota Yasuko, "Kanaami ni karamitsuita kanashii yokubo" (Sad desires entangled by wire fences), *Asahi Journal*, November 13,1987, p. 7.
26. Kudo, "Gaijin no otoko denakereba sekkusu dekinai onna," p. 411.
27. Subsequent research has shown that many Japanese women do hold a markedly idealized image of Western (white) men. The white male is often described as a "knight in shining armor" or "prince charming" (lit. prince on a white horse, *hakuba ni notta ojisama*) who is unfailingly chivalrous yet treats women with perfect equality. John Russell has called this image of the white male the "Messianic Mystic," and it is in some ways parallel to the Western male image of "Madame Butterfly," in that both serve indirect efforts at sexual control by acting as cautionary reminders to the opposite sex within the race/nation of the existence of competition.
28. See the works of Boye De Mente, especially the 1964 and 1991 editions of his classic guidebook *Bachelor's Japan*, for a blunt exposition of this Western male power fantasy.
29. For a discussion of these racial ideologies and the "alien"-ation of the foreigner, see Karen Kelsky, "Intimate Ideologies: Transnational Theory and Japan's 'Yellow Cabs'" *Public Culture* 6, no.3 (Spring 1994): 465-478.
30. Marilyn Ivy, "Discourses of the Vanishing" (Ph.D. diss., University of Chicago, 1988), p. 49.
31. See Karen Kelsky, "Postcards from the Edge: The 'Office Ladies' of Tokyo," *U.S.-Japan Women's Journal (English Supplement)* 6 (March 1994): 3-26.
32. See Roger Goodman, "Deconstructing an Anthropological Text: A 'Moving' Account of Returnee Schoolchildren in Contemporary Japan," in *Unwrapping Japan: Society and Culture in Anthropological Perspective*, ed. Eyal Ben-Ari et al. (Honolulu: University of Hawaii Press, 1990).
33. Akhil Gupta, "The Song of the Nonaligned World: Transnational Identities and the Reinscription of Space in Late Capitalism;" *Cultural Anthropology* 7, no. 1 (February 1992): 63.
34. James Clifford, "Traveling Cultures," in *Cultural Studies*, ed. Lawrence Grossberg, Cary Nelson, and Paula Treichler (London: Routledge, 1992), p. 109.
35. Kajiwara Hazuki, "Koron shuron-Hitomae de no kisu" (Debate—kissing in public), AERA, August 6, 1991, p. 58.
36. Ikushima Jiro, "Koron shuron-Hitomae de no kisu" (Debate—kissing in public), AERA, August 6, 1991, p. 58.
37. Kajiwara, "Koron shuron," p. 58.
38. Yoshimoto Mitsuhiro, "The Postmodern and Mass Images in Japan," *Public Culture* 1, no. 2 (Spring 1989): 22.
39. See also Anna Tsing, *In the Realm of the Diamond Queen* (Princeton: Princeton University Press, 1993), pp. 213-229 for a nuanced discussion of this complexity and its implications for the ethnographic encounter.
40. Marianna Torgovnick, *Gone Primitive: Savage Intellects, Modern Lives*

(Chicago: University of Chicago Press, 1990), p. 40.
41. One entirely unforeseen consequence of this research has been the large number of white Western male scholars and academics who have personally approached or contacted the author with the apparently self-therapeutic goal of explaining, justifying, rationalizing, or otherwise attempting to absolve themselves for a variety of unhappy personal relationships with Japanese women. I have been quite disturbed to find my research used to promote an identity as abused and misunderstood victim among white male academics; I have the odd, unpleasant sense of, in Lisa Yoneyama's words, "entertaining those I do not wish to entertain." At the same time, however, this latest, somewhat surreal, twist in the yellow cab saga has been instrumental in alerting me both to the ongoing issues of politics and agenda in academic work (whose purposes is it serving? Is it serving purposes that I do not intend?) and to my own culpabilities and responsibilities as ethnographer of such global sex "trades".
42. bell hooks, *Black Looks: Race and Representation* (Boston: South End Press, 1992), pp. 23-24.
43. Tony Rivers, "Oriental Girls: The Ultimate Accessory," *Gentlemen's Quarterly (British Edition)* (October 1990): 39-44.
44. hooks, *Black Looks*, p. 24.
45. Ibid.

LOS ANGELES 1965-1992: FROM CRISIS-GENERATED RESTRUCTURING TO RESTRUCTURING-GENERATED CRISIS[1]

EDWARD W. SOJA

Between 1965 and 1992, the metropolis of Los Angeles experienced a dramatic transformation. Always at the forefront of new urbanization trends ever since its rapid growth in the late nineteenth century, Los Angeles again came to exemplify the dynamics of yet another round of accelerated urban restructuring, in this case one that emerged from the various crises that ended the long postwar economic boom to profoundly reshape the American city in the closing decades of the Twentieth Century. Many new and different urban geographies took form in the aftermath of the Watts rebellion of 1965; they developed together with impressive synergy over nearly thirty years of rapid economic growth; and at the very point when the restructured Los Angeles was comfortably consolidated as one of the paradigmatic metropolises of the late Twentieth Century, the "new" Los Angeles exploded in the most violent urban insurrection in American history.

Compressed within the spatio-temporal brackets of this period and place is a remarkable story, one which has implications far beyond the local context. Through its telling can be seen a symptomatic history and geography of the contemporary world, a revealing glimpse of what it has meant to be alive over the past three decades not only in Los Angeles but nearly everywhere on earth. Many places provide similarly revealing viewpoints from which to make theoretical and practical sense of the contemporary world, but few offer such a vivid and variegated panorama of insights as that provided by the Los Angeles experience, from the crisis-generated restructuring that followed the events of 1965 to what I will describe as the restructuring-generated crisis that surfaced in 1992.

LOOKING BACK TO THE FUTURE: LOS ANGELES IN 1965

To outsiders and many of its own inhabitants, the Los Angeles that erupted in the Watts rebellion of 1965 was a virtually unknown city hidden behind the thick sheathing of a hyperactivated American imaginary. The academic world of urban studies, still being swayed by the appealing orderliness of Chicago and the indescribable density of power and culture in New York, steered clear of Southern California, leaving all hope of accurate understanding to other observers more in tune with the region's seemingly bizarre exceptionalism. What was more generally known about Los Angeles in both the academic and popular literatures was characteristically vicarious and impressionistic, built on a collection of heavily mediated images passing, almost by default, for the real thing.

Every city generates such imagery, internally and externally, but Los Angeles was (and is) more specialized in image production and more prone to be understood through its created imagery than any other urban region. On location here since the 1920s are the "dream factories" of what is still called "the industry," mass producing moving pictures of Los Angeles that insistently substitute reel stories for real histories and geographies. Camera crews "shooting" scenes depicting practically every place on earth (and often off-earth) are a familiar sight on the streets of the city, and a constant local reminder of the confusing interplay between fantasy and reality that pervades everyday urban life, especially in the City of Angels.

By 1965, ten years after its opening, Disneyland had added new layers to this landscape of vicarious unreality. Its imagineered protogeography of America reconfigured the mental maps of the national subconscious to fit the familiar artifice deposited in a tiny corner of Orange County. A cleverly concocted Main Street centered the map and led the all-consuming visitor to separate worlds of fantasy, the future, the frontier, the "happiest places" on earth. With the addition of mass audience television, the blanket of consciousness-shaping imagery was not only thicker than anywhere else, it was more creatively heterogeneous and diverting in Los Angeles, the place where urban imagineering was invented, commodified, mass produced, and projected to a worldwide scale and scope.

Behind these broadcast scenes, however, was another Los Angeles that is only now coming into focus through an almost archeological process of excavation, a digging process that Mike Davis describes in his *City of Quartz* as "excavating the future."[2] Amidst the imagic runes of this extendable past, a clearer picture of the "actually existing" Los Angeles of 1965 is beginning to take shape. What it depicts can be seen as both the darkest side of the American Dream and a crowning moment of twentieth century urban modernity, a particularly vivid representation of the simultaneously utopian and dystopian urbanization that has been infusing the development of Los Angeles since its origins.

More than a century of obsessive Anglofication (posing as Americanization) had increasingly "purified" the population of El Pueblo de Nuestra Senora la Reina de Los Angeles to the point that, in 1960, more than 80% of the population were non-Hispanic whites or "Anglos" (to use a term deeply and defiantly rooted in the recolonization of formerly Spanish America). Although the statisticians might quibble, this Anglo population was almost entirely suburban in lifestyle, not unlike the situation comedies of television, constructing places where city and countryside blended together in a new experiential synthesis. This situational synthesis was definitively WASPish, for Los Angeles had for decades contained the highest percentage of native-born Protestants of all the largest US cities. With a substantial dose of irony, Los Angeles in 1965 could be described quite figuratively as the first truly American metropolis. An almost crusade-like mentality pervaded this white, often anti-papist, and racially proud Christian majority, supremely confident in its successful inhabitation and preservation of an earthly and preternaturally American paradise.

Few areas of Los Angeles contained the conventional densities of urban life, even among the poor and working class communities of every color, for the city's ghettoes and barrios were more suburban than anywhere else in America. "Sixty Suburbs in Search of a City" became the catchall description of life in Los Angeles in the 1960s and many of those suburbs wore blue collars. Built into this homogeneously un-urban sprawl of American Dream-like communities was what two of the best academic treatments of Los Angeles at the time called a "fragmented metropolis" and a "non-place urban realm,"[3] the former reflecting the mass production of suburban municipalities (what a later observer would call "cities by contract"),[4] the latter tapping the rootlessness and artificiality of place-named identities and "proximate" community. Having escaped the claustrophobic tightness of small town America and the imperfect urbanity of the big cities, well-off Angelenos atomistically constructed far-flung networks of contacts and activities centered around increasingly protected homespaces rather than in well-defined neighborhood communities. The unlisted telephone number and the gated and walled-in residence symbolized this most privatized of urban landscapes. Truly public spaces were few and far between, as what the social theorists call "civil society" seemed to melt into the airwaves and freeways and other circuitries of the sprawling urban scene.

Mass suburbanization and other centrifugal forces had emptied the gridlocked downtown of the 1920s, leaving only a decaying financial and retail center, a few hotels, and the still imposing Civic Center, which had been recently philanthropically revived by the opening in December, 1964, of the Music Center, a product of a fantastically successful effort by the Anglo elite to put their acropolitan culture high up on the map of the city. Still towering over downtown, however, was City Hall, which by 1965 had become a global symbol of the American justice system after being portrayed each week on Dragnet and other no-nonsense TV crime shows. Dragnet's sober Sgt. Joe Friday curtly epitomized modernist justice for white America by always insisting on "just the facts, ma'am" in scripts that were checked for verisimilitude by then police chief William H. Parker of the LAPD. No fluffy imagery here, for there was a threatening dark side to life in the brightness of the simulated City of Angels, a tough counterpoint landscape that teemed with stygian dangers, never very far from the glittering surface.

Downtown Los Angeles has been the dystopian Main Street of the world's most visible Noir City at least since the 1920s, a lineage that traces easily from the gritty Bunker Hill of Raymond Chandler to the acid-rain swept streets of Ridley Scott's only slightly futuristic "Blade Runner." And by 1965, the contrapuntal dark side of the Southern California dreamscape seemed to be particularly rife with what many upholders of the peace were convinced was their greatest threat ever, nothing short of a global alliance of evil forces bent on planetary domination, echoing the many villainous scripts shot on Los Angeles' meaner streets. When Watts exploded in the summer of 1965, the unfolding events immediately appeared to many as the products of a maniacal noir-Disney staging an evil spectacular in Negroland, the darkest and most secretive annex to Noir City. Police Chief Parker, whose name now enshrines the riot-damaged downtown headquarters of LAPD that was a primary target in the 1992 uprising, not unexpectedly saw everything in black and white, with a little red thrown in for good measure. The revolutionary "monkeys" in the "zoo" of Negroland were running amok, he said, stirred by the "Communists" and their hordes of Hollywood sympathizers. With little accurate knowledge and understanding to distinguish the difference between the two, the real Los Angeles once again seemed to collapse into vivid imagineering. How else could one understand the latest event staged in this dystopic utopia, this place where the unique and the paradoxical are somehow universalized for all to see?

Only well after the rioting, burning, and looting spread to other cities, did a different picture begin to develop of late modern Los Angeles and the deeper – and wider – meaning of the Watts rebellion. Spurred by its increasing role as America's military arsenal for three successive Pacific wars, the Los Angeles region had experienced the most rapid industrial growth of any region in the country after the Great Depression. Federally subsidized suburbanization combined with federally fostered industrial growth to create an exceedingly efficient urban machine for simultaneously stimulating both mass production and mass consumption, one of the crown jewels of the Fordist-Keynesian "social contract" that allowed Big business, Big labor, and Big government to lead the great American post-war boom.

After 1942, when Executive Order 8802 forced war contractors to stop their racist hiring practices, another federally-induced ingredient was added to the local mix.[5] One of the largest internal migration streams in American history brought nearly 600,000 African Americans into Los Angeles County alone between 1942 and 1965. They carried with them the cutting edge of national black politics, enhanced by the growing power of the civil rights movement, the War on Poverty, the dreams of Martin Luther King, and the raised fist of black nationalism. A second large migration stream, similarly attracted to the hyperactive Los Angeles job machine ever since the Great Depression, added almost equal numbers of relatively poor white southerners to the cultural mix of the city once called "Iowa's seaport."[6]

Not surprisingly perhaps, both groups concentrated around the huge urban industrial zone (then probably the second largest in the world, after the Ruhr) stretching from downtown to the twin ports of Los Angeles and Long Beach, a zone bounded on its western edge by Alameda Avenue, which in 1965 had become one of the most pronounced racial divides in any American city. On one side of this so-called Cotton Curtain were the factories and jobs and such exemplary white working-class suburbs as South Gate; immediately on the other was a string of equally exemplary African American sub-urban communities, many on unincorporated county land and all strikingly bereft of major industrial establishments as well as basic social services: Florence, Watts, Willowbrook, Compton. Despite a tantalizing physical proximity to one of the largest pools of high-wage, unionized, blue collar jobs in the country, nearly one-third of the African American workforce was unemployed and almost sixty percent lived on welfare. This southside racial geography provided the immediate backdrop to the urban "civil war" that was part of the events of 1965, once again illustrating how race divides America in ways that often cut across powerful class divisions.

Although concentrated in the Watts district of the City of Los Angeles, the rebellion peaked along the entire corridor just west of Alameda, an area which had become one of the major local, national, and global centers of radical black consciousness in the 1960s. Perhaps nowhere else were conditions more ripe for rebellion. Los Angeles, after a long history of racist administration, zoning, and violence, had become one of the most segregated cities in the country; its mayor, police chief, and dominant newspaper had given sufficient indications that this tradition of recalcitrant racism was still flourishing in the centers of political power; and another obsessive tradition, of McCarthyesque anti-communism, fed by the vicious trials of Hollywood "sympathizers" and the defeat of a vigorous "socialist" public housing movement in the 1950s, had excitedly centered its attention on uppity blacks as the great revolutionary threat to the White American dream. The mood of the time was captured one month before the August insurrection. In an attempt to stem what seemed to be a rising tide of police brutality, then LAPD lieutenant Tom Bradley formally protested against the widespread posting of John Birch Society literature on LAPD bulletin boards, literature that labelled Martin Luther King and other Black leaders as dangerous communists and implicitly promoted white and thin-blue-line terrorism against the enemy within.

At the national level, urban blacks had assumed, both by default and by active choice, the leadership of American social movement politics and were thus the most powerful voice of resistance against the status quo and racially uneven development of the Fordist/Keynesian economic boom. Although African-Americans in Los Angeles had probably benefitted from the boom more than those of any other major urban region, the segregated social geography of the larger metropolis all too visibly presented itself as an extraordinarily polarized mosaic of extreme and conspicuous wealth and poverty, a consciousness-raising tableau of racially-intensified relative deprivation. That the worst civil disturbance of the century would occur where and when it did was therefore as predictable as the immediate reaction to it. Thirty-four people were killed (31 by police gunfire), 1,032 were injured, and 3,952 were arrested (the vast majority African-American). Property damage topped $40 million and 6000 buildings were damaged, most heavily along 103rd Street, which came to be called Charcoal Alley.

Looked at myopically, the riots, burning, and looting appeared to be a self-inflicted local wound instigated by the particular frustrations and impatience of a long impoverished and racially isolated population. In retrospect, however, the events were of more global significance. They can be seen today as a violent announcement that "business as usual" in urban and industrial America could no longer continue without explosive resistance, even in the most successful boomtown of the twentieth century. The Watts rebellion and the series of urban uprisings which followed it in the late 1960s all over the world (and again in Los Angeles in August, 1970, with the Chicano Moratorium, the largest mass protest of Mexican-Americans in U.S. history) marked one of the beginnings of the end of the post-war economic boom and the social contract and Fordist/Keynesian state planning that underpinned its propulsiveness. As occurred a century earlier, the peculiar articulations of race and class in the US ruptured the booming space economy at about the time it was reaching its peak performance. The worldwide recession of the early 1970s, the worst since the Great Depression, helped to confirm the turning-pointedness of the preceding decade, but even more convincing confirmation can be derived from the dramatic restructuring process that has been far-reachingly transforming the urban landscape and the very nature of urban modernity over the past two decades. As seen from the present, the urban worlds of 1965 have not only been "deconstructed", they have also become increasingly "reconstituted" in many different ways. How this crisis-generated deconstruction and reconstitution took place in Los Angeles provides a particularly revealing story.

URBAN TRANSFORMATIONS

Until the early 1980s, Los Angeles remained as understudied and theoretically incomprehensible as it was in 1965. The little wave of attention that followed the Watts rebellion had passed into the forgetful busyness of a national economy trying to deal with stagflation, industrial decline, and the broadly felt downturn in real income that would later be described as the "Great U-Turn."[7] As another severe recession hit urban America (1979-1982) and Reaganomics began to take hold, Los Angeles was "discovered" by a group of local urban analysts who sought to construct in their studies not only a deeper understanding of what was happening in Los Angeles but also a picture of how these local developments might provide insight into the changes taking place in the regional, national, and global economies. Urban restructuring was the central theme of this new literature on the greater Los Angeles region. In the decade from 1982 to 1992, it would generate more significant scholarly writings on Los Angeles than had been produced in the preceding two centuries.

The most influential discovery shaping this new literature came from the realization that the urban region of Los Angeles had developed from the 1920s as one of the world's largest industrial growth poles, that those distracting dream factories of Hollywood stood amidst what was becoming the largest manufacturing city in North America. That this industrial expansion was continuing apace during a period of extensive deindustrialization elsewhere intensified the challenge of making practical and theoretical sense of the apparently anomolous Los Angeles experience. Between 1970 and 1980, the entire country experienced a net addition of less than a million manufacturing jobs and New York lost well over 300,000, triggering descriptions of wholesale industrial decline and the rise of "postindustrial" society. In the same decade, however, the far from post-industrial Los Angeles region added 225,000 new manufacturing jobs, as well as 1,300,000 people and an even larger number of total jobs in all categories of employment. How could this extraordinary countercurrent be explained? Why had it been so invisible for so long? What impact was it having on the local economy? Was this industrialization in Los Angeles merely a continuation of post-war trends or was it taking new forms and directions? How could this aggregate picture of a booming regional economy be reconciled with increasing local indications of intensifying poverty, unemployment, and homelessness?

These and other questions initiated an empirical and theoretical exploration of the dynamics of urban restructuring in Los Angeles that was attuned to the particularities of the regional context and, at the same time, connected to more general debates on the changing organization of the national and global political economies. Reflecting the spatial perspective that has informed much of this urban restructuring research, its findings can be summarized around six "geographies", each representing an important dimension of accelerated urban change as well as a particular approach to interpreting the "new" Los Angeles that took shape in the period between 1965 and 1992. As will become evident, the study of urban restructuring has expanded well beyond the initial focus on industrial change to raise issues of much broader local and global significance.

I. EXOPOLIS: THE RESTRUCTURING OF URBAN FORM

Los Angeles has been participating in the redefinition of urban form throughout the twentieth century. The classic model of urban form, built primarily around the nineteenth century industrial capitalist city, presented a monocentric picture of increasing geographical regularity patterned by the dynamics of employment and residential agglomeration.

Everything revolved around the singular city center. From its peak densities of population, jobs, and fixed capital investment rippled concentric zonations of residential land use, household composition, and family life. Stretching these concentricities outward were radial sectors that developed particular cross-cutting specializations: zones of industry and commerce, usually one high income residential area extending from the center to the suburban fringe, and one or more working class zones, typically associated with tightly segregated communities of racial and ethnic minorities. Cities that had grown large before the nineteenth century surge in urban industrialization displayed much less regularity, but even in these cases regularities could be found by those who assiduously searched for them.

From its first major urban boom in the late nineteenth century, Los Angeles seemed to have a morphological mind of its own. The classic urban forms were never entirely absent and glimmerings of them are discoverable even today, but from the beginning the Los Angeles urban fabric took on a very different texture. Although the centrality of downtown Los Angeles has been recognizable for more than two hundred years, the surrounding urban region grew as a fragmented and decentered metropolis, a patchwork quilt of low density suburban communities stretching over an extraordinarily irregular terrain of mountains, valleys, beaches, and deserts. Both tying the fabric together and giving it its unusual elasticity was first a remarkable network of inter-urban electric railways and then an even more remarkable freeway system, each visibly focused on the downtown node but spinally tapping a multiplicity of increasingly outlying centers and peripheries.

This more flexible and resilient urban ecology seemed to stimulate eccentric specializations and segregations. By 1965, the patchwork of Los Angeles contained a tightly circumscribed African American ghetto and Mexican American barrio, and, as previously noted, a vast urban industrial zone and a well-defined area of poor whites from the southern states. There were also mini-ghettoes and mini-barrios scattered over the landscape, as well as smaller but still significant clusters of industrial production and other specialized land uses, often enshrined in the names of particular municipalities: City of Industry, City of Commerce, Studio City.

By 1965, Los Angeles had become simultaneously eccentric and paradigmatic, a peculiar place yet one that seemed to be symptomatic of the newest trends in American urbanization and modernity. In the 1950s, it was the only one of the fifteen largest cities in the country to grow in population and even its fiercely ghettoed African American community was named by the Urban League in 1964 as the best among 68 cities for blacks to live. What then has happened since 1965? The answer, as will be true for all the geographies of urban restructuring, involves both significant continuities and pronounced changes in the urbanization process and attendant patternings of urban life and experience. First of all, the population continued to grow at an unusually rapid rate, matched only by other western and LA-like cities such as Houston and Phoenix. By 1992, the sprawling regional metropolis had filled in most of a sixty-mile circle drawn around the downtown Civic Center, encompassing the built-up area of five counties and a constellation of more than 160 cities and municipalities. With a population approaching 15 million, Los Angeles today has become one of the world's largest "megacities" (another of the many new terms devised to capture contemporary urbanization trends) and was rapidly catching up to the three other megacities of the so-called First World: Tokyo, New York, and London.

This growth was marked by continued decentralization of residential population, industrial establishments, corporate offices, and retail activities into the outer reaches of the sixty-mile circle, following trends established in nearly all North American cities since the end of the nineteenth century. But between 1965 and 1992, this decentralization seemed to break out from its conventional metropolitan boundaries. As before, manufacturing and office development in particular moved outward through the concentric rings and along sectoral zones into satellite cities and suburban green spaces. But increasingly, they burst out even further to fuel what, after the 1980 census, was called (somewhat prematurely, it now seems) the "great non-metropolitan turnaround," when for the first time in U.S. history, small towns and non-metropolitan counties grew more rapidly than either the central cities or the suburban rings. The suburbs at least were able to rebound in the 1980s, but what became clearer was that the scale and scope of decentralization was becoming increasingly globalized, that American manufacturing was not only leaving its metropolitan concentrations, it was leaving the country entirely. This meant that the dynamics shaping urban form could no longer be seen as confined within the metropolitan space, even when expanded to include the larger national system of cities. The local was becoming global more than ever before, and this was demanding new ways of understanding the "specificity" of the urban.

The restructuring of Los Angeles exemplified all of these decentralization trends. At the same time as decentralization was occurring, however, there was another major development that was reshaping urban form in Los Angeles and many other metropolitan regions even more dramatically, a recentralization process that would place much greater stress on the traditional conceptual frameworks of urban analysis. The primary form of this recentralization can be described most simply as peripheral urbanization or the urbanization of suburbia, but within this slightly oxymoronic phrase is contained what some contemporary observers claim is one of the most radical transformations of urban life and landscape ever seen, a far-reaching deconstruction and reconstitution of urban form. By 1990, the population census would show another historical turn. For the first time, the majority of Americans were living in megacities, sprawling metropolitan regions of more than one million inhabitants.

At the simplest descriptive level, peripheral urbanization refers to the growth of cities in suburbia, the increasing concentration of jobs, factories, offices, shopping centers, entertainment and cultural activities, heterogeneous populations, new immigrants, gangs, crime, and a host of other attributes once thought to be specifically urban in areas that never before had experienced such intensive agglomeration. In recent years, this urbanization of suburbia has triggered a burst of descriptive invention to provide a vocabulary commensurable with the new forms taking shape, with what some have described as "the city turned inside out." Counterurbanization and the growth of Outer Cities are perhaps now the most widely used terms, but the list of alternatives is expanding: post-suburbia, edge cities, urban villages, metroplex, technopoles, technoburbs, technopolis.

Drawing particularly on the Los Angeles experience, I have added another summative term, Exopolis, literally the city "without" in the double sense of the expanding Outer (vs. the Inner) City as well as the city that no longer is, the ex-city.[8] This double meaning signals an explicit attack on our conventional usage of the terms urban, suburban, exurban, and non-urban to describe divisions within contemporary metropolitan areas. As geographical restructuring works increasingly to blur these distinctions, we must not only revamp our vocabulary but also reconceptualize the very nature of urban studies, to see urban form more as a complex and polycentric regional mosaic of geographically uneven development affecting and affected by local, national, and global forces and influences. Studying Los Angeles (or Tokyo, or São Paulo, or Little Rock) thus becomes a window on to a wider panorama of subject matter than has traditionally been treated in the field of urban studies.

Four major Outer Cities can be identified in the Los Angeles regional exopolis. None of the four have conventional urban place names or identities and they do not appear clearly in official statistical tabulations, but each has been among the fastest growing "urban" areas in the country over the past thirty years. If identified as distinct cities, each would rank among the fifteen largest in the country. The largest and perhaps most paradigmatic of all Outer Cities is multiply centered in Orange County, an agglomeration of about 50 incorporated municipalities (none much over 300,000 in size) with a total population of more than two and a half million. Orange County has been an especially significant focus of restructuring research in all its dimensions and has become a model of sorts for comparative urban studies throughout the world.[9]

Of similar size and even more expansive in recent years is what might be called the "Greater Valley," stretching from Glendale and Burbank through the San Fernando Valley, once the epitomization of American suburbia, to Chatsworth-Canoga Park (administratively part of the City of Los Angeles) and beyond into adjacent Ventura County, with another extension northward into the high desert and canyon country of northern Los Angeles County.

A third Outer City has grown along the Pacific shores of Los Angeles County from Malibu to Long Beach, which, with its twin port of San Pedro, has risen to challenge the Randstad and Tokyo-Yokahama as the world's largest port complex. At the center of this Outer City region is Los Angeles International Airport (LAX) and the large agglomeration of office buildings, hotels, and high technology research and manufacturing establishments that surround it. Sometimes called "Aerospace Alley," this region contains what is probably the country's largest concentration of the American military-industrial complex and has been the seedbed of US weapons and warfare research from the development of the DC-3 to Star Wars.

The fourth Outer City extends from the eastern edge of Los Angeles County to the most developed parts of San Bernardino and Riverside Counties. Called the Inland Empire after its wartime industrial expansion in the 1940s and 50s, this subregion of Exopolis is the least developed of the four in terms of industrial employment and office growth, having suffered significantly from the deindustrialization process over the past thirty years. Its rapid population growth, fed by the sprawling development of relatively cheap housing, has created some of the cruelest repercussions of the restructuring of urban form, especially in terms of what the policy-makers call the "jobs-housing balance." Lured by the success stories of other Outer Cities, hundreds of thousands of people have moved to planned new communities in anticipation of soon finding local employment opportunities. All too often, however, the promised jobs do not arrive, leaving huge populations stranded up to sixty miles from their places of employment.

To take perhaps the extreme example, the city of Moreno Valley, located in the far eastern edge of the sixty-mile circle of greater Los Angeles, has reached national attention as an exemplar of the new problems arising in the housing-rich job-poor areas of the Outer City. The 1990 census listed Moreno Valley as the fastest growing city over 100,000 in the entire country (of the top ten, seven were in Southern California). With local employment growth far below what was promised by the community developers, large numbers of residents are forced to rise well before dawn to drive or be taken by vans and buses, often for more than two hours, to the places of employment they held before moving to Moreno Valley. Without a large commercial or industrial tax base, public services are poor, schools are overcrowded, freeways are gridlocked, and family life is deeply stressed as residents contend with the psychological and financial costs of living in a new "Edge City" of more than 120,000 inhabitants that is becoming what might be called a new exopolitan slum.

The four Outer Cities of the re-regionalized Exopolis of Los Angeles box in a residual Inner City that has been experiencing a dramatic recentralization of its own. Reversing decades of suburban drain (but not the "white flight" that has been an important part of the formation of Outer Cities), downtown Los Angeles and its surrounding Inner City ring has probably doubled in population since 1965 to more than five million. This reversal of fortune, like the transformation of suburbia, has been geographically uneven and the highs and lows of development have been changing rapidly over the past thirty years. With seeming irony, while many Inner Cities further east have experienced continued reductions in population and job densities, that paragon of low-density urbanization has been packing them in. Many sections of the Inner City of Los Angeles now have population densities higher than Chicago or St. Louis, often without significant changes in the built form of housing, creating severe problems of residential overcrowding and homelessness. But to gain better insight into the changing exopolitan Inner City, as well as to understand better the shifting regional mosaic of geographically uneven development in the Outer Cities, we must turn to other restructuring processes.

II. FLEXCITIES: THE CHANGING GEOGRAPHY OF PRODUCTION

Accompanying the changing urban morphology of Los Angeles have been substantial shifts in the urban social division of labor and in the corporate organization and technology of industrial production. This important link between industrial restructuring and the restructuring of urban form has been a key focus for much of the new literature on Los Angeles. It has also contributed to a changing emphasis within urban studies more generally and in the practices of urban and regional planning. For most of this century, urban analysis and urban planning have given primary attention to matters of collective consumption: housing, the provision of social services, public welfare policies and anti-poverty programs, the development of mass transit systems, land-use regulation, and the emergence of urban social movements around these issues. Today, more and more attention (in money, time, and effort) is being given to the production side of the urban economy and to such questions as how to attract new businesses to stem economic decline and contend with the larger forces of global economic restructuring.

Academic analyses of this powerful relation between industrial and urban restructuring have hinged around a pronounced shift in industrial organization and technology from the Fordist-Keynesian practices of mass production and mass consumption that dominated the post-war economic boom in the US, to what is increasingly described today as a Post-Fordist system of flexible production and corporate development that has been at the forefront of urban economic restructuring since at least 1965. Fordist mass production was rooted in dedicated assembly lines and vertically integrated production systems feeding off increasing internal economies of scale that were sustainable only by huge oligopolistic corporations engaged in a relatively stable social contract with the largest trade unions and a federal government dedicated to priming the consumption pump of the national economy through Keynesian practices of demand stimulation and social welfare provision. Under these conditions, it was no great exaggeration to claim that as General Motors or Ford goes, so would go the American economy, for in the automobile industry the entire gamut of Fordist and Keynesian practices were most characteristically manifested.

Fordism continues to be important in the national economy, but the crisis-generated restructuring of the past thirty years has led to the emergence of new leading sectors and new technological and organizational innovations that have coalesced in what some have called a new regime of accumulation, more capable of competing successfully in a restructured national and increasingly global economy. This new regime is characterized by more flexible (vs. hierarchical) production systems located in transactions-intensive clusterings of predominantly small and middle size firms intertwined to achieve increasing "external" economies of scope through complex subcontracting arrangements, improved inventory control, the use of numerically controlled (i.e., computerized) machinery, and other techniques that allow for easier responses to market signals, especially in times of economic recession and intensified global competition. With the increasing disintegration of the post-war social contract through union-busting, wage give-backs, corporate restructuring, government withdrawal from most sectors of the economy (with the major exception of the defense industry), and the weakening of the federally sustained welfare safety net (signalling what some have described as a shift from the welfare state to the warfare state), traditional Fordism was no longer sustainable at its former level.

The result of all this was a complex process of unprecedented deindustrialization linked to an initially experimental but increasingly focused reindustrialization that has had significant repercussions on the regional economic geography of America. Sunrise industries and the growing Sunbelt contrasted with the setting sun of heavy industrial Fordism in the Frostbelt signalled one of the most dramatic regional role reversals in U.S. history, although these metaphors captured only part of the story. What lay behind the shifting regional geography came into clearer focus in Southern California. Still primed by the federal munificence of military Keynesianism and the Cold-Warfare state that peaked in the Reagan-Bush years, the greater Los Angeles region traced a particularly revealing and apparently economically successful pathway through this profound industrial restructuring. Since 1965, Los Angeles has experienced an almost complete destruction of its Fordist industries, once the largest cluster west of the Mississippi, in a smaller scale version of what was happening in Detroit, Cleveland, and other centers in the American Manufacturing Belt. At the same time, the resilient regional space economy, built upon a few large "systems houses" (as in aerospace and film studios) and many thousands of small and middle size, often craft based, industrial firms, flexibly retuned its productive capacity to emerge as one of the world's prototypical Post-Fordist industrial metropolises.

Reflecting national trends, the more characteristically Fordist industrial sectors in Los Angeles, including what were once the second largest concentrations of automobile assembly and tire manufacturing in the country, were wiped out entirely between 1965 and 1992, as was much of the large steel and consumer durables industries. Industrial unions were decimated and tens of thousands of well-paid, often quite senior, and to a significant extent minority and women blue-collar workers, lost their jobs in widespread layoffs and plant closures. Particularly hard-hit was the domestic working class (Anglo, Chicano, and Black) in the Inner City and in the Outer Cities of the Inland Empire and the eastern San Fernando Valley. Massive white flight from the Inner City, begun in the aftermath of the Watts rebellion, accelerated to near-total abandonment in certain working class neighborhoods, while large numbers of African Americans who could afford to do so left the region entirely, triggering in the 1990 census the first decline ever in the Black population of Los Angeles County.

The African American communities left behind in the old riot zone suffered even deeper immiseration than existed at the time of the Watts rebellion, sinking into what came to be described nationally as the formation of a permanent and predominantly black urban underclass—a sad symbol of the degree to which industrial restructuring worked to discipline and punish the main instigators of urban unrest in the late 1960s. More locally, the descriptions were less benign. Urban restructuring in all its forms was correlated closely with "The Killing of South Central" and "The Making of an American Bantustan," an impounded enclave left to its own subsistence and survival economy of racially defined separate development.[10] Some even equated this abandonment and implosion with a new form of indirect genocide, as mortality rates increased dramatically for almost every African American age-group, especially infants and young male adults. Whatever its deeper causes, deindustrialization and the attendant decline of the welfare state had particularly devastating effects on African Americans in Los Angeles whose major channels of upward economic mobility had been heavily concentrated in manufacturing and government employment.

Meanwhile, the great Los Angeles job machine continued to churn out new employment opportunities at an almost record pace, oblivious to the decimation of African American and to a lesser extent Mexican American communities. For most of the period between 1965 and 1992, job generation was even greater than net population growth. The vast majority of these jobs were in non-unionized occupations and most paid much lower wages (with fewer or nonexistent benefits) than those lost through Fordist deindustrialization, creating, among many other effects, a health care crisis of unprecedented proportions as more than a third of the population was left without health insurance. But something else was going on as well, a process of Post-Fordist industrial development that was rapidly reconstituting the regional economy in at least three different ways. Receiving the most analytical and popular attention was the development of the "technopoles" of Southern California, the high-technology based complexes of industrial estates, research and development offices, and supportive business services that propelled the growth of the Outer Cities and clustered around them what is reputed to be the world's largest urban concentration of engineers, physical scientists, mathematicians, computer technicians, and military weapons specialists. It is no surprise that Los Angeles became one of the "textbook" cases for studying the new pathways of Post-Fordist industrialization and regional development.

While the technopoles have spun their eddies of industrial growth primarily in the Outer (Flex) Cities, two other forms of flexible specialization have sustained the redevelopment of the Inner City and especially downtown Los Angeles. The first revolves around craft-based production networks and the dense clustering of many small and middle sized firms highly adaptive to national and global market signals and changes in style and consumer preferences; while the second is built primarily on the provision of specialized financial services and technologically advanced communications and information processing. For each, the Inner City of Los Angeles has been particularly receptive. The garment industry more than matched the aerospace industry (another craft-centered rather than mass production sector) in the volume of job growth and is now probably the largest in the country, having recently passed New York City. Significantly, the Los Angeles garment industry is highly specialized in sportswear and other clothing that is particularly fad and fashion sensitive and also less susceptible to easy mechanization. Major specializations also exist in furniture, jewelry, printing, industrial design, and the array of services connected to the entertainment industry, where Los Angeles leadership has been established since the 1930s but has grown even more intense since 1965.

Growth in the FIRE sector (finance, insurance, and real estate) has fueled the emergence of Los Angeles as a major challenger to the triumvirate of Tokyo, London, and New York atop the global hierarchy of the "capitals of capital." While extending the region's global reach, this growth has become localized in a dense web of consumer banking, mortgage lending, business accounting, credit checking, information processing, personnel management, building maintenance, and legal services that pulse through the regional economy in ways that probably have greater positive impact than the more cocooned and externally oriented financial districts of New York and London. At the heart of this web is the downtown financial district, but, as might be expected, the FIRE stations are broadly dispersed, with major subcenters in Century City (along the Wilshire Corridor) and Newport Beach in Orange County.

Helping to sustain these flexibly specialized districts is a teeming underground economy and an immigrant-fed pool of low wage labor that makes the crackhouse and the sweatshop, the pirate video store and the swap meet, as well as a vast reservoir of underpaid janitors, gardeners, dishwashers, street vendors, homeworking chipboard polishers, and household servants as much a part of the Post-Fordist Flexcities of Los Angeles as anything else I have described. Understanding more about this double-sided industrial geography leads us to another key dimension of urban restructuring.

III. COSMOPOLIS: GLOBALIZATION AND WORLD CITY FORMATION

Central to the transformation of Los Angeles has been an expansive internationalization process that accelerated after the major changes in federal immigration policy that took place in that turning point year of 1965. It has compressed within the region the most culturally heterogeneous population of investors, entrepreneurs, workers, and families any city has ever seen. Perhaps as many as five million migrants have moved to Los Angeles since 1965, with the vast majority coming from the Latin American and Asian countries of the Pacific Rim. Accompanying this immigration has been an equally global and heterogeneous inflow of capital investment, especially from Japan, Canada, the European Economic Community, the East Asian NICs (newly developing countries), and the oil-rich states of the Middle East. Together these flows of labor and capital have probably been more responsible than any other restructuring process for the continued economic growth of the region and the radical changes that have taken place in the regional built environment and the character of everyday urban life.

If the industrially restructured Exopolis has turned the city inside-out, the new Cosmopolis has turned it outside-in again in a far-reaching globalization of the local, a process that has given birth to a new term: "glocalization". After years of relatively unsuccessful local promotion, the development of downtown Los Angeles accelerated dramatically in the 1970s with the influx of foreign capital and the availability of a cheap, unorganized, and seemingly limitless supply of immigrant workers. For the first time, a high profile central city appeared that was almost commensurable with the size and complexity of the regional economy. Although still far from the heights and densities of Manhattan or Chicago's Loop, downtown development in Los Angeles more directly reflected the effects of economic and cultural glocalization. Its specific geography was split in two, with a half-city of First World skyscrapers and financial power standing starkly above a half-city of Third World cultures and street scenes.

Capping this divisive moiety and holding it together is the governing domestic "Citadel-LA,"[11] a band of social control and surveillance that contains, in addition to the so-called cultural acropolis (the Music Center, Museum of Contemporary Art, and the soon to be built Gehry-designed Disney Concert Hall) and the adjacent headquarters of the LAPD, the Times-Mirror Company, and the country's largest Catholic archdiocese, what has become the second heaviest concentration of local, state, and federal government employment in the country, after Washington, D.C. (the center of the east coast's most expansive Exopolis). Here, the impact of glocalization on domestic governance and planning is most direct, as local decision-making is increasingly affected by global constraints and opportunities. To illustrate, the City of Los Angeles several years ago obtained a loan from the government of Japan to meet its budget shortfall, the first time any local government unit in the country ever turned to a foreign source for financial assistance.

Most studies of world city formation have emphasized the concentration of global financial control functions. For the exceedingly heterogeneous world city of Los Angeles, this focus must be expanded to include not only the huge industrial base (eliciting comparisons with Tokyo more than any other major world city), but even more emphatically the extraordinarily global labor force, especially in the corona of diverse ethnic communities that surrounds and sustains the downtown financial, commercial, and government complex. This inner ring is the heartland of the Los Angeles Cosmopolis, a special type of world city where the very nature of urban cosmopolitanism, glocalization, and modern world cityness is currently being redefined.

In this ring of ethni-cities is a dazzling constellation of global cultures that simultaneously reaches out to every corner of the world and draws into Los Angeles an amazing array of "foreign" influences. It also provides an unusually rich testing ground for urban multiculturalism and what can be described as the new cultural politics of identity and difference, far removed from the imagic melting pot of Anglofying Americanization. Reproduced on the streets and in its neighborhoods are microcosms of Hong Kong and Taiwan, Vietnam and the Philippines, Bombay and Beirut, São Paulo and Medellin. There is a Little Tokyo and a vast Koreatown, a huge long-established Mexican barrio and a new barrio filled by a dense mix of Central American migrants representing every faction of the politics of Guatemala, El Salvador, and Nicaragua. An old (from the former Soviet Union) and a new (from Lebanon, Iran, and elsewhere) Armenian community splits its animosities between Turks and Azerbaijanis. Jewish diasporan settlers from Iran, Russia, and New York City debate Middle East politics, while African marketplaces teem with discussions of current events in Cape Town and Addis Ababa, and the construction of Afrocentric school curricula.

The list of separate cultural worlds microcosmed in Los Angeles seems endless, but there is still another dimension to this complex panorama of urban multiculturalism, a growing cultural syncretism that may prove be the most important new development arising from the contemporary Cosmopolis. Multiculturalism is usually described in two ways, first as the formation of segregated ethnic spaces (ghettoes, barrios, Koreatown, Chinatown, etc.), and second as a proliferation of conflictful edges and turfs where different cultural worlds frequently collide in struggles to maintain cultural identity and cohesion. But something else is also happening in the urban borderlands. Multiform "composite" cultures are slowly taking shape and expressing their admixture on the local landscape and daily life: in the creation of new cuisines, designs, clothing, and styles of popular art and music; and in the development of new cultural and political identities. Los Angeles, for example, has been a major center for the assertion of Latino identity (vs. such imposed categories as Hispanic or Spanish-speaking) as a means of uniting the diverse populations whose homelands stretch from Cape Horn to the Rio Grande. Even greater heterogeneity is being synthesized in the growth of Asian American identity, with Los Angeles again taking a leading role. Many other forms of cross-cultural fusion and coalition building are taking place in the schools and neighborhoods, in community organizations and housing projects, in local government and cultural festivals, in ways that we are only beginning to recognize and understand.

IV. SPLINTERED LABYRINTH: THE REPOLARIZED METROPOLIS

The first three geographies of urban restructuring are tightly interwoven and, taken together, present the most powerful explanatory arguments outlining the causes of the new urbanization processes that have been reshaping Los Angeles and, to varying degrees, other metropolitan regions of the world. The next three geographies can be seen primarily as consequences of or reactions to metropolitan transformation, although they too are marked by the same restructuring dynamic of deconstruction (the breaking down of an older order) and reconstitution (the creation of new or significantly different forms of urban modernity). We begin with the changing social order and, in particular, the increasing and many-sided socio-economic inequalities that have been so integrally associated with the crisis-generated restructuring of the past thirty years.

Paralleling the spatial structure of the globalized Post-Fordist Exopolis of Los Angeles is a social and economic structure that has become increasingly fluid, fragmented, decentered, and rearranged in ways that differ significantly from the old class-divided city of the bourgeoisie and proletariat; the neatly apportioned hierarchical city of the wealthy, the middle class, and the poor; and the "two Americas" city of Black vs. White that was described in the aftermath of the 1960s urban insurrections. This polychotomous segmentation and repolarization has begun to reconstitute the extremes of wealth and poverty and derigidify the social boundaries of class, race, and income grouping, challenging our old ways of understanding the sociology of urbanism.

There are now, for example, more millionaires than ever before in Los Angeles, many constituting a reserve army of the wealthy that includes rock stars and baseball players, computer software specialists and real estate agents, hairdressers and employment headhunters, drugdealers and dentists, as well as thousands of homeowners who were lucky enough to buy at the right time in the right place. Never before has the top ten percent of the income ladder been so heterogeneous, so segmented, and so politically unpredictable. And in many ways, the same can be said for the bottom twenty percent, which now contains representatives from the same occupations and backgrounds as the millionaires and displays much the same political unpredictability.

As is by now clear, urban restructuring in Los Angeles deepened poverty even under conditions of rapid regional economic growth and job generation. As many as 80,000 people are now homeless on any given night in the region and perhaps three times as many are homeless at some point in the average year. But this is only the most visible tip of an iceberg of extreme poverty that broadens into a population of well more than half a million living precariously in housing conditions little better than those of the worst Third World squatter settlements and shantytowns, a situation that has created what is arguably the most severe urban housing crisis in America. Many of the more than 1.3 million living below the poverty line in L.A. County in 1989 (the numbers have increased since) are unemployed and welfare dependent, an unquestionable core of what urban sociologists and policy makers have recently begun to call the "permanent urban underclass." But just as many, perhaps more, are part of the rapidly growing and primarily Latino contingent of the working poor, often laboring for well more than forty hours a week on more than one job for wages that are insufficient to feed and clothe a family.

A perverse symbiosis has developed between the extremes of wealth and poverty in Los Angeles, each feeding the growth of the other. Occasionally, the perversity is exposed in startling ways, as in several clear cases of what can only be called slavery. Immigrants from Indonesia, China, and Central America have been imported (in one case as "entertainers" with cultural visas) and sold to wealthy households as live-in domestic servants. Their passports are kept by their "owners" who provide limited room and board for their services. This new slavery, however, is just one step below what is present in the sweatshops and many other businesses (and households), where undocumented workers are paid sub-minimal wages at often hazardous worksites and under the constant threat of deportation. The bottom of the poverty iceberg and the new urban social division of labor is indeed broad and deep.

As is clearly shown in many chapters of *The City: Los Angeles and Urban Theory at the End of the Twentieth Century*, the book from which this essay is drawn, the great Los Angeles job machine has had a "missing middle," bifurcating instead into a small stream of high-paying jobs feeding the new technocracy and a raging torrent of low wage work (much also involved in feeding the new technocracy) that barely deserves the adjective subsistence. This multivalent polarization is no longer easily definable by simple racial, ethnic, occupational, class, or immigrant status categories and binary oppositions. A recent national survey has shown, for example, that Los Angeles contains both the richest and the poorest predominantly African American communities in urban America and my guess would be that similar results would be found if such a study were done for Mexican-Americans and Asian-Americans. There are also some indications from unpublished comparative studies of U.S., Canadian, and Australian cities that the polarization and inequality measured among recent immigrant populations extends from the Inner to the Outer Cities, with Los Angeles-Long Beach, Orange County, and San Bernardino-Riverside ranking as the three highest of all metropolitan areas surveyed.

The impact of repolarization also extends deeply into the middle classes which, as in most of the country, have been increasingly destabilized in their class position over the past thirty years, splitting away from the once robust middleground of the income ladder in two directions, some upwardly mobile or at least maintaining their comfortable living standards in increasingly multiple-job households, while many more, especially women and children, slide downward toward the working poor, the new underclass, and the homeless. The reconstitution of the American middle class has spawned a new vocabulary for urban sociology, with yuppies, guppies (groups of young urban professionals), dinks (double income-no kids couples), woopies (well-off older people), infomerchants and the high technocracy, hyperghettoization and gentrification, glass ceilings and the feminization of poverty. A growing population of "new orphans" fill the streets with children abandoned by their parents and the elderly abandoned by their children. Workers are "K-Marted" or "Burger Kinged" as their income is cut in half in the shift from manufacturing to the burgeoning services economy.

With the socio-economic landscape becoming more fluid and kaleidoscopic, there has been an accompanying statistical decline in major indices of racial and ethnic segregation, as Latinos and Asians in particular increase rapidly in numbers and move out from their older staging settlements into new grounds and different lifestyles. The City of Cerritos, for example, near the border of Los Angeles and Orange counties has recently been named the most racially mixed city in America, with a population in 1990 that was 44% Asian, 36% Anglo, 13% Latino, and 7% Black. In Gardena, also a city of around 50,000, the four groups are almost equal in size, approaching a racial balancing that may never before have been achieved for any city in history: 32% Asian (mainly Japanese), 23% for Blacks and Latinos, and 21% Anglo. Asians have been the fastest growing segment in nearly all of the wealthiest (and still more than 80% Anglo) areas of L.A. County and have become the largest ethnic group in several cities and the majority in Monterrey Park, which has received national attention for its interethnic struggles over language use, with Latinos and Anglos often combining to stop the exclusive use of Chinese and to declare English the "official language."

Equally indicative has been a rapid "recycling" of cities and communities, as one majority is replaced by another. Southeast of downtown, municipalities such as Huntington Park and Maywood have seen their population shift from almost 80% Anglo in 1965 to more than 90% Latino in a demographic wave that has flowed even further, into South Central, where Latinos will very soon form the majority of the more than 250,000 inhabitants of this once overwhelmingly African American section of the City of Los Angeles. The broad spread of the Latinos has been so extensive that nearly all the 163 communities listed in a report on the 1990 census, including Beverly Hills, Bel Air, and Brentwood, had populations that were at least 5% Latino. The exceptions were all on the far western flanks of the county, near the border with Ventura County, in some of the stubbornly Anglo beach communities and Black elite Ladera Heights, and in the gated communities of the Palos Verdes peninsula.

The number of cities and communities with more than 60% Black population has shrunk to five: the large (169,000) West Adams-Baldwin Hills-Leimert district within the City of Los Angeles and four small pockets of unincorporated county land (Westmont, West Compton, West Athens, and View Park-Windsor Hills), with a total population of about 55,000. The very names of these areas signal the pronounced westward shift, as well as overall shrinkage, of the core of Black Los Angeles. With the growth of Koreatown and Anglo gentrification pushing from the north, and Latinoization obliterating the old Cotton Curtain and spreading through the Watts-Willowbrook-Florence-Compton corridor from the east, Black L.A. has not only been compacted, it has become increasingly polarized, with the richest and poorest African American communities more visibly locked together in their inequalities than ever before. And still further west, across the San Diego Freeway, a new racial barrier looms in the great Anglo redoubt that runs along the Pacific shores south of Los Angeles International Airport. In this prime stretch of surfurbia, as Reyner Banham once called it, 1603 African Americans were counted in the 1990 census in five cities with a total population of nearly 140,000.[12]

V. UNENDING EYES: REVAMPING THE CARCERAL CITY

The new topography of race, class, gender, age, income, and ethnicity has produced an incendiary urban geography in Los Angeles, a landscape filled with violent edges, colliding turfs, unstable boundaries, peculiarly juxtaposed lifespaces, and enclaves of outrageous wealth and despair. How this immanently conflagratory metropolis was kept from socially exploding until 1992 is wound up in the development of the Carceral City, a geography of war-like fortification and enclosure, of ever-watchful surveillance and creative means of social and spatial control, a place where police has become an insistent substitute for polis. Provocative descriptions of the Carceral City feature prominently in Mike Davis' *City of Quartz*, probably the best and most widely read of all the books to have been written about contemporary Los Angeles. Merely listing some of the chapter headings and topic outlines of *City of Quartz* provides a telling synopsis of the history and geography of the Carceral City.

Most direct is Chapter Four, "Fortress L.A.," a tour de force through the built environment of security-obsessed urbanism. Its headings include "The Destruction of Public Space" (described as a "security offensive" to meet "the middle-class demand for increased spatial and social insulation"); "The Forbidden City" ("taking the form of a brutal architectural edge or glacis that defines the new Downtown as a citadel"); "Sadistic Street Environments" ("hardening the city surface against the poor," with bum-proof bus benches, absent public lavatories, razor-wire protected trash bins, and overhead sprinkler systems that work randomly through the night to discourage sidewalk sleepers); "Frank Gehry as Dirty Harry" (on the fortress-like "stealth houses" of this leading L.A. architect); "The Panopticon Mall" (from the "mall-as-panopticon-prison" to the "housing-project-as-strategic-hamlet"); "From Rentacop to Robocop" (the "frenetic effort" of affluent neighborhoods to "insulate home values and lifestyles" in gated communities, "high-tech castles," "belligerent lawns," and the "voracious consumption of private security services"); "The LAPD as Space Police" (the LAPD's Star Wars-like "metamorphosis into a techno-police"); "The Carceral City" (honing in on the prisons around downtown that contain "the largest incarcerated population in the nation"); and finally, "The Fear of Crowds" (on the increasing attempts to control or prevent all public gatherings and to erase the last vestiges of public space).

Another dimension of the Carceral City is the "sunbelt bolshevism" Davis explores in Chapter Three. These "revolutionary" homeowner-backed slow-growth insurgencies have created "white walls" of zoning regulations, agile NIMBY protest movements, increasing "suburban separatism," and new "homeowner's soviets" in the attempt to turn back the tide (and the clock) of urban restructuring. In what has been called "the Watts riots of the middle classes," in part to commemorate the victorious tax revolts of the 1970s but also evoking images of the gang power and turf wars of wealthy white adults, there has been what Davis calls "a reassertion of social privilege" by the Anglo middle classes just in the nick of time, given their diminishing numbers and increasingly confusing class identities.

In Chapter Five, "The Hammer and the Rock," Davis takes on the police state and the secret and not so secret LAPD-FBI-CIA wars on crime, gangs, drugs, "expendable youth," and the "revolutionary lumpenproletariat." Here one finds one of the most flagrant continuities in the history and geography of Los Angeles between 1965 and 1992, a persistent streak of racism, police brutality, right-wing conspiracy theories, secret spy networks, and Blue Knight crusades to save the world from imminent god-forsaken destruction, a streak that spans the chiefly generations from William Parker to Ed Davis to Daryl Gates. Los Angeles remains less densely foot-policed than any other major U.S. city, but it has continued to build on its military defense, space surveillance, and weapons production tradition to produce the most technologically advanced urban armed forces, on the ground and in the air, another vital organ of the mighty militarized technopolis of Southern California.

The policed metropolis is augmented by the quieter presence of what may be the most extensive network of military installations around any major city, a global strike force allegedly prepared to take on any challenge anywhere in the universe. Several military enclosures are scheduled to close down in the 1990s, but their abundance and versatility guarantees a continued impact even if converted to peacetime functions. To illustrate, troops were able to prepare for the Persian Gulf War in the deserts of Southern California, replicating conditions so faithfully that there were special manouevers around the desert hamlet of Bagdad. At a more intimate scale, lethal weapons are also kept in most households and in many automobiles, creating a heterogeneous, fragmented, and highly mobile militia that also patrols the turfs and edges of the Carceral City, attempting with violence to keep everyone in their place and, increasingly along the freeways, in their proper lane and going at appropriate speeds. In restructured Los Angeles, the potential for violence has been raised to new heights, triggering often fatal attractions to a disciplinary technology of security and surveillance that patrols the region with endless eyes.

An important and all too easily neglected side effect of these intensified locality struggles has been to focus grassroots political consciousness and energy on what Michel Foucault, who first used the term Carceral City, described as "the little tactics of the habitat," or what contemporary urban scholars call "the politics of place." This recharging of locale and spatial location with active political attachment and identity has spread to the poorest neighborhoods and kindled what have been the most powerful forms of social resistance to the Carceral City and to the other oppressive effects of urban restructuring. Some of these micropolitical struggles have consciously crossed racial, ethnic, class, and gender boundaries to engage in a new multicultural politics of space and place that is significantly different from the polarized politics of binary opposition (black vs. white, labor vs. capital, women vs. men) that formed the basis for most earlier urban social movements. Perhaps never before have the people of Los Angeles, once the quintessential non-place urban realm, been so politically involved in their immediate neighborhoods and localities, another of the major changes that have occurred between 1965 and 1992 and one which, like the cultural syncretisms of Cosmopolis, must be recognized and built upon by all those who retain some optimism about the future of the region.

CODA FOR 1992[13]

The preceding descriptions of the Los Angeles experience over the past thirty years have been bracketed between two key turning points. The first is more confidently and hindsightfully defined by the Watts rebellion in 1965, one of the most portentous sparks for the concatenation of crises that marked the end of the post-war economic boom and the beginning of the search for new strategies to restore robust economic growth and avoid even greater social unrest. The six geographies of restructuring can be locally traced back to Watts, and through the window of the Los Angeles experience after 1965 can be seen many comparable crisis-generated restructurings affecting many other areas of the world. This is not to say that Watts in itself was the cause of urban restructuring or that restructuring would not have happened without it. What can be said, however, is that for Los Angeles 1965 was a significant turning point and that, for the rest of the world, what happened after 1965 in Southern California provides a particularly interesting and revealing case study in urban restructuring.

The second turning point, 1992, is more tentatively proclaimed, for its sighting is immediate and not subject to the same degree of retrospective understanding. Nevertheless, the events which took place in Los

Angeles just before and just after May 1, 1992, seem to be signalling another beginning of the end of an era, a forceful local disruption of (restructured) business as usual that may be a precursor to a more widespread crisis of postmodernity and Post-Fordism, just as Watts exemplified the crisis of modernity that marked the end of the Fordist post-war economic boom. This new crisis can be seen emerging from the very practices and strategies that have proved most successful in restoring robust economic growth and effectively controlling social unrest over the past thirty years: in the restructuring of urban form into the stretched fabric of Exopolis; in the flexibly specialized and productive industrial landscapes of Post-Fordism; in the formation of a globalized multicultural Cosmopolis; in the widening income gaps and mixed-up class boundaries of the new socio-economic (dis)order; in the protective fortresses and violent edges of the Carceral City; and in the rise of a neoconservative urban imaginary of enchanting and duplicitous hypersimulations. What all this portrays, I contend, can be summarized as a movement from crisis-generated restructuring to restructuring-generated crisis.

Up to the first years of the 1990s, the bright side of the new Los Angeles increasingly stood out to define one of the great success stories of the late twentieth century. By April, 1992, however, the mood had already shifted as all that was so compellingly bright seemed to be self-destructing. Perestroika (that potent Russian word for restructuring) and the end of the Cold War simultaneously pulled the propulsive rug from underneath the Post-Fordist regional economy and removed one of the key ideological pillars that had supported the tightening of social control by local and federal keepers of the peace. As the technopolis went into crisis, so too did its supportive FIRE sector, a coalescence of economic stress that spun into a recessionary spiral that seemed to go deeper in Southern California than in most other regions of the country. Massive job losses hit hard at the upper "bubble" of the bimodal labor market: bankers and brokers, highly paid aerospace workers and the new technocracy, lawyers and real estate agents, yuppies and beamers: those who had rode the crest of the most recent boom.

Meanwhile, the Cosmopolis became increasingly unsettled. For every new multicultural achievement in the arts, in business, and in local politics, there appeared new kinds of inter-ethnic violence and conflict as scores of different cultural worlds collided without mixing. More and more poor immigrants were added to the population, but the inflow of foreign capital slowed down and even Japanese owned hotels, office buildings, and businesses went into bankruptcy. Homelessness dramatically widened its scope and visibility, turning once sympathetic observers into edgy not-in-my-back-yard antagonists. Bulging prisons began releasing thousands of allegedly non-threatening criminals, and even the most enchanting urban villages seemed to be not far enough away to escape from the growing cosmopolitan violence. In 1992, a record number of violent crimes were committed in Los Angeles County, including 2,589 homicides and more than 800 gang-related killings. There were forewarnings of what might occur, especially in the domestic music of the streets, but the "rap" was incomprehensible to most or was reduced to a mixture of noise and entertainment.

On April 29, Los Angeles exploded in what appeared to many as a stubborn continuity with the past: police brutality, racism, and social injustice provoking an equally brutal, racially-motivated, and Watts-like riot of burning and looting marauders. The more things change, as some would say, the more they seemed to remain the same. Yet there was another dimension to the specific events of 1992 that challenged these appeals to historical continuity left, right, and center. It was difficult to identify and label, but seemed to be coming from another side of postmodernity, from a postmodernism of resistence that had been bred in the new multicultural politics of place, space, and local identity; in a deepened awareness of the surveillant webs controlling the geography the Carceral City and how to defend against them; in a more sophisticated understanding of the racially and locationally uneven impact of deindustrialization and reindustrialization; in the slowly growing empowerment of a "minority majority" in local politics; and, not least, from the tactical use of media-transported hypersimulations as a means of countering and encountering the neoconservative scamscape. What I am suggesting is that the largest urban insurrection in U.S. history differed significantly from the second largest in being both a consequence and a strategic political expression of the postmodern transition.

Stated differently, whereas Watts marked the first major rebellion against the late modernism of post-war America, the civil disturbances of

1992 may represent the first explosion of resistance to neoconservative American postmodernism and post-Fordism. Both took place in the urban region that was in the developmental vanguard of their respective eras, and each reflected the specific political and economic conditions of their time and place. In 1965, the insurrection was concentrated in the African-American community and emanated directly from the modernist politics of the civil rights movement and black nationalism. In 1992, although initially concentrated in nearly the same areas and led again by young Black men, the insurrection was decidedly more global and cosmopolitan, and was fought more like Operation Desert Storm than like the Vietnam War. As the word of the Rodney King verdict spread from the courthouse in Simi Valley (the primarily Anglo working-class Edge City in Ventura County that had become a favorite place for policemen and white families escaping the now foreign Inner City) to the symbolic corner of Florence (the name of one of the major communities affected by the burning and looting of 1965, now primarily Latino) and Normandie (a street running north into the heart of the new Koreatown), two series of events conjoined, one local and immediate, the other global and hypersimulated, with news networks broadcasting to the world more and lengthier images of Los Angeles than had ever been seen before.

The most memorable pictures, involving the beating of Reginald Denny, were characteristically ambiguous. To most, they conveyed clear visual evidence of violent frustration and anarchy, the absence of order and the lack of concern for human life. To others, there was another reality here, one arising from the consciously televisual enactment of resistance and rage to a long history of unpunished police brutality brought to a head when the "truth" conveyed by the all-seeing video camera had been denied in a Simi Valley courthouse. As if to reassert the power of one visual hypersimulation against another, Police Chief Gates donned the war apparel of his SWAT teams to arrest the presumed gang-bangers so visible on everyone's TV screens. This gave rise to a disturbing question, one which the beaters of Reginald Denny may have intentionally wanted to raise: If the videotape of many white men kicking and beating up a lone black man could be dismissed as a misleading picture of reality, would it be possible for the same result to occur with a videotape of many black men kicking and beating up a lone white man? For many, this was an irrelevant question. For some, it was and is crucial.

The local events and images spread well beyond South Central Los Angeles. With less well reported details, Long Beach, the region's second largest city, exploded as violently as anywhere else. The Salvadoran barrio in Pico-Union was also particularly active, drawing in a small army of immigration officials who, against established local policies, quickly deported hundreds of allegedly undocumented workers. More than 50% of those arrested at the peak of the riots were Latino vs. 36% Black, and it was not only Blacks and Latinos that participated in the looting. Anglo yuppies with carphones raided computer stores and camera shops, while others gathered into vigilante groups to defend their neighborhoods against all intruders. In another symbolic act, an especially ecumenical group immediately struck deep into the Citadel-LA, attacking the Parker Center headquarters of the LAPD as well as City Hall and other institutional centers of power and surveillance. The flames fanned outward into the San Fernando Valley, Pomona, Long Beach, the South Bay, and other parts of the Outer City and leapfrogged to the region's outermost satellite, Las Vegas. Sympathetic rebellions were sparked in the Bay Area, Atlanta, Omaha, Minneapolis, Toronto. Moment by moment, the local events became regional, national, and global at the same time and at an unheard of speed and intensity.

Again, there is much more to tell as Los Angeles rebuilds, or perhaps more accurately and hopefully, begins another round of crisis-induced restructuring, for if there is one general conclusion to be derived from the events of 1992 it is that the restructuring processes of the past thirty years, especially where they appear to have been most advanced and successful as in Los Angeles, produce new conditions for economic decline, racial and ethnic oppression, and social upheaval. This dialectic of extremes, of utopian dreams and dystopian nightmares, of paradigmatic successes and exemplary failures, has always characterized the history and geography of Los Angeles, giving pause to any categorical predictions about its future. All that can be said in closing is that Los Angeles, as always, is worth watching.

1. Reprinted with minor modifications from Chapter 14 in Allen J. Scott and Edward W. Soja (eds), *The City: Los Angeles and Urban Theory at the End of the Twentieth Century*, Berkeley and Los Angeles: University of California Press, forthcoming 1996.

2. Mike Davis, *City of Quartz: Excavating the Future in Los Angeles*, New York and London: Verso (1990).

3. Robert M. Fogelson, *The Fragmented Metropolis: Los Angeles, 1850-1930*, Cambridge MA: Harvard University Press (1967); reissued with a forward by Robert Fishman, Berkeley and Los Angeles: University of California Press (1993). The vision of Los Angeles as a "non-place urban realm" can be found in Melvin Webber, "Culture, Territoriality, and the Elastic Mile," *Papers of the Regional Science Association* 11 (1964), 59-69.

4. Gary Miller, *Cities by Contract: The Politics of Municipal Incorporation*, Cambridge MA: MIT Press (1981).

5. 1942 was an especially interesting year for Los Angeles. The first concentration camps were created to remove Japanese-Americans from their property and businesses in the city, a Japanese submarine shelled an oil field near Santa Barbara, and a purely imaginary air raid led to a crazed scenario in which a "hostile aircraft" was reported to have been shot down on Vermont Avenue. Five citizens died in this imaginary invasion, three from car crashes and two from heart attacks. In the same year, Camp Pendleton Marine corps base was founded and the "Sleepy Lagoon" murder triggered another racist-enhanced frenzy in which as many as 150 Mexican-American "boy gang" members (as they were then called) were arrested for the death of one youth at a party in East Los Angeles.

6. Significant changes in U.S. immigration laws were made in 1965, following the end of bracero program in the previous year. The continuing hunger for cheap foreign labor to feed industrial growth and assist in disciplining the burgeoning domestic workforce would stimulate the extraordinary immigration from Mexico, Central America, and Asia in the succeeding decades.

7. Bennett Harrison and Barry Bluestone, *The Great U-Turn: Corporate Restructuring and the Polarizing of America*, New York: Basic Books (1988).

8. Edward W. Soja, "Inside Exopolis: Scenes from Orange County," in Michael Sorkin (ed.), *Variations on a Theme Park: The New American City and the End of Public Space*, New York: Noonday Press (1992), 94-122.

9. Soja (1992), op.cit.; Allen J. Scott, *Metropolis: From the Division of Labor to Urban Form*, Berkeley and Los Angeles: University of California Press (1988); and R. Kling, S. Olin, and M. Poster, *Postsuburban California: The Transformation of Orange County since World War II*, Berkeley and Los Angeles: University of California Press (1991).

10. See Cynthia Hamilton, "The Making of an American Bantustan," and other articles under the heading "The Killing of South Central" in Institute for Alternative Journalism, *Inside the L.A. Riots: What Really Happened and Why it will Happen Again*, 1992.

11. Edward W. Soja, "Heterotopologies: A Remembrance of Other Spaces in the Citadel-LA," *Strategies* 3 (1990), 6-39.

12. The number of census tracts in Los Angeles County with no African American residents has dropped, however, from nearly 400 in 1960 to as few as four in 1990, a mark of the success of anti-racist legal struggles in the Los Angeles housing market.
13. Chapter VI. SIMCITIES: RESTRUCTURING THE URBAN IMAGINARY dealing with hyperreality had to be eliminated because of the length of the article.

IMPORTED – A READING SEMINAR in Relationship with my "A Portable (Not so Ideal) Imported Library, Or How to Reinvent the Coffee Table: 25 Books for Instant Use (German Version)," 1995/96
Künstlerhaus Stuttgart, Stuttgart, January 1996

BÖSE BEMERKUNGEN ZWISCHEN LOS ANGELES UND MOSKAU

BENJAMIN H. D. BUCHLOH - RAINER GANAHL

Rainer Ganahl: Wann und weshalb sind sie aus Deutschland in die USA gekommen?

Benjamin H. D. Buchloh: Ich bin 1977 aus Düsseldorf nach Halifax gegangen und hatte dafür verschiedene private Gründe. Zum einen hatte man mir eine Professur angeboten und die Redaktion der *Nova Scotia Series*. Dies interessierte mich zu dem Zeitpunkt sehr. Zum anderen waren die Arbeitsverhältnisse an der Kunstakademie Düsseldorf sehr unzufriedenstellend, obwohl die Studenten, die mit mir arbeiteten, sehr begeistert waren. Die Arbeitsumstände jedoch waren unakzeptabel. Über das private und das ökonomische Beziehungsfeld hinaus gab es noch andere, komplexere Gründe, die die Abwanderung leichter machten; zum einen die Tatsache, daß ich mich, zumindest seit den frühen 70er Jahren, zunehmend mit amerikanischer Gegenwartskunst, aber mehr noch vielleicht mit amerikanischer Gegenwartskunstkritik und Kunstgeschichtsschreibung, beschäftigt hatte. In diesem Bereich gab es, wie Sie wissen – zumindest damals und in gewisser Hinsicht auch heute noch – ein unvorstellbares Vakuum, d.h. die Fähigkeit, Gegenwartskunst oder auch Kunstgeschichte des 20. Jahrhunderts zu denken und zu schreiben war in Deutschland zum damaligen Zeitpunkt noch sehr schwach entwickelt. Also fand ich den Entschluß plausibel, mich in jenen kulturellen Kontext zu begeben, der meiner eigenen Arbeit und meinen Interessen am nächsten stand. Das galt dann auch für mein Interesse an der Arbeit jener Künstler, mit denen ich in vielen Fällen persönlich bekannt war. Mir schien es, daß, abgesehen von wenigen wichtigen Ausnahmen, die wesentlichen Arbeiten zum damaligen Zeitpunkt alle aus Amerika kamen. Auch von daher ist mir der Übersiedlungentschluß leichter ge-fallen.
R. G.: An wen denken Sie hier speziell?

B. B.: Ich glaube, daß zu diesem Zeitpunkt Dan Graham, Michael Asher und Lawrence Weiner für mich von besonderer Bedeutung waren. Als Modelle von Gegenwartskunstpraxis, die mich damals – und auch heute noch – sehr beschäftigten. Das wären drei Künstler, die ganz wesentlich an meiner Entscheidung mitgewirkt haben, nach Nordamerika zu übersiedeln. Mit denen habe ich ja dann in der Nova Scotia Series auch drei wichtige frühe Bücher produziert.

R. G.: Wurden nicht diese Künstler zur damaligen Zeit hauptsächlich in Europa gezeigt?

B. B.: Ja, das ist natürlich ein Paradox, daß deren Arbeit in Europa viel bekannter war als in Amerika. Das heißt aber nicht, daß deren Arbeit in Europa hätte entstehen können. Die Modelle, Praktiken, Denkansätze oder Verhaltensformen, die mit dieser Praxis assoziiert werden, bzw. auch real liiert waren, kamen eben aus einem kulturellen Kontext, der sich ganz anders verstand und auch definitiv anders gesehen werden wollte als die Definition der kulturellen Praxis in Europa.

R. G.: Wollen Sie damit sagen, daß die Rezeption von amerikanischer Kunst in Europa zu jenem Zeitpunkt auf einem Mißverständnis basierte?

B. B.: Das wäre wahrscheinlich zuviel gesagt. Sie meinen die europäische Rezeption? ...

R. G.: ... ja, die europäische Rezeption ...

B. B.: Ich glaube, das würde zu weit gehen, wenn man das so formulierte. Ich glaube, daß die Rezeption in vielen Fällen die Praktiken verfälscht hat. Das findet immer noch statt. Das ist einer der wesentlichen Unterschiede zwischen amerikanischer und europäischer Gegenwartskunstrezeption. Die europäische Rezeption amerikanischer Kulturpraxis hat immer die Tendenz, die Arbeiten aus ihrem eigenen Kontext herauszulösen; d. h. Isolierung der Praxis aus der Alltagssphäre ist eine ganz wesentliche Differenz: die Definition der Kultur als eine von der Gegenwartspolitik separate Sphäre im Gegensatz zu einer Definition von Kultur, die sich in unmittelbarer Auseinandersetzung mit gegenwärtigem Alltagsleben befindet und immer wieder aufs Neue versucht, sich in diesen Zusammenhang zu setzen, anstatt sich von vornherein als institutionell oder gar autonom zu begreifen. Dies scheint mir immer noch ein großer Unterschied zwischen den beiden Kontinenten zu sein, da, bei aller Assimilierung, das Distanzvermögen oder das Distanzverlangen der kulturellen Praxis in Europa immer noch viel intensiver auf die Verläßlichkeit von Kulturbegriffen und Kulturinstitutionen aus ist. Diese akademischen und institutionellen Distanzen sind letzlich Distanzen der Traditionalität. Das scheint mir immer noch eines der Rezeptionsprobleme zu sein: in dem Maße, in dem man zum Beispiel Dan Grahams Arbeit als "Skulptur" akkulturiert hat oder, indem man Michael Ashers Arbeit als institutionelle Kritik akkulturiert hat, war natürlich die Dynamik der Arbeiten in vieler Hinsicht neutralisiert, wenn nicht verfälscht worden. Das würde ich Ihnen schon zugeben.

R. G.: ... und ästhetisiert ...

B. B.: ... ja, dies trifft für alle drei Künstler zu.

R. G.: Was für ein intellektuelles und kulturelles Klima haben Sie damals in Amerika angetroffen?

B. B.: Ich glaube, ich muß vorerst noch betonen, daß ich meine ersten drei Jahre in Nordamerika in Kanada verbracht habe, und ich war zunächst naiv genug zu glauben, daß Kanada und die USA das gleiche seien. Aber das begreift man sehr schnell, wenn man in Kanada lebt, daß dies überhaupt nicht der Fall ist. Es wäre für mich jetzt sehr leicht zu behaupten, daß ich von 1977 bis 1980 wirklich ein intellektuelles Klima in Amerika kennengelernt hätte. Was ich jedoch tatsächlich kennengelernt habe, waren einzelne Künstler, einzelne Kritiker und einzelne Historiker, die ich entweder durch meine Reisen oder durch meine Teilnahme an Seminaren, Konferenzen, Vorträgen mehr oder minder als Kollegen kennenlernte und die schließlich dann auch Freunde wurden. Es war der Zeitpunkt, an dem ich Leute wie Rosalind Krauss, Douglas Crimp und

Annette Michelson kennengelernt habe, und die Freundschaft mit diesen Herausgebern der Zeitschrift "October" datiert tatsächlich aus dem Jahre 1978, als ich einen Vortrag in Montreal auf einer Konferenz gehalten habe. Während dieser Konferenz lernte ich auch Serge Guilbault kennen, der sich in einem ganz anderen Kontext bewegte. Dies wäre also die konkreteste Form eines intellektuellen Milieus, daß spezifisch auf Kunstkritik und Kunstgeschichte ausgerichtet war. Darüber hinaus habe ich Künstler kennengelernt, die für mich sehr wichtig wurden, und mit denen ich als Herausgeber ihrer Schriften oder Ihrer Bücher im Kontext der *Nova Scotia Series* direkt gearbeitet habe. Sehr wichtig wurden aber auch die jungen Künstler der folgenden Generation, die sich von der konzeptuellen Situation sehr kritisch abgewendet hatten. In mancher Hinsicht wurde diese Generation für mich sogar noch wichtiger, weil sich intellektuelle, methodologische und philosophische Parallelen herausstellten, die ich mit der früheren Generation der konzeptuellen Künstler in viel geringerem Maße teilte. Ich hatte mit der früheren Generation ästhetische Interessen gemein, aber weniger philosophische, politische und methodologische Interessen. Ich spreche jetzt ganz spezifisch von Künstlern wie Martha Rosler oder Allan Sekula, bei denen ich also plötzlich eine marxistische Theorie der Kunstproduktion wiederfand, die ich zuletzt in Europa gesehen hatte, der ich aber in Amerika nie begegnet war.

R. G.: Das sind also die späteren Künstler?

B. B.: Ja, das ist tatsächlich ein Generationsunterschied. Ich meine, Asher, Graham und Weiner sind genau meine Generation, wohingegen Rosler und Sekula insbesondere, fünf Jahre zumindest, wenn nicht zehn Jahre jünger sind. Ihre Arbeit entstammt einer anderen Generation, einer postkonzeptuellen Position. Man weiß eigentlich gar nicht, wie man diese Generation und diese Künstler nennen soll, weil sie im Grunde auch keine Rezeption gefunden haben. Ich habe damals das erste wichtige Buch mit Allan Sekula und das erste Buch mit Martha Rosler gemacht. Aber bis zum heutigen Tag sind diese Künstler relativ unbekannt geblieben. Diese Generation formulierte erstmals eine kritische Revision der konzeptuellen Kunst, insbesondere deren Anspruch auf Neutralität und deren Anspruch auf ein universales Sprachmodell, sowie auch die Tatsache, daß die konzeptuelle Kunst in ihrer institutionellen Kritik ganz wesentliche Aspekte einer politischen Kritik außer Acht ließ.

R. G.: die Problematik der Moderne ...

B. B.: Wesentlich für mich war auch, durch den Kontakt mit Serge Guilbaut im Jahre 1978, die Entdeckung der ersten Phase einer sich neu formierenden sozialen Kunstgeschichte. Ich glaube, daß meine Entdekkung der Arbeit von Timothy Clark, die ich Serge verdanke – Clark war ja Serge Guilbauts Lehrer – ungemein wichtig wurde. Zu entdecken, daß es in den Vereinigten Staaten ein Modell von marxistischer Kunstgeschichte gab, war eine wichtige Erfahrung. Ich wußte natürlich, daß es dies in Europa in der Vorkriegszeit gegeben hatte, aber in der Nachkriegszeit war es ja kaum denkbar gewesen, einen Autor wie Max Raphael überhaupt noch auszugraben. Diese Tradition der sozialen Kunstgeschichte war paradoxerweise, wie vieles andere in Amerika, fortgesetzt oder erneuert worden, da sich die Erbschaft der deutschen marxi-stischen Kunstgeschichtsschreibung durch Antal und Klingender nach England verlagert und dann weiter nach Amerika gewandert war.

R. G.: Paradoxerweise wurde diese Art Kunstgeschichtsschreibung dann auch wieder unter dem englischen Titel in Europa, in Deutschland als *social art history* weiterrezipiert.

B. B.: Ja, *social art history*, es gibt ja auch gar keine deutsche Übersetzung dafür.

R. G.: Sie haben für einige europäische Künstler hier in den USA eine ausgezeichnete Rezeptions- und – wie letzthin bei Marian Goodman – auch Präsentationsarbeit geleistet, die einen gewissen männlichen, heterosexuellen Kanon etabliert hat: Broodthaers, Richter, Haacke, Buren. Was ist Ihr persönlicher Bezug zu diesen Künstlern und wie sehen Sie heute Ihre eigene Rezeptionsarbeit für diese Künstler?

B. B.: Ja, diese Frage habe ich mehrmals gelesen um mir vorzustellen, was ich darauf antworten würde, wenn sie mir gestellt würde, real. Das ist sehr kompliziert, weil ich mir natürlich durchaus inzwischen über die Problematik einer solchen heterosexuell, maskulinistischen Auswahl im klaren bin. Das hat mich aber leider, oder zum Glück, das ist schwierig zu sagen, im Moment noch nicht davor bewahrt oder nicht dazu gebracht, das nun zeitgemäß zu revidieren. Zeitgemäße Revisionen wären ebenso problematisch wie das starrsinnige Festhalten am einmal formulierten Kanon. Ich würde sagen, meine Revisionen dieses maskulinistischen Kanons haben durchaus stattgefunden, aber sie haben sich nicht notwendigerweise in eigenen Schriften niedergeschlagen oder in kritischer, kuratorischer Arbeit. Gleichzeitig möchte ich betonen, daß mein Kanon, wenn man das wirklich so nennen muß, mir immerhin erlaubte, bereits 1982 in einem Aufsatz in "Artforum" Künstler wie Dara Birnbaum, Jenny Holzer, Louise Lawler, Sherrie Levine und Martha Rosler ausführlich zu diskutieren und zum Teil auch Bücher mit diesen Künstlerinnen zu produzieren. Also von daher würde ich sagen, daß meine Begrenzungen vielleicht nicht ganz so hartnäckig sind, wie sie in der Auswahl der Namen, die Sie zitiert haben erscheinen ...

R. G.: ... ich dachte an europäische Künstler...

B. B.: Es stimmt, daß ich in Europa ausschließlich mit männlichen Künstlern enger zusammengearbeitet habe. Entweder als Kritiker und Historiker oder als Herausgeber, Katalogautor oder Kurator. Das stimmt. Ich würde dann allerdings auch dazusagen, daß die Situation in Deutschland, zumal Mitte bis Ende der 70er Jahre, keine sehr emanzipierte Situation war. Das heißt, die feministischen Kunstpraktiken, die man kannte oder die ich kannte, würden auch heute noch nicht mein Interesse finden. Aber die Situation, aus einem maskulinistisch sexistischen Milieu zu stammen, das man wenig verändert hat, ist mir als durchaus pro-blematische vor Augen. Ob mich das dann im nachhinein dazu bringen sollte, spezifisch historisch gewordene Interessen oder spezifisch entwik- kelte identifikatorische Beziehungen retrospektiv zu annullieren, ist mir nicht unmittelbar klar. Ich glaube zum Beispiel, daß die Arbeit am Rezep-tionsprozeß von Broodthaers, der mich immer wieder aufs Neue beschäftigt, oder die Fortsetzung meiner Arbeit an meiner Richtermonographie, durchaus gerechtfertigt werden könnte, ohne daß man mir daraus einen maskulinistischen Strick drehen muß. Ich würde sehr gerne, wenn ich Zeit hätte, einen großen Aufsatz über Hanne Darboven schreiben, oder ich würde sehr gerne, wenn ich die Zeit hätte und das könnte, einen großen Aufsatz über Eva Hesse schreiben. Also ich glaube nicht, daß meine Begrenzungen so tief eingefurcht sind, daß es da gar keinen Überblick mehr gibt über die real notwendigen methodologischen Veränderungen. Ich bin sehr an feministischer Kritik und sehr an feministischer Theorie interessiert. Ich glaube aber nicht, daß die Konsequenz dessen nun wäre, unmittelbar den eigenen Identifikationskanon umzubauen, um unter dem Druck politischer Korrektheit Anpassungsmaßnahmen vorzunehmen.

R. G.: In diesem Zusammenhang drängen sich heute nicht nur im nordamerikanischen Kontext Fragen zur *gender* Problematik und zur sexuellen Identität auf. Komplexe Zusammenhänge also, die in Ihren bekanntesten Texten weniger eine Rolle gespielt haben. Welche Relevanz haben heute diese Diskurse für Sie? Auch natürlich die Frage der ethnischen Zugehörigkeit.

B. B.: Ich glaube, daß man sich als Historiker und Kritiker, ein relativ begrenztes Kompetenzfeld erarbeitet, und natürlich hofft man, daß Entwicklungen und Ausweitungen ständig möglich bleiben. Natürlich hofft man, daß einmal erarbeitete Lese- und Sprachkompetenzen unausgesetzt kritisch revidiert und kritisch entwickelt werden. Ich glaube aber, daß man gerade, um die Definition der Kompetenz gültig zu halten, daß man eine solche Kompetenz nicht mutwillig oder willkürlich dem Druck radikal veränderter Interessen anzupassen hat. Ich würde sagen, daß die disziplinären Verpflichtungen des eigenen Gebietes, des eigenen Feldes und die einer relativ strengen Definition dessen, was Kunstgeschichtsschreibung oder Kunstkritikschreibung sein könnte oder zu sein habe, eine Verpflichtung für Kontinuität, Solidität und Komplexität auferlegen, die nicht ohne weiteres durch ein ständiges Erweitern, ständiges Verwandeln, ständiges Verschieben eine neue methodologische Perspektive gewinnt. Das heißt, wenn ich die Frage klären will, warum die Arbeit von Broodthaers in vielen Fällen eine Kritik der konzeptuellen Kunst und nicht ein Teil der konzeptuellen Kunst ist und welche Modelle von Broodthaers Ende der 60er Jahre schon entwickelt worden sind, die heute in vieler Hinsicht erst sichtbar und verständlich werden, dann scheint mir das eine wichtige Frage zu sein. Anders formuliert, inwieweit Broodthaers Foucaultianer oder Habermasianer gewesen ist, das scheint mir eine komplexe und wichtige Frage zu sein, die meiner Meinung nach niemand angemessen angegangen ist. Diese Fragestellung kann nun nicht einfach unter dem Druck von *gender politics* oder *identity politics* zurückgelassen werden. Ich kann nicht aus Broodthaers einen Postkolonialisten machen, so sehr mich postkoloniale Theorie auch interessiert, und ich glaube, das wäre eine doch zutiefst ahistorische Unternehmung, sich plötzlich mit allen Diskursen der Gegenwartspraktiken zu dekorieren, um am Zug zu bleiben. Das scheint mir sehr viel mehr verdächtiger zu sein, als methodologisch zu erstarren, was natürlich die gegenteilige Gefahr ist.

R. G.: Wobei aber gerade Broodthaers mit einer sehr kolonialen Ästhetik und typisch kolonialistischen Themen gespielt hat ...

B. B.: Ja, deshalb habe ich es auch bewußt erwähnt.

R. G.: Woran denken Sie genau, wenn Sie von vom Habermas-Modell und einem Foucault-Modell in Bezug auf Broodthaers sprechen?

B. B.: Ganz spezifisch denke ich an die Konzeption und Definition der Funktion des Museums in der Arbeit von Broodthaers. Die Frage stellt sich, ob Broodthaers das Museum als eine Institution der individuellen Differenzierung in der Sphäre der bürgerlichen Öffentlichkeit definiert hat und ob er diese Institution deshalb in ihren letzten Zügen gesehen hat, als eine, die sich unter dem Eindruck der Kulturindustrie und der Spektakelkultur hoffnungslos im Abbau befindet. Oder ob er diese Institution als eine konservativ zu verteidigende und als eine zu rettende bürgerliche Institution verstanden hat, und ob er durchaus im Sinne von Habermas die Möglichkeit gesehen hat, eine solche Institution der bürgerlichen Öffentlichkeit in der nachbürgerlichen Sphäre aufrechtzuerhalten. Ob er es als sinnvoll angesehen hätte, am Museumsmodell zu arbei-ten, sodaß es sich also tatsächlich nicht um einen historisch bereits abgeschlossenen Prozeß handelt. Oder ob er vielmehr das Museum in einer Foucaultschen Definition verstanden hat, als einen Ort, an dem Kultur kontrolliert, diszipliniert und als Indoktrination weitergereicht wird, als intellektueller Diskurs der Kontrolle und der historischen Angleichungen, der von innen heraus gesprengt und kritisiert werden muß – etwa in dem Sinne wie Buren das vorgeschlagen hatte. Also ich glaube, daß es bei Buren letztlich um eine ganz andere Auffassung von Museumsdiskurs geht als bei Broodthaers, obwohl die beiden sehr eng befreundet waren, sehr viel voneinander wußten und miteinander gearbeitet haben. Ich glaube, wenn man das im Detail untersuchen würde, so ist der Museumsbegriff Burens und die Kritik der Institution, die aus der Arbeit Burens hervorgeht, im Grunde sehr viel anders als der Museums-begriff von Broodthaers, und das ist nur ein Beispiel einer komplexen Frage.

R. G.: Sie glauben, daß Broodthaers mehr auf der Seite von Habermas steht und ans Museum glaubt?

B. B.: Ja, ich glaube, letztlich würde ich mehr in diese Richtung tendieren, obwohl das alles noch differenziert werden müßte. Ich glaube schon, daß Broodthaers tatsächlich eine zutiefst traditionalistische, um nicht zu sagen konservative Dimension hatte, in der er die Dimension des Museums in seiner Arbeit zu retten versuchte gegenüber den Zugriffen und den zunehmend stärker werdenden Kontrollen der *corporate culture* und der Kulturindustrie, deren Resultate wir jetzt ja in voller Blüte sehen und deren Resultate wahrscheinlich auch irreversibel sind. Von daher ist also die Position von Broodthaers wahrscheinlich eine groteske bzw. eine tragische oder allegorische Position gewesen – oder vielleicht auch eine tragikomische Position und das ist ja auch in seiner Arbeit durchaus immer wieder angelegt.

R. G.: Das erinnert mich an den erst jetzt erschienenen Briefverkehr von Horkheimer, in dem dieser sich Adorno gegenüber über Habermas beschwerte, daß dieser zu revoltierend, zu revolutionär sei ...

B. B.: ... ja, als Habermas Horkheimers Assistent war. Der hat ja auch seine Habilitation blockiert ...

R. G.: ... wobei Adorno Habermas verteidigte. Es ging dabei genau um die Frage, inwieweit eine bürgerliche Kultursphäre noch zu verteidigen sei, für die sich Horkheimer ausgesprochen hat. Nun würde mich aber auch ihre persönliche Meinung zu diesem Komplex interessieren. Teilen Sie eher die Auffassung von Habermas oder von Foucault über das Museum? Können Sie sich vorstellen, daß es zwischen beiden Modellen auch einen Bezugspunkt geben kann, also daß es auch Foucault nicht unbedingt auf eine Auflösung dieser Institution abgesehen hat und daß umgekehrt Habermas nicht auch eine Kritik an dieser Institution implizierte?

B. B.: Das glaube ich ist richtig. Aber daß Foucault die Institution sehr viel kritischer gesehen hat und sehr viel weniger Emanzipationspotential in der Institution des Museums sah als Habermas es gesehen hatte oder sieht, das scheint mir doch ein wesentlicher Unterschied zu sein.

R. G.: Und wie sehen Sie das heute?

B. B.: Da würde ich wahrscheinlich antworten müssen, daß ich dem in absoluter Ambivalenz gegenüberstehe, d.h. an einem Morgen wache ich auf und denke, daß es besser wäre, das Museum so schnell wie möglich den Korporationen komplett zu überlassen ...

R. G.: ... Guggenheim ...

B. B.: ah, Sie haben das gelesen, das war naürlich nicht ganz ernst gemeint – und am nächsten Morgen wache ich auf und denke darüber nach, welche Strategien man entwickeln könnte, um die bürgerlich-öffentliche liberaldemokratische Funktion des Museums als relativ autonome Institution des Sozialstaates retten zu können, was ja durchaus denkbar ist. Ich meine, es ist ja nicht solange her, daß man das in durchaus machbaren Umständen noch sehen konnte.

R. G.: ... in Europa zumindest, wobei die Europäer jetzt auch anfangen, amerikanischen Management- und Sponsoringmodellen zu folgen ...

B. B.: ... es ist ja nicht so, als wäre es vollkommen undenkbar geworden, das Museum als öffentliche Institution zu sehen ... aber vielleicht ist es völlig naiv und sentimental, immer noch daran zu glauben, daß es eine Institution der bürgerlich liberaldemokratischen Öffentlichkeit geben könnte, die die Funktion des Museums übernimmt oder weiterhin aufrechterhält.

R. G.: Interessant, wie Max Beckmann wieder herhalten mußte, der von den Nazis vertrieben, von der DDR vereinnahmt und nun für deutsches, an die New Yorker Börse drängendes Kapital erneut im Guggenheim PR machen muß. Nebenbei frißt die *Corporate Culture* nicht nur das Museum und den Staat, sondern auch die Universität, die sich ebenfalls in ein riesiges Servicemanagement verwandelt, für das nur noch profitorientierte Kriterien der "Exzellenz" und Kompatibilität gelten.

Aber nun zur nächsten Frage: Hal Foster warf Ihnen in der in "October" abgedruckten Diskussion zur Rezeption der 60er Jahre vor, daß für Sie Geschichte eine "rastlose Subtraktion von Möglichkeiten" sei. Können Sie sich mit solch einem Kunstgeschichtsverständnis identifizieren? Hat dieses Geschichtsmodell für Sie jemals eine Rolle gespielt?

B. B.: Ich glaube, daß dieser Vorwurf, wenn es denn ein Vorwurf war, durchaus wohl formuliert war. Mit einer Einschränkung: nämlich der, daß eine Subtraktion von Möglichkeiten natürlich immer auch die Eröffnung von anderen Möglichkeiten beinhaltet. Um ein Beispiel zu nennen: Im Moment der Erfindung des *ready mades* im Jahr 1913 wurde eine beträchtliche Anzahl von künstlerischen Möglichkeiten subtrahiert. Gleichzeitig muß man aber erkennen, daß durch die Erscheinung des *ready mades*, das ja nur die Artikulation eines viel komplexeren Prozesses ist, eine Unzahl anderer Denk-, Seh- und Produktionsmöglichkeiten freigesetzt wurde. Und nun ist das ein altes Modell, und wieweit sich das in die Gegenwart übertragen läßt, ist eine andere Frage. Mir scheint es immer noch eine der wichtigsten Definitionen der gegenwärtigen Kultur-praxis zu sein, einer ihrer wesentlichsten Anfangspunkte, genau diesen aktuell gültigen Status der Subtraktion überhaupt verstanden zu haben. Also das heißt, sich darüber ins Klare zu setzen, warum bestimmte Möglichkeiten einfach nicht mehr gegeben sind. Und wenn man sich darüber noch immer hinwegtäuscht, dann braucht man eigentlich gar nicht mehr anzufangen. Oder man kann anfangen und "vorsichher-basteln". Aber wenn man nicht einmal in der Lage ist, eine historische Analyse zu entwickeln, aus der die subtrahierten Möglichkeiten offen-kundig werden, dann hat man, glaube ich, schon einen schlechten Start oder einen Start fürs Irrelevante. Die Tatsache, daß man diese Analyse erfolgreich durchführt, ist im Gegensatz dazu dann wiederum keine Garantie für eine relevante Praxis, sie ist lediglich die Voraussetzung für eine relevante Praxis. Ich glaube, der nächste Schritt, die Klärung dessen, was aus der Subtraktion dann als Möglichkeit hervorgeht oder was aus der subtrahierten Situation als Notwendigkeit entspringt, das scheint mir die sehr viel schwierigere Frage zu sein. Dies ist ein sehr viel schwieri-gerer Sprung, den der Künstler, der Kritiker oder der Historiker in verschiedener Weise dann auch machen muß. Und man muß zum Beispiel verstehen, um beim Beispiel zu bleiben, daß das *ready made* bei aller Subtraktion in gewisser Weise auch eine Subtraktion des *ready made* war, daß es im Grunde ein Mißverständnis war, zu glauben, es gäbe nun die Lizenz für unausgesetzte Variationen des *ready made* Prinzips. Das ist ja eines der fatalen Mißverständnisse, unter dem Künstler bis in die heutige Zeit noch leiden, daß sie glauben, daß das *ready made* Tür und Tor geöffnet habe. Ich glaube viel mehr, mit Barnett Newman, daß wichtige Kunst alle Türen schließt und nicht, daß sie sie öffnet.

R. G.: Sozusagen Subtraktion als Negation im Sinne Hegels.

B. B.: Ja, und ich glaube, das ist tatsächlich ein Prinzip, das noch eine gewisse Gültigkeit hat. Es gibt ja verschiedene Beispiele in der Gegenwartskunst, wo Leute glauben, daß Broodthaers ein Modell sei, das man so fortsetzen könnte. Das ist wirklich ein fatales Mißverständnis. Man kann Broodthaers nicht zum Modell einer Gegenwartspraxis machen, obwohl er vielleicht in vieler Hinsicht einer der wichtigsten gegenwärtigen Künstler ist, immer noch. Genauso wie man Robert Ryman nicht zum Modell einer Gegenwartsmalerei machen kann. Ich glaube, das ist eine der schwierigsten Schwellen, die man überschreiten muß, auch im Denken, nicht nur als praktizierender Künstler. Man kann also auf

Rymans Malerei keine Theorie der fundamentalen Malerei als Historiker oder Kritiker begründen. Da ist man schon ganz falsch gelaufen.

R. G.: Sehr früh haben Sie für "October" gearbeitet und geschrieben. Was für eine Rolle spielte und spielt heute noch die Übersetzung und Aufarbeitung europäischer Texte für ein amerikanisches Publikum?

B. B.: Die Frage hat eine subtil kritische Dimension, d.h. daß Sie wohl die Frage stellen wollten, wie sinnvoll es sei, daß in der Zeitschrift "October" Texte der 30er und 40er Jahre aus Europa publiziert werden, die nie übersetzt wurden. Das ist natürlich auch eine komplexe Geschichte. Wenn man es zu rechtfertigen hätte, würde ich sagen: zum einen, weil jede philosophische oder theoretische oder ästhetische Position immer verschiedene Rezeptionsphasen haben wird, d. h., es gibt eine 60er Jahre Rezeption von Wittgenstein, eine 70er Jahre Rezeption von Wittgenstein und vielleicht eine 90er Jahre Rezeption. Und das rechtfertigt an sich schon ein erneutes und ständiges Wiederaufgreifen, ein Wiedererarbeiten von historischem Material. Es gibt eine 60er Jahre Bataille-Rezeption in Europa, in Frankreich zumindest, und es gibt eine 90er Jahre Bataille-Rezeption in Amerika – und diese sind sehr verschieden. Und daß man Bataille in *October* vor längerer Zeit schon hat lesen können, bevor die Baraillewelle wirklich in Gang kam, ist in gewisser Hinsicht eine Bestätigung, daß die Archivarbeit von *October* realkulturpolitische Funk-tion haben kann. Ich glaube nicht, daß jedes historische Dokument, das man ausgräbt, nun unmittelbar aktivistische Konsequenzen haben muß, um gerechtfertigt zu werden. Aber ich glaube durchaus, daß in mancher Hinsicht die Rezeptionsarbeit oder die kulturelle Archäologie, die "Octo-ber" betreibt, durchaus in diesen Termini gerechtfertigt werden könnte. Die andere Dimension, die mir in der Archivarbeit immer wieder wichtig erscheint, ist, daß, zumal in Amerika, historisches Gedächtnis und historische Kompetenz nur schwer aufrechtzuerhalten sind, sagen wir einmal so in der Alltagssphäre und natürlich nicht in der akademischen Sphäre oder im Leben von Spezialisten, von hochentwickelten und hochgebildeten Kontexten. Aber das eine Zeitschrift, die sich als kulturpolitische Zeitschrift versteht, immer wieder nicht nur auf die Gegenwart, sondern auch auf die Geschichte und die unmittelbar zurückliegende Geschichte verweisen sollte und zum geschichtlichen Prozeß damit beiträgt, scheint mir durchaus eine zu rechtfertigende Position zu sein. Ob die Zeitschrift damit von jeder Avantgardeposition disqualifiziert wird, ist eine durchaus angemessene Frage. Ich glaube, daß "October" sich schon seit langem nicht mehr wirklich als Avantgardezeitschrift versteht, in der nun wirklich die neuesten Positionen und die wichtigsten Praktiken vorgestellt werden, obwohl es das in den 70er Jahren durchaus gegeben hat, als *October* in gewisser Hinsicht als theorievermittelnde Zeitschrift fungierte. Aber diese Frage stellt sich erneut ganz deutlich in der nächsten Nummer über den "Situationismus". Wenn man in Frankreich war oder häufig ist, wird einem klar, wie merkwürdig diese Diskrepanz ist, wie Debord und der "Situationismus" in Frankreich absolut musealisiert worden sind. Sie können in Paris genauso Malraux oder Debord kaufen oder lesen oder präsentiert sehen ...

R. G.: ... oder pantheonisiert sehen ...

B. B.: In Frankreich weiß man nicht mehr recht, was Gegenwart ist, aber man weiß sicherlich was Geschichte ist. Wohingegen hier – und ich weiß, daß die Franzosen die USA in dieser Hinsicht als lächerlich ansehen – natürlich eine merkwürdige Situation existiert, wo man zumindest in der Unterhaltung mit jüngeren Künstlern, Akademikern, Kritikern und Historikern sich die Frage stellt, inwieweit das Erbe von Guy Debord, das Erbe der "Internationalen Situationisten" revitalisiert werden könnte. Und das scheint mir zwar eine etwas naive Haltung zu sein, die typisch amerikanisch ist und von der wir alle betroffen sind, solange wir hier arbeiten und leben, die aber durchaus eine produktive Haltung ist. Ob man neuerliche Geschichte reaktivieren und für die Gegenwart brauchbar machen kann oder ob man argumentiert, wie die Franzosen es sehr gerne tun, daß zum Beispiel die Theorien des Feminismus schon seit den 60er Jahren obsolet seien, dies schient mir immer noch eine wichtige Frage zu sein.

R. G.: Wie stehen Sie zu Eurozentrismuskritiken, die in westlichen kulturellen Institutionen eine Verlängerung eurozentristischer Hegemonieansprüche sehen?

B. B.: Das ist natürlich eine der wichtigsten Fragen der Gegenwart, die uns alle betrifft. Dies schließt an die Frage an, inwieweit man Institutionen der bürgerlich-demokratischen Öffentlichkeit zu retten versuchen, und inwieweit man sich damit abfinden sollte, daß sie historisch hinfällig, längst Teil der Kulturindustrie geworden sind und definitiv dieser Sphäre der *corporate culture* zugeschlagen werden sollten. Im glei-chen Sinne könnte man sich auch fragen, mit welchen Gründen und in welcher Weise könnte man ein eurozentrisches Kulturmodell überhaupt noch retten, wenn man es retten möchte, und wie ließe sich das rechtfertigen. Da kann ich Ihnen eine Anekdote erzählen, die mir sehr nahe liegt und an der ich einige Zeit festgehangen habe, weil ich darüber gerne geschrieben hätte, aber ich habe es leider nicht gemacht. Als ich vor einigen Wochen in Paris war, wurde am gleichen Tag, an dem André Malraux ins Pantheon überführt wurde, eine Pariser *Banlieue*-Rapper-gruppe, die NTM, zu sechs Monaten Gefängnis verurteilt, um sie für ihre aufrührerischen Texte zu bestrafen. Das schien mir eine sehr prägnante und signifikante Situation zu sein: auf der einen Seite diese sehr komplexe und politisch schillernde Figur Malraux, der trotz seiner linksradi-kalen Vergangenheit nun hier zum republikanischen Kulturheroen stilisiert, und in eine so merkwürdige Institution wie das Pantheon überführt wurde, die wohl nirgends auf der ganzen Erde ihresgleichen hat. Es ist ja an sich schon erstaunlich, daß es so etwas überhaupt noch gibt, und in gewisser Weise vielleicht ja auch sehr bewundernswert. Auf der anderen Seite stehen die Praktiken der *Banlieue*, die aus dem Gegenwarts-kulturverständnis, in Frankreich zumal und in Deutschland im gleichen Maße, ausgeschlossen werden, und wo man glaubt, zensierend in diese eingreifen zu können.

In den Vereinigten Staaten gibt es dann doch eine sehr interessante Situation, wo dieses Prinzip einer eingreifenden zensierenden Interven-tion in Massenkultur schon aus kommerziellen Gründen eigentlich undenkbar ist, obwohl es immer wieder Versuche gegeben hat und geben wird. Das heißt also, wie ließe sich eine politisch motivierte und politisch definierte Theorie rechtfertigen, die von der Fortsetzung und der Aufrechterhaltung von Standards der Sublimierung, der Komplexität und der Ausdifferenzierung in der gegenwärtigen Kulturpraxis ausgehen würde? Das ist der erste Teil Ihrer Frage, glaube ich, ohne eurozentrisch zu sein. Das ist für mich eine der schwierigsten Fragen, die ich nicht beantworten möchte, weil ich sie nicht beantworten kann, aber die ich durchaus als eine der wichtigsten Fragen ansehen würde. Ich glaube, daß es darauf keine einfache Antwort geben kann. Ich glaube, ... und da kann ich mich nur auf Beispiele beziehen, die allemal leider aus den 60er Jahren stammen, statt aus den 90ern, wo sie herkommen sollten. Ich kann zum Beispiel auf die Positionen von Jean-Marie Straub und Danielle Hulliet verweisen: für sie war es immer undenkbar, eine radikale kritische Kultur zu konzipieren, die die historischen Standards der kognitiven Ausdiffe-renzierung, der ästhetischen Ausdifferenzierung, der psychosomati-schen, psychosexuellen Ausdifferenzierung unterschlägt. Das heißt, Sinnlichkeitsmodelle, Erfahrungsmodelle, kognitive Modelle können in der ästhetischen Produktion der Gegenwart nicht zum Opfer von politi-schen, aktivistischen Ansprüchen gemacht werden und das gleiche gilt, würde ich sagen, für Modelle von Kunstpraxis, die sich in Fragen der Identitätspolitik und bei Fragen der *gender*-Problematik engagieren. Ich glaube, daß es ein Phänomen des historischen Widerstands gibt, das in der gegenwärtigen ästhetischen Praxis (genau so wenig wie in der literarischen oder philosophischen Praxis) nicht ungestraft beiseitegeschoben werden kann. Die "Strafe", ein schlimmes deutsches Wort, das mir da entfährt, die nun mal unvermeidlich scheint, ist die "Strafe" des eigenen Versagens. Die Banalität und die Irrelevanz vieler gegenwärtiger Kunst-praktiken, die sich als aktivistisch in *gender politics* oder aktivistisch in *identity politics* geben, ist meiner Meinung nach der beste Beleg dafür, daß die Fragen einer untragbaren eurozentrischen Tradition, die ich durchaus und in vielerlei Hinsicht als unerträglich sehe, nicht mit einfachen Handstreichen gelöst werden können. Ich hoffe, daß ich wenigstens eine Position klargemacht habe.

R. G.: Es ist interessant, daß jene asiatischen Länder, die zu Reichtum gekommen sind, jetzt anfangen, in das westliche Modell von Kunst zu investieren. Museen entstehen und Biennalen werden geschaffen ...
B. B.: Ja, Kwangju in Korea zum Beispiel, haben Sie dafür eine Erklärung?

R. G.: Ich glaube, daß das Kulturmodell westlicher Prägung in den reichen asiatischen Ländern, insofern es im großen Stil mit staatlichen Mitteln oder Geldern der jeweiligen *corporate world* organisiert, gesponsert und importiert wird, vor allem eine legitimierende Funktion spielt, wie das auch zur Zeit des Schahs von Persien der Fall war ...

B. B.: ... Legitimierug wovon?

R. G.: Die Legitimierung und Selbstrepräsentation der jeweiligen Gesellschaft als eine moderne, aufgeschlossene, liberale, westlich orientierte, kapitalistische Nation, die westliche Wertstandards akzeptiert und ihnen nacheifert. Zur ökonomischen Macht gesellt sich so ein kulturelles Pendant. Auch die USA wußte nach 1945 kulturelle Hegemonieansprüche gegenüber Europa geltend zu machen. Interessanterweise aber funktioniert ein dubioser Kulturbegriff vor allem als letzter wichtiger Identifikations- und Abgrenzungs*token* in den rassistischen Zirkeln von weißen Europäern, Amerikanern und Australiern, die ich in asiatischen *Gaijin*gemeinden[1] angetroffen habe. Der Besitz von dem, was jeweils als "Kultur" angenommen wird, ist ein arrogantes, ideologisch sehr wichtiges Identifikationskissen, um das nicht nur in Asien gestritten wird. Man kennt doch auch in Europa chauvinistische Sätze wie "die haben das Geld, wir haben die Kultur".

B. B.: Man sollte aber wahrscheinlich auch den Entertainment-Wert nicht unterschätzen, den Kultur mitbringt, obwohl das vielleicht gering ist im Vergleich.

R. G.: Dann könnten sie aber auch nur den Zirkus bringen.

B. B.: Aja...

R. G.: In fast allen Seminaren für das *Whitney Progam* haben Sie Texte der Frankfurter Schule präsentiert. Was für eine Bedeutung hat für Sie die Frankfurter Schule gehabt oder hat sie immer noch, und wie sehen Sie deren Rezeption in den USA?

B. B.: Ja, das ist wiederum eine Frage, die einen gewissen berechtigten und notwendigen kritischen Unterton hat, im Sinne einer Anspielung auf die Möglichkeit, daß es sich da um ein relativ sklerotisches Unterfangen handelt, da es ja in keiner Weise eine offensichtliche Verbindlichkeit der Frankfurter-Schule-Theorie in der gegenwärtigen Situation gibt. Man könnte eher sagen, wenn irgend etwas offensichtlich ist, dann die Tatsache, daß es keine Anwendbarkeit der Frankfurter-Schule-Theorie gibt, wenn man das so generell sehen möchte. Was hat man denn zum gegenwärtigen Zeitpunkt der elektronischen Bildmedien, der Digitalphotographie oder des Internets noch mit dem Kunstwerk-Aufsatz Benjamins zu tun? Relativ wenig, wenn überhaupt noch etwas. Dann würde ich zum Teil auf das zurückgreifen, was ich vor wenigen Minuten schon gesagt habe bezüglich der Archäologieaufgabe des Kritikers und des Historikers, bestimmten Texten immer neue Rezeptionsphasen zukommen zu lassen. Das wäre also ein Argument. Ich glaube, daß man als Leser und Studierender, als angehender Künstler, Kritiker oder Theoretiker, durchaus einen Anspruch auf eine relativ komplexe und solide Formation hat. Warum das in meinem Falle immer wieder Frankfurter Schule gewesen ist, statt Strukturalismus, statt Psychoanalyse zu werden, ist mit meinen eigenen Begrenzungen zu erklären. Es ist also keineswegs ein Anspruch, daß dies das einzige Modell sei, mit dem man sich zu beschäftigen habe. Das hat tatsächlich sehr viel mehr mit der Frage einer bestimmten Lese- und Interpretationskompetenz zu tun, genauso wie es mit der Frage bestimmter historischer Identifikationen zu tun hat, wie wir es schon am Anfang angesprochen haben. Es ist nun einmal für mich sehr viel wichtiger, mich mit Broodthaers zu beschäftigen als mit Janine Antoni.

Und das wäre in der Frage der Theorie-Instruktion dann auch noch anders zu formulieren: daß natürlich bei aller offensichtlichen Obsoletheit bestimmter Theoriemodelle aus der Frankfurter Schule andere Modelle wiederum ungemein aktuell sind und immer wieder neu aktualisiert werden können und müssen. Daß die Frage der Beziehung zwischen Avantgarde-Kulturindustrie, meiner Meinung nach, immer noch vollkommen untertheoretisiert ist und im Grunde immer noch nicht verstanden wird, obwohl Leute daran arbeiten und dauernd darüber nachdenken, scheint mir ein Beispiel dafür zu sein, wie wichtig es ist, gewisse Texte, z. B. die "Dialektik der Aufklärung" durchaus bereitzuhalten oder immer neu zu lesen.

R. G.: Auch die gesamte Phänomenologiekritik ist in Amerika komplett übergangen worden.

B. B.: ... speziell die Heideggerkritik.

R. G.: Auch die an Husserl. Der "Jargon der Eigentlichkeit" wurde erst jetzt übersetzt, ebenfalls die drei Hegelaufsätze von Adorno. Darüber hinaus wurde die Kulturkritik Adornos in den USA auf seinen sicherlich problematischen Jazzaufsatz reduziert.

B. B.: Ja, also von daher glaube ich schon, daß man eine Fortsetzung der Rezeptionsarbeit der Kritischen Theorie rechtfertigen kann. Keinesfalls würde ich damit behaupten wollen, daß das ein Modell ist, das Ausschließlichkeitsanspruch vertritt. Im Gegenteil.

R. G.: Die Frankfurter Schule selbst hat das schon in ihren eigenen Schriften antizipiert.

B. B.: Ja.

R. G.: In Ihrem letzten in "October" veröffentlichten Text zu Richters "Atlas" beschäftigen Sie sich mit dem Problem von "post-traditioneller Identität". Wie können Sie sich aus der Distanz solch eine post-traditionelle Identität für das wiedervereinte, verstärkt xenophobische Deutschland vorstellen? Und was bedeutet so eine post-traditionelle Identität für Sie als private Person, sozusagen als in den USA lebender Deutscheuropäer ?

B. B.: Das ist in gewisser Hinsicht meine liebste Frage, weil diese mich vor vollkommen unlösbare Probleme stellt und mir gleichzeitig auch Gelegenheit gibt, ein paar böse Bemerkungen zu machen, die ich gerne öffentlich machen möchte. Das scheint mir bei aller Faszination, die ich für die deutsche Situation und spezifisch für die Berliner Situation habe, eine der fatalsten Problematiken der Gegenwartskultur und der Gegenwartspolitik in Deutschland zu sein. Daß es sowenig Verständnis und so wenig Reflexion zu geben scheint – es kann ja sein, daß es viel mehr gibt, als mir bekannt ist – bezüglich der Frage, ob es alternative oder konträre Modelle der Identität geben könnte, auf die man sich einlassen könnte. Das wird nun sehr akut und konkret im Falle Berlins, das ja nun als neue "Hauptstadt" deklariert worden ist und nun als neue "Hauptstadt" aufgebaut wird ...

R. G.: ... in Granit und Marmor.

B. B.: ... ja, daß also da keinerlei Bewußtsein vorhanden zu sein scheint, um zum einen über die historische Krise, um nicht zu sagen das definitive Ende der Ideologie des Nationalstaates zu reflektieren – das wäre immerhin doch noch eine Möglichkeit sich diesem Problem anzunähern – ode, auf der anderen Seite, sich ganz praktisch aus dem Blickwinkel der Architekturgeschichte oder der Urbanistik real vor Augen zu führen, daß Agglomerationen von der Größe Berlins inzwischen weltweit Metropolisformen schaffen, die keineswegs mehr durch nationalstaatliche Identität gezeichnet oder definiert werden können. Also daß man sich zumindest darüber klar werden muß, daß Faktoren wie globale Industrieproduktion, globale Migration, globale ökonomische Verflechtungen das Modell einer nationalstaatlich definierten Hauptstadt vollkommen ad absurdum geführt haben. Und das man im besten Falle in Berlin etwas herstellen kann, das so eine hybride Fusion werde könnte wie eine Synthese von Los Angeles und Moskau, nehme ich an. Und daß es von daher sehr hilfreich wäre, wenn man sich über die Problematik einer rekonstituierten nationalen Identität und die Problematik einer rekonstituierten nationalstaatlichen Hauptstadt etwas klarer werden könnte. Das scheint mir in Deutschland gegenwärtig wirklich zu unentwickelt zu sein. Diese Unfähigkeit oder Unwilligkeit, über andere Identitätsmodelle zu reflektieren, macht es nach zwanzig Jahren Auslandsaufenthalt auch hart und immer schwieriger, sowohl nach Deutschland als auch nach Frankreich zurückzukehren. Das ist, muß ich sagen, vielleicht eine bloße Rationalisierung des Verlustes, aber vielleicht auch eine affirmative Bejahung einer real gewonnenen Freiheit. Und ich würde natürlich für das letztere optieren. Ich glaube, daß genau so, wie man sich von bestimmten Kinderkrankheiten oder frühen Glaubensformen emanzipiert, wie man sich von bestimmten Ideologieformationen emanzipiert und wie man sich von unfreiwillig erfahrener oder erlittener religiöser Indoktrination emanzipieren kann, so kann man sich halt auch von der nationalstaatlichen Identifikation emanzipieren. Ob man das freiwillig oder unfreiwillig tut, ist eine andere Geschichte: die meisten Menschen in der ersten und zweiten Hälfte des 20. Jahrhunderts haben das unfreiwillig, mit beträchtlichen Schmerzen und Verlusten gemacht. Ich habe das Glück gehabt, dies freiwillig zu tun und trotzdem sehe ich in meiner eigenen Geschichte immer deutlicher, wie sehr das als Bruch und als Verlust gesehen werden muß. Aber ich glaube, es wäre wirklich falsch zu behaupten, daß es sich nicht auch um eine reale Entwicklung handelte. Es ist ja nicht zufällig, daß immer mehr Menschen, zumindest in unserem kulturellen Milieu (schwächlich signifikant wie das auch sein mag), sich zumindest in Ansätzen über die Problematik einer nationalstaatlich definierten Identität klar geworden sind. Von daher würde ich also sagen, daß der Verlust der nationalstaatlichen Identität, so sehr man diesen bedauert, einhergeht mit einem realen Emanzipationsgewinn, der einen durchaus für diesen Verlust kompensieren kann. Bei der Rückkehr in die forciert aufrechterhaltene nationalstaatliche Ideologie in europäischen Ländern, nicht nur in Deutschland, sondern auch in Italien und Frankreich, kann man nur noch erschüttert sein über die Blindheit dieser Identifikationen. Man kann auch amüsiert sein über die Verkrüppe-lungsformen, die diese Identifikationen erzeugt haben, im Zuge einer immer weiter hinausgezögerten und immer weiter hinausgeschobenen Aufklärung. Ob das nun Bayern ist, Österreich oder Frankreich: die unzähligen grotesken Auswüchse der nationalstaatlichen Ideologien kann man immer wieder aufs Neue entdecken und zumindest in Ihren grotesken Formen belächeln. Wahrscheinlich nicht in ihren realpolitisch bedrohlichen Formen, die es zum Glück vielleicht zum gegenwärtigen Zeitpunkt noch nicht in Deutschland oder Frankreich, wohl aber in Serbien und Kroatien gibt ...

R. G.: ... also post-traditionelle Identität im Sinne von post-nationalstaatlicher Identität ...

B. B.: Ja, das ist sicherlich keine ausreichende Definition aber in diesem

Zusammenhang würde ich das so definieren. Es gibt andere Kriterien für post-traditionelle Identität, aber das ist der Aspekt auf den ich geantwortet habe.

R. G.: Vielen Dank.

1. *gaijin* - Ausländer (japanisch)

"TEUFELSKREISE" – GEOGRAPHISCHE VORSTELLUNGEN DEUTSCHER JUGENDLICHER ZUM THEMA "AFRIKANISCHE ENTWICKLUNGSLÄNDER"

WULF SCHMIDT-WULFFEN

Was denken Jugendliche über die ihnen von Medien und Schule als unterentwickelt präsentierte fremde "Dritte Welt"? Was haben sie an Vorstellungen und Wissen "im Kopf"? Welches Bewußtsein prägt sie? Was ändert sich daran im Verlaufe der Schulzeit zwischen dem fünften und zehnten Schuljahr? Haben sie überhaupt ein Interesse an der psychisch fernen Welt, die aber gleichwohl über Informationen wie das Fernsehen, Waren und zunehmend auch Menschen (Flüchtlinge, Asylbewerber) zugleich schon Teil der eigenen Welt ist?

Fragen der "Entwicklung" sind längst fester Bestandteil des Unterrichts der Sekundarstufe I geworden. Zwar ist die Zahl der Themen z. B. im Geographieunterricht eher gering, jedoch sind sie nicht auf ein einziges Fach begrenzt. Schüler werden aus unterschiedlichen Blickwinkeln mit dieser Thematik konfrontiert: aus einer historischen Perspektive in Geschichte, aus politischer Sicht in Politik/Sozialkunde, aus einem ethischen Blickwinkel in Religion/Werte und Normen. Fraglich ist allerdings, ob die in den Schulen üblichen didaktischen und methodischen Vermittlungsverfahren geeignet sind, ein realistisches Bild von den Lebensbedingungen und Problemen der Menschen und Gesellschaften zu entwerfen. Jugendlichen sind heute Informationen in Hülle und Fülle zugänglich, auch solche über die "Dritte Welt": Bücher und Bibliotheken, Zeitungen und Fernsehen, reich bebilderte moderne Schulbücher. Fraglich ist allerdings, ob diese Angebote die Schüler erreichen, über deren Bewußtseinslagen und Lerninteressen fast nur bekannt ist, daß organisiertes schulisches Lernen für sie von geringerer subjektiver Bedeutung ist als Erfahrungslernen im außerschulischen, privaten Bereich, d. h. vornehmlich in sozialen Bezügen von Freundschaftsgruppen.

Offene Fragen wie diese, aber auch Skepsis gegenüber den Formen organisierten schulischen Lernens, veranlaßten mich zu einer Untersuchung über die Fragestellungen, Erwartungen und Interessen Jugendlicher zum Problemkreis "Entwicklung". Diese Untersuchung ist inzwischen abgeschlossen und in verschiedenen, leicht zugänglichen Publikationsorganen nachlesbar[1]. Daher werde ich nur kurz auf die Ergebnisse dieser Untersuchung am Schluß dieses Beitrages eingehen. Diese Untersuchung mit zirka 1700 Jugendlichen offenbarte ein krasses Mißverhältnis zwischen den Erwartungen der Schüler und ihren eigenen Fragestellungen an den Unterricht und den Fragestellungen und Inhalten, die über Schulbücher angeboten werden, und vermutlich den Kern des Unterrichts ausmachen. Daher begann ich im Sommer 1996 mit einer Nachfolgeuntersuchung, die Aufschluß über die Ergebnisse stattgefundenen Unterrichts geben sollte. Diese ist noch nicht abgeschlossen, und es fehlt daher noch eine systematische Auswertung. Dennoch lassen sich wesentliche Befunde bereits ausmachen.

"Wie ich Ghana (oder Schwarzafrika) sehe – beschreibe, zeichne oder male!" Auf meine Bitte hin schickten mir Lehrerinnen und Lehrer der Sekundarstufe I aus bisher zwanzig Städten der alten Bundesländer insgesamt zirka 1500 geschriebene, gemalte oder gezeichnete Antworten ihrer Schüler zu. Es hatten sich in vielen Fällen nicht nur die angeschriebenen und mir persönlich bekannten Lehrer an der Umfrage beteiligt, sondern auch weitere Kolleginnen und Kollegen der gleichen Schule. So sind alle Jahrgänge der Schultypen Hauptschule, Realschule, Gesamtschule und Gymnasium vertreten. Das von mir den Lehrern zugeschickte Formblatt, das auch Fragen zu einigen Rahmenbedingungen enthielt, war nicht in allen Fällen verwendet worden. Daher fehlen bei den Klassen, in denen die Schüler statt des vervielfältigten Formblattes ein Blatt aus einem Block oder Heft verwendet hatten, Angaben zu den Fragen: "Hast Du etwas über Afrika im Unterricht erfahren?" und "in welchem Fach?" Die nachfolgenden Zitate und Zeichnungen stammen, soweit nicht anders angegeben, von 8. Klässlern (zirka Dreizehn- bis Vierzehnjährigen), also von Sekundar-I-Schülern bei "Halbzeit". Danach werden die Äußerungen von 5. und 10.Klässlern zueinander in Beziehung gesetzt. Wiedergegebene Zitate und Zeichnungen zeichnen sich durch ihre Häufung aus, so daß sie auch ohne quantifizierende Auswertung als bewußtseinsbesetzend angesehen werden können.

"Die dingliche Erfüllung des Raumes" – In Afrika "sind die Menschen schwarz", "gibt es dunkelhäutige Menschen". In Afrika "ist es sehr heiß ... ungefähr bis 50 Grad ... durch die Hitze kann man schlecht anbauen." "Die Menschen haben Hunger ... und sie sind arm. Deshalb haben Sie nichts Richtiges anzuziehen. ... Viele machen sich ihre Klamotten selbst, aus Bananenblättern. ... Die Menschen leben in ärmlichen Hütten, aus Lehm und Stroh (oder aus Palmblättern) gemacht." "Afrika verbinde ich mit Tieren ... Da gibt es viele wilde Tiere ..." Die Schüler präsentieren ihre Vorstellungen über das Leben in Ghana bzw. Schwarzafrika in Form von symbolhaften Kennzeichnungen, die "Teufelskreise" und geodeterministische Ableitungen Hitze-Hunger-Armut erahnen lassen. Durchwegs definieren sie Afrikaner über ihre im Vergleich zu uns ins Auge fallenden materiellen Defizite. Diese kommen in Zeichnungen mit Kegeldach- und Rundhäusern am stärksten zum Ausdruck. In den Texten ist von Hütten, selten von Häusern die Rede. Über alle Jahrgänge hinweg geben 91% aller Zeichnungen "Hütten" wieder; bei den verbleibenden 9% "Häusern" ist unsicher, ob bewußt an Stadt gedacht wurde, da viele Zeichnungen im Stil des heimischen "Landhauses" bzw. "Bauernhauses" angefertigt wurden. Eines scheint aber sicher: Afrika, das ist Leben auf dem Lande. Fähigkeiten und menschliche oder kulturelle Qualitäten finden sich nicht im "Bild" der Jugendlichen. Die ständige Erwähnung der Hautfarbe in Verbindung mit Armut und materiellen Defiziten, legt eine zumindest unterschwellige Kausalerklärung zwischen "schwarz" und "arm" nahe. Dieses Afrika-"Bild", zu dem auch die Verbindung "Afrika-Tiere/Wildtiere" gehört, geht offensichtlich auf vorschulische Prägungen durch Kinderbücher und -filme, gleichermaßen aber auch auf Fernsehkonsum zurück. Unterricht bleibt anscheinend gegenüber den verbreiteten Klischees unwirksam, bzw. "reichert" sie noch "an", indem klimatische Verhältnisse als vermutliche Erklärungsvariable in den Vordergrund gerückt werden. Einige Lehrer, die die "Werke" ihrer Klassen wohl mit Interesse analysiert haben, gaben mir (sie entschuldigende) bestätigende Hinweise: "Ich habe die Klasse gerade erst übernommen. (Ich bin dafür also nicht verantwortlich). In der 7. Klasse wurden die Klima- und Landschaftszonen Afrikas behandelt (also nicht die konkreten Lebensbedingungen der Menschen)."

Afrika ohne "Moderne"? – Wie die Stadt, so fehlen auch andere

Akzentuierungen modernen Lebens: Hochhäuser wie in vielen Großstädten, Autoverkehr, Industrie – nichts davon taucht auf. Eine Ausnahme: Zwei Zeichnungen zeigen Reisebusse. "Modernes" verbindet sich ansonsten nur mit der Urlauberperspektive. Viele Zeichnungen zeigen Sonne, Strand, Palmen und ein Hotel "Palma". Hotels und Strände sind auch hin und wieder mit Zeichnungen wilder Tiere verbunden. Eine Lehrerin fragte während der Anfertigung der Zeichnungen einige Schüler, warum sie denn keine Hochhäuser oder Autos zeichnen würden. "Sie verneinten dies ganz entrüstet und sagten, in Afrika hungern die Menschen und sind sehr arm. Da gibt es doch keine Autos wie bei uns!"

Die Menschen in Afrika sind ganz anders als wir! – Nur einige Mädchen äußerten sich zu den Menschen direkt, vor allem zu den ihnen unterstellten Verhaltensweisen. Sie knüpften dabei am Motiv der Armut an: "Wenn Menschen arm sind, halten sie fest zusammen." Der syrische Politologe Bassam Tibi sieht in solchen Gedanken Projektionen, in denen der Verlust erwünschter Verhaltensweisen auf fremde Gesellschaften übertragen wird, die dadurch verklärt und romantisiert werden. Die Realität mit ihren realen gesellschaftlichen Brüchen kann nicht wahrgenommen werden. Wenn Sekundarstufen-I-Schüler an Menschen denken, sind das in erstaunlich vielen Fällen Kinder. Kinder kommen aber in Schulbüchern kaum als handelnde Personen vor.

Alltag-Gesellschaft-Politik: die großen Unbekannten? – Bemerkungen zum Alltagsleben, insbesondere zu seinen gesellschaftlichen Aspekten, sind in den Schüleräußerungen eher spärlich anzutreffen. Im Bewußtsein der Jugendlichen ist am stärksten noch der Umstand der Kinderarbeit verankert, ein Indiz auf die grundsätzliche Wahrnehmung von Jugendlichen durch Jugendliche. Ähnlich häufig werden Kriege bzw. Bürgerkriege genannt. Auch die Vorstellung der Hilfsbedürftigkeit wird des öfteren hervorgehoben. Wirklich politische Äußerungen werden nur von einigen wenigen Gesamtschülern gemacht. Neben der Wiedergabe einer Karikatur zum Aspekt "Hunger durch Agrarexporte" wird hin und wieder auf diktatorische Staatsführungen hingewiesen.

"Koks" in Afrika? – Häufig unterstellen Schüler Afrikanern eine hohe Kriminalität, die aber nicht mit Biertischparolen in unserer Gesellschaft in Zusammenhang gebracht wird, sondern aus den Lebensbedingungen in Ghana gefolgert wird: "Armes Land, viel Bevölkerung, hohe

Kriminalität" – offensichtlich so etwas wie ein Naturgesetz. In Zeichnungen wird Kriminalität mit dem Anbau von Drogen begründet. Hier wird ein Problem deutlich, das auch bei anderen Sachbereichen anzutreffen ist: Einmal mit der "Dritten Welt" bzw. mit Afrika in Zusammenhang gebrachte Erscheinungen werden verallgemeinert oder auf Ghana übertragen. Das offensichtlich aus lateinamerikanischem Kontext über die Medien entnommene Problem des Kokainanbaus wird auf Afrika übertragen. Gleichermaßen werden "Rassenunruhen" und "Bürgerkriege", bekannt aus anderen Ländern, auch Ghana unterstellt. Das im Geographieunterricht angestrebte Ziel der regionalen Differenzierung ist offensichtlich schwerer zu erreichen als geglaubt und bedarf wohl neuer Überlegungen. Einmal erkannte Phänomene, die nicht in das Bild der eigenen Welt passen, werden offensichtlich als typisch für die "Dritte Welt" angesehen und verallgemeinert. Ist das eine Folge des verbreiteten schulischen Vorgehens, "Dritte Welt" anhand von Defizite pointierenden Unterentwicklungsmerkmalen zu definieren?

Klasse 5 und 10 im Vergleich: Ob Zeichnungen, Texte oder Merkmalskataloge, die Ergebnisse des 10. Jahrganges müssen als Ausdruck eines fünfjährigen Lernprozesses schockieren. Die "Bilder" sind, was Erkenntniszuwachs und -tiefe anbetrifft, kaum von denen der 5. Klasse unterscheidbar. Einige "Irrläufer" lassen ein noch katastrophaleres Ergebnis befürchten: Irrtümlicherweise wurde einmal im 3. Schuljahr, ein anderesmal in der 11. Klasse das "Ghanabild" ermittelt – in beiden Fällen ohne merkliche Qualitätsunterschiede. Die erklärliche Vordergründigkeit bei den "Anfängern" dominiert weiterhin, wie eine Lehrerin in ihrem Begleitbrief kommentiert: "Bei der Auswertung der Zeichnungen fiel mir auf, daß in allen Zeichnungen die Elemente "einfache Hütten", "wilde, gefährliche, aber auch schöne Tiere" und "schwarze Menschen" angesprochen sind, die vermeintlich traditionell gekleidet sind. Nur geringfügig weniger wurde symbolhaft auf Hitze, karges Land und Urwald verwiesen."

Lassen wir weiter Lehrer sprechen: "Wie schon bei der Klasse von vor vier Wochen finde ich persönlich die Ähnlichkeiten im "Bild Klasse 8" und im "Bild Klasse 10" erschreckend! Waren zwei Jahre Bemühungen umsonst?" "Ein Kollege, der nicht richtig zugehört hatte und statt in die Sekundarstufe-I in die 11. ging, war reichlich schockiert über das Ergebnis. Er war aber nicht bereit, darüber zu diskutieren." "Als ich meinen Kolleginnen die Ergebnisse zeigte, waren wir erschrocken über die Naivität und das Fehlen politischer Bezüge. Wir haben uns gleich hingesetzt, haben versucht, uns in die Lage der Schülerinnen und Schüler zu versetzen und mal aufgeschrieben, was wir vielleicht geschrieben hätten. In einem waren wir uns einig: "Dritte Welt" und "Ausbeutung" wäre da bestimmt vorgekommen." "... auch diese Klasse war sich nicht sicher, ob Afrika überhaupt schon mal im Unterricht vorgekommen wäre." "Bemerkenswert vielleicht, daß die Klasse meinte, sie hätten "Afrika noch nicht gehabt." Vielleicht lag's am Schwerpunkt. In der 7. waren die Landschaftszonen und in der 8. die ökologischen Probleme des Sahel behandelt worden." "Beide 9. Klassen behaupteten steif und fest, sie hätten noch nie etwas über Afrika gehabt. Das ist aber Quatsch. Die Klima- und Landschaftszonen müssen sie auf jeden Fall gehabt haben."

Die auf analytisches Bemühen der Lehrerinnen und Lehrer gerichteten Aussagen bedürfen eigentlich nur noch einer Ergänzung: Das "Bild" der Jugendlichen ist nicht nur vergangenheitsbezogen, es ist auch statisch. Über Wandel und Entwicklungsprozesse gibt es keine Auskunft. Solch eine Erwartung wird aber aus mitunter eingestreuten Bemerkungen deutlich, von denen Lehrer auch in ihren Begleitbriefen häufig berichteten. Eine Schülerin schrieb: "Ich würde gern mal sehen, wie die heute in Ghana leben." Die selbstkritischen Lehrerinnen und Lehrer haben durch die Äußerungen ihrer Schüler klar erkannt: der herkömmliche, an Fachkategorien orientierte Unterricht, wie er sich in der Sekundarstufe I besonders am Schwerpunktthema "Klima- und Landschaftszonen" festmacht, erreicht die Köpfe (kognitiv) und die Gemüter und Herzen (emotional) unserer Schülerinnen und Schüler nicht. Das bezeugt schon das geringe Erinnerungsvermögen der Jugendlichen: Nur in 9 von 30 Klassen gaben die Schüler mehrheitlich an, Themen zu Afrika seien behandelt worden. Offensichtlich verbauen die Schwierigkeiten, die z.B. mit Klimadiagrammen, planetarischer Zirkulation/Passatkreislauf verbunden sind, den Zugang zu Alltagshandeln als Ausdruck von Entwicklungsbedingungen und -prozessen. Für das Mißverhältnis zwischen Aufwand und Ertrag scheint mir allerdings weniger Geographieunterricht als Unterricht schlechthin verantwortlich. Bezeichnend aber ist auch die Beziehungslosigkeit zu den möglichen

Fragestellungen, die die Jugendlichen selbst haben. Wo sich die Schüler an den Unterricht erinnerten, gaben sie zweimal Erdkunde, viermal Gesellschaftslehre, einmal Deutsch und zweimal "im Unterricht" an.

Ein Befund inhaltlich eher marginaler Bedeutung bestätigt diese Interpretation und könnte wegweisend zugleich sein: Für nicht wenige Jungen erschließt sich Ghana über Fußball. Sie kennen Anthony Yeboah und Abedi Pele, nennen die Vereine, bei denen diese spielen bzw. spielten. Wie könnte es anders sein: Auch die Nigerianer Okotcha und Akpobori werden Ghana zugeschlagen. Im Vergleich verschiedenster Sachbereiche erweist sich das Wissen dieser Schüler über Fußball als das präziseste. Sogar die nicht gerade sehr geläufigen Vor- und Familiennamen der Spieler werden korrekt geschrieben. Offensichtlich liegt hier ein tieferes Interesse zugrunde, das sich als geeigneter Zugang zu Ghana und der afrikanischen Lebenswelt erweist. Es lohnt sich daher, an dieser Stelle die Frage nach den Interessen der Jugendlichen an der "Dritten Welt" aufzuwerfen.

JUGENDLICHE UND IHRE FRAGEN ZUR "DRITTEN WELT"

1677 Schülerinnen und Schüler kreuzten zwölf von zweiundzwanzig vorgelegten Fragestellungen gemäß ihren Interessen an. Sie hatten die Auswahl zwischen Fragen, die die Schüler einer 7. und einer 9. Klasse (mindestens fünfmal) genannt hatten (x) und einer gleichen Zahl von Fragen, die ich aus Schulbuchüberschriften gebildet hatte (y): (1y)Klima und Böden (2x)Aufwachsen Jugendlicher (3x)Vorbilder (4y)Landwirt-schaft und Industrie (5x)Alltagsprobleme der Menschen (6y)Räumliche Gegensätze (7x)Schulalltag, Einstellungen zur Bildung (8y)Merkmale eines EL (9x)Freizeit (10x)Zukunftspläne (11x)Kleidung, Musik, Sport (12y)Wirtschaftliche Verflechtungen IL/EL (13x)Bedeutung des Geldes (14y)Umweltprobleme (15y)Regenwald (16y)Handel IL/EL (17y)Welche Hilfe (18y)Hunger und Armut (19x)Vorstellungen über Leben bei uns (20y)Entwicklungshilfe (21x)Stellung der Frau (22x)Lebensgefühl Jugendlicher.

Die Jugendlichen gaben mit weitem Abstand jenen Fragen den Vorzug, die sozial-ethischen Inhalts sind, die Beziehungen zwischen Menschen zum Inhalt haben. Dies sind Fragen, die Schüler sich in bezug auf die eigene Person stellen, die also für sie selbst wichtig sind. Sie sind hochgradig emotional besetzt. Diese Fragen setzen eine Auseinandersetzung mit Werten und Normen der eigenen wie der fremden Gesellschaft voraus. "Denken, handeln und sind fremde Menschen anders oder gleichen sie uns" könnte die zentrale Frage lauten. Demgegenüber finden die Fragen nach Beziehungen zwischen eher abstrakten gesellschaftlichen Subsystemen oder kausal verbundenen, kognitiven Sachverhalten nur geringen Zuspruch. Letztere beherrschen Schulbücher. Diese reduzieren die Begegnung mit dem Fremden, mit Afrika, praktisch auf kognitive Aspekte, schließen hingegen psychische und emotionale Bedürfnisse weitestgehend aus. Es gibt dabei allerdings ermutigende Ausnahmen: Die stark problemorientierten Themen der jüngsten Rahmenrichtliniengeneration, die Fragen nach Hunger und Armut, Regenwald und Umweltzerstörung treffen auf ähnlich starken Widerhall wie die Schülerfragen. Bei diesen problemorientierten Themen richtet sich das Frageinteresse zweifellos auf die handlungsleitenden Normen, die in der fremden Gesellschaft Deformationen hervorgerufen haben, die die eigene Lebenswelt bedrohen könnten. Über die Frage nach der richtigen Hilfe, die auch die eigene Person einschließt, gewinnen aber auch diese Themen einen sozial-ethischen Charakter.

Postscriptum: Aus den 1500 "Ghanabildern" werde ich typische Zeichnungen sowie musterhafte Beschreibungen mit nach Ghana nehmen und sie dort in Schulen mit Schülerinnen und Schülern diskutieren. Anschließend werde ich diese bitten, auf der freien Rückseite ihr eigenes "Ghanabild" aufzuschreiben oder zu zeichnen. Dieses sollte geeignet sein, die deutsche Sicht zu korrigieren. In allen Schulklassen, in denen die Lehrer dieses Vorgehen ankündigten, baten die Schülerinnen und Schüler inständig um eine Rückmeldung. Dieses große Interesse legt einen weitergehenden Gedanken nahe: An zwei Schulen[2] wird durch Sammeln eine Videoeinrichtung für eine ghanesische Schule angeschafft und ein gegenseitiger Austausch von selbstgefilmten Videos in die Wege geleiten. Die afrikanischen und deutschen Schüler erhielten den Auftrag, einen Film zu den Fragen ihrer ausländischen Partner zu drehen.

1. Praxis Geographie 11/1996, Eine Welt in der Schule 3/1996, Materialien zur

Didaktik der Welt- und Wirtschaftskunde, Bd. 16/1997: Kinderalltag in Afrika – (k)ein Kinderspiel?
2. KGS Drochtersen und KGS Neustadt a. Rbbg. signalisierten bereits ihr Interesse

IMPORTED – A READING SEMINAR in Relationship with my "A Portable (Not so Ideal) Imported Library, Or How to Reinvent the Coffee Table: 25 Books for Instant Use (Austrian Version)," 1994/96
Depot, Vienna; no reading seminar was held because of organizational difficulties.

LESEN, SPRECHEN, LERNEN, LEHREN

RAINER GANAHL

...
per tag zwi mozart

each day one mozart pink a smithy
pink in the petal of a smithy stop
stop the buds stop the keys and learn
how to drop your mozarts in a smithy
each lilty day one drop of mozart
....
bahia blanca narvico
pernambuco tant bleu
bart ferraguts verne
fortsetzen
dreieinhalb hier
monsterreally
daheim und abroad
...
H.C. Artmann, aus "flaschenposten", Malmö 1964

I

Was hat es mit Lesen und Sprechen, Lernen und Lehren auf sich? Für die Anthropologen wie auch die Psychologen markieren Lesen und Sprechen wichtige Etappen in der Entwicklungsgeschichte des Menschen. Lesen und Sprechen sind keine bloß natürlichen Phänomene, sondern im wesentlichen sozial vermittelte Prozesse, die Lernen und Lehren verlangen. Diese elementaren Fähigkeiten subjektivieren jedes Individuum und stellen die Bedingungen für eine differenzierte gesellschaftliche Organisation dar. Es ist dabei schwierig, die einzelnen Potentiale und Tätigkeiten in ihrer gegenseitigen Bedingtheit klar einander zuzuordnen, sie voneinander zu unterscheiden und zu trennen. Damit eine Gesellschaft fortbestehen und sich entwickeln kann, muß sie diesen elementaren Kulturtechniken die allergrößte Aufmerksamkeit schenken.

In Europa wie auch in den meisten anderen Industrieländern sind heute diese gesellschaftsreproduzierenden Techniken institutionalisiert und staatlich geregelt. Der Subjektivierungsprozeß einer Person wird nicht der Willkür überlassen, sondern ist institutionell vorgeschrieben. Er wird schulisch und medizinisch geregelt, diszipliniert und kontrolliert. Vom Lesen-, Sprechen- und Lernenkönnen werden alle anderen individuell wichtigen Entscheidungen wesentlich beeinflußt. Meist stellen sie sogar eine soziale Bedingung dar. In Europa ist das Schulsystem z. B. im wesentlichen hierarchisch und ausschließend organisiert, damit es sich nur kegelartig in den gesellschaftlichen Gesamtkörper eintreiben kann. Gesellschaftliche und ideologische Produktions- und Reproduktionsverhältnisse sind somit objektiviert und vorhersehbar: Abitur, Universitätsabschlüsse, Bac, Bac +2, Bac +5. Was das verschulte Indivi-duum oft als verzweifelten, sinnlosen, singulären und nicht zuletzt exi-stentiellen Kampf in den Schulen und Prüfungskommissionen wahr- nimmt, ist einem Kalkül verpflichtet, das in vielen Bereichen unange-messen ist und die Realität oft nur wenig tangiert. Hier verstecken sich die schwerwiegenden ideologischen, sozialen und technologischen Konflikte. Mittels dieser pädagogischen Apparate produzieren und re-produzieren sich gesellschaftliche Realitätsverhältnisse nicht nur, sondern werden auch erkennbar und bewertbar gemacht.

Hinter der Schlichtheit und Einfachheit von Lesen, Sprechen, Lernen und Lehren in ihrer scheinbaren Privatheit verstecken sich komplizierte Verhältnisse, die es wert sind, reflektiert zu werden. Gerade weil sich im Lesen und Lernen, Sprechen und Lehren eine mehr oder weniger gut abgeschirmte Unscheinbarkeit vor die Konflikte stellt, werden hier ideale Mischverhältnisse für alte, bestehende und zukünftige Macht- und Gewaltkonstellationen jeder Art ablesbar und studierbar. Privilegien, strukturelle Ungleichheiten und Ungerechtigkeiten, Einteilungen in Inländer und Ausländer, Gastarbeiter, Asylanten und Asylbewerber, Zentrum und Peripherie und nicht zuletzt rassistische, geschlechts- und klassenspezifische Vorurteile entstehen. Sie verlängern und verstärken sich mit versteckter oder offener Aggressivität in pädagogischen Apparaten, wo gelesen, gesprochen, gelernt und gelehrt wird. Nur als ein Beispiel darf genannt werden, daß es bis zum Ende des 19. Jahrhunderts gesetzlich verboten war, Afro-Amerikanern in den USA lesen oder schreiben beizubringen.

Andererseits sind es gerade wiederum diese pädagogischen Institutionen mit ihren stabilisierenden Konzeptionen, die gewonnen, mobilisiert und verteidigt werden müssen, um Ausgleiche zu schaffen, um anderen, noch mächtigeren Apparaten wie z. B. den Medien und deren Industrien etwas zu entgegnen. Es dürfen auch jene Kämpfe nicht vergessen werden, die dieses schulische Universum schufen und garantierten, etwas, das heute selbst in Mitteleuropa nicht mehr selbstverständlich ist. Eine fundamentale Kritik an den pädagogischen Staatsapparaten darf nicht die Auflösung dieser zum Ziel haben, sondern muß den Demokratisierungsprozeß vorantreiben und versuchen, deren Entscheidungen als ideologische und politische zu verstehen.

Das Lesen ist eine Tätigkeit, die nur in besonderen Kontexten als gesellschaftliche Praxis anerkannt wird. Während des Studiums und in intellektuellen Berufen wird den Lesenden das Lesen als eine produktive, gesellschaftliche Aktivität zugestanden. In den meisten anderen Fällen wird das Lesen, sofern überhaupt noch gelesen wird, dem Bereich Freizeit und Müßiggang zugerechnet. Wenn es sich bei den Lesenden um in den allgemein geregelten Arbeitsprozeß eingegliederte Personen handelt, wird Lesen als Regeneration oder Weiterbildung verbucht. Wird aber gelesen um des Lesens Willen und das überdies noch ohne offiziell zu arbeiten, so rückt es als unanerkannte Arbeit in ein dubioses, ungeklärtes Licht. Gegen alle Formen geregelter Arbeit "anzulesen" ist als Arbeit selbst nicht anerkannt, auch dann nicht, wenn sich dadurch aus dem Leser oder der Leserin eine gegen gesellschaftliche Zwänge imprägniertere Person entwickelt. Unheimlichkeit mag sich dabei einstellen.

Mit dem Sprechen verhält es sich ähnlich. Wird zu bestimmten Zeiten, in bestimmten Institutionen, an bestimmten Orten, für bestimmte Interessen gesprochen, so kann damit Geld und Prestige verbunden sein. Das Sprechen ohne anerkannten Kontext wird nicht als Arbeit verstanden. Dabei erzeugt es Gesprächsstoffe, Themen und soziale Gemeinschaften, die wesentlich sind. Wird außerhalb von Gemeinplätzen gesprochen, so kann sich auch beim Sprechen Unheimlichkeit einstellen, was besonders dann der Fall sein wird, wenn es kritisch und vorerst machtlos ist. Kritik und Machtlosigkeit beim Sprechen ergänzen sich zu einer Geometrie, die das Zentrum ausspart, es aber nicht ignoriert.

Lernen kennen wir in den meisten Fällen als institutionell stark eingerahmtes Tun bestimmter Altersgruppen. Aber auch wenn die Lernenden noch so fleißig das Wort Arbeit für sich beanspruchen, wird Lernen im allgemeinen nicht als Arbeit verstanden, außer es handelt sich um firmenangeregte Aus- oder Weiterbildungskurse. Wo nicht der Staat langwierige Investitionen und aufwendige Vorbereitungen vorschreibt, anbietet und bezahlt, müssen andere Geldgeber für diese Studien aufkommen und können somit versuchen, sie zu beeinflussen. Was, wie, wann und wo gelernt wird, ist mitunter denselben konformistischen Zwängen unterworfen, die sich auch beim Lesen und Sprechen bemerkbar machen. *Unheimlich* kann einem nicht nur vor Prüfungen, sondern auch vor dem Angebot der Lernstoffe werden. Hier reihen sich die Lernenden in unterschiedliche Welten ein. Manche dieser Wissenswelten sind extrem arbeitsaufwendig, erfordern langjährige Studien und endlose Lektüre, wirken sich stark auf die Persönlichkeitsstruktur der Lernenden aus, ohne jedoch den Absolventen direkt einer bezahlten Arbeitsnische zuzuspielen. Es kann so vieles gelernt werden, ohne daß es auch nur geringes Öl ins Getriebe des leistungsfähigen Gesellschaftsapparates abgibt. Probleme und Fragestellungen können von solch spezialisierten Köpfen nicht nur abstrakt gelöst, sondern unter Umständen auch neu formuliert und geschaffen werden.

Anders als das Lesen, Sprechen und Lernen, wird das Lehren als Arbeit anerkannt und somit im allgemeinen auch bezahlt. Professionalität und Kontrolle verschränken sich, realisiert sich ein Lehrverhältnis meistens doch nur in einer sozial eindeutig definierten, hierarchisierten Konstellation. Die Kunst des Lehrens, wenn es sie je gab, reduzierte sich auf ein Überangebot von Lehrveranstaltungen, in denen in dosierter und geregelter Form Wissen für Schulklassen vermittelt wird. Dem Lehrpersonal sind Lehrpläne und Unterrichtszeiten verbindlich vorgegeben. *Unheimlichkeit* stellt sich weniger beim Material oder in der Vermittlungsarbeit ein, sondern ist Faktor im Alltagsleben der von Lehrplänen, Aufsichtskommissionen, Schüler- und Studententerror verbrauchten Lehrer. Resignation und Zynismus lösen in vielen Fällen den einst ge-hegten Willen, etwas verändern und bewirken zu wollen, ab. In den Werkstätten gesellschaftlicher Produktion herrschen leider oft deswegen unbefriedigende und entmutigende Umstände.

II

Unbefriedigend und entmutigend sind auch die Konditionen, in denen die Kunst sich seit der Entlassung aus den sicheren Armen bestimmter Auftragsgeber gegen Ende des 18. Jahrhunderts versucht. Nicht nur Künstlerexistenzen, sondern auch Kunstpraktiken wanderten in den letz-ten 150 Jahren aus den verabredeten Orten herkömmlicher Zeichenpro-duktionen ab. Seit den diversen *ready made*-Paradigmen ist nichts vor den Aneignungen durch die Kunst gefeit. Was sich allgemein unter dem Verzeichnis "konzeptuelle Kunst" verbuchte, könnte problemlos als ernsthafter Versuch mißverstanden werden, mit Methodeansprüchen diverser wissenschaftlicher Disziplinen Ordnung und Akademismus zu reinthronisieren, bevor die letzten Enklaven visueller Kulturversprechen sich völlig den multimedialen Kulturindustrien angeglichen haben. Kunst, wenn an diesem "Generalsubjekt" noch festgehalten werden darf, migrierte von der Produktion ihrer Objekte zur Rezeption ihrer Kontexte und Operationsmodalitäten, wo der Künstler nicht mehr selbst der "Staat" ist, sondern er/sie vielmehr nur seinen ersten Bürger neben vielen darstellt. Rollenspiele sind seither zur ernsten Sache avanciert. *Unheimlich* muten mitunter die Rezeptionsangebote mit ihren täuschenden Echtheitsvorgaben an, die oft zwischen dem Alltäglichen und seinem Kritisch-Entgegengesetzten oszillieren.

Um in der Rolle des Künstlers das Lesen, Sprechen, Lernen und Lehren "materialfähig" zu machen und in ein Dialogfeld einzuführen, das mit dem Prädikat Kunst seine gesellschaftliche Legitimation erfährt, bedarf es bestimmter Verschiebungen und Eingriffe, sowohl auf den institutionellen als auch auf den kontextuellen und den rezeptionellen Ebenen. Diese Interventionen sind jedoch in meinem Falle weniger professioneller, sondern eher dilletantischer und autodidaktischer Natur, könnte ich doch in keiner Weise mit den Lern-, Lehr-, Wissens- und Methodenansprüchen der dafür vorgesehenen Institutionen – Schulen, Universitäten oder Sprachinstituten – konkurrieren.

"IMPORTED – A READING SEMINAR .... (Different National Versions)" – mein schon im Vorwort erklärtes Leseseminarprojekt, das diese Publikation hier zum Ergebnis hat – privilegiert den verbal-kriti-schen Aspekt einer objektlosen, an Vermittlungs- und Austauschprozessen ori-

entierten Kunst, die ihre Abfallprodukte, sofern sie in den an Exponaten interessierten Ausstellungsbetrieb zurückgeführt werden, indexikalisch und dokumentarisch definiert. Die Hauptsache jedoch bleibt das gemeinsame Lesen und Sprechen der verbliebenen Interessenten in einem Betrieb, der an Interessensschwund leidet, obwohl die Vermarktung von Kunst zur Industrie avancierte. Auch ist es für mich in der Rolle des Künstlers entscheidend, direkt mit den Personen, die sich herkömmlicherweise als Publikum definieren, in eine oft herausfordernde Beziehung zu treten. Da in den meisten Fällen die Sprache der importierten Bücher von der Sprache der Teilnehmer abweicht und auch ich meistens eine sogenannte Fremdsprache sprechen muß, nimmt das Sprach- und Übersetzungsproblem, wenn auch indirekt, eine zentrale Stelle ein. Diese Sprachgrenzen sind konstitutiv für diese Projektserie wie auch für meine Arbeit im allgemeinen, die sich besonders am Problem der Vermittlung, der Übersetzung, der Schnittstelle, des Interfaces und den dazugehörigen Werkzeugen orientiert. Das erschwer-te Lesen von mitunter komplizierten, fremdsprachigen Originaltexten ist für alle Beteiligten produktiv, da es kritisches Unterscheidungsver-mögen und das Abarbeiten und Verlernen von Vorurteilsstrukturen fördert.

III

Vorurteile sind es auch, die unsere Einstellungen gegenüber Fremdsprachen und deren Schwierigkeitsgrad prägen. Generell verlaufen unsere Einschätzungen an den Grenzen des Bekannten und Vertrauten entlang. So wird Albanisch als schwieriger eingeschätzt als Spanisch. Die Sprachen Asiens und des Nahen Ostens mit ihren unterschiedlichen Schreibsystemen werden als nahezu unlernbar eingestuft. Rassismus und Unverständnis überlagern sich mit den exotischen Betrachtungsweisen, die man allen asiatischen, arabischen und afrikanischen Sprachen entgegenbringt. Der Umgang mit der Einschätzung von Fremdsprachen an sich reflektiert aus westlicher Sicht leider oft nicht viel mehr als eurozentristische Arroganz oder neugierigen, touristischen Exotismus.

Was hat es aber mit dem Erlernen von sogenannten Fremdsprachen überhaupt auf sich? Wer lernt was, wann, wo und warum? Seit der Renaissance und dem Humanismus wurde die Kenntnis der klassischen Sprachen – Latein, Griechisch, Hebräisch – eine Notwendigkeit auch jenseits des bloß geistigen Lebens. Das Studieren dieser Sprachen war die *conditio sine qua non* für den Zugang an die Universitäten, die das Bildungsmonopol innehatten und anfingen, eine verstärkte Rolle in der Verteilung von Macht und Einfluß in einer sich säkularisierenden Welt zu spielen.

Seit der Französischen Revolution und den entstehenden Nationalismen in Europa wurden nationale Sprachen geschaffen, standardisiert und der Gesamtheit der Bevölkerung aufgezwungen. Andere Sprachen und Idiome wurden zu Dialekten erniedrigt oder zum Verschwinden gebracht , ein Prozeß, der bis heute andauert. Es darf dabei erinnert werden, daß 1789 nur ein Drittel der französischen Bevölkerung französisch sprach. In Italien waren es nur gebildete 15 %, die das heutige Italienisch 1871 im Alltag anwandten[1]. Nur in Deutschland ist dieser Prozeß der Standardisierung des Deutschen schon seit der Übersetzung der Bibel (Luther) zu beobachten. Mit dem Auftreten der Geistes- und Geschichtswissenschaften des 19. Jahrhunderts wurden die "neuen" Nationalsprachen studiert und zu einem Hauptinstrument in der Formation der diversen Nationalismen und Nationalstaaten gemacht. Das polyglotte Habsburgerreich zerbrach nicht zuletzt daran.

Im 19. Jahrhundert wurden auch Sprachen in die Lehrpläne aufgenommen, die scheinbar nicht direkt nationales Bewußtsein reflektierten. Allerdings waren mit dem Studium diverser orientalischer Sprachen auch andere Interessen verbunden. Kolonialismus und Imperialismus der Europäer bewirkten bemerkenswerte und anhaltende geolinguistische Verschiebungen und verursachten, daß in manchen Kolonialländern die dort gesprochenen Sprachen verboten wurden (z. B. Arabisch in Algerien). Orientalismus wurde ein Phänomen, das nicht nur eine Handvoll Gelehrter anhielt, kulturell schöngeistiges Wissen zu produzieren, sondern auch ein ideologischer Faktor, der Bevormundung, Unterdrückung, kulturelle, ökonomische und politische Ausbeutung direkt und indirekt legitimierte[2].

Lesen, Lernen, Lehren und Sprechen produzieren und reproduzieren so Repräsentationen und Vorstellungsverhältnisse von sich und den anderen, die sich für die einen von Vorteil und für andere von Nachteil erweisen können. Das Geschäft mit solchen Repräsentationsverhältnissen war und ist das *Business* der Macht und ihrer Interessen, die im Falle der letzten 150 Jahre nicht nur Gewürze, Edelmetalle und Arbeitskräfte, sondern auch Masken, Skulpturen, Bilder, Vorstellungen und Wissen abzwangen. Die jeweilige Repräsentation sollte diese Zugriffe auf die anderen rechtfertigen.

Um die in den westlichen Zentren gemachten Repräsentationen besser in die in Abhängigkeit gebrachten Territorien tragen zu können, wurden und werden oft gleich die Sprachen der Hegemonialmächte mitgeliefert. Das Lernen dieser Sprachen ist dann Zwang, Privileg und Notwendigkeit. Die neuen Sprachen – Englisch, Französisch, Portugiesisch, Spanisch, Russisch usw. – wurden akzeptiert, gesprochen und letztendlich (wie in einzelnen Fällen) als einzig mögliche sprachliche Verständigung internalisiert. Erst mit dem Auseinanderbrechen der Macht zerfallen auch sprachliche Identifikationen, sofern sie nicht völlig gefestigt sind: Wer im abgefallenen Teil des Sowjetimperiums möchte noch Russisch als *Lingua Franca* lernen und benützen, sind doch mit der sprachlichen Hartwährung Englisch viel größere Vorteile zu erschließen?

Nach dem II. Weltkrieg wurde Englisch die am meisten gelernte Sprache im von den Westmächten befreiten Europa. In den von der Roten Armee befreiten, (man sagt auch) besetzten Teilen Mittel- und Osteuropas war es Russisch. In beiden Fällen wurden diese sprachlichen Anliegen staatlich institutionalisiert und geregelt. Mit den auseinandergeglittenen Machtkonstellationen haben sich auch die Einstellungen zu den Sprachen verändert. Die Russen lernen nun alle Englisch und auch die Amerikaner und Engländer fangen an, sich im Fremdsprachenlernen Mühe zu geben. Schwäche verpflichtet auch sprachlich.

Das Beherrschen von Sprachen verschafft Privilegien, Vorteile und neue Identitäten. Die europäischen Schulbildungssysteme, mit deren Hilfe die Sozialstruktur der Gesellschaften reproduziert, kontrolliert und stabilisiert wird, strukturieren sich großteils entlang der Wahl der zu erlernenden Fremdsprache. Das Lernen von Englisch, Französisch, Deutsch, Latein usw. ist ein gesellschaftlicher Differenzierungsfaktor, der nicht unterschätzt werden darf und der sich in fast jedem Stellenangebot erneut bestätigt. In den ehemaligen Ostblockstaaten ist die Beherrschung einer Hartwährungssprache im wesentlichen entscheidend dafür, an welcher Ökonomie man teilhat. Informationsflüsse mäandern fast immer parallel zu monetäre, entlang den Ufern von bestimmten Sprachen und verbreitern sich mit ihnen in all jenen Ländern, die strukturell Geld-, Entwicklungs- und Informationsmängel aufweisen.

Migrationsbewegungen sind im postkolonialen Zeitalter Spätprodukt des installierten Kolonialisationsprozesses und finden oft entlang sprachlicher Verbindungslinien statt, was in Paris und London besonders auffällt. Dort, wo Immigranten die Gastsprache noch nicht beherrschen, müssen sie sie oft umständlich erlernen, wobei sie jedoch gerade auf sprachlicher Ebene wieder große Diskriminierungen erfahren. Legal oder illegal sind Immigranten, Flüchtlinge, Asylanten und Asylbewerber nicht nur ihren ursprünglichen sozialen Kontakten, sondern auch ihrem sprachlichen Umfeld entrissen, was sie mitunter mit Scham für ihre eigene Sprache, Kultur und Herkunft erfüllt. Die weltweit zahlreichen Flüchtlinge und Asylanten zählen zu den schwächsten, hilflosesten und auch sprachlich zu den am meisten diskriminierten Bevölkerungsgruppen.

Anders verhält es sich mit den sogenannten Gastarbeitern, ein Begriff, der auch in allen nicht-deutschsprachigen Industrieländern ein ebenso bezeichnendes, dubioses wie pejoratives Äquivalent kennt. Gastarbeiter, die aus Arbeitermangel in das Land geholt wurden und die westlichen Industrien seit den 60er Jahren mitaufbauten, sprechen oft die Landessprache mit einem Akzent und einer ihnen speziell zugestandenen, denn so angelernten Syntax: "Du machen Arbeit ganz." Ohne daß sich die meisten der Inländer der Implikationen voll bewußt sind, entspricht dieses verzerrte Lehrverhalten der Arroganz und Ignoranz einer Bevölkerung, die es nicht schafft, kulturelle und sprachliche Vielfalt anders als negativ zu bewerten.

Die Angst vor fremden Sprachen und die Angst vor dem Sprechen von Fremdsprachen läßt sich u. a. mit der Angst vor dem Unverständlichen, dem *Unheimlichen,* als auch den Hilflosigkeiten und Unsicherheiten des Sprechers erklären. Das Einlassen auf fremde Sprachen relativiert aber auch die eigene Sprache, die Muttersprache, und erlaubt eine Distanzierung vom vertrauten Sprachfeld, welches an sich schon von den unterschiedlichsten Diskursformen durchzogen ist. Diese jede Sprache durchlaufenden Sprachdifferenzierungen sind Produkte unterschiedlichster Faktoren: topographischer, historischer, ausbildungsspezifischer, sozialer, klassenspezifischer, generationsspezifischer, geschlechtsspezifischer, sowie mode- und medienspezifische Faktoren, um nur einige davon zu nennen.

Das Eintreten in eine neue Sprache ist ein langwieriger und qualvoller Prozeß, der das lernende Subjekt "entsprachlicht" und teils in die bereits durchlaufene frühkindliche Entwicklungsstufe der Spracherlernung zurückversetzt. Der Lernende wird hilflos, wird man doch im wesentlichen überall anhand der Sprachbeherrschung eingeschätzt. Sprachliches, bzw. fremdsprachliches Unvermögen eröffnet auch einen Raum jenseits linguistischer Normen, wo gegen Etiketten verstoßen, richtiger Sprachgebrauch geschmäht und Einstufungen erschwert werden. Auch bei diesen Abweichungen verursachen die jeweiligen Umstände Reaktionen. Ob Fehler und abweichende Aussprache Charme oder verachtendes Übergehen bewirkt, hängt leider nicht vom sich bemühenden Sprecher selbst, sondern von den (Gruppen)Einstellungen der einheimischen Interakteure ab, welche offen, verständnisvoll und entgegenkommend oder diskriminierend, fremdenfeindlich und rassistisch sein können. Amerikanische oder französische Studenten in Heidelberg oder Wien erfahren in den einschlägigen Amtsstellen eine andere Behandlung als kurzbefehlsempfangende sprachlose Arbeiter oder Asylanten, die oft nur Tagalog, Tamil oder Kantonesisch sprechen.

Der Amerikaner Louis Wolfson hat mit zwei Büchern die psychologischen Aspekte des Fremdsprachenlernens bestens angesprochen. In den 70er Jahren schrieb er "*Le schizo et les langues*" (Der Schizo und die Sprachen) und kurz darauf "*Ma mère musicienne est morte*" (Meine musizierende Mutter ist tot). Beide Bücher, die er in einer für ihn fremden Sprache verfaßte, hatten einen besonderen Zweck: das Sich-Entledigen seiner Muttersprache, was ihm u. a. auch dadurch besonders gut gelang, daß er anfing, den Bedeutungsprozeß durch ein teilweise unverständliches Sprachgemisch zu spalten und zu zersetzen. Sein delirierendes Sprachgebräu treibt ihn in ein sprachliches Niemandsland ab, wo seine Instrumente nur noch zwiespältig für sich selbst räsonieren. Das ist sicherlich neben der Aphasie (das Nicht-Sprechen-Können) die radikalste Abrech-nung mit einer Muttersprache.

IV

Im Hinblick auf diese politischen, ideologischen und psychologischen Dimensionen integrierte ich das Fremdsprachenlernen in meine künstlerische Praxis. Aus dem *"ready made"* ist ein *"trying hard"* geworden, was ironischerweise auch jene Qualitäten wieder ins Spiel bringt, welche das traditionelle *"ready made"* ausschließen wollte: Lernen, Übung, Meisterschaft, Zeit, Prozeß und Ausdauer. Das Japanischlernen eröffnete diesen Prozeß. Gefolgt wurde Japanisch von den Sprachen Russisch, Neugriechisch und Koreanisch. Ich versuche, diese Sprachen weiterzulernen. Es braucht kaum dazugesagt zu werden, daß es sich dabei immer nur um *Basic Japanese, Basic Russian, Basic Modern Greek* und *Basic Korean* handelt. Perfektion wird beim Lernen nicht angestrebt.

Allerdings können die mit dem Fremdsprachenlernen einhergehenden Kontakte und Auswirkungen auf meine Lebens- und Arbeitsumstände so weit führen, daß ich über die Jahre hinweg anfange, einige dieser Sprachen auch frei und problemlos zu sprechen. Diese Sprachprojekte verursachen einschneidende Überlappungen verschiedener Sphären. In eines dieser Projekte involviert zu sein, heißt, über lange Zeit hindurch dieser Tätigkeit nachzugehen, mit ihr zu leben und ihre Konsequenzen zu erleben.

Japanisch wie auch Koreanisch wird wie alle nichteuropäischen, in Europa zumindest völlig unterrepräsentierten Sprachen als schwierig, ja als unlernbar eingestuft. Den Schriftzeichen gegenüber herrscht noch eine größere Skepsis. In diesem Zusammenhang ist es interessant, daß auch im Jugoslawienkrieg die kyrillische Schrift einen Angriffspunkt darstellte und die Losung der Serben auch dementsprechend hieß: "Ein Land, eine Sprache, eine Religion und ein Alphabet". Auch konstruierten Europäer und Nordamerikaner eine Abneigung gegenüber Japan bzw. Asien im allgemeinen. Diese negativen Vorurteile sind alt und neu. Zurückgehend bis u. a. auf das Zeugnis des Nibelungenlieds stellt sich der Westen Asiaten oft nur als Horden vor, was heute in den westlichen Medien aus den Japanern die verächtliche Figur manipulierter, entindividualisierter Massenmenschen macht. Man stellt sich Japaner wie auch andere Asiaten nur als Gruppenmenschen vor, denen keine Individualität zugestanden wird. Um dieses Vorurteil etwas zu durchbrechen und dem gigantischen Mißverhältnis zwischen wirschaftlichem und kulturellem Austausch etwas entgegen zu steuern, lernte und lerne ich immer noch Japanisch wie auch Koreanisch.

Das Erlernen von asiatischen Sprachen hat aufgrund dieser Vorurteile etwas *Unheimliches* an sich. Koreanisch ist insofern auch interessant, als im Westen kaum eine genauere Vorstellung von diesem Land (oder diesen beiden getrennten Ländern) vorhanden ist. Meine wenigen, vagen Vorstellungen von Korea sind genährt von der voreingenommenen Haltung des Korea gegenüber abgeneigten Japan und den Koreanern, die ich in den USA als große Koreaemigrationsgesellschaft antreffe. Die Auseinandersetzung mit der Sprache macht mich nun dem Land und seinen Einwohnern oder Emigranten gegenüber sensibel. Dank des Spracherwerbs können sich Beziehungen einstellen, die ein Leben lang von Wichtigkeit sind.

Neugriechisch ist eine Sprache, für die es heute kaum ein Interesse gibt. Anders jedoch ist Altgriechisch die Sprache, die vor allem die deutschen Gemüter vom 18. bis ins 20. Jahrhundert philologisch in Atem hielt. Es wurde aber nicht nur fleißig studiert und geforscht, kulturelle, moralische, philosophische und staatsphilosophische Einbil-dungs- und Projektionsarbeit geleistet, sondern auch reichlich für die ideologische, deutsch-nationale Landschaft Vergangenheit konstruiert. Kulturgüter wurden minutiös aus- und abgetragen und nach Deutschland in die Museen verfrachtet. In Athen wurde mit Otto dem Bayern 1833 das griechische Königtum wiederbelebt. Griechenland war so ein klassisches Land eines hauptsächlich – nicht ausschließlich – deutschen Orientalismus. In der Nachkriegszeit sahen sich die etwas weniger geschätzten, aber für die Industrie umso nützlicheren Nachkommen der Alten Griechen als Gastarbeiter gezwungen, Deutsch zu lernen und zu erfahren, was es heißt, eine Sprache nicht perfekt zu beherrschen. In den Ferienzeiten zählten und zählen immer noch die Deutschen und Österreicher im griechischen Süden zu den Haupt-besuchern, die, bis auf wenige Ausnahmen und wenige Worte, nichts von der Landessprache verstehen oder zu verstehen brauchen. Abgesehen davon haben die Griechen in ihrem Land nicht anerkannte sprachliche Minderheiten (albanische, mazedonische, türkische) und äußerst problematische Nachbarschaftsverhältnisse, die sich nicht immer auf einen Nenner mit Toleranz und

Verständnis für die anderen bringen lassen.

Die russische Sprache ist für mich, als Kind des "Kalten Krieges" an den Grenzen zum sogenannten Ostblock, ebenfalls ein Kulturell-Anderes. Des öfteren versuchte ich, Russisch schon während meiner Studienzeit zu erlernen, wobei ich jedoch immer scheiterte. Erst mit dem Fall des Eisernen Vorhangs überwand ich alle Schwierigkeiten und studierte seit 1990 regelmäßig in New York. Mehrere längere Rußlandauf-enthalte in Verbindung mit kontinuierlichem Lernaufwand ermöglichten es mir, ein Russisch zu erwerben, in dem ich mich verständlich machen kann.

Was man glaubt zu können, kann man auch weitergeben. *Basic linguistic services* nenne ich jene Praxis, in der ich Sprachen weitervermittle: *basic linguistic services, basic german, basic english, basic french, basic japanese* ... sind Vermittlungsarbeiten, in denen ich Interessierten in Rußland (*Basic English*), in Japan (*Basic French*) und in den USA und Frankreich (*Basic German*) elementare Sprachkenntnisse beizubringen versuchte. Auch dabei zeigte sich sehr schön, weshalb die einzelnen Teilnehmer an einer neuen Sprache Interesse fanden. Diese Servicelei-stungen sind auch eine ideale Voraussetzung, um Gespräche, wenn nicht sogar Freundschaften, zu entwickeln.

V

Es ist schwer, die Kunst des 20. Jahrhunderts nicht in Beziehung zu den Paradigmen des *ready made*'s und der Fotografie zu sehen. Wie auch immer diese beiden Produktionsmodi aufeinander bezogen werden, so teilen doch beide eine bezeichnende Struktur: sie sind schnell, "*ready made*". Mit den Verfahren von Lesen, Sprechen, Lernen und Lehren verhält es sich umgekehrt: sie sind langsam, fragil, kaum repräsentierbar und gehören einem Lebens- und Erfahrungsbereich an, durch den jeder Mensch durchgeht und der in seinen Auswirkungen kaum überschätzt werden kann. Es ist dies auch ein Bereich, in dem Privilegien und Benachteiligungen sich offen zeigen, bestätigen und multiplizierend fortsetzen. Mit ihm werden ideologische, ökonomische und kulturelle Konstellationen gespiegelt, produziert und reproduziert. Meine Arbeit ist ein Versuch, mich auf das Lesen, Sprechen, Lernen und Lehren mit der konsensarmen, fragilen Legitimation als Künstler einzulassen, um mich erneut dem gefalteten Feld von Überlappungen mit ihren Konsequenzen und Zwängen auszusetzen. Nicht zuletzt kann diese Praxis des Lesens, Sprechens, Lernens und Lehrens ein Versuch sein, sich den paternalen, nationalen und eurozentrischen Über-Ich-Funktionen der Erziehungsmaschinerien zu widersetzen. Das Motto dazu lautet: Lernen als Verlernen als Lernen.

1. vgl. E. J. Hobsbawm, Nations and Nationalism since 1780, Cambridge University Press, 1992, p. 38, 60.
2. vgl. Edward W. Said, Orientalism, Vintage Books, New York 1979.

ZUR REKONSTRUKTION DES FRANZÖSISCHEN FEMINISMUS: VERDINGLICHUNG, MATERIALISMUS UND GESCHLECHT. DIE VERDINGLICHUNG DES "FRANZÖSISCHEN FEMINISMUS"

LISA ADKINS UND DANA LEONARD

Seit mehr als zehn Jahren ist nicht nur bei Feministinnen ein besonderes Interesse an Analysen der Geschlechterdifferenz zu beobachten. Dabei hat sich die Aufmerksamkeit vor allem auf psychoanalytische und dekonstruktivistisch literaturwissenschaftliche Analysen konzentriert, insbesondere auf die der französischen Autorinnen Luce Irigaray, Julia Kristeva und Hélène Cixous. In der Tat gibt es, wie viele Kommentare bemerken, eine wahre Flut von Publikationen über ihre Arbeiten. Uns geht es hier jedoch nicht so sehr um das Pro und Contra der Arbeiten dieser drei Autorinnen, noch um die Frage, ob der "französische Feminismus" nicht eigentlich (wie Christine Delphy argumentiert[1]) aus der englischsprachigen Sekundärliteratur besteht, da diese drei Autorin-nen verschiedene Standpunkte vertreten und zwei von ihnen sich deutlich gegen den Feminismus aussprechen. Vielmehr geht es uns darum, wie ihre Arbeiten als die Gesamtheit der aus Frankreich kommenden "feministischen" Theorie dargestellt worden sind. Uns scheint, daß diese Konstruktion zum Ausschluß anderer französischer feministischer Auto-rinnen beigetragen hat – sowohl der hier vorgestellten radikalen Feministinnen als auch der sozialistischen Feministinnen.

Darin zeigt sich eine Parallele zu den Auseinandersetzungen in Frankreich selbst, wo seit dem Beginn der zweiten Welle des Feminismus nach 1968 eine gut organisierte und finanzierte Gruppe namens *Psychanalyse et Politique* (oder *Psych et Po*) ganz andere Analysen entwik-kelte als der Rest der Frauenbewegung (*Mouvement de libération des femmes*, abgekürzt *MLF*).[2] Letztere ging von Beauvoirs berühmtem Satz aus, daß "man nicht als Frau geboren wird", doch *Psych et Po* "bezogen sich intensiv auf die Psychoanalyse und insbesondere auf Lacan, um zu behaupten, daß es 'die Frau nie gegeben hat'. Sie setzten die psychoanalytische Spezifität der Frauen voraus, argumentierten aber, daß das Patriarchat Frauen in einer solchen Weise unterdrückt hat, daß wir heute nicht mehr wissen, was die Frau von sich selbst aus wäre. [...] Die Gruppe, die sich um Antoinette Fouque als Schlüsselfigur herum organisierte, [...] war erklärtermaßen gegen den 'Feminismus'"[3].

"Der Konflikt zwischen *Psych et Po* und dem Rest der feministischen Bewegung war eine französische Besonderheit, die uns bis heute verfolgt. *Psych et Po* [...] unterhält den Verlag 'des femmes' [...], der 1979 [...] das feministische Symbol [die geballte Faust im Frauen-Symbol] und den Namen *Mouvement de libération des femmes* als sein gesetzlich geschütztes Warenzeichen eintragen ließ und 1980 die Editions Tierce, einen anderen feministischen Verlag, wegen unlauterer Geschäftspraktiken verklagte, als Tierce zusammen mit dem Rest der Bewegung gegen diesen Akt der Enteignung protestierte. [...] Das Fehlen formaler Strukturen [begründet im alten feministischen Mißtrauen gegenüber Institutionen] ermöglichte es [...] der Leiterin von *Psych et Po,* [...] sich gegenüber der Regierung und den Medien als Sprecherin der Frauenbe-wegung auszugeben."[4]

"Die für den Standpunkt [von *Psych et Po*] so zentrale Idee der weiblichen Differenz [...] entwickelte sich rapide in der Mitte der 70er Jahre. Drei bedeutende Theoretikerinnen veröffentlichten wichtige und einflußreiche Texte, [...] die sich zwar in wichtigen Aspekten voneinander unterschieden, jedoch alle eine Rolle in der Herbeiführung der von *Psych et Po* so bezeichneten 'Revolution des Symbolischen' spielten, einer Revolution [...], die darauf abzielte, das Weibliche sichtbar zu machen. Luce Irigarays 'Speculum. De l'autre femme' ['Speculum. Spiegel des anderen Geschlechts'], 1974 erschienen, versucht, das 'männlich Weib-liche' zu lokalisieren und zu definieren, das, wie sie argumentiert, zu-nächst erforscht werden muß, bevor wir das 'weiblich Weibliche' durch- denken können. Julia Kristevas [...] 'La révolution du language poétique' ['Die Revolution der poetischen Sprache'], ebenfalls 1974 erschienen, wurde als ein besonders wichtiger Text angesehen, der das Weibliche im Prä-Ödipalen lokalisiert und es als eine notwendigerweise marginale und revolutionäre Kraft charakterisiert, welche mittels der Kraft des von Kristeva so genannten Semiotischen die Sprache aufbricht [...]. Im folgenden

Jahr begann Hélène Cixous in 'Le rire de la Meduse' ['Das Lachen der Medusa'] und einem anderen Essay, 'Sorties' ['Auswege'], darüber zu theoretisieren, was die Praxis einer *écriture féminine* [eines weiblichen Schreibens] sein könnte, eines aus der vielfältigen Natur der weiblichen libidinösen Ökonomie hervorgehenden Schreibens. Sie rief die Frauen auf, 'mit ihrem Körper' zu schreiben."[5]

Um nachzuvollziehen, wie es außerhalb Frankreichs zur Gleichsetzung des französischen Feminismus mit Irigaray, Kristeva und Cixous kam, müssen wir uns den Arbeiten zuwenden, welche die französische feministische Theorie erstmals einem englischsprachigen Pub-likum vorstellten. Die erste Textsammlung war "New French Feminisms" (1981) von Marks und Courtivron; im selben Jahr erschienen außerdem in den USA zwei Sondernummern von Zeitschriften ("Signs and Feminist Studies"). Mitte der 80er Jahre folgten "Feminism in France: From May 68 to Mitterand" von Claire Duchen (1986) und "French Connecions: Voices from the Women's Movement in France" (1987) sowie "French Feminist Thought" von Toril Moi (1987). Sie alle präsentieren eine Reihe verschiedener Standpunkte, und einige kritisieren auch scharf die Aktionen von *Psych et Po*.[6] Dennoch suggerieren sie alle, insbesondere Moi, daß die Arbeiten von Cixous, Irigaray und Kristeva besonders interessant sind – und ihren Arbeiten wird insgesamt weitaus mehr Raum und Beachtung gewidmet.

In der Folgezeit konzentrierte sich die Aufmerksamkeit so sehr auf diese drei Autorinnen[7], daß es in den späten 80er und frühen 90er Jahren nicht mehr möglich war, einen Überblick über den gegenwärtigen Stand des englischsprachigen feministischen Denkens zu geben, ohne auf die Auswirkungen ihrer Arbeiten einzugehen. In den frühen 90ern entstanden sogar komplette Essaysammlungen, die sich mit der Bedeutung der von ihren Ideen ausgelösten Veränderungen im anglophonen Feminismus befassen.[8]

In der Einleitung zu einem dieser Bände ("Revaluing French Feminism" von Fraser und Bartky, 1992) - der sich mit der Einwirkung des "französischen Feminismus" auf die US-amerikanische feministische Politik auseinandersetzt – argumentiert Fraser, daß der "französische Feminismus" seit längerem zu einer weitgehenden Umgestaltung des US-amerikanischen Feminismus beiträgt, indem einige der innerhalb des "französischen Feminismus" aufgeworfenen Problematiken (z.B. die "Differenz") nahezu pauschal auf die US-amerikanische feministische Diskussion übertragen werden. Fraser ist sich völlig darüber im klaren, daß "die Rezeption des französischen Feminismus partiell und selektiv verlaufen ist. Sie hat sich fast ausschließlich auf ein oder zwei Richtungen – die dekonstruktive und die psychoanalytische – aus einem weitaus größeren, vielfältigeren Feld konzentriert. Das Resultat ist eine merkwürdige synekdochische Reduktion"[9].

Diese Reduktion führt sie zurück auf die Publikation des Readers von Marks und Courtivron, der erstmals französische Femini-stinnen einem englischsprachigen Lesepublikum vorstellte und den Grundstein zur Konstruktion des "französischen Feminismus" als einem eigenständigen kulturellen Objekt legte (und, möchten wir hinzufügen, ihn zugleich attraktiv machte und ihn verdinglichte). Fraser merkt an, daß die "merkwürdige [...] Reduktion" eintrat, obwohl der Band von Marks und Courtivron den "französischen Feminismus" nicht in dieser Weise darstellte. Er enthielt zwar keine Texte des französischen "'Syn-diko-Feminismus' und feministischer Strömungen innerhalb der Linksparteien", bot aber ansonsten eine vielseitige (oder "relativ umfassende") Auswahl.[10] (Anzufügen ist hierzu noch, daß Marks und Courtivron in der Tat das erste Editorial des *Questions féministes*-Kollektivs abgedruckt haben, sowie kurze Auszüge aus einem frühen Artikel von "C.D." – Christine Delphys "Pour un matérialisme féministe" von 1975 – und aus einem der Romane von Monique Wittig.)

Obwohl sie bemerkt, wie eingeschränkt der "französische Feminismus" innerhalb der anglophonen Diskussion erscheint, versucht Fraser nicht, die Ursachen dafür zu erklären. Sie scheint diesen Tatbe-stand vielmehr unerklärlich und unbegründbar zu finden und schreibt:

"Zweifellos könnten wir mehr darüber lernen, wie unsere Kultur und ihre Institutionen funktionieren, wenn wir den genauen Prozeß dieser synekdochischen Reduktion rekonstruieren könnten, der umso auffälliger wirkt, als er sich gegen den unermüdlichen Protest von Monique Wittig, Simone de Beauvoir und den Herausgeberinnen von *Questions féministes* vollzog."[11]

Die Vorgänge dieser Reduktion sind allerdings weniger unerklärlich, als es Fraser andeutet. Denn, wenn wir uns der Darstellung des "französischen Feminismus" bei Marks und Courtivron zuwenden, finden wir in der Einleitung der Herausgeberinnen das Argument, daß "Frauen, die sich in Frankreich mit der Frauenfrage befassen, die Wörter 'Feminismus' und 'feministisch' seltener verwenden als Frauen in den USA", was sie begründen mit einem "Wunsch, mit einer bürgerlichen Vergangenheit – mit den Unzulänglichkeiten und den feststehenden Kategorien des humanistischen Denkens, einschließlich des Feminismus – zu brechen, was sowohl eine der einflußreichsten und radikalsten Frauengruppen (die ursprünglich unter dem Namen *Psychoanalyse et Politique* bekannt war [...]) als auch Hélène Cixous zu heftiger Kritik an diesen Bezeichnungen motiviert hat"[12].

Marks und Courtivron stellen also nicht nur von Anfang an die gesamte französische Frauenbewegung in Distanz zum "Feminismus" dar, sondern situieren auch *Psych et Po* als die "einflußreichste und radikalste" Gruppe in Frankreich, als das Zentrum der französischen feministischen Diskussion und als die interessanteste und innovativste Variante des Feminismus: "*Psychanalyse et Politique* besitzt die größte Originalität von allen Frauenbefreiungsgruppen in Frankreich und vielleicht in der gesamten westlichen Welt"[13].

Führende Feministinnen in Frankreich haben jedoch immer wieder argumentiert, daß diese Variante des französischen Feminismus innerhalb Frankreichs *nicht* so einflußreich war, wie die US-amerikanische feministische Literatur behauptet, und nur diese eine Gruppe hat sich tatsächlich von der Bezeichnung "Feminismus" distanziert. Die Mehrheit protestierte lange und lautstark und betonte die Wichtigkeit einer autonomen, nicht zum Warenzeichen gemachten, aktivistischen Frauenbewegung.

"Die französische Frauenbewegung [...] ist permanent gefährdet von solchen Gruppen wie *Psych et Po*, die sich als *die* Frauenbewegung ausgeben und einen bedeutenden Einfluß ausüben, da die allgemeine Öffentlichkeit ihre Ideologie – eine bequeme Neo-Femininität, die von Autorinnen wie Hélène Cixous, Annie Leclerc und Luce Irigaray entwickelt wurde – leider allzu bereitwillig aufgenommen hat. [...] Dies ist leider auch derjenige Aspekt der französischen Frauenbewegung, der in den USA am besten bekannt ist. Bücher wie [...] "New French Feminism" liefern ein völlig verzerrtes Bild des französischen Feminismus, indem sie ihn einerseits darstellen, als existierte er nur in der Theorie und nicht im praktischen Handeln, und andererseits, als ginge die Gesamtheit dieser Theorie von der Schule der Neo-Femininität aus, die den weiblichen Zyklus und weibliche Rhythmen und Körperflüssigkeiten zelebriert, die 'Körperschrift' [*écriture du corps*] und das weibliche 'zirkuläre Denken'."[14]

"Es ist ironisch, daß *Psych et Po*, die sich selbst die Bewegung nannten und zugleich den Feminismus denunzierten, von Feministinnen in anderen Ländern so offen aufgenommen wurden. So ist es beispielsweise weitgehend die Arbeit dieser Gruppe und ihrer Anhängerinnen, die in den USA "französischer Feminismus" genannt wird, trotz zahlreicher Proteste aus der Bewegung – worin sich eine nicht geringe Arroganz seitens der amerikanischen Feministinnen zeigt."[15]

Die meisten französischen Feministinnen betrachten also den Reader von Marks und Courtivron nicht als eine relativ ausgewogene Einführung und Darstellung des französischen Feminismus, wie Fraser es sieht, sondern als einen wesentlichen Beitrag zu eben dem Reduk-tionsprozeß, den sie so merkwürdig findet. Ein anderer interessanter Aspekt von "New French Feminisms" ist, auf welche Weise die Heraus-geberinnen einige der mit "Questions féministes" assoziierten Feministin-nen darstellen. Spezifisch situieren sie, wie es häufig in der englisch- sprachigen feministischen Literatur der Fall ist, Beauvoir und Wittig als zentrale Figuren innerhalb des anregenden und innovativen "neuen französischen Feminismus", ohne die Diskrepanz zwischen ihnen, *Psych et Po* und Cixous zu erwähnen.[16] Und während Marks und Courtivron zwar in ihrer Geschichte der französischen Frauenbewegung die Grün-dung und die Existenz von "Questions féministes" würdigen, nennen sie als Grund, weshalb die Zeitschrift ein "bedeutendes politisches und literarisches Ereignis"[17] sei, daß Beauvoir und Wittig gemeinsam *in* ihr veröffentlichten - aber nicht, daß sie (und andere) gemeinsam sich an der Entwicklung und der Herausgabe der Zeitschrift als einer Form von politischem Aktivismus beteiligten. Sie beachten kaum, daß Beauvoirs Unterstützung der französischen Frauenbewegung weithin bekannt und umfassend war, aber "die Wahl von Beauvoirs Kontakten [in den 70er Jahren] kein Zufall war: Es waren, damals wie heute, immer Frauen, die auch auf dem Boden einer materialistischen Analyse der Lage der Frauen (und der Welt) stehen und jeglichen Glauben an eine 'Natur der Frau' strikt ablehnen. Frauen wie Anne Zelensky zum Beispiel, die mit ihr in der 'Liga der Frauenrechte' aktiv ist; Christine Delphy, die die feministische Theoriezeitschrift *(Nouvelles)* "Questions féministes" herausgibt, oder auch die Gruppe von Frauen, mit denen sie seit Jahren die festen Seiten über den *sexisme ordinaire* (den alltäglichen Sexismus) in "Les Temps Modernes" redigiert"[18].

Die "merkwürdige synekdochische Reduktion" des französischen Feminismus auf die Arbeiten der dekonstruktiven und psychoanalytischen Autorinnen hängt auch wesentlich mit dem fachlichen Hintergrund der meisten englischsprachigen Frankreich-Expertinnen (d.h. derjenigen, die am ehesten historische Darstellungen und Textsammlungen des "französischen Feminismus" lesen, schreiben, kommentieren, übersetzen und herausgeben) zusammen. Ihr fachlicher Hintergrund liegt meistens in der Sprach- oder Literaturwissenschaft, so daß sie weitaus eher eine Verbindung zu denjenigen französischen Feministinnen finden, die Literatur oder Literaturtheorie schreiben, als zu denen aus Soziologie, Psychologie und Anthropologie. Das heißt, die englischsprachigen Feministinnen, die sich am wahrscheinlichsten mit der Verbreitung oder der Kritik der französischen Autorinnen befassen, sind weitaus mehr an Literaturwissenschaft und an der Konstruktion von Subjektivitäten durch Sprache und Texte interessiert als an denjenigen französischen Theoretikerinnen, die die Bedeutung der gesellschaftlichen Verhältnisse und der Ökonomie für ein Verständnis der Geschlechterverhältnisse und der Konstruktion des individuellen Bewußtseins betonen.[19] So ist die Darstellung des "französischen Feminismus" in der englischsprachigen Diskussion (und die Auswahl der übersetzten Texte) weitgehend von der fachlichen Verortung der Frankreich-Spezialistinnen beeinflußt.

Die besonderen Eigenheiten der akademischen und politischen Debatten in den USA haben diese Tendenz dort noch verstärkt. Der Materialismus hatte in den USA historisch eine geringe Bedeutung. Der Marxismus hatte beispielsweise nie einen solchen Einfluß auf das akademische Denken in Politik, Ökonomie und Soziologie und auf den politischen Aktivismus, wie er ihn in Europa ausübt. Andererseits sind sozialpsychologische und bestimmte psychoanalytische Diskurse in der nordamerikanischen Theorieszene immer populär und von zentralem Einfluß gewesen und spielen in den Geistes- und Gesellschaftswissenschaften eine Rolle, die sie in Europa nicht haben.[20] Außerdem ist die postmoderne Theoriebildung, deren Ursprung zwar oft auf europäische Autoren (Derrida, Barthes, Baudrillard, Lyotard) zurückgeführt wird, innerhalb des Feminismus in den USA am weitesten entwickelt. In diesem Kontext ist es also nicht überraschend, daß die psychoanalytische und dekonstruktive Variante in den USA die meisten Sympathien und die größte Verbreitung gefunden hat – und daß sie heute für die Gesamtheit des "französischen Feminismus" gehalten wird.

Hinzu kommt Delphys These (ein Echo auf den von Ezekiel und Moses[21] erhobenen Vorwurf des Imperialismus), daß Anglo-Amerikanerinnen den "französischen Feminismus" erfunden haben, um die Verantwortung für gewisse Ideen, die US-amerikanische Feministinnen gefährlich attraktiv finden, bei sich selbst aber nicht zulassen wollen, damit auf einen anderen abzuschieben – so daß sie diese Ideen dann aufgreifen können.[22] Das heißt, unter Zuhilfenahme der Französinnen, die in anglophonen Intellektuellenkreisen das Prestige des Exotischen haben, wird "eine veraltete [additive] epistemologische Struktur" (wieder) in die englischsprachige feministische Diskussion eingeführt, um damit den "Essentialismus [zu] rehabilitieren"[23], ihn zugleich seriös und "sexy" aussehen zu lassen.

Die "merkwürdige Reduktion" des "französischen Feminismus" auf bestimmte Autorinnen und ihre nachfolgende Erotisierung und Vermarktung ist also keinesfalls so unerklärbar, wie Fraser behauptet – und sie wirft in der Tat ein Licht darauf, "wie unsere [amerikanische] Kultur und ihre Institutionen funktionieren". Doch ironischerweise sind sowohl ihr eigener als auch die Mehrzahl der anderen Beiträge in dem von Fraser und Bartky herausgegebenen Sammelband auf eben diese "merkwürdig reduzierte" Version der feministischen Theorie in Frank-reich konzentriert (wenn auch in oft kritisch beurteilender Form). So ist dieses Buch *selbst* Bestandteil des Prozesses, den Fraser als seltsam und (zumindest zu einem gewissen Grade) problematisch ausgemacht hat. Es unterzieht den "französischen Feminismus" einer eingehenden kritischen Überprüfung, geht jedoch kaum auf neue Lektüren anderer Varianten der französischen feministischen Theorie ein.[24] Diejenige Version, mit der wir uns hier befassen – der radikal-materialistische Feminismus – wird überhaupt nur insofern erwähnt, als er mit der psychoanalytischen und dekonstruktiven Variante kontrastiert und dann als veraltet abgetan wird.[25]

Ähnliche Darstellungen von materialistischen Analysen – in denen festgestellt wird, wie sie sich von anderen Analysen unterscheiden, und/oder diese als für die gegenwärtige Debatte wenig förderlich abgetan werden – sind im Feminismus gang und gäbe. Im nächsten Abschnitt werden wir uns daher Auffassungen des "Materialismus" zuwenden, insbesondere der Rolle des "Materialismus" in der britischen feministischen Diskussion, um zu sehen, wie diese wiederum zu einer Marginalisierung des französischen materialistischen Feminismus führte.

MATERIALISMUS

Um den Gründen nachzugehen, weshalb in Großbritannien nur eine eingeschränkte Beschäftigung mit der Gruppe um "Questions féministes" stattfand, müssen wir uns mit frühen Darstellungen ihrer Ideen befassen, insbesondere mit der Darstellung, die britische Feministinnen Anfang der 80er Jahre von Christine Delphys Arbeiten geben. Wie bereits gesagt, sind Delphys Arbeiten, insbesondere die zur häuslichen Arbeit, in Großbritannien relativ gut bekannt. Sie nahm in den frühen 70er Jahren an einigen Konferenzen britischer Feministinnen teil; Delphy, Guillaumin, Mathieu und Plaza arbeiteten in gemeinsamen Workshops mit britischen Feministinnen[26], ihre Arbeiten wurden von einigen Leuten übersetzt und verbreitet, und Mitte der 70er wurden einige ihrer Vorträge auf Englisch veröffentlicht.[27] 1980 war sie als Gastdozentin an der Universität von Bradford. Der bedeutendste Faktor zur Begründung ihres Ruhms, oder besser: Ihrer Bekanntheit im britischen Kontext, war jedoch die Publikation eines Überblicks über ihre Arbeiten in der ersten Ausgabe der Zeitschrift "Feminist Review".[28]

Dieser Artikel von Michele Barrett und Mary McIntosh war deswegen wichtig, weil die Autorinnen prominente feministische Soziologinnen und marxistisch/sozialistische Feministinnen waren und die marxistisch feministische Soziologie damals in Großbritannien die dominante Form feministischer theoretischer Analysen war. Barrett und McIntosh selbst hatten bei der Durchsetzung dieser Ausrichtung – und bei der

Gründung von "Feminist Review" – eine Schlüsselrolle inne. So wurde Delphy (zumindest ihr Name) dank Barretts und McIntoshs Auseinandersetzung mit ihren Arbeiten in der ersten Ausgabe dieser Zeitschrift weit bekannt.

Der Artikel erschien zu einem Zeitpunkt, als die Suche nach einer materialistischen Analyse des sozialen Geschlechts (*gender*) auf der Tagesordnung stand. Wie Barrett selbst vor einigen Jahren formulierte, war es eine Zeit, als "'die Dinge' – seien es geringere Löhne, Vergewaltigung oder die Tötung weiblicher Föten"[29] hauptsächlich in marxistisch-feministischen Kategorien durchdacht wurden, d.h. in bezug auf die kapitalistische Produktionsweise. Im übrigen wurden in dieser Theorierichtung sowohl das Kapital als auch die Arbeit als geschlechtslose Kategorien angesehen.[30] In ihrem 1980 veröffentlichten Buch "Women's Oppression Today" lehnte Barrett jede Form von Materialismus ab, die versuchte, das soziale Geschlecht in nicht marxistisch spezifizierten Kategorien zu analysieren oder in der Form eines "Materialismus, der den Widerspruch zwischen Arbeit und Kapital aus seiner zentralen Funktion für die Analyse der kapitalistischen Gesellschaft verdrängt"[31]. Barrett erörterte die Geschlechterverhältnisse primär in Kategorien der Ideologie. So kritisierte sie beispielsweise den "kapitalistisch-funktionellen" Ansatz in der damals aktuellen Debatte über die Frage, wer aus der häuslichen Arbeit Nutzen ziehe. Sie argumentierte dagegen, daß das Familienleben in anderen Kategorien zu verstehen sei – daß nämlich der Kapitalismus *historisch* geschlechtsspezifische Momente enthielte, weil seine Entwicklung von früher bestehenden Familienformen beeinflußt sei, daß aber der häusliche Bereich *heute* in Kategorien der ideologischen Prozesse und der Strukturierung der Familien aus geschlechtsspezifi schen Subjekten analysiert werden müsse.[32]

Es überrascht also nicht, daß die von Delphy vorgebrachten Ideen – daß die Ehe ein spezifisches ökonomisches Verhältnis ist, in dem Männer und Frauen in verschiedenen Produktionsverhältnissen situiert sind; daß die Arbeit der Frauen durch "nicht-kapitalistische Prozesse" verdinglicht und ausgebeutet wird; und daß die "materiellen" Determinanten des sozialen Geschlechts vom Widerspruch zwischen den sozialen Kategorien "Männer" und "Frauen" konstituiert werden – ein äußerst explosives Potential darstellten. Die dominante Form des Materialismus, wie sie Barrett und McIntosh (und andere britische marxistische Feministinnen) formulierten, konnte solche Ideen nicht tolerie-ren, und so fiel ihre Beurteilung von Delphys Arbeiten erwartungsgemäß sehr kritisch aus.

Sie warfen Delphy u.a. vor, daß sie den Marxismus mißverstehe (insbesondere in ihrer Abweichung von einem Verständnis des Materiellen auf der Grundlage des Widerspruchs zwischen Arbeit und Kapital) und daß sie die marxistische Terminologie nicht korrekt anwende; daß ihre Analyse des sozialen Geschlechts nicht materialistisch, sondern ökonomistisch sei (d.h. daß sie Ehe und häusliches Leben in rein ökonomischen Kategorien als eine Produktionsweise sehe und daher weite Bereiche der Erfahrung von Frauen außer acht lasse); daß sie sich allein auf die Ehe konzentriere und die Mutterschaft ignoriere; daß sie die "Frauen" in ahistorischer Weise zu einer unveränderlichen ökonomischen Klasse reduziere; daß sie schließlich ethnozentristisch vorgehe, wenn sie von Daten von französischen Bauernfamilien auf andere Länder verallgemeinere (d.h., die Position der Frauen universalisiere).

Wir wollen hier Barretts und McIntoshs Argumente nicht vollständig wiedergeben – und auch nicht Delphys nicht minder robuste Antwort in Nr. 4 (1980) der "Feminist Review", wo sie entgegnete, daß Barrett und McIntosh "die materialistische Methode, die [...] Marx verwendete" mit seiner "Analyse des Kapitalismus, die er mit Hilfe dieser Methode erstellte" verwechselten[33] und daß Barrett und McIntoshs Analysen in sich widersprüchlich seien - und daß dies überhaupt nur durch einen "verzweifelten Wunsch, die Männer weiterhin nicht für die Unterdrückung der Frauen verantwortlich machen zu müssen"[34], zu erklären sei. Wichtig ist hier, daß wegen der damaligen Dominanz des marxistischen Feminismus der Eindruck entstand, der gesamte radikal-materialistische Feminismus sei mit der Kritik von Barrett und McIntosh erledigt. Obwohl Delphy nachwies, daß Barrett und McIntoshs Aufsatz "viele verzerrte Darstellungen" ihrer Arbeiten enthielt und daß "ihre theoretisch-politischen Positionen sie daran hinder[te]n", Delphys Ideen zu verstehen, wurden die Ansichten von Barrett und McIntosh weithin akzeptiert und ein ums andere Mal als die Probleme (d.h. als eine *vollständige Widerlegung*) des (französischen) radikal-materialistischen Feminismus wiederholt.[35] Mit anderen Worten, die Definitionsmacht des marxistischen Feminismus über den Materialismus in Großbritannien zu Anfang der 80er Jahre bedeutete, daß Delphys Analyse seither von einer großen Zahl von Autorinnen als ein problematischer Modus der feministischen Analyse abgelehnt wird.[36]

Ironischerweise ist jedoch eben die Version des Materialismus, die damals von Barrett und anderen verfochten wurde (d.h. das Verständnis des Materiellen ausschließlich in Kategorien des Widerspruchs zwischen Arbeit und Kapital – in bezug auf das, was als *die* ökonomische Produktionsweise angesehen wurde) inzwischen von mehr oder minder denselben Autorinnen unter dem Aspekt der Analyse des sozialen Geschlechts für bankrott erklärt worden. Mehr noch, sie haben nicht nur das Bemühen um eine materialistische Analyse von *gender* aufgegeben, sondern eine weitreichende Kritik des "Materialismus" innerhalb des Feminismus und darüber hinaus formuliert[37] – einschließlich der Behauptung, daß der Materialismus ein reduktives Verständnis von *gender* darstelle.

Diese Kritik geht davon aus, daß in materialistischen Darstellungen die ökonomischen Beziehungen (d.h. diejenigen zwischen Kapita-listen und Arbeitern) immer als dominant aufgefaßt werden und daß damit notwendigerweise eine ganze Reihe von Faktoren unbeachtet bleiben, die für das soziale Geschlecht von konstitutiver Bedeutung sind, wie z.B. Sexualität, Körper und Subjektivität. Darüber hinaus (und in bezug darauf) werden nun im Materialismus eine Reihe von anderen Problemen für die feministische Theorie (und in einem weiteren Rahmen für eine Gesellschaftstheorie) gesehen, u.a. daß er zu universalistischen Interpretationen und zu einem mechanistischen Verständnis der Konstitution gesellschaftlicher Formationen führt. Das heißt, die damals gegen Delphy gerichtete Kritik wird heute mehr oder weniger pauschal auf *alle* materialistischen Analysen angewandt. Wir möchten dagegen behaupten, daß diese Notwendigkeit, in Analysen von *gender* auf den "Materialismus" vollständig zu verzichten, nicht direkt auf diesen Modus der Analyse zurückzuführen ist, sondern auf das dominante (d.h. das damalige marxistisch-feministische) Verständnis des "Materiellen".

Einige Interpretationen des sozialen Geschlechts leiden an Ökonomismus, d.h. sie verstehen *gender* ausschließlich in bezug auf die ökonomischen Verhältnisse und/oder halten die Ökonomie für den bei der Strukturierung der Verhältnisse einzigen oder dominanten Faktor. Solche Erklärungen sind ungenügend, aber ihre Unzulänglichkeit liegt nicht nur darin, daß sie beweisen wollen, daß die ausschließliche oder hauptsächliche Verantwortung für die Unterdrückung der Frauen bei der kapitalistischen Ökonomie liegt, sondern ebenso in der reduktiven Auffassung des ökonomischen Bereichs und seiner konstitutiven Elemente.

Das marxistisch/sozialistische feministische Projekt hat zwar Jahre darauf verwandt, eine materialistische Interpretation von *gender* zu entwickeln, ist dabei jedoch zu keiner neuen Analyse des ökonomischen Sektors gekommen. *Die* Ökonomie (was als "der ökonomische Sektor" oder "das ökonomische System" bezeichnet wurde) wurde unhinterfragt vorausgesetzt. Statt dessen wurde versucht, durch neue Analysen des ideologischen und kulturellen Bereichs zu einem Verständnis des sozialen Geschlechts zu kommen. Diese neuen Analysen waren daher in einem bereits bestehenden Modell der gesellschaftlichen Formation lokalisiert, in dem der Bereich der Ökonomie als geschlechtsneutral galt und die konstituierenden Momente von *gender*, wie z.B. die Sexualität, nicht nur als außer-ökonomisch deklariert wurden, sondern auch als sekundär gegenüber dem Ökonomischen. Mit anderen Worten, diese Versuche geschahen innerhalb eines Modells der gesellschaftlichen Formation, in der eine feststehende Hierarchie erklärte, was wovon determiniert wird.[38]

Die marxistischen Feministinnen, die die Anwendung dieses Modells für problematisch hielten, unternahmen (in den frühen und mittleren 80er Jahren) verschiedene Versuche, den Materialismus zu überarbeiten, um eine umfassendere Berücksichtigung des sozialen Geschlechts zu ermöglichen. Sie brachten zwar zahlreiche wichtige Erkenntnisse hervor, konnten aber, rückblickend beurteilt, das Problem nicht lösen, weil einige Auffassungen über das Materielle und insbesondere die Konstruktion des ökonomischen Bereichs unverändert beibehalten wurden.

So versucht beispielsweise Cynthia Cockburn in ihrem Essay "The Material of Male Power" (1981), den Materialismus zu überarbeiten, um die Fehler früherer marxistisch-feministischer Analysen zu vermeiden – insbesondere ihren Ökonomismus. Sie argumentiert für eine umfassendere Auffassung des "Materiellen", das nicht nur das Ökonomische umfassen soll, sondern auch das, was sie das Physische nennt, wozu sie Fragen "der Körperlichkeit und der technologischen Extensionen des Körpers, des Hausbaus und der Kleidung, des Raums und der Bewegung" zählt, sowie das Sozio-Politische, wozu "männliche Organisationen und Solidarität, die Rolle von Institutionen wie Kirchen, Vereinen, Gewerkschaften und Clubs" zählen.[39] Cockburn behauptet, daß diese überarbeitete Version des Materialismus ein Verständnis von *gender* ermöglicht, welches "über die größeren Verdienstmöglichkeiten und Eigentumsvorteile der Männer hinausgehen"[40] und es damit ermöglichen würde, die uneingeschränkte Bedeutung der materiellen Verhältnisse für die Konstitution von *gender* zu erforschen.

Diese Öffnung der materialistischen Analyse scheint weit über alles frühere hinauszugehen. So scheint beispielsweise Cockburns Argument, daß das Physische ein Teil des Materiellen ist, auf den ersten Blick zu ermöglichen, die Bedeutung zuvor marginalisierter Faktoren, z.B. des Körpers, zu thematisieren. Doch während sie zwar den Primat der Ökonomie in der Analyse des sozialen Geschlechts in Frage stellt, bleibt die Kategorie des Ökonomischen selbst unhinterfragt. Es wird vielmehr weiterhin angenommen, daß das Ökonomische geschlechtsneutral sei und daß es restlos in der kapitalistischen Produktionsweise aufgehe. *Gender* dagegen – das, was Cockburn das *Sex-Gender*-System nennt - sei durch physische und sozio-politische Prozesse konstituiert. Dies wird z.B. dann deutlich, wenn sie explizit zuläßt, daß innerhalb ihrer Darstellung "'das Ökonomische' in den Hintergrund zurücktritt", um sich bei der Suche nach einem Verständnis von "gender" allein auf das Physische und das Sozio-Politische zu konzentrieren. Ihre strikte Trennung zwischen dem (geschlechtsneutralen) Ökonomischen und dem *Sex-Gender*-System wird auch sichtbar in Äußerungen wie:

"Ich will hier Aspekte des Prozesses der gegenseitigen Bestimmung untersuchen, in dem Männer und Frauen eingeschlossen sind, *und* solche (ebenfalls sich gegenseitig hervorbringende Prozesse), in denen Arbeiterklasse und kapitalistische Klasse historisch befangen sind."[41]

Und: "Daß eine Produktionsweise und ein *Sex-Gender*-System zwei parallele Grundzüge der Organisation menschlicher Gesellschaften sind, sollte uns nicht zu der Erwartung verleiten, eine exakte Vergleichbarkeit zwischen beiden vorzufinden, ob es sich nun um das Paar Kapitalismus und 'Patriarchat' handelt oder um ein beliebiges anderes."[42]

Was in dieser Darstellung ebenfalls auffällt ist, ironischerweise, daß die Bedeutung von Faktoren, die in früheren materialistischen Analysen der Konstitution von *gender* unbeachtet geblieben waren, immer noch nicht thematisiert werden konnte. So war es innerhalb dieses Rahmens immer noch nicht möglich, die Bedeutung der Sexualität für das soziale Geschlecht im Hinblick auf den Arbeitsmarkt zu untersuchen.[43]

In neueren Arbeiten unterscheidet Cockburn weiterhin zwischen dem Ökonomischen und *gender*. Sie distanziert sich nun, wie andere auch, von ihrer Beteiligung an einer materialistischen Interpretation von *gender* und gibt ihr früheres Projekt einer Überarbeitung des Materialismus auf, um nun das soziale Geschlecht mit Hilfe von Konzepten der institutionellen und kulturellen Macht zu analysieren. Doch obwohl dies wiederum einen Bruch mit ihren früheren Analysen zu beinhalten scheint, wenn sie nun ihre Aufmerksamkeit auf die Auswirkungen von Sexualität und Emotionen am Arbeitsplatz richtet, kann damit die volle Bedeutung des Sexuellen und des Affektiven für das soziale Geschlecht immer noch nicht thematisiert werden. Beispielsweise schreibt Cockburn, daß Sexualität in den Prozeß der Arbeit Eingang findet, indem Arbeitgeber die Sexualität zu ihrem Profit ausbeuten: "Das 'sexy' Kostüm einer Kellnerin in einem Club ist eine Ausbeutung sowohl ihrer weiblichen Sexualität als auch der männlichen Sexualität des Kunden."[44] Das heißt, Sexualität kann eine Produktivkraft sein. Doch die Implikationen dieser Tatsache, daß die Sexualität eine Produktivkraft darstellt, werden nicht unter dem Aspekt von *gender* thematisiert. Im Gegenteil, die Produktion wird ausschließlich in Kategorien des Kapitalismus aufgefaßt, so daß die Sexualität am Arbeitsplatz ausschließlich zum Profit ausgebeutet wird. Fragen wie die, ob die Ausbeutung der Sexualität am Arbeitsplatz ein geschlechterspezifisches Phänomen ist – warum z.B. Kellnerinnen, nicht aber Kellner bei der Arbeit 'sexy' gekleidet sein müssen – werden nicht gestellt. Das Ökonomische wird weiterhin als eine geschlechtsneutrale Kategorie behandelt, nicht als eine potentielle Quelle von *gender* – und folglich bleiben das soziale Geschlecht und Ökonomie voneinander getrennt.

So bleibt trotz einiger ziemlich weitgehender Veränderungen in den feministischen Analysen eine Auffassung weiterhin vorherrschend, nach der das Ökonomische geschlechtsneutral ist und soziales

Geschlecht und Ökonomie in keinem Zusammenhang stehen. Wie wir gezeigt haben, verhindert diese Auffassung eine uneingeschränkte Erkenntnis der an der Konstitution des sozialen Geschlechts beteiligten Prozesse. Ein Verständnis des Ökonomischen ausschließlich in Kategorien einer geschlechtsneutralen kapitalistischen Produktionsweise ignoriert, daß die Ökonomie selbst geschlechtsspezifische Züge tragen kann. Dagegen bestehen einige der wichtigsten Beiträge der "Questions féministes"-Position zur feministischen Theorie gerade in einer entgegengesetzten Konzep-tion des Ökonomischen, in der Betonung anderer Formen der Arbeitsteilung und in der Erkenntnis, daß die Definitionen der "Arbeit" und des "Materiellen" Veränderungen unterworfen sein können. Angesichts der innerhalb der anglophonen feministischen Diskussion ungebrochenen Dominanz einer aus den frühen marxistisch-feministischen Analysen herrührenden Auffassung vom "Materialismus" ist es allerdings nicht überraschend, daß diese alternative Version eines materialistischen Feminismus wenig Verbreitung gefunden hat.[45] Auch überrascht es nicht, daß Arbeiten, die einen Schwerpunkt auf das Ökonomische legen, als engstirniger Ökonomismus abgelehnt werden, solange die vorherrschende Interpretation des Ausdrucks "das Ökonomische" derart eingeschränkt wird.

Die Arbeiten der französischen radikal-materialistischen Feministinnen leiden jedoch nicht an Ökonomismus, sondern sie entwickeln *eine Neubestimmung der Bedeutung des "Ökonomischen"*, die höchst interessante Möglichkeiten eröffnet und aus einer Anzahl von Sackgassen herausführt, welche die feministischen Analysen beeinträchtigt hatten. Die hier vorgestellten Autorinnen haben die Definition des Ökonomischen nie auf den Widerspruch zwischen Kapital und Arbeit (auf die kapitalistische Produktion) beschränkt. Sie haben im Gegenteil das "Ökonomische" stets viel umfassender situiert, nämlich als ein gesellschaftliches und politisches Produkt in einem weitaus umfassenderen Sinne. Nach ihrer Auffassung umfaßt es auch *gender*, ist sogar intrinsisch durch Geschlechterkategorien strukturiert – d.h. durch die Widersprüche, die real existierenden Ausbeutungsverhältnisse zwischen den gesellschaftlichen Gruppen von "Männern" und "Frauen".

Während es den marxistisch-materialistischen Feministinnen im allgemeinen kaum gelungen war, die Bedeutung beispielsweise von Sexualität, Sex, dem Körper und Subjektivität für das soziale Geschlecht zu erfassen (insbesondere nicht in Bereichen wie dem Arbeitsmarkt, wo die politisch-ökonomischen Rahmensetzungen besonders einflußreich sind), hat die Position von "Questions féministes" den Begriff der "Produk- tion" nicht auf die organisierenden und ausführenden Aktivitäten bei der Produktion von Waren und Dienstleistungen für Kapital beschränkt. Die Produktion ist nach ihrer Ansicht vielmehr in eine Reihe gesellschaftlicher Verhältnisse zwischen Männern und Frauen eingebettet. Dies eröffnet die Möglichkeit eines viel umfassenderen Verständnisses des sozialen Geschlechts, und die hier vorliegenden Texte betrachten Ehe und Sexualität, Hausarbeit, symbolische Arbeit, affektive Beziehungen und körperliche Praktiken wie Geschlechtsverkehr, Schwangerschaft und Kinderpflege alle – simultan – als Formen geschlechtsspezifischer Produktion. Diese Version des "Materialismus" enthält auch weder eine klare Trennung noch eine Hierarchie zwischen verschiedenartigen "gesellschaftlichen" Formationen. So werden das "Sexuelle" und das "Ökonomische" nicht in einer Weise unterschieden, die es unmöglich machen würde, das Verhältnis zwischen beiden zu analysieren. Vielmehr gelten beide als sich gegenseitig konstruierend. So hat beispielsweise Tabet argumentiert, daß Schwangerschaft, Geburt und Stillen als Arbeit betrachtet werden sollten, und zwar als ausgebeutete Arbeit[46], an anderer Stelle analysierte sie verschiedene Formen des sexuell-ökonomischen Tauschs – der Tausch von Sex gegen etwas anderes als Sex – und die Bedeutung dieser Tauschformen für die Konstitution von *gender*.[47]

Damit wird die Sackgasse vermieden, in die die marxistischen Feministinnen gelaufen sind. Weil sie *gender* und Ökonomie als strikt voneinander getrennt betrachten, verlieren sie, wenn sie sich mit Themen wie Sexualität, Sex, Körper und Subjektivität befassen – wie sie es in neuerer Zeit vermehrt tun – das "Materielle" aus den Augen (und umgekehrt). Sie tendieren daher dazu, ersatzweise auf die Unterscheidung zwischen "Materiellem" und "Kulturellem" aufzubauen, mit dem Resultat einer oft nur partiellen Konzeption des sozialen Geschlechts.[48] Barrett bemerkte vor einigen Jahren zur Verschiebung von Fragestellungen der gesellschaftlichen Struktur zu solchen des politischen Handelns, der Sexualität etc. (und zu der damit verbundenen Verlagerung von den Gesellschafts- zu den Geisteswissenschaften), daß das Kulturelle zwar als ein Gegengewicht gegen das Materielle/Sozio-Ökonomische fungiert hat, es jedoch nicht "angemessen ist, den Blick bloß in diese oder jene Richtung zu lenken. [...] Die Frage, welches Gewicht den diversen Thematiken (z.B. dem Ökonomischen und dem Ästhetischen) beizu-messen sei, muß in Zukunft neu durchdacht werden"[49].

Die Position von "Questions féministes" war jedoch nie auf das traditionelle Verständnis des "Materiellen" noch auf das des "Kulturellen" beschränkt.[50] In dieser Situation ist es ironisch, daß, wenn der radikal-materialistische Feminismus in der englischsprachigen feministischen Diskussion erwähnt wird, er immer noch wegen seines angeblichen veralteten "Materialismus" auf Ablehnung stößt. Ihm wird z.B. vorgeworfen, an einer strikten Unterscheidung zwischen dem Materiellen und dem Ideellen festzuhalten. Tatsächlich stellen die aus dieser Perspektive kommenden Arbeiten diese problematische Dichotomie permanent in Frage, so z.B. die Idee, daß das Sexuelle eindeutig unterschieden ist vom Materiellen, oder daß das Ästhetische vom Ökonomischen zu trennen ist. Und sie konnten, was noch wichtiger ist, eine Darstellung des sozialen Geschlechts leisten, welche besser als viele andere dazu in der Lage ist, eine Reihe von strukturierenden Elementen zu integrieren.

"SEX" UND "GENDER"

Daß das soziale Geschlecht in den hier besprochenen Texten nicht in den Kategorien von materiell vs. kulturell oder real vs. ideal analysiert wird, wird besonders deutlich sichtbar im Vergleich mit der heutigen Debatte über den Gebrauch der Ausdrücke *sex* (biologisches Geschlecht) und *gender* (soziales Geschlecht). Die Destabilisierung der angeblichen orthodoxen Lehrmeinung bezüglich des Verhältnisses von *sex* und *gender* gilt als eine der wichtigsten Entwicklungen in der englischsprachigen feministischen Theorie Anfang der 90er Jahre. Das Geschlecht gilt nicht mehr als eine "natürliche" oder "biologische" Kategorie, der die soziale oder kulturelle Konstruktion des Geschlechts irgendwie übergestülpt ist. Immer mehr setzt sich die Auffassung durch, daß das "Geschlecht" keine fixe, transhistorische oder unhinterfragbare Kategorie ist, sondern ein soziohistorisches Produkt.

Diese Destabilisierung hat verschiedene Ursprünge[51], doch erst in letzter Zeit scheint die volle Reichweite der Implikationen erkannt worden zu sein, die aus dem Konstruktionscharakter des "Geschlechts" folgen. Innerhalb des nordamerikanischen Feminismus waren Judith Butlers Arbeiten zur Dekonstruktion der *Sex/Gender*-Unterscheidung, in denen sie die Fixiertheit des Geschlechts problematisiert, besonders einflußreich.[52]

Butler stellt die Grundannahme in Frage, daß das Geschlecht (*sex*) der Geschlechtsidentität (*gender*) vorgängig sei, und argumentiert, daß das Geschlecht vielmehr durch den regulatorischen Apparat der Heterosexualität materialisiert wird. Sie setzt die radikale Unterschei-dung zwischen *sex* und *gender* in Verbindung mit solchen unhaltbaren Dichotomien wie real vs. ideal und Natur vs. Kultur (letztere begründet in der *Sex/Gender*-Dichotomie die These, daß das Sozio-Kulturelle auf eine vor-soziale, fixierte Natur aufsetzt). Damit negiert sie nicht nur die historische Konstruktion des Geschlechts, sondern auch des Körpers. Überdies zeigt sich, daß diese Destabilisierung von *sex* vs. *gender* auf der Grundlage von Kritiken der oben erwähnten materialistischen Modelle der Gesellschaftsformation entwickelt ist. Butler selbst sagt, daß das problematische Modell des *gender* "für die Beauvoirsche Version des Feminismus von zentraler Bedeutung"[53] war.

Zwar haben sich in der Tat viele "materialistische" feministische Analysen auf eine strikte Unterscheidung zwischen biologischem und sozialem Geschlecht bezogen, dies gilt jedoch kategorisch *nicht* für die Gruppe um "Questions féministes" – die wohl am ehesten den Anspruch erheben kann, die "Beauvoirsche Version" zu sein. Im Gegenteil haben sich viele Autorinnen aus dieser Richtung lange Zeit explizit geweigert, den Ausdruck *gender* überhaupt zu verwenden, gerade *weil* die *sex/gender*-Unterscheidung zu einer Naturalisierung des Geschlechts führt. Statt von *gender* sprechen sie, wie die meisten Feministinnen in Frankreich, von den *rapports sociaux du sexe* ("soziale Geschlechterverhältnisse"[54]) und von *différence*[55], wobei sie die neo-feministische *Aufwertung* der weiblichen Differenz heftig bekämpfen.[56] Sie analysieren auch in konkreten Beispielen den Konstruktionscharakter[57] des Geschlechts, der Reproduktion, der Sexualität und des Körpers, und, weit davon entfernt, das Geschlecht als eine fixe, "biologische" Kategorie zu verorten, suchen sie vielmehr "ein Verständnis derjenigen Verhältnisse, welche die sozialen Kategorien des Geschlechts konstituieren und konstruieren"[58].

Wir wollen kurz einige Texte aus der Gruppe um "Questions féministes" vorstellen, deren gemeinsames Thema die Bezüge zwischen "Geschlecht", "*gender*" und "Sexualität" sind. Dies ist keine vollständige und erschöpfende Darstellung all dessen, was der französische materialistische Feminismus zu bieten hat, doch sie repräsentiert eine bedeutende, seit langem bestehende, weit entwickelte Perspektive auf einen Themenbereich, der in der englischsprachigen feministischen Debatte derzeit eine wichtige Rolle spielt.

"The Category of Sex" (1982)[59] bietet eine hervorragende kurze Einführung in die gemeinsamen Schlüsselideen der Gruppe. Die Romanautorin und Literaturtheoretikerin Monique Wittig argumentiert in diesem Text, daß die Teilung der Gesellschaft in zwei Geschlechter nicht die Ursache, sondern das Ergebnis der Unterdrückung ist; daß "Geschlecht" eine politische Kategorie ist und es ohne Unterdrückung kein "Geschlecht" geben würde; daß schließlich die Heterosexualität von zentraler Bedeutung ist, um die Geschlechter als natürlich, verschieden und zueinander komplementär zu definieren. "Geschlecht" wird solchermaßen als ein Produkt der Machtverhältnisse zwischen zwei entgegengesetzten Gruppen, "Männern" und "Frauen", verstanden[60] – und als etwas, das sich in einem Klassenverhältnis konstituiert, welches durch die Ausbeutung der Arbeit der einen Gruppe durch die andere charakterisiert ist. Es gibt hier keine Trennung zwischen dem Körper, der "Biologie" und anderen körperlichen Prozessen auf der einen und Elementen dessen, was im Englischen *gender* genannt wird, auf der anderen Seite.

In "Penser le genre: Quels problèmes?" [1991; "Rethinking Sex and Gender", 1993] skizziert Christine Delphy – eine Soziologin, die seit langem in die englischsprachigen Debatten einbezogen ist – die Geschichte des englischsprachigen Konzepts von *gender* in Arbeiten von Margaret Mead und Ann Oakley sowie in verschiedenen Theorien der Geschlechterrollen. Sie zeigt auf, wie die Arbeitsteilung und die psychologischen Differenzen zwischen Männern und Frauen zunehmend entnaturalisiert und statt dessen verstärkt die kulturellen Variationen betont wurden. Doch keine dieser Autorinnen, sagt sie, hat je in Frage gestellt, daß *gender* auf einer natürlichen, sexuellen Dichotomie beruht. Ebenso wie Butler insistiert sie darauf, daß die Verbindungen zwischen *sex* und *gender* – und zwischen Sex, Sexualität und Fortpflanzung – hinterfragt werden müssen und daß *gender* vorgängig vor dem biologischen Geschlecht existiert. Die gesellschaftliche Arbeitsteilung und damit assoziierte hierarchische Verhältnisse führen dazu, daß das physiologische Geschlecht dazu benutzt wird, zwischen denen zu differenzieren, die eine dominante Position erhalten, und denen, die dem untergeordneten *gender* bzw. der untergeordneten Klasse angehören. Sie meint, daß das Konzept von *gender* zwar bei der Entwicklung unseres Denkens geholfen hat, schlägt dann aber vor, daß wir versuchen sollten, uns ein *non-gender* vorzustellen: Wie würde eine nicht-hierarchische Gesellschaft – eine Utopie (vgl. die Romane von Wittig) – aussehen?

In "Identité sexuelle/sexuée/de sexe?" (1989) erarbeitet die Anthropologin Nicole-Claude Mathieu mittels ethnographischer und strukturalistischer Analysen eine Klassifikation von drei verschiedenen Weisen, wie das Verhältnis zwischen *sex* und *gender* konzeptualisiert werden kann:

Im ersten, in der westlichen Gesellschaft am weitesten verbreiteten Modus wird das biologische Geschlecht (*sex*) als individuelles anatomisches Schicksal erfahren, dem man durch die entsprechende Geschlechtsidentität (*gender*) Folge leistet. *Gender* fungiert hier als Übersetzung von *sex*; beide sind homolog.

Im zweiten Modus, der häufig in den Gesellschaftswissenschaften und bei sozialistischen und kulturalistischen Feministinnen anzutreffen, ist sowie auch bei den meisten von der Anthropologie erforschten "traditionellen" Gesellschaften, beruht die Geschlechtsidentität auf der gelebten Erfahrung innerhalb einer Gruppe (d.h. auf der "Sozialisation" und dem Leben als Frau in der Gruppe der Frauen). *Gender* symbolisiert hier *sex* (und *sex* symbolisiert *gender*); beide sind analog.

Im dritten Modus, der bei Radikalfeministinnen und politischen Lesben zu finden ist, wird eine gesellschaftliche/politische Logik im Verhältnis zwischen biologischem und sozialem Geschlecht gesehen, und die Identität beruht auf einem "Geschlechter-Klassenbewußtsein" ("*'sex-class'-consciousness*"), d.h. auf dem Bewußtsein der männlichen Herrschaft. *Gender* konstruiert hier *sex* (und die Heterosexualität wird als eine gesellschaftliche Institution betrachtet); beide sind heterogen.

Delphys Ideen sind also ein Beispiel von Mathieus drittem Modus; doch wo Delphy meint, daß das Konzept des *gender* bei der Entwicklung feministischer Ideen hilfreich gewesen sei, ist Mathieu davon weniger überzeugt. Doch beide würden wahrscheinlich (mit Butler) übereinstimmen, daß der heutige Gebrauch des Ausdrucks *gender* oft politisch kompromittiert und intellektuell verworren ist.

Eine ausführlichere Darstellung der von Wittig kurz vorgestellten Ideen findet sich in Colette Guillaumins "Pratique du pouvoir et idée de nature" [1978; "The Practice of Power and Belief in Nature", 1981]. Im ersten Teil dieses Artikels befaßt sie sich mit der Ausbeutung von Frauen, doch ihre Interpretation der Form dieser Ausbeutung unterscheidet sich von Delphys[61], welche englischsprachigen Leserinnen wahrscheinlich besser bekannt ist. Während sich Delphy auf die Ausbeutung der Arbeit von Ehefrauen (und anderen Familienmitgliedern) innerhalb von Familienverhältnissen konzentriert, argumentiert Guillaumin, daß *gender* generell eine körperliche Ausbeutung aller Frauen impliziert. Unter diesem Aspekt untersucht sie, inwiefern für Frauen sowohl die allgemeinen Beziehungen zu Männern als auch das individuelle Verhältnis der Ehe in einer solchen Ausbeutung besteht. Sie weist nach, auf welche Weise das Eigentum am Körper geschlechtsspezifisch geregelt ist, und hinterfragt damit die Nützlichkeit einer vom Körper abstrahierenden Konzeption der Arbeit, die nach ihrer Ansicht für die Klasse der Frauen inadäquat ist. Und sie entwickelt das Konzept der *sexage* ("Vergeschlechtlichung"), welches besagt, daß die spezifische Unterdrückung der Frauen in ihrer Reduktion auf den Status von natürlichen Objekten besteht, in der direkten physischen Ausbeutung ihrer Zeit und der Produkte ihrer Körper durch Männer, sowie in ihrer sexuellen Verpflich-tung und ihrer Verpflichtung, für andere Gruppenmitglieder zu sorgen.

Der zweite Teil ihres Artikels untersucht die verschiedenen Arten, wie die Komplementarität der Geschlechter erzeugt wird, einschließlich der biologischen Kategorisierung und der Konstruktion des Körpers. Die westlichen Gesellschaften verfügen über eine lange Geschichte der Herrschaft durch Rationalisierung und durch die Zuschreibung von Überlegenheit oder Unterlegenheit zu vorgeblich inhärenten und stabilen Eigenschaften wie IQ, Physiologie, "Rasse" oder Geschlecht. Doch "das 'Geschlecht' (*sex*) ist nichts a priori Gegebenes, kein *fait de nature;* [und] ihre Analyse macht die Prozesse sichtbar, die zu [seiner] Naturalisierung führen"[62]. Guillaumin hinterfragt damit die Kategorie der "Natur" oder des "Natürlichen", d.h. die Auffassung, daß inhärente Merkmale von Dingen oder Personen bestimmen, welche Eigenschaften sie haben. In ihrer Analyse der Geschlechterverhältnisse wie auch in ihrer Arbeit über das Konzept der "Rasse" betont sie, daß Frauen (und Nicht-Weiße) "naturalisiert" werden – d.h. daß ihnen ein bestimmtes natürliches Wesen zugeschrieben wird – *weil* sie eine untergeordnete Position haben, und nicht umgekehrt.

Paola Tabet bedient sich in "Fertilité naturelle, reproduction forcée" (1985) der gegenwärtig weniger populären Praxis der vergleichenden Anthropologie, um die Zuschreibung der Reproduktion zur "Natur" in effektiver Weise zu hinterfragen und Variationen in der Organisation der Reproduktion zu untersuchen. Sie beginnt mit einer Kritik des Konzepts der "natürlichen Fruchtbarkeit", wie es in der Demographie und der Anthropologie verwendet wird, und beweist, daß es die "natürliche Fruchtbarkeit" nicht gibt. Vielmehr werden im Gegenteil weltweit "permanent Eingriffe in die Sexualität unternommen [...], die dazu tendieren, einen auf die Reproduktion spezialisierten weiblichen Organismus hervorzubringen. Diese Interventionen bilden eine intensive und komplexe Transformation der biologischen Bedingungen der Reproduktion und, damit einhergehend, eine äußerst intensive und komplexe soziologische Manipulation der biologischen Bedingungen der menschlichen Sexualität"[63]. Tabet betont, daß Reproduktion und Sexualität keine gegebenen biologischen Fakten sind, sondern vielmehr gesellschaftlich konstituiert und zugleich konstitutiv für weibliche (in einem geringeren Grad auch für männliche) Individuen: Die Reproduktion ist ein Dreh- und Angelpunkt von Geschlecht und aller sexuellen Verhältnisse.

In "Nos dommages et leurs intérêts" (1978) befaßt sich Monique Plaza – besser bekannt für die Kritik, die sie als Sozialpsychologin und praktizierende Psychiaterin an Irigarays "Mißbrauch" der Psychoanalyse äußerte[64] – mit Aspekten der Arbeiten von Michel Foucault. Insbesondere kritisiert sie Foucaults Versuch, Gewalt und Sexualität voneinander getrennt zu halten, wenn er sagt, daß zwar Vergewaltigung als Gewalt unakzeptabel ist und bestraft werden sollte, es jedoch eine Form von Unterdrückung sei, Sexualität unter Strafe zu stellen. Plaza argumentiert, daß Vergewaltigung sich von anderen Gewaltakten unterscheidet, z.B. von einem Faustschlag ins Gesicht, da die Frage, ob eine Handlung als Vergewaltigung anzusehen ist, von der Einwilligung oder Nicht-Einwilligung abhängt, während ein Faustschlag nicht unter diesem Aspekt bewertet wird. Die Ursache dafür ist, daß Männer diejenigen vergewaltigen, die sozial Frauen sind / als sexuelle Wesen definiert sind / deren Körper von Männern ausgebeutet werden. Die Vergewaltigung beruht also auf der sozialen Differenz zwischen den Geschlechtern / auf der gesellschaftlichen Vergeschlechtlichung / auf der Heterosexualität als sexuellem Besitzverhältnis; sie ist daher essentiell sexuell. Plaza argumentiert, daß Foucaults Arbeiten zur Sexualität radikal sind, insofern sie die Sexualität nicht als etwas Gegebenes oder als ein Ding an sich betrachten, sondern als das Produkt sozialer Machtverhältnisse über den Körper. Sie sind jedoch reaktionär in ihrer Weigerung, den Antagonismus zwischen Männern und Frauen/das *gendering* der sexuellen Praxis zur Kenntnis zu nehmen. Foucault sieht nicht, welche Konsequenzen die "permanente Erregung"/"Verbreitung" der Sexualität in der heutigen Gesellschaft *für Frauen* hat (die *Gender*-Dimension). Wo er versucht, das Gesetz gegen Vergewaltigung so umzuschreiben, daß es weiterhin die Gewalt bestraft, aber die Sexualität entkriminalisiert, verteidigt er die bestehenden Besitzrechte von Männern an den Körpern von Frauen.

Diese Autorinnen zeigen, wie die materialistische Analyse der Bedeutung von Geschlecht, Sexualität und Körper zu einem besseren Verständnis der Konstitution von *gender* beitragen kann. Sie zeigen auch, daß der feministische Materialismus keineswegs an einen ökonomischen Determinismus gebunden ist und daß er nicht in naiver Weise unterstellt, das Bewußtsein sei von der Materie oder das Handeln von der Struktur determiniert.[65] Die in dieser Ausrichtung der feministischen Theorie aufgeworfenen Probleme und die Art ihres Umgangs mit diesen Problemen stellen einen originären und wirkungsvollen Zugang zu aktuellen feministischen Fragestellungen dar. Mit ihrem nachhaltigen Engagement für eine Analyse der sozialen Kategorien als gesell-schaftliche Instrumente der Unterdrückung, indem sie "die Klassifika-tion der Menschen in zwei Geschlechter für ebenso unberechtigt [erachten] wie die Klassifikation der Menschen in siebenunddreißig Rassen; anatomische und physiologische Unterschiede zwischen Perso-nen nur als einen Vorwand für die Herrschaft einer gesellschaftlichen Gruppe über eine andere"[66] ansehen, haben die französischen Radikal-feministinnen extrem wichtige Beiträge zum Verständnis der Geschlech-terverhältnisse geleistet, die eine direkte Relevanz für die gegenwärtigen Debatten im anglophonen Raum besitzen. Wir wollen dazu anregen, sich nicht nur mit den hier vorgestellten Texten auseinanderzusetzen, sondern mit der Gesamtheit ihrer Ideen.

Übersetzung aus dem Englischen von Christoph Hollender für "Texte zur Kunst", Mai 1996, Nr. 22; Wiederabdruck mit Genehmigung von "Texte zur Kunst". Isabelle Graw hat diesen Text als ihren Beitrag zu diesem hier vorliegenden Textband vorgeschlagen.

1. Christine Delphy, The Invention of French Feminism: An Essential Move, in: *Yale French Studies*, Nr. 87, S.190-221.
2. Für englischsprachige Kommentare über "Psych et Po" vgl. Nancy Huston, French Feminism, in: *Camera obscura,* Nr. 3-4, S.237-244; C. A. Douglas, Interview mit Christine Delphy and Monique Wittig, in: *Off Our Backs*, Vol. 10, Nr. 1, S.6; Joan Lewis, The Registration of "MLF" in France, in: *Spare Rib*, Nr. 108; Claire Duchen, Feminism in France: From May 68 to Mitterand, London: Routledge, 1986; Claire Duchen (Hrsg.), French Connections: Voices from the Women's Movement in France, London: Hutchinson, 1987; Nicole Ward-Jouve: White Woman Speaks with Forked Tongue: Criticism as Autobiography, London, New York: Routledge, 1991, S.61-74; Gisela Kaplan: Contemporary European Feminism, London: UCL Press, 1992, S.165; sowie Simone de Beauvoir, France: Feminism Alive, Well and in Constant Danger, in: Robin Morgan (Hrsg.), Sisterhood is Global, New York: Anchor Press/Doubleday, 1984, S.229-235. Für eine Bibliographie der französischsprachigen Kritik vgl. Judith Ezekiel, Radical in Theory: Organized Women's Studies in France, the Women's Movement, and the State, in: Women's Studies Quarterly, Vol. 20, Nr. 3-4, 1992, S.75-84; sowie vor allem: Chronique d'une imposture: du mouvement de libération des femmes à une marque commerciale, Association pour les Luttes Féministes, 1981.
3. Elizabeth Fallaize, French Women's Writing: Recent Fiction, Basingstoke: Macmillan, 1993, S.8-9.
4. Ezekiel, Radical in Theory, a.a.O., S.78.
5. Fallaize, French Women's Writing, a.a.O., S.8-9.
6. Vgl. z.B. Elaine Marks and Isabelle de Coutivron (Hrsg.), New French Feminism: An Anthology, Brighton: Harvester, 1981, S.31; und Duchen, Feminism in France, a.a.O., S.37.
7. Z.B. von Judith Butler in Das Unbehagen der Geschlechter (Frankfurt/M.: Suhrkamp, 1991), und von Elizabeth Grosz, die in Sexual Subversions: Three French Feminists (London: Allen and Unwin, 1989) auf Kristeva, Irigaray und die ziemlich anders gearteten Arbeiten von Michèle Le Doeuff eingeht.

8. Vgl. z.B. Nancy Fraser, Introduction, in: Nancy Fraser and Sandra Lee Bartky (Hrsg.), Revaluing French Feminism: Critical Essays on Difference, Agency and Culture, Bloomington: Indiana University Press, 1992; Delphy, The Invention of French Feminism, a.a.O., S.198f, Fn. 11. Daß Yale French Studies, die führende Zeitschrift für Anhänger des "französischen Feminismus", jetzt Christine Delphys drastische Attacke veröffentlich hat, deutet vielleicht eine neue Einschätzung von Seiten der US-amerikanischen Feministinnen an. Delphy formuliert jedoch keineswegs den ersten Protest in dieser Art; vgl. z.B. Alison Gibbs et al., Round and Round the Looking Glass: Responses to Elaine Marks and Isabelle de Courtivron: New French Feminisms [...], in: *Hecate*, 1980, S.23-45; Claire Moses, French Feminism's Fortunes, in: *The Women's Review of Books*, Vol. 5, Nr. 1, Oktober 1987, S.16f.

9. Fraser, Introduction, a.a.O., S.1.

10. Ebd., S.19, Fn. 2.

11. Ebd., S.19, Fn. 2.

12. Marks and Courtivron, New French Feminism, a.a.O., S.x.

13. Ebd., S.33.

14. Simone de Beauvoir, France: Feminism alive, a.a.O., S.234f.

15. Ezekiel, Radical in Theory, a.a.O., S.84.

16. Wittig, obwohl "manchmal irrtümlich zusammen mit Cixous und Irigaray unter der Rubrik der 'écriture féminine' (weibliches Schreiben) gruppiert [...], ist entschieden gegen die Exaltierung der weiblichen Differenz. Sie befürwortet das 'lesbische Schreiben', in dem die Kategorie des Geschlechts eliminiert und die Sprache von den Fesseln der männlichen Herrschaft befreit wird." (Diane Griffin Crowder, Monique Wittig, in: Eva Sartori and Dorothy Zimmerman (Hrsg..), French Women Writers, Lincoln: University of Nebraska Press, 1994, S.531.)

17. Marks and Courtivron, New French Feminisms, a.a.O., S.35.

18. Alice Schwarzer, Simone de Beauvoir heute. Gespräche aus zehn Jahren 1972 - 1982, Reinbek: Rowohlt, 1986, S.11f.

19. Vgl. Michele Barrett, Words and Things: Materialism and Method in Contemporary Feminist Analysis (in: Michele Barrett and Anne Phillips (Hrsg.), Destabilizing Theory. Contemporary Feminist Debates, Cambridge: Polity, 1992) für eine Erörterung der heutigen Probleme der Fachbezogenheit, insbesondere von Geistes- vs. Gesellschaftswissenschaften, bei Analysen zur Gender-Thematik.

20. Vgl. Gail Pheterson, Group Identity and Social Relations: Divergent Theoretical Conceptions in the United States, the Netherlands and France, in: *European Journal of Women's Studies*, Vol. 1, Nr. 2, 1994, S.257-264, für eine Erörterung der Unterschiede zwischen den feministischen Sozialwissen-schaften in den USA, den Niederlanden und Frankreich.

21 In einem Vortrag auf der Berkshire Conference on Women's History, Juni 1992, zitiert in Delphy, The Invention of French Feminism, a.a.O.

22. Delphy, The Invention of French Feminism, a.a.O.

23. Ebd., S.194+213.

24. Abgesehen von Simons "Two Interviews with Simone de Beauvoir" finden

sich nur einige kleinere Kommentare zu nicht-psychoanalytischen französischen Feministinnen. So diskutiert Fuss beispielsweise materialistisch-feministische Einwände gegen Irigarays Analyse der Lust (insbesondere Monique Plaza, Pouvoir "phallomorphique" et psychologie de "la femme": un bouclage patriarcal, in: *Questions féministes*, Nr. 1, 1977, S.91-119; englische Übersetzung: "Phallomorphic Power" and the Psychology of "Woman": A Patriarchal Chain, in: *Ideology and Consciousness*, Nr. 4, 1978, S.4-36) und die Auffassung von "Natur" und "Geschlecht" als gesellschaftlich konstituierte Entitäten, welche sie mit den "Materialistinnen" Wittig, Delphy und Plaza in Verbindung bringt - doch ihr Hauptanliegen ist eine kritische Auseinandersetzung mit Irigaray.
25. Beispielsweise beschreibt Fraser, wiederum in ihrer Einführung, wo sie auf Veränderungen in der englischsprachigen feministischen Theorie und Diskussion eingeht, wie (nach ihrer Darstellung) eine Bewegung weg von der Auffassung des frühen Zweite-Welle-Feminismus stattgefunden hat, daß es "das Ziel der Frauenbefreiung war, die Fesseln der Weiblichkeit abzuwerfen, die Unterschiede zwischen den Geschlechtern zu eliminieren und zu universalen menschlichen Subjekten zu werden" (Introduction, a.a.O., S.5). Dieser Konsens - und insbesondere die Auffassung von der Frau als universalem menschlichen Subjekt - wurde, so argumentiert sie, durch verschiedene Entwick-lungen diskreditiert (sic), u.a. durch die Analysen von "französischen Feministinnen" wie Cixous und Irigaray, die den Universalismus verwarfen und Differenzen befürworteten. Im folgenden erwähnt Fraser eine Strömung (beschreibt sie aber nicht) innerhalb des französischen Feminismus - den radikal-materialistischen Feminismus -, welche "an einer humanistisch-feministischen Verpflichtung auf den Universalismus und an einer negativen Sicht der Differenz festhält" (Introduction, a.a.O., S.7). Obwohl Fraser selbst in der anti-universalistischen Position Probleme sieht (z.B. in bezug auf die Destabilisierung des "Feminismus"), wertet sie den (nicht näher betrachteten) französischen radikal-materialistischen Feminismus implizit ab, indem sie ihn als eine Form der Analyse beschreibt, die an gewissen Annahmen festhält, die die meisten anderen hinter sich gelassen haben.
26. Von französischer Seite nahmen auch Noëlle Bisseret, Colette Capitan Peter und Emmanuèle de Lesseps teil. Die Workshops waren ursprünglich vom Social Science Research Council und der Maison des Sciences de l'Homme finanziert worden.
27. Christine Delphy, Continuities and Discontinuities in Marriage and Divorce, in: Diana Leonard Barker and Sheila Allen (Hrsg.), Sexual Divisions and Society: Process and Change, London: Travistock, 1976; dies., The Main Enemy, London: Women's Research and Resources Center, 1977 (wieder abgedruckt in: Christine Delphy, Close to Home: A Materialist Analysis of Women's Oppression, London: Hutchinson, 1984).
28. Michele Barrett and Mary McIntosh, Christine Delphy: Towards a Materialist Feminism?, in: *Feminist Review*, Nr. 1, 1979, S.229-235.
29. Barrett, Words and Things, a.a.O., S.201.
30. Für eine Kritik dieser Auffassung vgl. Maria Mies, Patriarchy and Accumulation on a World Scale, London: Zed, 1986; Joan Acker, The Problem with Patri-

archy, in: *Sociology*, Vol. 23, Nr. 2, 1989, S.235-240; Cynthia Cockburn, In the Way of Women: Men's Resistance to Sex Equality in Organizations, Basingstoke: Macmillan, 1991 (deutsch: Blockierte Frauenwege: Wie Männer Gleichheit in Institutionen und Betrieben verweigern, Hamburg: Argument, 1993); Christine Delphy and Diana Leonard, Familiar Exploitation: A New Analysis of Marriage in Western Societies, Cambridge: Polity, 1992; Lisa Adkins and Celia Lury, The Sexual, the Cultural and the Gendering of the Labour Market, in: L. Adkins and V. Merchant (Hrsg.), Sexualizing the Social Power and the Organization of Sexuality, Basingstoke: Macmillan, 1996.

31. Michele Barrett, Women's Oppression Today, London: NLB, 1980, S.252.

32. Ebd., S.173.

33. Delphys zwei Begründungen des Materialismus sind: "daß er 'eine Geschichtstheorie ist, [...] in der die Geschichte in Kategorien der Beherrschung gesellschaftlicher Gruppen durch andere gesellschaftliche Gruppen geschrieben ist'" (Delphy, Continuities and Discontinuities in Marriage and Divorce, a.a.O.). "Das letztendliche Motiv der Beherrschung ist die Ausbeutung. Dieses Postulat erklärt eine zweite Begründung, und wird zugleich von dieser erklärt: daß nämlich die Art, in der das Leben materiell produziert und reproduziert wird, die Grundlage für den Aufbau aller Gesellschaften ist, also fundamentale Bedeutung sowohl für die individuelle als auch für die kollektive Ebene besitzt." (Christine Delphy, A Materialist Feminism is Possible, in: *Feminist Review* Nr. 4, 1980, S.87f.)

34. Delphy, A Materialist Feminism is Possible, a.a.O., S.83+79.

35. So schreiben beispielsweise 12 Jahre später Landry und McLean 1993 in ihrem Werk über materialistische Feminismen: "Christine Delphy [...], die wir im Vorwort zitierten [ein Artikel aus dem Jahr 1975 - der einzige Text von Delphy in ihrer Bibliographie] schrieb Manifeste für einen materialistischen Feminismus. Wir finden ihre Beschreibung dieses Projekts [...] letztendlich aber enttäuschend, und wir würden z.T. dieselben Kritikpunkte anbringen wie bei Zillah Eisenstein [...] (vgl. für eine umfassende Kritik an Delphi auch Barry und McIntosh, Christine Delphy: Towards a Materialist Feminism?, a.a.O.)." (Donna Landry and Gerald MacLean, Materialist Feminisms, Oxford: Blackwell, 1993, S.15).

Im weiteren stellen sie fest, daß Eisenstein die marxistische Terminologie inkorrekt verwende, Status und Klasse verwechsle, zu Unrecht annehme, daß Frauen wegen ihres Bewußtseins von sich selbst als Frauen eine eigenständige Klasse bilden und daß die Auffassung von Frauen als einer Klasse unsere theoretische Durchdringung der Beziehung zwischen Kapitalismus und Patriarchat nicht befördere, sondern vielmehr die radikaleren Erkenntnisse des marxistischen (oder sozialistischen) Feminismus aus dem Blick verliere - und daß Eisenstein ethnozentrisch sei (ebd., S.33f) - alles Vorwürfe, die Barrett und McIntosh gegen Delphys Analyse gerichtet hatten.

36. Die marxistisch-feministische Kritik an Delphys Arbeiten war dermaßen einflußreich, daß die Parallelen zwischen ihrem Ansatz der "dualen Systeme" und dem von Heidi Hartmann entwickelten (Heidi Hartmann, Capitalism, Patriarchy and Job Segregation by Sex, in: Zillah R. Eisenstein (Hrsg.), Capital-

ist Patriarchy and the Case for Socialist Feminism, New York, Monthly Review Press, 1979; dies., The Unhappy Marriage of Marxism and Feminism: Towards a More Progressive Union, in: Lydia Sargent (Hrsg.), The Unhappy Marriage of Marxism and Feminism: A Debate on Class and Patriarchy, London: Pluto, 1981), dem in der feministischen Diskussion große Bedeutung zuerkannt wurde (vgl. Mica Nava, From Utopian to Scientific Feminism? Early Feminist Critiques of the Family, in: Lynne Segal (Hrsg.), What is to be Done About the Family? Harmondsworth: Penguin, 1983), allgemein nicht wahrgenommen wurden.

Inzwischen ist der Ansatz der dualen Systeme bekanntlich problematisiert worden (vgl. z.B. Mies, Patriarchy and Accumulation on a World Scale, a.a.O.; Carole Pateman, The Sexual Contract, Cambridge: Polity, 1988; Acker, The Problem with Patriarchy, a.a.O.; Cockburn, In the Way of Women, a.a.O.; Lisa Adkins, Gendered Work: Sexuality, Family and the Labour Market, Buckingham: Open University Press, 1995), und Delphy selbst vertritt heute eine andere Position (vgl. Delphy and Leonard, Familiar Exploitation, a.a.O.).
Die Ablehnung in den 80er Jahren war allerdings nicht total. Einige britische feministische Soziologinnen verwendeten Delphys Ideen in ihren eigenen Analysen. So bezieht sich beispielsweise Sylvia Walbys Arbeit über patriarchalische Beschäftigungsverhältnisse auf Delphys Analyse der häuslichen Produktionsweise, um das Verhältnis zwischen der Segregation auf dem Arbeitsmarkt bzw. dem Ausschluß der Frauen vom Arbeitsmarkt einerseits und der Ausbeutung ihrer häuslichen Arbeit in der Familie andererseits zu betrachten (Sylvia Walby, Patriarchy at Work: Patriarchal and Capitalist Relations in Employment, Cambridge: Polity, 1986); und Janet Finch bezieht sich in ihrer Untersuchung über die Ausnutzung der unbezahlten Arbeit von Ehefrauen durch den Arbeitgeber ebenfalls auf Delphy (Janet Finch, Married to the Job: Wives' Incorporation in Men's Work, London: Allen and Unwin, 1983).

37. Barrett, Words and Things, a.a.O.

38. Wir sollten betonen, daß dies eine besondere Auffassung des Marxismus war.

39. Cynthia Cockburn, The Material of Male Power, in: *Feminist Review*, Nr. 9, 1981, S.43.

40. Ebd., S.43.

41. Ebd., S.42; unsere Hervorhebung.

42. Ebd., S.56.

43. Vgl. Adkins, Gendered Work: Sexuality, Family and the Labour Market, a.a.O.; Adkins and Lury, The Sexual, the Cultural and the Gendering of the Labour Market, a.a.O.

44. Cockburn, In the Way of Women, a.a.O., S.149.

45. Wie es auch nicht überraschend ist, daß Delphys Arbeiten oft im Zentrum der Kritik standen, denn wegen ihrer früheren Konzentration auf die häusliche Arbeit waren ihre Analysen diejenigen, die innerhalb von *Questions féministes*-Gruppe am nächsten an einer klassischen marxistischen Position waren. Ihre neuere Arbeit mit Leonard ist jedoch umfassender und berücksichtigt auch die emtionale, sexuelle und reproduktive Arbeit in Familien.

46. Paola Tabet, Fertilité naturelle, reproduction forcée, in: Nicole-Claude Mathieu (Hrsg.), L'arraisonnement des femmes: essais en anthropologie des sexes, Paris: Editions de l'EHESS, 1985 (englische Übersetzung in Lisa Adkins and Diana Leonard (Hrsg.), The Sex in Question: French Materialist Feminism, London: Taylor & Francis, 1996).
47. Paola Tabet, Du don au tarif. Les relations sexuelles impliquant une compensation, in: *Les Temps modernes*, Nr. 490, 1987, S.1-53.
48. Für einen Kommentar zu solchen Schwierigkeiten in bezug auf neuere feministische Analysen des Arbeitsmarktes vgl. Adkins and Lury, The Sexual, the Cultural and the Gendering of the Labour Market, a.a.O.
49. Barrett, Words and Things, a.a.O., S.204.
50. So wird beispielsweise das "Kapital" nicht als etwas Gegebenes aufgefaßt, sondern seine Bedeutung wird als ein Produkt historischer Klassenkämpfe verstanden. Ebenso hat der französische materialistische Feminismus erkannt, daß "häusliche Arbeit" durch eine Reihe verschiedener Prozesse strukturiert ist, u.a. durch Ästhetisierung, Emotionalisierung und technologische Veränderungen - daß aber das Verhältnis zwischen Männern und Frauen für die Beziehung jedes Geschlechts zu dieser Arbeit unter den Aspekten von Eigentum, Ausbeutung und Tauschverhältnissen bestimmend ist. In diesem Sinn kann eine Parallele gezogen werden zwischen Bourdieus Revision des Klassenbegriffs (Pierre Bourdieu, Die feinen Unterschiede. Kritik der gesellschaftlichen Urteilskraft, Frankfurt/M.: Suhrkamp, 1982) und der von den französischen materialistischen Feministinnen entwickelten Analyse zum sozialen Geschlecht.

Bourdieu betont in seiner Untersuchung des Konsums und der Bedeutung des Konsums für die Formation der Klassen, welche Bedeutung dabei der Akkumulation und der Mobilisierung sozialen und kulturellen Kapitals zukommt. Er revidierte damit den Klassenbegriff, um gleichzeitig die Bedeutung der Kreisläufe sowohl des ökonomischen als auch des sozialen und kulturellen Kapitals zu berücksichtigen. Seine Arbeiten sind jedoch von feministischer Seite kritisiert worden, weil sie den Geschlechteraspekt vernachlässigen - insbesondere die Tatsache, daß der Besitz und der Tausch kulturellen Kapitals für Frauen nur eingeschränkt möglich ist, was wiederum mit Prozessen der Unterdrückung in Verbindung gebracht werden kann (vgl. z.B. Delphy and Leonard, Familiar Exploitation, a.a.O.; Beverly Skegg, Becoming Respectable: An Ethnography of White Working Class Women, London: Sage, 1996.; Celia Lury, Consumer Culture, Cambridge: Polity, 1996). So haben z.B. Delphy und Leonard nachgewiesen, daß Frauen innerhalb der Familienökonomie kulturelles Kapital erzeugen können, sie aber nicht über die gleiche Freiheit verfügen wie Männer, dieses Kapital auf dem Markt oder in anderen Kreisläufen in den Tausch einzubringen. Bourdieu sieht allerdings (ebenso wie die französischen materialistischen Feministinnen) keine strikte Trennung oder hierarchische Ordnung zwischen den verschiedenen Modi der Klassenformation. Das "Ökonomische", das "Soziale" und das "Kulturelle" verfügen zwar über eine je verschiedene Vergangenheit, werden jedoch alle gemeinsam als "Materielles" verortet.

51. Vgl. u.a. Michel Foucault, Sexualität und Wahrheit I: Der Wille zum Wissen, Frankfurt/M.: Suhrkamp, 1977/1986; Moria Gatens, A Critique of the Sex/Gender Distinction, in: Judith Allen and Paul Patton (Hrsg.), Beyond Marxism? Interventions after Marx, New South Wales Intervention Publications, 1983 (wieder abgedruckt in: Sneja Gunew (Hrsg.), A Reader in Feminist Knowledge, London: Routledge, 1991); Thomas Laqueur, Auf den Leib geschrieben. Die Inszenierung der Geschlechter von der Antike bis Freud, Frankfurt/M.: Campus, 1992.

52. Butler, Das Unbehagen der Geschlechter, a.a.O.; dies., Körper von Gewicht. Die diskursiven Grenzen des Geschlechts, Berlin: Berlin Verlag, 1995.

53. Butler, Körper von Gewicht, a.a.O., S.25.

54. Der französische Ausdruck hat einen oppositionellen Beigeschmack, der in der Übersetzung verloren geht.

55. In der Bedeutung dessen, was im Französischen "la différence" genannt wird: die eine Differenz, der Unterschied zwischen Männern und Frauen. Natürlich sind sie sich dessen bewußt, daß die Modalitäten dieser Differenz je nach Klasse, historischer Epoche, Rasse und Nation variieren und daß andere Systeme der Ungleichheit manchen Frauen Macht über andere Frauen verleihen, d.h. daß es auch Differenzen zwischen Frauen gibt. Doch sie halten keine dieser Differenzen zwischen Frauen für so "transzendental, fundamental, feststehend [oder] transkulturell" (Danielle Juteau-Lee, Reconstructing the Categories of "Race" and "Sex": The Work of a Precursor, in: Colette Guillaumin, Racism, Sexism, Power and Ideology, London: Routledge, 1995, S.21), wie sie in Formen der Identitätspolitik oft dargestellt werden.

56. Vgl. Nicole-Claude Mathieu, Paternité biologique, maternité sociale, in: Andrée Michel (Hrsg.), Femmes, sexisme et sociétés, Paris: PUF, 1977, S.39-48 (englische Übersetzung: Biological Paternity, Social Maternity: On Abortion and Infanticide as Unrecognised Indicators of the Cultural Character of Maternity, in: C.C. Harris et. al. (Hrsg.), The Sociology of the Family: New Directions for Britain, University of Keele: *Social Review Monographs*, Nr. 28, S.232-240); Colette Guillaumin, Question de différence, in: *Questions féministes*, Nr. 6, 1979, S.3-21 (englische Übersetzung: The Question of Difference, *Feminist Issues*, Vol. 2, Nr. 1, S.33-52; und in: Colette Guillaumin, Racism, Sexism, Power and Ideology, London: Routledge, 1995); Delphy, Continuities and Discontinuities in Marriage and Divorce, a.a.O.

57. Ihre Version des "sozialen Konstruktivismus" kann jedoch nicht mit einer "sozialen Konditionierung" verglichen werden, noch führt sie zu einer Entkörperlichung von "sex" und "gender". Sie beruht auch nicht auf einer radikalen Trennung zwischen "Natur" und "Sozialem". Sie steht daher im Widerspruch zu neueren Kritiken, die allen konstruktivistischen Analysen diese Eigenschaften zuschreiben (vgl. Butler, Körper von Gewicht, a.a.O.; Henrietta L. Moore, A Passion for Difference. Essays in Anthropology and Gender, Cambridge: Polity, 1994).

58. Juteau-Lee, Reconstructing the Categories of "Race" and "Sex", a.a.O., S.20.

59. Die Jahreszahlen in Klammern beziehen sich im folgenden auf die Erstveröffentlichung eines Buchs oder Artikels; bei französischen Erstveröf-

fentlichungen ist gegebenenfalls auch die Übersetzung ins Englische angegeben. [Die im folgenden vorgestellten Texte sind in englischer Sprache abgedruckt in Lisa Adkins and Diana Leonard (Hrsg.), The Sex in Question: French Materialist Feminism, London: Taylor & Francis, 1996.]

60. "Wittig geht davon aus, daß biologische Unterschiede außerhalb eines (hetero)sexistischen Diskurses keine Bedeutung haben, und behauptet, daß selbst die Begriffe 'Frau' und 'Mann' politische Konstrukte sind, die dem Zweck dienen, die Frauen den Männern unterzuordnen. Die Ablehnung der Kategorisierung von Menschen nach ihrem Geschlecht ist eine notwendige Phase auf dem Weg zur vollständigen Abschaffung der Unterdrückung der Frauen, weshalb die Wörter 'Frau' und 'Mann' in ihren literarischen Texten fast nie erscheinen." (Crowder, Monique Wittig, a.a.O., S.526.)

61. Christine Delphy, L'ennemi principal, in: *Partisans*, 1970 (englische Übersetzung: The Main Enemy, a.a.O.)

62. Juteau-Lee, Reconstructing the Categories of "Race" and "Sex", a.a.O., S.21.

63. Tabet, Fertilité naturelle, reproduction forcée, a.a.O.

64. Monique Plaza, Pouvoir "phallomorphique" et psychologie de "la femme", a.a.O.; dies., Psychoanalysis: Subtleties and other Obfuscations, in: *Feminist Issues*, Vol. 4, Nr. 2, 1984, S.51-58.

65. Die Überwindung dieser Einstellung wird häufig Foucaults Archäologie des Wissens zugeschrieben (Michel Foucault, Archäologie des Wissens, Frankfurt/M.: Suhrkamp, 1973.

66. Pheterson, Group Identity and Social Relations, a.a.O., S.262.

BIBLIOGRAPHIES

A PORTABLE (NOT SO IDEAL) IMPORTED LIBRARY, OR HOW TO REINVENT THE COFFEE TABLE: 25 BOOKS FOR INSTANT USE (JAPANESE VERSION), 1993

– Adorno, Theodor W., *Drei Studien zu Hegel*, Frankfurt am Main: Suhrkamp Verlag, 1991.
– Appadurai, Arjun, ed., *The Social Life of Things: Commodities in Cultural Perspective*, Cambridge: Cambridge University Press, 1986.
– Asher Michael, *Writings 1973 – 1983 On Works 1969 – 1979*, Halifax: The Press of the Nova Scotia College of Art and Design, 1986.
– Balibar, Etienne, *Ecrits Pour Althusser*, Paris: Editions la Découverte, 1991.
– Boudjedra, Rachid, *Topographie idéale pour une agression caractérisée*, Paris: Editions Denoël, 1975.
– Bourdieu, Pierre, *Homo Academicus*, Paris: Les Editions de Minuit, 1984.
– Djebar, Assia, *Femmes d'Alger dans leur appartement*, Paris: des femmes, 1980.
– Fabian, Johannes, *Time and the Other: How Anthropology Makes its Objects*, New York: Columbia University Press, 1983.
– Ferguson, Russell, Martha Gever, Trinh, T. Minh-ha, Cornel West, eds., *Out There: Marginalization and Contemporary Cultures*, New York: The New Museum of Contemporary Art and Cambridge: The MIT Press, 1990.
– Foucault, Michel, *Discipline and Punish: The Birth of the Prison*, New York, Vintage Books, 1979.
– Gates, Henry Louis Jr., *The Signifying Monkey: A Theory of African-American Literary Criticism*, New York: Oxford University Press, 1988.
– Graham, Dan (Edited by Brian Wallis), *Rock My Religion: Writings and Art Projects, 1965 – 1990*, Cambrige: The MIT Press, 1993.
– Gramsci, Antonio, *Selections from the Prison Notebooks of Antonio Gramsci*, New York: International Publishers and London: Lawrence and Wishart, 1992.
– Guilbaut, Serge, ed., *Reconstructing Modernism: Art in New York, Paris, and Montreal; 1945 – 1964*, Cambridge, London: The MIT Press, 1992.
– Krauss, Rosalind, *The Originality of the Avant-Garde and Other Modernist Myths*, Cambridge, London: The MIT Press, 1993.
– *L'Art Conceptuel, Une Perspective*, Paris:. Paris-Musées, 1989.
– Michelson, Annette, Rosalind Krauss, Douglas Crimp, Joan Copjec, eds., *October: The First Decade, 1976 – 1986*. Cambridge, London: The MIT Press, 1988.
– *October, 65*, Cambridge: The MIT Press, Summer 1993.
– Said, Edward W., *Culture and Imperialism*, New York: Alfred A. Knopf, 1993.
– Said, Edward W., *The World, the Text and the Critic*, Cambridge: Harvard University Press, 1983.
– Schiller, Herbert I., *Culture Inc.: The Corporate Take over of Public Expression*, New York and Oxford: Oxford University Press, 1989.
– Spivak, Gayatri Chakravorty, *Outside in the Teaching Machine*, New York Lon-

don: Routledge, Chapman and Hall, Inc., 1993.
- Spivak, Gayatari Chakravorty (Edited by Sarah Harasym), *The Post-Colonial Critic: Interviews, Strategies, Dialogues*, New York and London: Routledge, Chapman and Hall, Inc., 1990.
- Stewart, Susan, *On Longing; Narratives of the Miniature, the Gigantic, the Souvenir, the Collection*, Durham, London: Duke University Press, 1993.
- Yahia, Emna Bel Haj, *Chronique Frontalière*, Paris: Noël Blandin, 1991.

TEXTS READ IN THE READING SEMINAR (JAPANESE VERSION) AT HAIZUKA, HIROSHIMA PREFECTURE, AUGUST, SEPTEMBER 1995

- Bourdieu, Pierre, Hans Haacke, *Free Exchange*, Standford University Press, 1995
- Kafka, Franz, *The metamorphosis* in Kafka, Franz, *The metamorphosis and other stories,*, New York : Charles Scrib-ner's Sons, 1993.
- Freud, Sigmund, "The May-Beetle Dream", in Sigmund Freud, *The Interpretation of Dreams*, March: Avon Books, 1965.
- Foucault, Michael, "The Panopticon", in Michael Foucault, *Discipline and Punishment*: *The Birth of the Prison*, New York, Vintage Books, 1979.
- Said, Edward, "Traveling Theory", in Said, Edward, *The World, the Text, and the Critique*, Cambridge: Harvard University Press, 1983.

A PORTABLE, (NOT SO IDEAL) IMPORTED LIBRARY, OR HOW TO REINVENT THE COFFEE TABLE: 25 BOOKS FOR INSTANT USE, (US-VERSION), 1994

– Wellmer, Albrecht, *Endspiele: Die unversöhnliche Moderne*, Frankfurt am Main: Suhrkamp 1993.
– Magas, Branka, *The Destruction of Yugoslavia: Tracking the Break-Up 1980-92*, London, New York: Verso, 1993.
– Said, Edward W., *Orientalism*, New York: Vintage Books, 1978.
– Storey, John, *An Introductory Guide to Cultural Theory and Popular Culture*, Athens: The University of Georgia Press, 1993.
– Zizek, Slavoj, *Tout ce que vous avez toujours voulu savoir sur Lacan sans jamais oser le demander à Hitchcock*, France: Navarin Editeur, 1988.
– Al-Azmeh, Aziz, *Islams and Modernities*, London, New York: Verso, 1993.
– Deleuze, Gilles, Guattari, Felix, *Qu'est-ce que la philosophie*, Paris: Les Editions de Minuit, 1991.
– Luhmann, Niklas, *Die Wissenschaft der Gesellschaft*, Frankfurt am Main: Suhrkamp Verlag, 1992.
– Parker, Andrew, Russo Mary, Sommer, Doris, Yaeger, Patricia (Ed.), *Nationalisms & Sexualities*, New York, London: Routledge, 1992.
– Achternbusch, Herbert, *Die Alexanderschlacht*, Frankfurt am Main: Suhrkamp Verlag, 1986.
– Diederichsen, Diedrich, *Freiheit macht arm: Das Leben nach Rock'n'Roll 1990-93*, Kiepenheuer & Witsch, 1993.
– Musil, Robert, *Der Mann ohne Eigenschaften*, Band 1, Hamburg: Rowohlt, 1978.
– *"Curated by" Markus Brüderlin: Das Bild der Ausstellung*, Vienna: Hochschule für Angewandte Kunst, 1993.
– Spivak, Gayatri Chakravorty, (Harasym, Sarah, ed.), *The Post-Colonial Critic: Interviews, Strategies, Dialogues*, New York, London: Routledge, 1990.
– Bourdieu, Pierre, *Homo Academicus*, Paris: Les Editions de Minuit, 1984.
– Boudjedra, Rachid, *Topographie idéal pour agression caractérisée*, Editions Denoël, Paris 1975.
– Hadamitzky, Wolfgang, Spahn, Mark, *Kanji & Kana*, Rutland, Tokyo: Charles E. Tuttle Company Inc., 1981.
– Bornoff, Nicholas, *Pink Samurai: Love, Marriage & Sex in Contemporary Japan*, New York, London, Toronto, Sydney, Tokyo, Singapor: Bornoff, 1991.
– Screen, *The Sexual Subject: A Screen Reader in Sexuality*, London, New York: Routledge, 1992.
– Adorno, Theodor W., *Philosophie und Gesellschaft: Fünf Essays*, Stuttgart: Reclam, 1984.
– Wittgenstein, Ludwig, *Über Gewißheit*, Frankfurt am Main: Suhrkamp, 1990.
– Freud, Sigmund, *Schriften über Liebe und Sexualität*, Frankfurt am Main: Fisch-

er Verlag, 1940.
– Starobinski, Jean, *Les mots sous les mots: Les anagrammes de Ferdinand de Saussure*, Paris: Editions Gallimard, 1985.
– Foucault, Michel, *Naissance de la clinique,*, Paris: Presses Universitaires de France, 1963.
– Djebar, Assia, *Femmes d'Alger dans leur appartement*, Paris: des femmes, 1980..

TEXTS READ IN THE READING SEMINAR (US-VERSION) AT THE POLK MUSEUM LAKELAND, FLORIDA, NOVEMBER, DECEMBER 1995

– Hohendahl, Peter Uwe, "Recasting the Public Sphere," in: *October 73*, Summer 1995, pp. 27-54.
– Said, Edward W., "The Empire at Work: Verdi's Aida," in Said, Edward, *Culture and Imperialism*, New York: Alfred A. Knopf, Inc., 1993.
– Wittig, Monique, "The Straight Mind," in Ferguson, R. et alt. (Ed.), *Out There: Marginalization and Contemporary Cultures*, New York, Cambridge: The MIT Press, 1992.
– Spivak, Gayatri, "The Problem of Cultural Self–Representation," in: Spivak, Gayatri, *The Post–Colonial Critic: Interviews, Strategies, Dialogues*, New York, London: Routledge, 1990.
– Al–Azmeh, Aziz , "Prologue: Muslim 'Culture' and the European Tribe", in Al–Azmeh, Azis, *Islams and Modernities*, London, New York: Verso, 1993.
– Said, Edward, "Imaginative Geography and its Representations," "Orientalizing the Oriental," in: Said, Edward, *Orientalism*, Vintage Books, New York, 1979.
– Buchloh, Benjamin, "Cold War Constructivism," in Guilbaut Serge (Ed.), *Reconstructing Modernism: Art in New York, Paris, and Montreal 1945 – 1964*, Cambridge, London: The MIT Press, 1990.
– Storey, John, "What is Popular Culture?", in Storey, John, *An Introductory Guide to Cultural Theory and Popular Culture*, Athens: University of Georgia Press, 1993.

A PORTABLE, (NOT SO IDEAL) IMPORTED LIBRARY, OR HOW TO REINVENT THE COFFEE TABLE: 25 BOOKS FOR INSTANT USE, (FRENCH VERSION), 1994

– S. Ahmed, Akbar: *Postmodernism and Islam: Predicament and Promise*, London, New York: Routledge,1992.

– R. O'G. Anderson, Benedict, *Language and Power: Exploring Political Cultures in Indonesia*, Ithaca and London: Cornell University Press, 1990.

– Begag, Azouz, *Le gone du Chaâba*, Paris: Edition du Seuil, 1986.

– Bhabha, Homi K., *The Location of Culture*, London, New York: Routledge, 1994.

– Césaire, Aimé, *La Poésie*, Paris: Editions du Seuil, 1994.

– Classen, Constance, *Worlds of Sense: Exploring the Senses in History and Across Cultures*, London, New York: Routledge, 1993.

– Clifford, James, *Person and Myth: Maurice Leenhardt in the Melanesian World*, London: Duke University Press, Durham, 1992.

– Colomina, Beatriz, *Sexuality & Space*, Princeton: Princeton Papers on Architecture, 1992.

– Crimp, Douglas, *On the Museum's Ruins*, Cambridge, London: The MIT Press, 1993.

– Jarman, Derek, Butler, Ken, *Wittgenstein: The Terry Eagleton Script, The Derek Jarman Film*, London: The British Film Institute, 1993.

– Fanon, Frantz: *Les damnés de la terre*, Paris: folio actuel, Gallimard, 1961.

– Gates, Jr., Henry Louis, (Ed.), *"Race," Writing, and Difference*, Chicago, London: The University of Chicago Press, 1986.

– Graham, Dan, (Wallis, Brian,ed.), *Rock my Religion: Writings and Art Projects 1965 – 1990*, Cambridge: The MIT Press, 1993.

– Grossberg, Lawrence, Nelson, Cary, Treichler, Paula, *Cultural Studies*, New York, London: Routledge, 1992.

– Hooks, Bell, West, Cornel, *Breaking Bread: Insurgent Black Intellectual Life*, Boston: South End Press, 1991.

– Kraus, Karl, *Hüben und Drüben: Aufsätze 1929 – 1936*, Frankfurt am Main: Suhrkamp Taschenbuch Verlag, 1993.

– Magas, Branka, *The Destruction of Yugoslavia: Tracking the Break-Up 1980 – 1992*, London, New York: Verso, 1993.

– Negt, Oskar, Kluge, Alexander, *Machverhältnisse des Politischen: 15 Vorschläge des Politischen zum Unterscheidungsvermögen*, Frankfurt am Main: Fischer Verlag, 1993.

– Rafael, Vicente L., *Contracting Colonialism: Translation and Christian Conversion in Tagalog Society under Early Spanish Rule*, Durham, London: Duke University Press, 1993.

– Richie, Donald, *Scenes from Japanese Lives: Geisha, Gangster, Neighbor, Nun,*

Tokyo, London, New York: Kodansha International Ltd., 1987.
– Said, Edward W., *Orientalism*, New York: Vintage Books,1978.
– Screen, *The Sexual Subject: A Screen Reader in Sexuality*, London, New York: Routledge, 1992.
– Wallace, Michele, *Invisibility Blues: From Pop to Theory*, London, New York: Verso, 1990.
– Wittgenstein, Ludwig, *Philosophische Grammatik*,, Frankfurt am Main: Suhrkamp Verlag, 1984.
– Kateb Yacine, *Nedjma*, Paris: Editions du Seuil, 1956.

TEXTS READ IN THE READING SEMINAR (FRENCH VERSION) AT THE VILLA ARSON, NICE, MAY, APRIL 1996

– Fanon, Frantz, "De la Violence," in Fanon, Frantz, *Les damnés de la terre*, Paris: folio actuel, Gallimard, 1961.
– Fanon, Frantz, "Guerre coloniale et troubles mentaux," in: Fanon, Frantz, *Les damnés de la terre*, Paris: folio actuel, Gallimard, 1961.
– Mulvey, Laura, "Visual Pleasure and Narrative Cinema," in Screen, *The Sexual Subject: A Screen Reader in Sexuality*, London, New York: Routledge, 1992.
– Crimp, Douglas, "Portraits of People with AIDS," in Grossberg, et alt., (Ed.), *Cultural Studies*, New York, London: Routledge, 1992.
– Ahmed, Akbar S. , "Introduction: Postmodernism and Islam," in: Ahmed, Akbar S., *Postmodernism and Islam: Predicament and Promise*, London, New York: Routledge, 1992.

A PORTABLE, (NOT SO IDEAL) IMPORTED LIBRARY, OR HOW TO REINVENT THE COFFEE TABLE: 25 BOOKS FOR INSTANT USE, (RUSSIAN VERSION), 1994

– Balibar, Etienne, *Masses, Classes, Ideas: Studies on Politics and Philosophy before and after Marx*, New York, London: Routledge, 1994.
– Benjamin, Walter, *Moskauer Tagebuch*, Frankfurt am Main, Edition Suhrkamp, 1980.
Bolton, Richard, (ed.), *The Contest of Meaning, Critical Histories of Photography*, The MIT Press, 1992.
– Butler, Judith, *Bodies that Matter: On the Discursive Limits of "Sex"*, New York, London: 1993.
– Clastres, Pierre, *La société contre l'état*, Paris, Les Editions de Minuit, 1991.
– Crary, Jonathan, Kwinter Sanford, (ed.) *Incorporations*, New York: Zone Books, 1992.
– Crimp, Douglas, Rolston, Adam, (ed.), *Aids Demo Graphics*, Seattle: Bay Press, 1990.
– Crimp, Douglas, *On the Museum's Ruins*, Cambridge, London: The MIT Press, 1993.
– During, Simon, (ed.) *The Cultural Studies Reader*, London, New York: Routledge, 1993.
Ferguson, Russell, Gever, Martha, Minh-ha, Trinh T., West, Cornel, (ed.) *Out There: Marginalization and Contemporary Cultures*, Cambridge, London: The MIT Press, 1990.
– Ferguson, Russell, Olander, William, Tucker, Marcia, Fiss, Karen, *Discourses: Conversations in Postmodern Art and Culture*, Cambridge, London: The MIT Press, 1992.
– Gever, Martha, Greyson, John, Parmar, Pratibha, (ed.), *Queer Looks: Perspectives on Lesbian and Gay Film and Video*, London, New York: Routledge, 1993.
– Horkheimer, Max, Adorno, Theodor, Wiesengrund, *Dialektik der Aufklärung: Philosophische Fragmente*, Frankfurt am Main: Fischer Taschenbuch Verlag, 1990.
– Kafka, Franz, *Amerika*, Frankfurt am Main: Fischer Taschenbuch Verlag, 1992.
– Kluge, Alexander, *Schlachtbeschreibung*, Frankfurt am Main: Edition Suhrkamp, 1983.
– Marin, Louis, *Utopiques: jeux d'espaces*, Paris: Les Editions de Minuit, 1973.
– Mellencamp, Patricia, *Indiscretions: Avant-Garde Film, Video, & Feminism*, Bloomington, Indianapoli: Indiana University Press, 1990.
– Minh-ha, Trinh T., *Woman, Native, Other, Writing Postcoloniality and Feminism*, Bloomington, Indianapolis: Indiana University Press, 1989.
– Stewart, Susan: *On Longing: Narratives of the Miniature, the Gigantic, the Souvenir, the Collection*, Duke University Press, Durham, London, 1993
– Williams, Raymond, *The Politics of Modernism: Against the New Conformists*,

London, New York: Verso, 1989.
– Williams, Patrick, Chrisman, Laura, (ed.), *Colonial Discourse and Post-Colonial Theory: A Reader*, New York: Columbia University Press, 1994.
– Wallace, Michele, *Invisibility Blues: From Pop to Theory*, London, New York: Verso, 1990.
– Wallace, Michele, Gina Dent, ed., *Black Popular Culture*, Seattle, Bay Press, 1992.
– Jonathan White (ed.), *Recasting the World: Writing after Colonialism*, Baltimore and London: The Johns Hopkins University Press, 1993.
Zizek, Slavoj, *Tarrying with the Negative: Kant, Hegel, and the Critique of Ideology*, Durham: Duke University Press, 1993.

TEXTS READ IN THE READING SEMINAR (RUSSIAN VERSION) ATCONTEMPORARY ART CENTER, MOSCOW, JANUARY – MARCH 1995

– Said, Edward, "Introduction," "Representations of the Intellectual," "Holding Nations and Traditions at Bay," "Intellectual Exile: Expatriates and Marginals," "Professionals and Amateurs", in Said, Edward, *Representations of the Intellectual: The 1993 Reith Lectures*, New York: Vintage Books, 1994.
– West, Cornel, "The New Cultural Politics of Difference", in Furguson, Russel et alt. (Ed.), *Out There: Marginalization and Contemporary Cultures*, Cambridge, London, The MIT Press, 1992.
– Butler, Judith, "Introduction", in Butler, Judith, *Bodies that Matter, On the Discursive Limits of "Sex"*, New York, London: Routledge, 1993.
– Turner, Frederick, "Biology and Beauty", in Crary, J., Kwinter S., (Ed.), *Incorporations*, New Yor: Zone Books, 1992.
– Phillipson, Robert, "ELT: Taking stock of a world comodity," "English for all?" "English, the dominant language," "Professional and ethical aspects of ELT 'aid'," "English in periphery-English countries," "Language promotion," "Opposition to the dominance of English," "Linguistic Imperialism: Theoretical Foundations", in Phillipson, Robert, *Linguistic Imperialism*, Oxford, New York, Toronto et alt.: Oxford University Press, 1992.
– Fiss, Karen, "When is Art not Enough? Art and Community", in Ferguson, R. et alt. (ed.), *Discourses: Conversations in Postmodern Art and Culture*, Cambridge, London: The MIT Press, 1992.
– Rose, Tricia, "Black Texts/Black Contexts", in Wallace, Michelle, *Black Popular Culture*, Seattle: Bay Press, 1992.
– Marin, Louis, "Thèse sur l'Idéologie et l'Utopie," "Dégénérescence Utopique: Disneyland", in Marin, Luis, *Utopiques: jeux d'espaces*, Paris: Les Editions de Minuit, 1973.
– Bordowitz, Greg, "The Aids Crisis is Ridiculous", in Gever M., et alt. (ed.), *Queer Looks: Perspectives on Lesbian and Gay Film and Video*, London, New York: Routledge, 1993.
– Williams, Raymond, "When was Modernism", in Williams, Raymond, *The Politics of Modernism: Against the New Conformists*, New York: Verso, 1989.
– Said, Edward, "Reflections on Exile", in Ferguson, R. et alt. (ed.), *Out There: Marginalization and Contemporary Cultures*, Cambridge, The MIT Press, 1992.

A PORTABLE (NOT SO IDEAL) IMPORTED LIBRARY, OR HOW TO REINVENT THE COFFEE TABLE: 25 BOOKS FOR INSTANT USE (CALIFORNIAN VERSION), 1995

– Adorno, Theodor, Wiesengrund, *Philosophische Terminologie*, Band 2, Frankfurt am Main: Suhrkamp, 1974.
– Alfred Arteaga, (ed.), *An Other Tongue, Nation and Ethnicity in the Linguistic Borderlands*, Durham, London: Duke University Press, 1994.
– Janet Beizer, *Ventriloquized Bodies, Narratives of Hysteria in Nineteenth-Century France*, Ithaca, London: Cornell University Press, 1993.
– Bhabha, Homi K. *The Location of Culture*, New York, London: Routledge, 1994.
– Breuer, Josef, Freud, Sigmund, *Studien über Hysterie*, Frankfurt am Main: Fischer Taschenbuch Verlag, 1991.
– Brewer, John, Porter, Roy, (ed.), *Consumption and the World of Goods*, New York, London: Routledge, 1993.
– Bouhdiba, Abdelwahab, *La sexualité en Islam*, Paris: Quadrige, PUF, 1975.
– de Certeau, Michel, *La culture au pluriel*, Paris: Editions du Seuil, 1974.
– Dissanayake Wimal, (ed.), *Colonialism and Nationalism in Asian Cinema*, Indiana: Indiana University Press, 1994.
– Fabian, Johannes, *Time and the Other: How Anthropology Makes its Object*, New York: Columbia University Press, 1983.
– Foucault, Michel, *Naissance de la clinique*, Paris: Quadrige, PUF, 1963.
– Hobsbawm, Eric J., *Nations and Nationalism since 1780, Programme, Myth, Reality*, Cambridge: University Press Cambridge, 1990.
– Irigaray, Luce, *Parler n'est jamais neutre*, Paris: Les Editions de Minuit, 1985.
– Lingis, Alphonso, *Foreign Bodies*, New York, London: Routledge, 1994.
– Marx, Karl, *Die Frühschriften, Von 1837 bis zum Manifest der kommunistischen Partei 1848*, Stuttgart: Alfred Kröner Verlag, 1971.
– Kristeva, Julia, *Powers of Horror, An Essay on Abjection*, New York: Columbia University Press, 1982.
– Phillipson, Robert, *Linguistic Imperialism*, Oxford, New York, Toronto: Oxford University Press, 1992
– Said, Edward W. *Representations of the Intellectual, The 1993 Reith Lectures*, New York: Vintage Books, 1994
– Silverman, Kaja, *Male Subjectivity at the Margins*, New York, London: Routledge, 1992
– Spivak, Gayatri Chakravorty, *Outside in the Teaching Machine*, New York, London: Routledge, 1993
– Studlar, Gaylyn, *In the Realm of Pleasure: Von Sternberg, Dietrich, and the Masochistic Aesthetic*, Urbana, Chicago: University of Illinois Press, 1988.
– Theweleit, Klaus, *Object-Choice: (All You Need Is Love)*, London: Verso, 1994.
– Todorov, Vladislav, *Red Square, Black Square, Organon for Revolutionary Ima-*

gination, New York: State University of New York Press, 1995.
– Walker, Samuel, *Hate Speech, The History of an American Controversy*, Lincoln, London: University of Nebraska Press, 1994.
– Wittgenstein, Ludwig, *Über Gewißheit. Bemerkungen über die Farben. Zettel. Vermischte Bemerkungen*, Werkausgabe Bd. 8, Frankfurt am Main: Suhrkamp, 1984.

TEXTS READ IN THE READING SEMINAR (CALIFORNIAN VERSION) AT OTIS SCHOOL OF ART, LOS ANGELS, APRIL, MAY 1995:

– Said, Edward, "Introduction," "Representations of the Intellectual," "Holding Nations and Traditions at Bay," "Professionals and Amateurs", in Said, Edward W., *Representations of the Intellectual: The 1993 Reith Lectures*, New York: Vintage Books, 1994.
– Silverman, Kaja, "A Woman's Soul Enclosed in a Man's Body: Femininity in Male Homosexuality" in Silverman, Kaja, *Male Subjectivity at the Margins*, New York, London: Routledge, 1992.
– Todorov, Tzvetan, "Dialogism and Schizophrenia", in: Arteaga, Alfred, (ed.), *An Other Tongue, Nation and Ethnicity in the Linguistic Borderlands*, Durham, London: Duke University Press, 1994
– Brewer, John, Porter, Roy, "Introduction", in Brewer, John, Porter, Roy, (ed.), *Consumption and the World of Goods*, New York, London: Routledge, 1993.

A PORTABLE (NOT SO IDEAL) IMPORTED LIBRARY, OR HOW TO REINVENT THE COFFEE TABLE: 25 BOOKS FOR INSTANT USE, (GERMAN VERSION), 1996

– Bender, Gretchen, Druckrey, Timothy, *Culture on the Brink: Ideologies of Technology*, Seattle: Bay Press, 1994.
– Bourdieu, Pierre, *Raison Pratique: Sur la théorie de l'action*, Paris, Seuil, 1994.
– Cohen, Sande, *Academia and the Luster of Capital*, Minneapolis, London: University of Minnesota Press, 1993.
– Deleuze, Gilles, *Présentation de Sacher-Masoch: La Vénus à la fourrure*, Paris: Les Edition de Minuit, 1967.
– Felshin, Nina (ed.), *But is it Art? The Sprit of Art as Activism*, Seattle: Bay Press, 1994.
– Fock, Holger et alt. (ed), *Zwischen Fundamentalismus und Moderne: Literatur aus dem Maghreb*, Hamburg: Rowohlt, 1994.
– Foucault, Michel: *Dits et écrits, IV 1980 – 1988*, Paris: Gallimard, 1994.
– Freud, Sigmund: *Der Mann Moses und die monotheistische Religion: Schriften über die Religion*, Frankfurt am Main: Fischer, 1975.
– Hartley, John, *The Politics of Pictures, The Creation of the Public in the Age of Popular Media*, New York, London: Routledge, 1992.
– Hooks, Bell: *Outlaw Culture: Resisting Representations*, New York, London, Routledge: 1990.
– Karatani, Kojin, *Architecture as Metaphor: Language, Number, Money*, Cambridge, London: The MIT Press, 1995.
– Kafka, Franz, *Sämtliche Erzählungen*, Frankfurt am Main: Fischer Verlag, 1970.
– Kroker, Arthur, Weinstein, Michael A., *Data Trash: The Theory of the Virutal Class*, New York, St. Martin's Press, 1994.
– Lecercle, Jean-Jacques, *The Violence of Language*, New York, London: Routledge, 1990.
– McClintock, Anne, *Imperial Leather: Race, Gender and Sexuality in the Colonial Contest*, New York, London: Routledge, 1995.
– Mernissi, Fatema, *Der politische Harem: Mohammed und die Frauen*, Freiburg, Basel, Wien: Herder, 1992.
– Oe, Kenzaburo, *Teach Us to Outgrow Our Madness*, New York: Grove Press, 1977.
– Richter, Stefan, et alt. (ed.) *Kopfbahnhof: Orient-Express*, Leipzig: Reclam Leipzig, 1991.
– Said, Edward W. *Representations of the Intellectual, The 1993 Reith Lectures*, New York: Vintage Books, 1994.
– Sappington, Rodney, Stallings, Tyler, (ed.), *Uncontrollable Bodies, Testimonies of Identity and Culture*, Seattle: Bay Press, 1994.
– Segalen, Victor, *Die Ästhetik des Diversen*, Frankfurt am Main: Fischer Verlag, 1994

– Silverman, Kaja, *The Acoustic Mirror: The Female Voice in Psychoanalysis and Cinema*, Bloomington: Indiana University Press, 1988.
– Tibi, Bassam, *Nationalismus in der Dritten Welt am arabischen Beispiel*, Frankfurt am Main, Europäische Verlagsanstalt, 1971.
– Spivak, Gayatri Chakravorty, *Outside in the Teaching Machine*, New York, London: Routledge, 1993.
– Wolfson, Louis, *Le Schizo et les Langues*, Paris: Editions Gallimard, 1970.

TEXTS READ IN THE READING SEMINAR (GERMAN VERSION) AT KÜNSTLLERHAUS STUTTGART, STUTTGART, JANUARYY 1996

– Said, Edward, Representations of the Intellectual, in *Representations of the Intellectual*, New York, 1994.
– McClintock, Anne, "Introduction," "Postcolonialism and the Angel of Progress;" "Soft–Soaping Empire," "Race," "Commodity Racism and Imperial Advertising" in *Imperial Leather, Race, Gender and Sexuality in the Colonial Contest*, New York, 1995.
– Debord, Guy E., "Perspektiven einer bewußten Veränderung des alltäglichen Lebens," (1967) in *Der Beginn einer Epoche, Texte der Situationisten*, Hamburg, 1995.
– Vienet, René, Die Situationisten und die neuen Aktionsformen gegen Politik und Kunst, (1967) in *Der Beginn einer Epoche, Texte der Situationisten*, Hamburg, 1995.
– Kroker, Arthur, Weinstein, Michael A., "Preface," in *Data Trash, The Theory of Virtual Class*, New York, 1994.
– Dot Tuer, "Is It Still Privileged Art? The Politics of Class and Collaboration in the Art Practice of Carole Condé and Karl Beveridge", in Nina Felshin, (ed.), *But is it Art? The Spirit of Art as Activism*, Seattle, 1995.

A PORTABLE, (NOT SO IDEAL) IMPORTED LIBRARY, OR HOW TO REINVENT THE COFFEE TAHLE: 25 BOOKS FOR INSTANT USE (AUSTRIAN VERSION) 1996

– Amirou, Rachid, *Imaginaire touristique et sociabilités du voyage*, Paris: PUF, 1995.
– Althusser, Louis, *Écrits sur la Psychanayse, Freud et Lacan*, Paris: STOCK /IMEC, 1993.
– Assima, Fériel, *Rhoulem ou le sexe des anges*, Paris: Arléa, 1996.
– Benjamin, Walter, *Illuminationen, Augewählte Schriften 1*, Frankfurt am Main: Suhrkamp, 1977.
– Chambers, Iain, Curti, Lidia, (ed.), *The Post-Colonial Question, Common Skies, Divided Horizons*, London, New York: Routledge 1996.
– Enloe, Cynthia, *The Morning After, Sexual Politics at the End of the Cold War*, Berkeley, London: University of California Press, 1993.
– Fanon, Frantz, *Peau noire masques blancs*, Paris: Edition du Seuil, 1995.
– Foucault, Michael, *Dits et écrits I, 1954–1988*, Paris: Gallimard, 1995.
– Gbadamosi, Gabriel: *Alto Quaryson, Redrawing the Map, Two African Journeys*, Cambridge: Prickly Pear Press, 1994.
– Grosz, Elizabeth, *Space, Time and Perversion*, New York, London: Routledge, 1995.
– Hebdige, Dick, *Hiding in the Light*, London, New York: Routledge, 1988.
– Heinich, Nathalie, *Etats de femme, L'identité féminine dans la fiction occidentale*, Paris: Gallimard, 1996.
– Kafka, Franz, *Reisetagebücher*, Frankfurt am Main: Fischer, 1994.
– Kracauer, *Von Caligari zu Hitler, Eine psychologische Geschichte des deutschen Films*, Frankfurt am Main: suhrkamp, 1984.
– Lyon, David, Zureik, Elia, (Ed.), *Computers, Surveillance & Privacy*, Mineapolis, London: University of Minnesota Press, 1996.
– Marx, Karl: *Die Frühschriften*, Stuttgart: Alfred Kröner Verlag, 1953.
– Mernissi, Fatema: *Die Angst vor der Moderne, Frauen und Männer zwischen Islam und Demokratie*, Hamburg, Zürich: Luchterhand Literaturverlag, 1992.
– Morley, David, Chen, Kuan-Hsing, (Ed.), *Stuart Hall, Critical Dialogues in Cultural Studies*, New York, London: Routledge, 1996.
– Ngal, M. a M., *Giambatista Viko, ou Le viol du discours africain*, Paris: Hatier 1988,
– Sacher–Masoch, Leopold von, *Venus im Pelz, Mit einer Studie über den Masochismus von Gilles Deleuze*, Frankfurt am Main: Insel Taschenbuch, 1980.
– Rühmkorf, Peter, *Über das Volksvermögen, Exkurse in den literatischen Untergrund*, Hamburg: 1969.
– Smith, Anthony, *Books To Bytes, Knowledge and Information in the Postmodern Era*, London: British Film Institute, 1993.
– Smith, Sidonie, Watson, Julia, (Ed.), *Getting A Life, Everyday Uses of Autobiography*, Minneapolis, London: University of Minnesota Press, 1996.

– Warner, Michael, (Ed.), *Fear of a Queer Planet, Queer Politics and Social Theory*, Mineapolis, London: University of Minnesota Press, 1993.
– De Zegher, M. Catherine, *Inside the Visible, An Elliptical Traverse of 20th Century Art in, of, and from the Feminine*, Cambridge, London: The MIT Press, 1996.

There was no reading seminar held in Austria because of administrative difficulties.

CONTRIBUTORS

BILL ARNING is a New York based independent curator, art critic and writer for *The Village Voice, Time Out New York, Art in America, World Art* and other magazines. From 1985 - 1996 he was chief curator of White Columns Alternative Space, New York.

ZEIGAM AZIZOV is an artist and writer currently living in London. Recent projects shown at the ICA London and at Lisson Gallery.

LISA ADKINS teaches in the department of Sociology and Social Anthropology at the University of Kent, Canterbury.

DAN BACALZO is a performance artist and writerbased in New York.

BENJAMIN H. D. BUCHLOH is an art critique and art historian teaching at Columbia University. He is also editor of *October.*

COCO FUSCO is a New York based writer and interdisciplinary artist. She is the author of *English is broken here; Notes on cultural fusion in the Americas*. She is an assistant professor at the Tyler School of Art of Temple University.

RAINER GANAHL is an artist based in New York.

KOJIN KARATANI is a Japan based literary and cultural critic and a professor of Literature at Kinki University in Osaka,Visiting Professor at Columbia University. He has published two books in English: *Origins of Modern Japanese Literature* and *Architecture as Metaphor*. He is currently working on books on Kant and Marx which will also be published in English.

KAREN KELSKY received her doctorate in athropology at the University of Hawaii at Manoa in 1995.

SABU KOHSO is a New York based translater and writer. He is currently at working on a critical new journal.

JULIA KRISTEVA is a practicing psychoanalyst and professor at Paris University VII. Her many acclaimed books include *Time and Sense: Proust and teh Experience of Literature; Strangers to Ourselves; Desire in Language; New Maladies of the Soul; Black Sun; Tales of Love; Revolution in Poetic Language; Sens et non-sens de la révolte.*

DANA LEONARD teaches at the Centre for Research and Education on Gender, University of London.
SYLVERE LOTRINGER is professor of French Literature and Philosophy at Columbia University and the General Editor of *Semiotext(e)* . He has published *Pure War,* with Paul Virilio; *Forget Foucault,* with Jean Baudrillard; *Overexposed, a post-Foucauldian book on sexuality in America*; and *Antonin Artaud.*
SAMI NAÏR is professor of political science at Paris University VIII and author or numerous books includin *Marx et Machiavel; Le Caire, la victorieuse; Le regard des vainquerurs, les enjeux français de l'immigration; Le Différend méditerranén; Lettre à Charles Pasqua; En el nombre de Dios.* He is also president de *l'Institut d'Études et de Recherches Europe-Méditerranée.*
EDWARD W. SAID is professor at Columbia University. As a literary and cultural critic he has written more than a dozen of books, including *Orientalism; Culture and Imperialism; The Politics of Dispossession* and most recently *Peace and its Discontents.*
EDWARD SOJA is geographer and professor at UCLA. He has published many articles and serveral books, including: *Postmodern Geographies* and most recently *Third Space.*
GAYATRI CH. SPIVAK is an Avalon Professor in the Humanities at Columbia University. She is author of *In Other Worlds; The Post-Colonial Critic; Outside in the Teaching Machine;* and *Imaginary Maps: Three Stories by Mahasweta Devi.*
VICTOR TUPITSYN is New York based independent writer and art critic. He is professor at Pace University New York.
WULF SCHMIDT-WULFEN is professor of Social Sciences at the University of Hannover and has published noumerous articles on geographical pedagogy, development theory, and on development of Africa with a focus on West-Afrika.

SEMIOTEXT(E), THE JOURNAL
Jim Fleming & Sylvère Lotringer, Editors

POLYSEXUALITY
François Peraldi, ed.

OASIS
Timothy Maliqalim Simone, et al., eds.

SEMIOTEXT(E) USA
Jim Fleming & Peter Lamborn Wilson, eds.

SEMIOTEXT(E) ARCHITECTURE
Hraztan Zeitlian, ed.

SEMIOTEXT(E) SF
Rudy Rucker, Robert Anton Wilson, Peter Lamborn Wilson, eds.

RADIOTEXT(E)
Neil Strauss & Dave Mandl, eds.

SEMIOTEXT(E) CANADAS
Jordan Zinovich, ed.

SEMIOTEXT(E) NATIVE AGENTS SERIES
Chris Kraus, Editor

IF YOU'RE A GIRL
Ann Rower

THE ORIGIN OF THE SPECIES
Barbara Barg

HOW I BECAME ONE OF THE INVISIBLE
David Rattray

NOT ME
Eileen Myles

HANNIBAL LECTER, MY FATHER
Kathy Acker

SICK BURN CUT
Deran Ludd

THE MADAME REALISM COMPLEX
Lynne Tillman

I LOVE DICK
Chris Kraus

WALKING THROUGH CLEAR WATER IN A POOL PAINTED BLACK
Cookie Mueller

THE NEW FUCK YOU
Adventures in Lesbian Reading
Eileen Myles & Liz Kotz, eds.

READING BROOKE SHIELDS
The Garden of Failure
Eldon Garnet

THE PASSIONATE MISTAKES AND INTIMATE CORRUPTIONS OF ONE GIRL IN AMERICA
Michelle Tea

SEMIOTEXT(E) DOUBLE AGENTS SERIES
Jim Fleming & Sylvère Lotringer, Editors

FATAL STRATEGIES
Jean Baudrillard

FOUCAULT LIVE
Collected Interviews of Michel Foucault
Sylvère Lotringer, ed.

ARCHEOLOGY OF VIOLENCE
Pierre Clastres

LOST DIMENSION
Paul Virilio

AESTHETICS OF DISAPPEARANCE
Paul Virilio

COLLECTED INTERVIEWS OF WILLIAM S. BURROUGHS
Sylvère Lotringer, ed.

SEMIOTEXT(E) FOREIGN AGENTS SERIES

Jim Fleming & Sylvère Lotringer, Editors

INSIDE & OUT OF BYZANTIUM
Nina Zivancevic

COMMUNISTS LIKE US
Félix Guattari & Toni Negri

ECSTASY OF COMMUNICATION
Jean Baudrillard

SIMULATIONS
Jean Baudrillard

GERMANIA
Heiner Müller

POPULAR DEFENSE & ECOLOGICAL STRUGGLES
Paul Virilio

IN THE SHADOW OF THE SILENT MAJORITIES
Jean Baudrillard

FORGET FOUCAULT
Jean Baudrillard

ASSASSINATION RHAPSODY
Derek Pell

REMARKS ON MARX
Michel Foucault

STILL BLACK, STILL STRONG
Dhoruba Bin Wahad, Mumia Abu-Jamal & Assata Shakur

LOOKING BACK ON THE END OF THE WORLD
Jean Baudrillard, Paul Virilio, et al.

SADNESS AT LEAVING
Erje Ayden

NOMADOLOGY: THE WAR MACHINE
Gilles Deleuze & Félix Guattari

PURE WAR
Paul Virilio & Sylvère Lotringer

METATRON, THE RECORDING ANGEL
Sol Yurick

BOLO'BOLO
P.M.

ON THE LINE
Gilles Deleuze & Félix Guattari

SPEED AND POLITICS
Paul Virilio

DRIFTWORKS
Jean-François Lyotard

69 WAYS TO PLAY THE BLUES
Jürg Laederach

THE POLITICS OF TRUTH
Michel Foucault

CHAOSOPHY
Félix Guattari

SOFT SUBVERSIONS
Félix Guattari

AUTONOMEDIA BOOK SERIES

Jim Fleming, Editor

MARX BEYOND MARX
Lessons on the Gründrisse
Antonio Negri

TROTSKYISM AND MAOISM
Theory & Practice in France & the U.S.
A. Belden Fields

ON AN(ARCHY) & SCHIZOANALYSIS
Rolando Perez

FILE UNDER POPULAR
Theoretical & Critical Writing on Music
Chris Cutler

RETHINKING MARXISM
Steve Resnick & Rick Wolff, eds.

CLIPPED COINS, ABUSED WORDS, CIVIL GOVERNMENT
John Locke's Philosophy of Money
Constantine George Caffentzis

HORSEXE
Essay on Transsexuality
Catherine Millot

FILM & POLITICS IN THE THIRD WORLD
John Downing, ed.

COLUMBUS & OTHER CANNIBALS
The Wétiko Disease & The White Man
Jack Forbes

ENRAGÉS & SITUATIONISTS
The Occupation Movement, May '68
René Viénet

MIDNIGHT OIL
Work, Energy, War, 1973–1992
Midnight Notes Collective

GONE TO CROATAN
Origins of North American Dropout Culture
James Koehnline & Ron Sakolsky, eds.

ABOUT FACE
Race in Postmodern America
Timothy Maliqalim Simone

THE ARCANE OF REPRODUCTION
Housework, Prostitution, Labor & Capital
Leopoldina Fortunati

BY ANY MEANS NECESSARY
Outlaw Manifestos & Ephemera, 1965–70
Peter Stansill & David Zane Mairowitz, eds.

¡ZAPATISTAS!
Documents of the New Mexican Revolution
EZLN

THE OFFICIAL KGB HANDBOOK
USSR Committee for State Security

THIS WORLD WE MUST LEAVE
Jacques Camatte

CRIMES OF THE BEATS
The Unbearables

THE MEDIA ARCHIVE
The Foundation for Advancement of Illegal Knowkedge

ESCAPE FROM THE NINETEENTH CENTURY
Essays on Marx, Fourier, Proudhon & Nietzsche
Peter Lamborn Wilson

DREAMER OF THE DAY
Francis Parker Yockey & Secret Fascist Underground
Kevin Coogan

THE ANARCHISTS
Portrait of Civilization at the End of the 19th Century
John Henry Mackay

BLOOD & VOLTS
Tesla, Edison, & the Birth of the Electric Chair
Th. Metzger

CARNIVAL OF CHAOS
On the Road with the Nomadic Festival
Sascha Altman Dubrul

PIONEER OF INNER SPACE
The Life of Fitz Hugh Ludlow
Donald P. Dulchinos

PSYCHEDELICS REIMAGINED
Introduced by Timothy Leary, Prefaced by Hakim Bey
Tom Lyttle, Editor

ROTTING GODDESS
The Origin of the Witch in Classical Antiquity
Jacob Rabinowitz